THE ENCYCLOPEDIA OF
DESSERTS

THE ENCYCLOPEDIA OF
DESSERTS

400 INTERNATIONALLY INSPIRED SWEETS AND CONFECTIONS

CIDER MILL
PRESS

BOOK
PUBLISHERS

CONTENTS

INTRODUCTION

They can signal that a grand celebration is underway, as the cake at a birthday party or wedding does. They can kindle a memory that warms the heart—recall that afternoon spent making Christmas cookies with nana—or transform human consciousness, as Marcel Proust did following that famous bite of a madeleine. They hold such sway that they can become an avatar for a level of fortune previously unimaginable, as seen in the apple pie's status as the symbol for all that is good in the American way of life. They can, like little else, deliver on the promises that the eye and mind make, as anyone who has had the good fortune to spend a week patisserie hopping in Paris will testify.

Desserts, due to the traditions, memories, and emotions attached to them, carry a greater weight than any other group of foods. So tremendous is their power that even the simplest desserts have the miraculous ability to put any unpleasantness firmly in the past and fix our attention on the encouraging aspects of the world before us.

Things being what they are, it is always better to take matters into your own hands when your palate sounds a cry for something sweet. Not only is a homemade dessert more likely to satiate, since you can tailor it exactly to your tastes, but taking a step back from the busy world to turn out something special means your satisfaction won't be limited to your consumption of it. By committing to making your own sweets, you continually get to enjoy the sensation of watching a series of seemingly disparate elements come together to form an appealing whole. This alchemy, which can be managed with little more than a few mixing bowls, a couple of simple implements, and a standard-issue stove and oven, is a process that never ceases to amaze.

To tap into that wonder, it helps to keep a few things in mind. Precision is important in all forms of cooking, but it is crucial when it comes to making desserts, and baking in particular. The taste and texture of your favorite confection hinge on a delicate balance of flavors and interactions between ingredients, meaning that, most often, getting the results you desire means a commitment to measuring the components by weight, especially for ingredients such as flour.

If you and a friend were both to measure a cup of flour and place each of them on a scale, the weights would be different. This discrepancy occurs because of inconsistencies that arise when packing and filling a cup of flour. This goes for any ingredient measured using spoons or cups. These dry measuring cups and measuring spoons do not have a universal standard and can vary from brand to brand. But no matter where you are or what you are measuring, weight is weight. .

Throughout this book, weights will be given for a number of ingredients, particularly in the recipes that will be baked. A liquid in ounces should be measured by volume unless otherwise specified. Liquids such as water have a density of 1, which means they have a 1:1 ratio of weight to volume—i.e., they can be weighed on a scale or measured by volume and produce the same result. Dry ingredients labeled by ounce should be measured on a scale.

Temperature is very important for certain ingredients, as most recipes call for you to emulsify items with different densities and structures. Having these various items at a similar temperature allows them to come together in a smooth and cohesive manner. Let us take butter that has softened at room temperature, for example.

The creaming method is the process of combining butter and sugar until airy, light, and fluffy. This process is only possible when the butter is warm enough that the friction from beating it opens up small pockets, which trap air as the sugar is being incorporated. As more air enters the mixture, it grows lighter, almost fluffy.

Eggs are another ingredient where various temperatures make a big difference in the final product. As a general rule, take your eggs out of the refrigerator at least one hour before starting your preparation.

You want everything to be at room temperature for baked goods where a lighter, delicate texture is paramount. Any dough or batter that must rest at room temperature or be refrigerated before going in the oven does not need to be made with room-temperature ingredients.

One of the most common and detrimental mistakes in cooking is starting preparations without reading the recipe all the way through. Reading the recipe carefully allows you to get organized, so that you can focus on executing it properly when the time comes. It's easy to leave something out or miss a key step when you're rushing to grab items and containers as you go. It's also much harder to pay attention to how a certain batter feels, or how a cookie smells as it turns toward the last minute of baking, hindering the sixth sense that is essential for overcoming the inevitable changes in conditions and ingredients.

Finally, the temptation to open the oven and take a closer look to ensure that whatever's in there is baking properly is overwhelming. Resist the temptation, especially when there's a cake in the oven, for at least three-quarters of the suggested baking time. A drop in temperature could cause the final product to deflate slightly, nullifying all the work you did to mix the dough or batter properly.

That's it. Now you're ready to indulge whatever craving arises, wipe out your next gray day, and/or provide a celebration with the perfect punctuation. Pulled from cuisines around the globe, each of the following recipes is a testament to this bit of wisdom: all that really matters is how you finish.

COOKIES

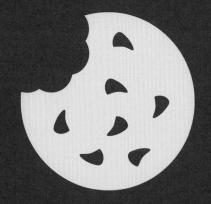

Chocolate Chip Cookies

YIELD: 16 COOKIES | **ACTIVE TIME:** 15 MINUTES | **TOTAL TIME:** 45 MINUTES

7 OZ. UNSALTED BUTTER

8¾ OZ. ALL-PURPOSE FLOUR

½ TEASPOON BAKING SODA

3½ OZ. SUGAR

5.3 OZ. DARK BROWN SUGAR

1 TEASPOON FINE SEA SALT

2 TEASPOONS PURE VANILLA EXTRACT

1 LARGE EGG

1 LARGE EGG YOLK

1¼ CUPS SEMISWEET CHOCOLATE CHIPS

1. Preheat the oven to 350°F. Place the butter in a saucepan and cook over medium-high heat until it is starting to brown and give off a nutty aroma (let your nose guide you here, making sure you frequently waft the steam toward you). Transfer to a heatproof mixing bowl.

2. Place the flour and baking soda in a bowl and whisk until combined.

3. Add the sugars, salt, and vanilla to the bowl containing the melted butter and whisk until combined. Add the egg and egg yolk and whisk until the mixture is smooth and thick. Add the flour-and-baking soda mixture and stir until incorporated. Add the chocolate chips and stir until evenly distributed. Form the mixture into 16 balls and place on parchment-lined baking sheets, leaving about 2 inches between each ball.

4. Working with one baking sheet at a time, place it in the oven and bake until golden brown, 12 to 16 minutes, rotating the sheet halfway through the bake time. Remove from the oven and let cool to room temperature before serving.

Classic Sugar Cookies

YIELD: 48 COOKIES | **ACTIVE TIME:** 40 MINUTES | **TOTAL TIME:** 3 HOURS

½ LB. UNSALTED BUTTER, SOFTENED

7 OZ. LIGHT BROWN SUGAR

1 EGG

12 OZ. ALL-PURPOSE FLOUR, PLUS MORE AS NEEDED

1 TEASPOON BAKING POWDER

½ TEASPOON KOSHER SALT

1. In the work bowl of a stand mixer fitted with the paddle attachment, cream the butter and brown sugar on medium speed until the mixture is very light and fluffy, about 5 minutes. Scrape down the work bowl and then beat the mixture for another 5 minutes.

2. Reduce the speed to low, add the egg, and beat until incorporated. Scrape down the work bowl and beat the mixture for 1 minute on medium.

3. Add the remaining ingredients, reduce the speed to low, and beat until the mixture comes together as a dough. Form the dough into a ball and then flatten it into a disk. Envelop the dough in plastic wrap and refrigerate for 2 hours.

4. Preheat the oven to 350°F and line two baking sheets with parchment paper.

5. Remove the dough from the refrigerator and let it sit on the counter for 5 minutes.

6. Place the dough on a flour-dusted work surface and roll it out until it is approximately ¼ inch thick. Use cookie cutters to cut the dough into the desired shapes and place them on the baking sheets. Form any scraps into a ball, roll it out, and cut into cookies. If the dough becomes too sticky or warm, place it back in the refrigerator for 15 minutes to firm up.

7. Place the cookies in the oven and bake until lightly golden brown at their edges, 8 to 10 minutes. Remove from the oven, transfer to a wire rack, and let cool for 10 minutes before enjoying or decorating.

Snickerdoodles

YIELD: 24 COOKIES | **ACTIVE TIME:** 25 MINUTES | **TOTAL TIME:** 1 HOUR

15 OZ. ALL-PURPOSE FLOUR

2 TEASPOONS CREAM OF TARTAR

1 TEASPOON BAKING SODA

2½ TEASPOONS CINNAMON

½ TEASPOON KOSHER SALT

½ LB. UNSALTED BUTTER, SOFTENED

11.6 OZ. SUGAR

1 LARGE EGG, AT ROOM TEMPERATURE

2 TEASPOONS PURE VANILLA EXTRACT

1. Preheat the oven to 375°F and line two baking sheets with parchment paper. Whisk the flour, cream of tartar, baking soda, 1½ teaspoons of the cinnamon, and the salt together in a mixing bowl.

2. In the work bowl of a stand mixer fitted with the paddle attachment, cream the butter and all but 2 oz. of the sugar together on medium speed until light and fluffy. Add the egg and vanilla and beat until combined, scraping down the work bowl as needed. With the mixer running on low, add the dry mixture in three increments, waiting until each portion has been incorporated until adding the next. A thick dough will form.

3. Roll 1-tablespoon portions of the dough into balls. Place the remaining cinnamon and sugar in a mixing bowl and stir to combine. Roll the balls in the mixture until coated and place them on the baking sheets.

4. Place in the oven and bake for 10 minutes, until puffy and very soft. Remove from the oven, press down with a spatula to flatten them out, and let cool on the baking sheets for 10 minutes before transferring to a wire rack to cool completely.

Cardamom Biscotti

YIELD: 8 SERVINGS | **ACTIVE TIME:** 30 MINUTES | **TOTAL TIME:** 1 HOUR AND 30 MINUTES

1½ CUPS ALL-PURPOSE FLOUR

¾ TEASPOON BAKING POWDER

PINCH OF FINE SEA SALT

¼ CUP SUGAR

⅓ CUP LIGHT BROWN SUGAR

¾ TEASPOON CARDAMOM

½ TEASPOON CINNAMON

¼ TEASPOON GROUND GINGER

⅛ TEASPOON GROUND CLOVES

⅛ TEASPOON FRESHLY GRATED NUTMEG

ZEST OF 1 ORANGE

2 EGGS

¼ CUP EXTRA-VIRGIN OLIVE OIL

1 TEASPOON PURE VANILLA EXTRACT

1. Preheat the oven to 350°F. Line a baking sheet with parchment paper. Place all of the ingredients, except for the orange zest, eggs, olive oil, and vanilla, in a mixing bowl and whisk until combined.

2. Add the remaining ingredients and work the mixture by hand until it comes together as a smooth dough. Roll the dough into a log that is about 6 inches long and about 2 inches wide. Place the log on the baking sheet, place it in the oven, and bake until golden brown, about 20 minutes.

3. Remove the biscotti from the oven and let it cool.

4. Cut the biscotti into the desired shape and size. Place the biscotti back in the oven and bake until it is crispy, about 20 minutes.

5. Remove the biscotti from the oven, transfer to a wire rack, and let them cool completely before enjoying.

Gluten-Free Biscotti

YIELD: 12 COOKIES | **ACTIVE TIME:** 15 MINUTES | **TOTAL TIME:** 2 HOURS

1½ CUPS ALMOND FLOUR

½ CUP GLUTEN-FREE ALL-PURPOSE FLOUR

½ TEASPOON BAKING SODA

¼ TEASPOON FINE SEA SALT

ZEST OF 1 LEMON

1 TEASPOON ALMOND EXTRACT

¼ CUP SUGAR

¼ CUP HONEY

½ CUP SLIVERED ALMONDS

1. Preheat the oven to 325°F. Line a large baking sheet with parchment paper. Combine the flours, baking soda, salt, and lemon zest in a mixing bowl. Add the almond extract, sugar, and honey and work the mixture until it comes together as a rough dough. Add the almonds and knead the dough to incorporate them.

2. Form the dough into a 1-inch log, place it on the baking sheet, and bake until set, about 15 minutes. Remove from the oven and carefully transfer the dough to a cooling rack. Let cool for 1 hour. Leave the oven on.

3. Slice the dough into ½-inch-thick slices and place them on the baking sheet, cut side up. Return the biscotti to the oven and bake until dry and set, about 15 minutes. Turn off the oven and open the oven door slightly. Let the biscotti cool completely in the oven before enjoying.

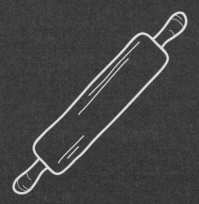

Gluten-Free Butter Cookies

YIELD: 24 COOKIES | **ACTIVE TIME:** 20 MINUTES | **TOTAL TIME:** 1 HOUR

⅓ CUP ALMOND MEAL

⅓ CUP SORGHUM FLOUR

½ CUP RICE FLOUR

⅓ CUP TAPIOCA FLOUR

½ CUP CORNMEAL

⅔ CUP SUGAR

½ TEASPOON GUAR GUM

1 TEASPOON GLUTEN-FREE BAKING POWDER

ZEST OF 1 LEMON

¾ TEASPOON GROUND CARDAMOM

PINCH OF KOSHER SALT

4 OZ. UNSALTED BUTTER, CHILLED AND DICED

2 TABLESPOONS WATER

1 LARGE EGG

½ TEASPOON PURE VANILLA EXTRACT

2 CUPS CONFECTIONERS' SUGAR

1 TEASPOON FRESH LEMON JUICE

HOT WATER (125°F), AS NEEDED

GROUND CARDAMOM, FOR TOPPING

GROUND ANISE, FOR TOPPING

1. Place the almond meal, flours, cornmeal, sugar, guar gum, baking powder, lemon zest, cardamom, and salt in a food processor and pulse to combine.

2. Add the butter and pulse until the mixture is coarse crumbs. Add the water, egg, and vanilla, and pulse until the mixture is just holding together. Cover the dough with plastic wrap and refrigerate for 30 minutes.

3. Preheat the oven to 350°F and line two baking sheets with parchment paper. Roll out the dough between two sheets of parchment paper and use cookie cutters to create the desired shapes.

4. Bake for 15 minutes, until a light golden brown. Remove from the oven and let cool on the baking sheets for a few minutes before transferring them to wire racks to cool completely.

5. Place the confectioners' sugar in a mixing bowl. Incorporate the lemon juice and enough hot water to give the frosting a thick consistency. Spread the frosting on the cookies or place it in a piping bag if a more decorative design is desired. When all of the cookies have been frosted, sprinkle the cardamom and anise over them.

Sfratti

YIELD: 6 SERVINGS | **ACTIVE TIME:** 30 MINUTES | **TOTAL TIME:** 3 HOURS

3 CUPS ALL-PURPOSE FLOUR, PLUS MORE AS NEEDED

1 CUP SUGAR

PINCH OF FINE SEA SALT

⅓ CUP UNSALTED BUTTER, CHILLED

⅔ CUP DRY WHITE WINE, CHILLED

1 CUP HONEY

2 CUPS CHOPPED WALNUTS

2 TEASPOONS ORANGE ZEST

¾ TEASPOON CINNAMON

¼ TEASPOON GROUND GINGER

DASH OF FRESHLY GRATED NUTMEG

¼ TEASPOON BLACK PEPPER

1 LARGE EGG

1 TABLESPOON WATER

1. Combine the flour, sugar, and salt in a mixing bowl. Add the butter and work the mixture with a pastry cutter until it resembles coarse crumbs. Add the wine a little at a time, mixing it in with a fork to moisten the dough. Continue adding wine until the mixture just comes together as a dough. Divide the dough in half and form each piece into a ball. Flatten the balls into disks, cover them with plastic wrap, and refrigerate for 1 hour. The dough will keep in the refrigerator for up to 3 days.

2. Remove the dough from the refrigerator and let it stand at room temperature until malleable but not soft.

3. Place the honey in a saucepan and bring it to a boil. Boil for 5 minutes, lowering the heat if the honey starts to foam over the edge of the pan. Add all of the remaining ingredients, except for the egg and water, and cook, stirring constantly, for another 3 to 5 minutes, and remove the pan from heat. If the mixture begins to turn dark, it is starting to burn—remove from heat immediately and keep stirring!

4. Let the mixture stand, stirring occasionally, until it is cool enough to handle. Pour the mixture onto a flour-dusted surface, divide it into six equal portions, and shape each portion into a 14-inch-long rod.

5. Preheat the oven to 350°F. Line a large baking sheet with parchment paper.

6. On a piece of parchment paper or on a flour-dusted work surface, roll each piece of dough into a 14 x 12–inch rectangle, then cut each rectangle lengthwise into three long rectangles. Place one of the strips of filling near a long side of each rectangle, then form the dough around the filling.

7. You will have six long sticks of dough with filling in each. Cut these into 2-inch-long sticks. Place the cookies, seam side down, on the baking sheet, leaving 1 inch between the cookies.

8. Place the egg and water in a cup and beat until combined. Brush the cookies with the egg wash.

9. Place the cookies in the oven and bake until golden brown, about 20 minutes.

10. Remove from the oven, transfer the cookies to a wire rack, and let them cool completely before serving.

Apricot Kolaches

YIELD: 32 COOKIES | **ACTIVE TIME:** 30 MINUTES | **TOTAL TIME:** 2 HOURS AND 30 MINUTES

½ LB. DRIED APRICOTS

3½ OZ. SUGAR

2.8 OZ. ALL-PURPOSE FLOUR, PLUS MORE AS NEEDED

¼ TEASPOON FINE SEA SALT

2 OZ. CREAM CHEESE, SOFTENED

4 OZ. UNSALTED BUTTER, SOFTENED

¼ CUP CONFECTIONERS' SUGAR, FOR DUSTING

1. Place the dried apricots in a saucepan and cover with water. Bring the water to a boil over medium-high heat and cook until the apricots are soft, adding more water if too much evaporates. Add the sugar and reduce the heat so that the mixture simmers. Cook, stirring to dissolve the sugar, until the liquid thickens into a syrup. Transfer the mixture to a blender or food processor and puree until smooth. Let stand until cool.

2. Sift the flour and salt into a mixing bowl. In the work bowl of a stand mixer fitted with the paddle attachment, beat the cream cheese and butter on high until the mixture is fluffy. Gradually add the dry mixture to the wet mixture and beat to incorporate. Divide the dough into two balls and cover loosely with plastic wrap. Flatten each ball to about ¾ inch thick and refrigerate until the dough is firm, about 2 hours.

3. Preheat the oven to 375°F and line a large baking sheet with parchment paper. Place one of the balls of dough on a flour-dusted work surface and roll it out into a ⅛-inch-thick square. Cut the dough into as many 1½-inch squares as possible.

4. Place approximately 1 teaspoon of the apricot mixture in the center of each square. Gently lift two opposite corners of each square and fold one over the other. Gently press down to seal and transfer to the baking sheet.

5. Place in the oven and bake for 12 to 14 minutes, until the cookies are golden brown. Remove, briefly let them cool on the baking sheet, and transfer to a wire rack to cool completely. Repeat with the remaining ball of dough. When all of the kolaches have been baked and cooled, dust with the confectioners' sugar.

Pignoli

YIELD: 36 COOKIES | **ACTIVE TIME:** 15 MINUTES | **TOTAL TIME:** 40 MINUTES

1¾ CUPS PLUS 1 TEASPOON UNSWEETENED ALMOND PASTE

1½ CUPS CONFECTIONERS' SUGAR

2 TABLESPOONS HONEY

PINCH OF CINNAMON

PINCH OF FINE SEA SALT

2 LARGE EGG WHITES, AT ROOM TEMPERATURE

ZEST OF 1 LEMON

¾ CUP PINE NUTS

1. Preheat the oven to 350°F and line two baking sheets with parchment paper. In the work bowl of a stand mixer fitted with the paddle attachment, beat the almond paste until it is thoroughly broken up. Add the confectioners' sugar and beat the mixture on low until combined.

2. Add the honey, cinnamon, salt, egg whites, and lemon zest, raise the speed to medium, and beat until the mixture is very thick, about 5 minutes.

3. Drop tablespoons of dough onto the prepared baking sheets and gently pat pine nuts into each of the cookies. Place the cookies in the oven and bake until golden brown, 12 to 14 minutes. Remove from the oven and let the cookies cool on the baking sheets.

Fig, Orange & Anise Honey Balls

YIELD: 20 BALLS | **ACTIVE TIME:** 30 MINUTES | **TOTAL TIME:** 2 HOURS

½ CUP PLUS ⅓ CUP SUGAR

1 CUP PLUS 2 TABLESPOONS WATER

2 TABLESPOONS HONEY

ZEST AND JUICE OF 1 ORANGE

SEEDS OF ½ VANILLA BEAN

2 CUPS DRIED FIGS

½ TEASPOON FENNEL SEEDS

1 CUP WALNUTS, TOASTED AND CHOPPED

1 TABLESPOON PERNOD

½ LB. FROZEN KATAIFI, THAWED

¼ CUP EXTRA-VIRGIN OLIVE OIL

1. Place ⅓ cup of the sugar, 2 tablespoons of the water, the honey, orange zest, orange juice, and vanilla seeds in a small saucepan and bring the mixture to a boil, stirring to dissolve the sugar. Reduce the heat and simmer the mixture until it is syrupy, about 5 minutes. Remove the pan from heat, let the syrup cool, and strain it. Set the syrup aside.

2. Line a baking sheet with parchment paper. Place the figs, fennel seeds, and remaining sugar and water in a saucepan and bring the mixture to a boil, stirring to dissolve the sugar. Reduce the heat and simmer the mixture until the liquid is syrupy, about 10 minutes. Remove the pan from heat and let it cool.

3. Place the cooled fig mixture in a food processor and puree until it is a paste, scraping down the sides of the work bowl frequently. Add the walnuts and Pernod and pulse until combined.

4. Form tablespoons of the mixture into balls and place them on the baking sheet. You should have about 20 balls. Place them in the refrigerator and chill for 30 minutes.

5. Preheat the oven to 350°F. Place the kataifi in a mixing bowl, slowly drizzle in the olive oil, and gently fold until the kataifi is evenly coated.

6. Grab a small amount of the kataifi and wrap it around one of the balls. Place the ball back on the baking sheet and repeat until all of the balls have been wrapped in kataifi.

7. Place the baking sheet in the oven and cook until the kataifi is golden brown, about 10 minutes, rotating the pan halfway through.

8. Remove the balls from the oven and let them cool.

9. Pour ½ tablespoon of the syrup over each ball and enjoy.

Pasteli

2 CUPS SESAME SEEDS

1 CUP HONEY

½ TEASPOON KOSHER SALT

1 TEASPOON PURE VANILLA EXTRACT

1. Preheat the oven to 350°F. Line a square 8-inch baking pan with parchment paper. Place the sesame seeds on a baking sheet, place them in the oven, and toast until golden brown, about 5 minutes. Remove from the oven and let the sesame seeds cool.

2. Place the honey in a small saucepan and warm it over medium-high heat. Boil the honey until it reaches 310°F.

3. Remove the pan from heat, stir in the salt, vanilla, and toasted sesame seeds, and pour the mixture into the baking pan. Let the mixture cool for 15 minutes.

4. Cut the bars into the desired shape; they should still be warm. Enjoy immediately or at room temperature.

Keto Chocolate Chip Cookies

YIELD: 20 COOKIES | **ACTIVE TIME:** 10 MINUTES | **TOTAL TIME:** 1 HOUR

½ LB. UNSALTED BUTTER

1½ CUPS ALMOND FLOUR

½ CUP COCONUT FLOUR

1½ TEASPOONS BAKING SODA

2 TABLESPOONS COCONUT OIL, MELTED

½ CUP STEVIA OR PREFERRED KETO-FRIENDLY SWEETENER

2 TEASPOONS PURE VANILLA EXTRACT

½ LB. SUGAR-FREE SEMISWEET CHOCOLATE CHIPS

1. Preheat the oven to 350°F and line two baking sheets with parchment paper. Place the butter in a saucepan and cook over medium-high heat until it is dark brown and has a nutty aroma. Transfer the browned butter to a heatproof mixing bowl and set it aside.

2. Place the flours and baking soda in a mixing bowl and whisk until combined. Set the mixture aside.

3. Add the coconut oil, sweetener, and vanilla to the bowl containing the melted butter and whisk until combined. Gradually add the dry mixture and stir until the mixture comes together as a dough. Add the chocolate chips and fold until evenly distributed. Form tablespoons of the mixture into balls and place them on the parchment-lined baking sheets, leaving about 2 inches between each ball. Gently press down on the balls to flatten them slightly.

4. Place the cookies in the oven and bake, rotating the sheets halfway through, until they are golden brown, about 12 minutes. Remove the cookies from the oven and let them cool on the baking sheets for 10 minutes before transferring to wire racks to cool completely.

Nutritional Info Per Serving: Calories: 178; Fat: 16.5 g; Net Carbs: 5.1 g; Protein: 2.5 g

Keto Peanut Butter Cookies

YIELD: 10 COOKIES | **ACTIVE TIME:** 10 MINUTES | **TOTAL TIME:** 45 MINUTES

½ CUP SALTED, NO SUGAR ADDED PEANUT BUTTER

1 TABLESPOON COCONUT OIL, MELTED

⅓ CUP STEVIA OR PREFERRED KETO-FRIENDLY SWEETENER

1 CUP ALMOND FLOUR

¾ TEASPOON BAKING SODA

1 TEASPOON PURE VANILLA EXTRACT

½ TEASPOON FLAKY SEA SALT

1. Preheat the oven to 350°F and line a large baking sheet with parchment paper. Place all of the ingredients, except for the salt, in a mixing bowl and stir to combine.

2. Drop tablespoons of the dough on the baking sheet, gently press down to flatten them, and then press down on them with a fork to leave a crosshatch pattern on top.

3. Place the cookies in the oven and bake until the edges are set and golden brown, about 10 minutes. Remove from the oven and let the cookies cool on the baking sheet for 10 minutes before transferring to a wire rack to cool completely.

4. Sprinkle the salt over the cookies and enjoy.

Nutritional Info Per Serving: Calories: 115; Fat: 9.6 g; Net Carbs: 2.6 g; Protein: 5.5 g

Keto Almond Clouds

YIELD: 24 SERVINGS | **ACTIVE TIME:** 10 MINUTES | **TOTAL TIME:** 35 MINUTES

4 TABLESPOONS UNSALTED BUTTER, SOFTENED

2 OZ. CREAM CHEESE, SOFTENED

⅓ CUP MONK FRUIT SWEETENER

1 LARGE EGG

1 TABLESPOON SOUR CREAM

1½ TEASPOONS PURE ALMOND EXTRACT

½ TEASPOON PURE VANILLA EXTRACT

PINCH OF KOSHER SALT

3 CUPS ALMOND FLOUR

24 BLANCHED ALMONDS

1. Preheat the oven to 350°F and line two baking sheets with parchment paper. Place the butter, cream cheese, and sweetener in the work bowl of a stand mixer fitted with the paddle attachment and beat at medium speed until light and fluffy. Add the egg, sour cream, extracts, and salt and beat until well combined.

2. Reduce the mixer's speed to low and incorporate the almond flour ½ cup at a time.

3. Form 1½-tablespoon portions of the dough into balls and place them on the baking sheets, making sure to leave about 2 inches between the cookies. Gently press down on the cookies to flatten them and press an almond into the center of each one.

4. Place the cookies in the oven and bake until the edges are set and lightly browned, about 15 minutes. Remove the cookies from the oven and let them cool on the baking sheets before enjoying.

Nutritional Info Per Serving: Calories: 117; Fat: 10.6 g; Net Carbs: 4.5 g; Protein: 3.7 g

Gluten-Free Chocolate & Hazelnut Cookies

YIELD: 36 COOKIES | **ACTIVE TIME:** 20 MINUTES | **TOTAL TIME:** 40 MINUTES

1½ CUPS HAZELNUTS, SKINS REMOVED

1¼ CUPS BITTERSWEET CHOCOLATE CHIPS

3 TABLESPOONS UNSALTED BUTTER

2 TABLESPOONS BROWN RICE FLOUR

2 TABLESPOONS UNSWEETENED COCOA POWDER

1 TABLESPOON CORNSTARCH

¼ TEASPOON GLUTEN-FREE BAKING POWDER

¼ TEASPOON XANTHAN GUM

¼ TEASPOON KOSHER SALT

2 LARGE EGGS

½ CUP SUGAR

2 TABLESPOONS HAZELNUT-FLAVORED LIQUEUR

½ TEASPOON PURE VANILLA EXTRACT

1 CUP SEMISWEET CHOCOLATE CHIPS

1. Preheat the oven to 350°F and line two baking sheets with parchment paper. Place the hazelnuts on a separate baking sheet and toast for 5 to 7 minutes. Remove from the oven and let cool.

2. Fill a small saucepan halfway with water and bring it to a gentle simmer. Place the bittersweet chocolate chips and butter in a heatproof bowl, place it over the simmering water, and stir until melted and smooth. Remove the mixture from heat and let it cool for 5 minutes.

3. Place the rice flour, cocoa powder, cornstarch, baking powder, xanthan gum, and salt in a mixing bowl and whisk to combine. Place the eggs, sugar, liqueur, and vanilla in a separate mixing bowl. Beat at high speed with a handheld mixer fitted with the paddle attachment until combined. Add the melted chocolate, beat to incorporate, and then gradually incorporate the dry mixture. Fold in the hazelnuts and semisweet chocolate chips.

4. Form tablespoons of the dough into balls and place them on the baking sheets. Bake for 10 to 12 minutes, until they are dry to the touch. Remove from the oven and let them cool on the baking sheets for a few minutes before transferring the cookies to wire racks to cool completely.

Macarons

YIELD: 30 MACARONS | **ACTIVE TIME:** 1 HOUR | **TOTAL TIME:** 4 HOURS

11 OZ. FINE ALMOND FLOUR

11 OZ. CONFECTIONERS' SUGAR

8 EGG WHITES

PINCH OF FINE SEA SALT

11 OZ. SUGAR

½ CUP WATER

2 DROPS OF GEL FOOD COLORING (OPTIONAL)

1. Place the almond flour and confectioners' sugar in a food processor and blitz for about 1 minute, until the mixture is thoroughly combined and has a fine texture. Place the mixture in a mixing bowl, add three of the egg whites and the salt, and stir with a rubber spatula until the mixture is almost a paste. Set the mixture aside.

2. Place the sugar and water in a small saucepan. Place a candy thermometer in the saucepan and cook the mixture over high heat.

3. While the syrup is coming to a boil, place the remaining egg whites in the work bowl of a stand mixer fit with the whisk attachment, and whip on medium until they hold firm peaks.

4. Cook the syrup until it is 245°F. Remove the pan from heat and carefully add the syrup to the whipped egg whites, slowly pouring it down the side of the work bowl. When all of the syrup has been added, whip the mixture until it is glossy, holds stiff peaks, and has cooled slightly. If desired, stir in the food coloring.

5. Add half of the meringue to the almond flour mixture and fold to incorporate. Fold in the remaining meringue. When incorporated, the batter should be smooth, very glossy, and not too runny.

6. Fit a piping bag with a plain tip and fill it with the batter. Pipe evenly sized rounds onto baking sheets, leaving an inch of space between each one. You want the rounds to be about the size of a silver dollar (approximately 2 inches wide) when you pipe them onto the sheet; they will spread slightly as they sit.

7. Gently tap each sheet pan to smooth the tops of the macarons.

8. Let the macarons sit at room temperature, uncovered, for 1 hour. This allows a skin to form on them.

9. Preheat the oven to 325°F.

10. Place the macarons in the oven and bake for 10 minutes. Rotate the baking sheet and let them bake for another 5 minutes. Turn off the oven, crack the oven door, and let the macarons sit in the oven for 5 minutes.

11. Remove the cookies from the oven and let them sit on a cooling rack for 2 hours. When the macarons are completely cool, fill as desired.

Almond Cookies

YIELD: 18 COOKIES | **ACTIVE TIME:** 15 MINUTES | **TOTAL TIME:** 1 HOUR

1¼ OZ. ALL-PURPOSE FLOUR

2 OZ. CONFECTIONERS' SUGAR

3½ OZ. SUGAR

2 EGG WHITES

½ LB. UNSWEETENED ALMOND PASTE

½ CUP SLIVERED ALMONDS

1. Preheat the oven to 350°F and line two baking sheets with parchment paper. Place the flour, confectioners' sugar, sugar, egg whites, and almond paste in a large mixing bowl and work the mixture with your hands until an extremely sticky dough forms.

2. Place the almonds in a bowl. Place teaspoons of the dough in the bowl of almonds and roll the pieces of dough until completely coated. Place on the baking sheets.

3. Place in the oven and bake for about 15 minutes, until golden brown. Remove and let cool on the baking sheets for a few minutes before transferring to a wire rack to cool completely.

Cornmeal Cookies

YIELD: 24 COOKIES | **ACTIVE TIME:** 20 MINUTES | **TOTAL TIME:** 3 HOURS

4 OZ. UNSALTED BUTTER

3 OZ. CONFECTIONERS' SUGAR

1 LARGE EGG, AT ROOM TEMPERATURE

½ TEASPOON PURE VANILLA EXTRACT

3.2 OZ. ALL-PURPOSE FLOUR

¼ CUP FINE CORNMEAL

2 TABLESPOONS CORNSTARCH

¼ TEASPOON FINE SEA SALT

1. In the work bowl of a stand mixer fitted with the paddle attachment, cream the butter and confectioners' sugar at medium speed until pale and fluffy, scraping down the sides of the bowl as needed. Add the egg and vanilla, reduce the speed to low, and beat to incorporate. Gradually incorporate the flour, cornmeal, cornstarch, and salt and beat until the mixture is a stiff dough.

2. Place the dough on a sheet of parchment paper and roll it into a log that is 2½ inches in diameter. Cover in plastic wrap and refrigerate for 2 hours.

3. Preheat the oven to 350°F and line two baking sheets with parchment paper. Cut the chilled dough into ⅓-inch-thick rounds and arrange the cookies on the baking sheets. Place the cookies in the oven and bake until the edges start to brown, about 10 minutes. Remove from the oven, let cool on the sheets for a few minutes, and then transfer the cookies to wire racks to cool completely.

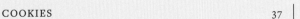

Macarons
SEE PAGE 36

Brownies from Scratch

YIELD: 12 BROWNIES | **ACTIVE TIME:** 30 MINUTES | **TOTAL TIME:** 3 HOURS

7½ OZ. DARK CHOCOLATE (55 TO 65 PERCENT)

1½ CUPS UNSALTED BUTTER

¾ LB. SUGAR

¾ LB. LIGHT BROWN SUGAR

¼ CUP PLUS 1 TABLESPOON COCOA POWDER

1 TEASPOON KOSHER SALT

5 EGGS

1½ TABLESPOONS PURE VANILLA EXTRACT

9½ OZ. ALL-PURPOSE FLOUR

1. Preheat the oven to 350°F. Line a 13 x 9–inch baking pan with parchment paper and coat it with nonstick cooking spray.

2. Fill a small saucepan halfway with water and bring it to a simmer. Place the dark chocolate and butter in a heatproof bowl, place it over the simmering water, and stir until they have melted and been combined. Remove from heat and set aside.

3. In a separate mixing bowl, whisk the sugar, brown sugar, cocoa powder, and salt together, making sure to break up any clumps. Whisk in the eggs, vanilla, and melted chocolate mixture and then gradually add the flour, whisking to thoroughly incorporate before adding the next bit.

4. Pour the batter into the baking pan and use a rubber spatula to even out the top. Lightly tap the baking pan on the counter and remove any air bubbles.

5. Place the brownies in the oven and bake until a cake tester comes out clean, 30 to 40 minutes.

6. Remove from the oven, transfer the brownies to a cooling rack, and let them cool completely. Once they are cool, transfer to the refrigerator and chill for 1 hour.

7. Run a paring knife along the sides of the pan, cut the brownies into squares, and enjoy.

Madeleines

YIELD: 30 MADELEINES | **ACTIVE TIME:** 40 MINUTES | **TOTAL TIME:** 3 HOURS AND 30 MINUTES

½ LB. SUGAR

½ LB. EGG WHITES

ZEST OF 1 LEMON

3.2 OZ. FINE ALMOND FLOUR

3.2 OZ. ALL-PURPOSE FLOUR

7 OZ. UNSALTED BUTTER

1 TEASPOON PURE VANILLA EXTRACT

CONFECTIONERS' SUGAR, FOR DUSTING

1. In the work bowl of a stand mixer fitted with the paddle attachment, beat the sugar, egg whites, and lemon zest on medium until the mixture is light and fluffy. Add the almond flour and flour and beat until incorporated. Set the mixture aside.

2. Place the butter in a small saucepan and melt it over low heat.

3. Set the mixer to low speed and slowly pour the melted butter into the mixer. When the butter has been incorporated, add the vanilla and beat until incorporated.

4. Place the madeleine batter mixture into two piping bags. Place the bags in the refrigerator until the batter is set, about 2 hours.

5. Preheat the oven to 350°F. Coat your madeleine pans with nonstick cooking spray. Cut a ½-inch slit in the piping bags and pipe about 1 tablespoon of batter in the center of each seashell mold.

6. Place the pans in the oven and bake until the edges of the madeleines turn golden brown, about 10 minutes. Remove from the oven, turn the cookies immediately out onto a cooling rack, and let them cool completely.

7. Once cool, lightly dust the tops of the madeleines with confectioners' sugar.

Keto Coconut Macaroons

YIELD: 36 COOKIES | **ACTIVE TIME:** 20 MINUTES | **TOTAL TIME:** 1 HOUR

8.4 OZ. UNSWEETENED SHREDDED COCONUT

5 LARGE EGG WHITES, AT ROOM TEMPERATURE

½ TEASPOON CREAM OF TARTAR

¼ TEASPOON KOSHER SALT

½ CUP GRANULATED ERYTHRITOL

½ CUP POWDERED ERYTHRITOL

1 TEASPOON PURE VANILLA EXTRACT

1. Preheat the oven to 350°F and line two baking sheets with parchment paper. Place the coconut on another baking sheet, place it in the oven, and toast the coconut until it is lightly browned, 7 to 10 minutes. Remove the coconut from the oven and let it cool. Reduce the oven temperature to 275°F.

2. Place the egg whites in a mixing bowl and beat them with a handheld mixer until frothy. Add the cream of tartar and salt and beat until the mixture holds soft peaks. Incorporate both forms of erythritol a tablespoon at a time and beat until the mixture holds stiff peaks. Stir in the vanilla and then fold the toasted coconut into the meringue.

3. Drop heaping tablespoons of the meringue onto the parchment-lined baking sheets, leaving about 1½ inches between each portion.

4. Place the macaroons in the oven and bake until they are dry to the touch. Remove the cookies from the oven and place the baking sheets on wire racks to cool.

Nutritional Info Per Serving (1 Serving = 3 Cookies):
Calories: 96; Fat: 9 g; Net Carbs: 2.1 g; Protein: 2.4 g

Keto Brownies

YIELD: 16 SERVINGS | **ACTIVE TIME:** 15 MINUTES | **TOTAL TIME:** 2 HOURS

½ LB. UNSALTED BUTTER, PLUS MORE AS NEEDED

1¼ CUPS GUINNESS

11 OZ. SUGAR-FREE CHOCOLATE CHIPS

3 LARGE EGGS

1 TEASPOON PURE VANILLA EXTRACT

¾ CUP ALMOND FLOUR

1 TEASPOON KOSHER SALT

¼ CUP UNSWEETENED COCOA POWDER

1. Preheat the oven to 350°F and coat a square 8-inch cake pan with butter. Place the stout in a medium saucepan, bring it to a boil, and cook until it has reduced by half. Remove the pan from heat and let the stout cool.

2. Place the chocolate chips and butter in a microwave-safe bowl and microwave on medium until melted, removing to stir every 15 seconds.

3. Place the eggs and vanilla in a large mixing bowl and whisk until combined. Slowly whisk in the chocolate-and-butter mixture and then whisk in the reduced stout. Add the almond flour and salt and fold the mixture until it comes together as a smooth batter. Pour the batter into the pan.

4. Place the brownies in the oven and bake until the surface begins to crack and a toothpick inserted into the center comes out with a few moist crumbs attached, about 35 minutes. Remove the brownies from the oven and let them cool in the pan.

5. Sprinkle the cocoa powder over the brownies, cut them into squares, and enjoy.

Nutritional Info Per Serving: Calories: 244; Fat: 20.3 g; Net Carbs: 11.8 g; Protein: 2.6 g

Ginger Molasses Sandwich Cookies

YIELD: 15 COOKIES | **ACTIVE TIME:** 30 MINUTES | **TOTAL TIME:** 1 HOUR

FOR THE COOKIES

3.2 OZ. MARGARINE

7.7 OZ. SUGAR, PLUS MORE AS NEEDED

6.7 OZ. BROWN SUGAR

11.6 OZ. ALL-PURPOSE FLOUR

2 TEASPOONS BAKING SODA

½ TEASPOON FINE SEA SALT

1 TEASPOON GROUND GINGER

1 TEASPOON CINNAMON

2 EGGS

2½ OZ. MOLASSES

FOR THE FILLING

7 OZ. MARSHMALLOW CREME

8.8 OZ. CONFECTIONERS' SUGAR

5.3 OZ. MARGARINE

2.1 OZ. COCONUT OIL

1 TABLESPOON COCONUT MILK

1. Preheat the oven to 325°F. Line a baking sheet with parchment paper.

2. To begin preparations for the cookies, place the margarine and sugar in the work bowl of a stand mixer fitted with the paddle attachment and beat on medium speed until the mixture is light and fluffy.

3. In a separate bowl, combine the remaining dry ingredients.

4. Add the eggs and molasses to the work bowl of the stand mixer and beat to incorporate. With the mixer running, gradually add the dry mixture in and beat until the mixture comes together as a dough.

5. Roll the dough into 1-oz. balls and then roll them in a bowl of sugar. Place the cookies on the parchment-lined baking sheet, making sure to leave plenty of room between each ball.

6. Chill the cookies in the refrigerator for 15 minutes.

7. Place the cookies in the oven and bake until the edges are set and their surfaces cracked, about 12 minutes, rotating the baking sheet halfway through. Even if the centers of the cookies look slightly wet, remove them from the oven. Transfer the cookies to a wire rack and let them cool completely before placing them in the refrigerator.

8. To prepare the filling, place all of the ingredients in a mixing bowl and whip until combined.

9. Place 1 tablespoon of cream filling between two cookies, and gently twist and press the cookies together until the cream gets to the edge. Repeat with the remaining cookies and filling and enjoy.

Gluten-Free Spicy Chocolate Cookies

YIELD: 12 COOKIES | **ACTIVE TIME:** 35 MINUTES | **TOTAL TIME:** 1 HOUR AND 45 MINUTES

3.2 OZ. GLUTEN-FREE ALL-PURPOSE FLOUR

2.6 OZ. COCOA POWDER

½ TEASPOON XANTHAN GUM (IF MISSING FROM ALL-PURPOSE FLOUR)

1 TEASPOON BAKING SODA

2 TEASPOONS CINNAMON

½ TEASPOON CAYENNE PEPPER

2 LARGE EGGS

7 OZ. SUGAR

½ CUP CANOLA OIL

1 TABLESPOON PURE VANILLA EXTRACT

1 CUP CHOCOLATE CHIPS

1. Place the flour, cocoa powder, xanthan gum, baking soda, cinnamon, and cayenne pepper in a bowl and whisk to combine. Set the mixture aside.

2. Place the eggs, sugar, canola oil, and vanilla extract in the work bowl of a stand mixer fitted with the paddle attachment and beat on medium until the mixture is well combined.

3. Add the dry mixture to the work bowl and beat on low until the mixture comes together as a smooth dough, about 5 minutes. Add the chocolate chips and fold until combined.

4. Place the dough in the refrigerator and chill it for 1 hour.

5. Preheat the oven to 325°F. Line a baking sheet with parchment paper. Form the dough into 1½-oz. balls and place them on the baking sheet.

6. Place the cookies in the oven and bake until the edges are set, about 12 minutes. Remove the cookies from the oven, transfer them to a wire rack, and let them cool completely before enjoying.

Coconut Macaroons

YIELD: 12 MACAROONS | **ACTIVE TIME:** 45 MINUTES | **TOTAL TIME:** 3 HOURS

1 (14 OZ.) CAN OF SWEETENED CONDENSED MILK

7 OZ. SWEETENED SHREDDED COCONUT

7 OZ. UNSWEETENED SHREDDED COCONUT

¼ TEASPOON KOSHER SALT

½ TEASPOON PURE VANILLA EXTRACT

2 EGG WHITES

CHOCOLATE GANACHE (SEE PAGE 523), WARM

1. Line a baking sheet with parchment paper. In a mixing bowl, mix the sweetened condensed milk, shredded coconut, salt, and vanilla together with a rubber spatula until combined. Set the mixture aside.

2. In the work bowl of a stand mixer fitted with the whisk attachment, whip the egg whites until they hold stiff peaks. Add the whipped egg whites to the coconut mixture and fold to incorporate.

3. Scoop 2-oz. portions of the mixture onto the baking sheet, making sure to leave enough space between them. Place the baking sheet in the refrigerator and let the dough firm up for 1 hour.

4. Preheat the oven to 350°F.

5. Place the cookies in the oven and bake until they are lightly golden brown, 20 to 25 minutes.

6. Remove the cookies from the oven, transfer them to a cooling rack, and let them cool for 1 hour.

7. Dip the bottoms of the macaroons into the ganache and then place them back on the baking sheet. If desired, drizzle some of the ganache over the tops of the cookies. Refrigerate until the chocolate is set, about 5 minutes, before serving.

Gluten-Free Chocolate Polvorones

YIELD: 24 COOKIES | **ACTIVE TIME:** 15 MINUTES | **TOTAL TIME:** 1 HOUR

⅓ CUP GROUND PECANS

1⅔ CUPS CONFECTIONERS' SUGAR, DIVIDED

1½ CUPS GLUTEN-FREE ALL-PURPOSE FLOUR

¾ CUP GLUTEN-FREE COCOA POWDER

½ TEASPOON PSYLLIUM HUSKS

¼ TEASPOON XANTHAN GUM

¼ TEASPOON FINE SEA SALT

½ LB. UNSALTED BUTTER, CHILLED AND CUBED

1 LARGE EGG

1. Preheat the oven to 350°F. Line two large baking sheets with parchment paper and coat with nonstick cooking spray. In a small mixing bowl, combine the pecans and ⅔ cup of confectioners' sugar.

2. Sift the flour, cocoa powder, psyllium husks, xanthan gum, and salt in a separate mixing bowl. Add the butter and work the mixture until it comes together as a coarse, crumbly dough. Add the pecan mixture to the dough and knead to incorporate. Add the egg and knead until the dough is smooth.

3. Form the dough into small balls and place them on the baking sheets, making sure to leave enough space between them. Place the cookies in the oven and bake until the cookies are golden brown, 12 to 15 minutes.

4. Remove the cookies from the oven and let the cookies cool on the sheets for 2 minutes. Sift the remaining confectioners' sugar into a mixing bowl, roll the cookies in it until coated, and transfer to a wire rack to cool completely.

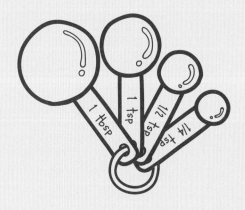

Gluten-Free Cornflake Cookies

YIELD: 18 COOKIES | **ACTIVE TIME:** 30 MINUTES | **TOTAL TIME:** 1 HOUR AND 45 MINUTES

¾ CUP CASTER SUGAR

6 OZ. UNSALTED BUTTER, DIVIDED INTO TABLESPOONS

7 TABLESPOONS HEAVY CREAM

¼ CUP HONEY

¾ CUP SLICED ALMONDS

2 TABLESPOONS CORNSTARCH

3½ CUPS GLUTEN-FREE CORNFLAKES

ZEST OF 1 LEMON

1 TABLESPOON CHOPPED CANDIED CITRUS PEELS

½ CUP CHOPPED CANDIED CHERRIES

⅔ CUP RAISINS

1¼ CUPS DARK CHOCOLATE CHIPS

1¼ CUPS WHITE CHOCOLATE CHIPS

1. Preheat the oven to 350°F and line a baking sheet with parchment paper. Place the sugar, butter, cream, and honey in a large saucepan, and warm, while stirring, over medium heat until thoroughly combined. Remove the saucepan from heat, and stir in the almonds, cornstarch, cornflakes, lemon zest, candied citrus peels, cherries, and raisins. Let the mixture cool.

2. Place tablespoons of the batter onto the baking sheet and flatten them. Bake for about 10 minutes, until the top starts to brown. Remove from the oven, transfer to a wire rack, and let cool.

3. Fill a small saucepan halfway with water and bring it to a gentle simmer. Place the dark chocolate chips in a heatproof bowl, place it over the simmering water, and stir until melted and smooth. Remove the mixture from heat and let it cool for 5 minutes. Repeat with the white chocolate chips. Dip half of the cookies in the dark chocolate, the other half in the white chocolate, and let them set before serving.

Gluten-Free Cranberry & Nut Bars

YIELD: 36 BARS | **ACTIVE TIME:** 20 MINUTES | **TOTAL TIME:** 45 MINUTES

¾ CUP CHOPPED WALNUTS

1 CUP BROWN RICE FLOUR

⅓ CUP POTATO STARCH

¼ CUP TAPIOCA STARCH

1 TEASPOON GLUTEN-FREE BAKING POWDER

¾ TEASPOON XANTHAN GUM

¼ TEASPOON KOSHER SALT

4 OZ. UNSALTED BUTTER, SOFTENED

1¼ CUPS FIRMLY PACKED LIGHT BROWN SUGAR

2 LARGE EGGS

½ TEASPOON PURE VANILLA EXTRACT

1 CUP CHOPPED FRESH OR FROZEN CRANBERRIES

1. Preheat the oven to 350°F and grease a 13 x 9–inch baking pan with nonstick cooking spray. Place the walnuts on a baking sheet, place it in the oven, and toast for 5 to 7 minutes. Remove from the oven and let cool.

2. Place the rice flour, potato starch, tapioca starch, baking powder, xanthan gum, and salt in a mixing bowl and whisk to combine. Place the butter and brown sugar in a separate mixing bowl. Beat at medium speed with a handheld mixer fitted with the paddle attachment until light and fluffy, scraping down the sides of the bowl as needed. Incorporate the eggs one at a time, and then add the vanilla. Beat until incorporated. Gradually add the dry mixture and beat until the dough just holds together. Fold the walnuts and cranberries into the dough and then press it into the baking pan.

3. Bake for about 20 minutes, until the top is brown. Remove from the oven and let cool in the pan before cutting into bars.

Gluten-Free Double Chocolate Cookies

YIELD: 18 COOKIES | **ACTIVE TIME:** 15 MINUTES | **TOTAL TIME:** 1 HOUR

1¼ CUPS ALMOND FLOUR

½ CUP GLUTEN-FREE COCOA POWDER

1 TEASPOON GLUTEN-FREE BAKING SODA

¼ TEASPOON FINE SEA SALT, PLUS MORE FOR TOPPING

1 CUP DARK CHOCOLATE CHUNKS

1 LARGE EGG, AT ROOM TEMPERATURE

¼ CUP SUGAR

½ CUP BROWN SUGAR

4 OZ. UNSALTED BUTTER, SOFTENED

1 TEASPOON PURE VANILLA EXTRACT

1. Preheat the oven to 350°F. Line two baking sheets with parchment paper and coat with nonstick cooking spray. In a mixing bowl, combine the almond flour, cocoa powder, baking soda, and salt.

2. Fill a small saucepan halfway with water and bring it to a simmer. Place half of the chocolate in a heatproof bowl, place it over the simmering water, and stir until melted and smooth.

3. In the work bowl of a stand mixer fitted with the paddle attachment, cream the egg, sugars, butter, and vanilla on medium speed until the mixture is very light and fluffy, about 5 minutes. Add the melted chocolate and gently stir to incorporate. Add the almond flour mixture and remaining chocolate and beat until the mixture comes together as a soft cookie dough.

4. Drop teaspoons of the dough on the baking sheets, making sure to leave enough space between them. Place in the oven and bake until set, 10 to 12 minutes. Remove from the oven, sprinkle salt over them, and let the cookies cool on the sheets for a few minutes before transferring to a wire rack to cool completely.

Chocolate Crinkle Cookies

YIELD: 20 COOKIES | **ACTIVE TIME:** 45 MINUTES | **TOTAL TIME:** 2 HOURS AND 30 MINUTES

9 OZ. DARK CHOCOLATE
(55 TO 65 PERCENT)

4½ OZ. UNSALTED BUTTER,
SOFTENED

7 OZ. DARK BROWN SUGAR

¾ TEASPOON PURE VANILLA
EXTRACT

2 EGGS

7 OZ. ALL-PURPOSE FLOUR

2½ OZ. COCOA POWDER

2 TEASPOONS BAKING
POWDER

1 TEASPOON KOSHER SALT

2 CUPS CONFECTIONERS'
SUGAR, FOR COATING

1. Line two baking sheets with parchment paper. Bring water to a simmer in a small saucepan over low heat. Place the chocolate in a heatproof bowl and place the bowl over the simmering water. Occasionally stir the chocolate until it is melted. Remove the bowl from heat and set it aside.

2. In the work bowl of a stand mixer fitted with the paddle attachment, cream the butter, dark brown sugar, and vanilla on medium speed until the mixture is very light and fluffy, about 5 minutes. Scrape down the work bowl and then beat the mixture for another 5 minutes.

3. Reduce the speed to low, add the melted chocolate, and beat until incorporated, scraping down the work bowl as needed.

4. Add the eggs one at a time and beat until incorporated, again scraping the work bowl as needed. When both eggs have been incorporated, beat for another minute.

5. Add the flour, cocoa powder, baking powder, and salt and beat until the mixture comes together as a smooth dough.

6. Drop 2-oz. portions of the dough on the baking sheets, making sure to leave enough space between them. Place the baking sheets in the refrigerator and let the dough firm up for 1 hour.

7. Preheat the oven to 350°F. Place the confectioners' sugar in a mixing bowl, toss the cookie dough balls in the sugar until completely coated, and then place them back on the baking sheets.

8. Place the cookies in the oven and bake until a cake tester comes out clean after being inserted, 12 to 14 minutes.

9. Remove the cookies from the oven, transfer them to a cooling rack, and let them cool for 20 to 30 minutes before enjoying.

Chocolate-Covered Marshmallow Cookies

YIELD: 24 COOKIES | **ACTIVE TIME:** 30 MINUTES | **TOTAL TIME:** 3 HOURS AND 30 MINUTES

13.2 OZ. ALL-PURPOSE
FLOUR, PLUS MORE AS
NEEDED

⅔ CUP SUGAR

½ TEASPOON FINE SEA SALT

¾ TEASPOON BAKING
POWDER

½ TEASPOON BAKING SODA

1 TEASPOON CINNAMON

6 OZ. UNSALTED
BUTTER, DIVIDED INTO
TABLESPOONS

3 LARGE EGGS, LIGHTLY
BEATEN

12 LARGE MARSHMALLOWS,
HALVED

2 CUPS DARK CHOCOLATE
CHIPS

1 TABLESPOON COCONUT
OIL

1. Place the flour, sugar, salt, baking powder, baking soda, and cinnamon in a mixing bowl and whisk to combine. Add the butter and work the mixture with a pastry blender until it is coarse crumbs. Add the eggs and stir until a stiff dough forms. Shape the dough into a ball, cover with plastic wrap, and refrigerate for 1 hour.

2. Preheat the oven to 375°F and line two baking sheets with parchment paper. Place the dough on a flour-dusted work surface and roll out to ¼ inch thick. Cut the dough into 24 rounds and place them on the baking sheets.

3. Place in the oven and bake for about 10 minutes, until the edges have browned. Remove from the oven and transfer the cookies to wire racks to cool completely. Leave the oven on.

4. When the cookies are cool, place a marshmallow half on each cookie. Place them back in the oven and, while keeping a close eye on the cookies, bake until the marshmallows start to slump. Remove from the oven and let cool completely on the baking sheets.

5. Bring water to a simmer in a small saucepan over low heat. Place the chocolate in a heatproof bowl and place the bowl over the simmering water. Occasionally stir the chocolate until it is melted. Remove the bowl from heat, add the coconut oil to the melted chocolate, and stir until incorporated.

6. Drop the cookies into the chocolate, turning to coat all sides. Carefully remove the coated cookies with a fork, hold them over the bowl to let any excess chocolate drip off, and place them on pieces of parchment paper. Let the chocolate set before serving.

Chocolate Crinkle Cookies
SEE PAGE 54

Fiori di Mandorle

YIELD: 24 COOKIES | **ACTIVE TIME:** 20 MINUTES | **TOTAL TIME:** 1 HOUR

10.2 OZ. FINE ALMOND
FLOUR

½ LB. CONFECTIONERS'
SUGAR, PLUS MORE FOR
DUSTING

ZEST OF 1 LEMON

2 LARGE EGGS, LIGHTLY
BEATEN

1 TABLESPOON MILK

24 CANDIED CHERRIES

1. Preheat the oven to 350°F and line two baking sheets with parchment paper. Place the almond flour, confectioners' sugar, and lemon zest in a large mixing bowl and stir to combine. Add the eggs and milk and work the mixture with your hands until a soft, slightly sticky dough forms.

2. Dust your hands with confectioners' sugar and then roll tablespoons of the dough into balls. Place them on the baking sheets and dust them with additional confectioners' sugar. Make an indent with your thumb in each piece of dough and fill with a candied cherry.

3. Place in the oven and bake for about 18 minutes, until golden brown and dry to the touch. Remove from the oven and transfer to wire racks to cool completely.

Orange Spice Cookies

YIELD: 24 COOKIES | **ACTIVE TIME:** 20 MINUTES | **TOTAL TIME:** 50 MINUTES

7 OZ. SUGAR

ZEST OF 1 ORANGE

11.2 OZ. ALL-PURPOSE FLOUR

1 TEASPOON BAKING SODA

1½ TEASPOONS CINNAMON

1½ TEASPOONS GROUND GINGER

½ TEASPOON GROUND CLOVES

¼ TEASPOON ALLSPICE

¼ TEASPOON BLACK PEPPER

¼ TEASPOON FINE SEA SALT

6 OZ. UNSALTED BUTTER, SOFTENED

2.7 OZ. DARK BROWN SUGAR

1 LARGE EGG YOLK

1 TEASPOON PURE VANILLA EXTRACT

½ CUP MOLASSES

1. Preheat the oven to 375°F and line two baking sheets with parchment paper. Place one-quarter of the sugar and 2 teaspoons of orange zest in a food processor and pulse until combined. Place the sugar mixture in a square baking dish and set aside. Place the flour, baking soda, spices, and salt in a mixing bowl, whisk to combine, and set aside.

2. In the work bowl of a stand mixer fitted with the paddle attachment, beat the butter, remaining orange zest, brown sugar, and remaining sugar at medium speed until pale and fluffy, scraping down the sides of the bowl as needed. Add the egg yolk and vanilla, reduce the speed to low, and beat to incorporate. Add the molasses and beat to incorporate. Add the dry mixture and beat until the dough just holds together.

3. Form tablespoons of the dough into balls, roll them in the orange sugar, and place them on the baking sheets. Working with one sheet of cookies at a time, place them in the oven and bake for about 10 minutes, until they are set at their edges but the centers are still soft. Remove from the oven and let cool on the baking sheets for 5 minutes before transferring them to wire racks to cool completely.

White Chocolate & Cranberry Cookies

YIELD: 48 COOKIES | **ACTIVE TIME:** 15 MINUTES | **TOTAL TIME:** 3 HOURS

13¼ OZ. ALL-PURPOSE FLOUR

1 TEASPOON BAKING SODA

1 TEASPOON FINE SEA SALT

½ LB. UNSALTED BUTTER, SOFTENED

7 OZ. LIGHT BROWN SUGAR

3½ OZ. SUGAR

2 LARGE EGGS, AT ROOM TEMPERATURE

2 TEASPOONS PURE VANILLA EXTRACT

1½ CUPS WHITE CHOCOLATE CHIPS

1 CUP SWEETENED DRIED CRANBERRIES

1. Place the flour, baking soda, and salt in a large mixing bowl and whisk to combine. Place the butter, brown sugar, and sugar in the work bowl of a stand mixer fitted with the paddle attachment and beat at medium speed until pale and fluffy, scraping down the sides of the bowl as needed. Reduce the speed to low and incorporate the eggs one at a time. Add the vanilla and beat to incorporate.

2. With the mixer running on low speed, gradually add the dry mixture to the wet mixture and beat until a smooth dough forms. Add the white chocolate chips and dried cranberries and fold until evenly distributed. Cover the dough with plastic wrap and refrigerate for 2 hours.

3. Preheat the oven to 350°F and line two large baking sheets with parchment paper. Drop tablespoons of the dough onto the baking sheets and, working with one baking sheet at a time, place the cookies in the oven and bake for about 10 minutes, until lightly browned. Remove from the oven and let cool on the baking sheets for 5 minutes before transferring to wire racks to cool completely.

Florentines

YIELD: 30 COOKIES | **ACTIVE TIME:** 10 MINUTES | **TOTAL TIME:** 45 MINUTES

¾ CUP SUGAR

1 TEASPOON PURE VANILLA EXTRACT

7 TABLESPOONS HEAVY CREAM

1½ OZ. UNSALTED BUTTER

1½ CUPS SLIVERED ALMONDS

⅓ CUP CANDIED CITRUS PEELS

⅓ CUP DRIED CHERRIES OR PLUMS, CHOPPED

⅓ CUP RAISINS

1¼ CUPS DARK CHOCOLATE CHIPS

1. Place the sugar, vanilla, and cream in a saucepan and bring to a boil. Remove from heat, add the butter, and let it melt. Stir in the almonds, candied citrus peels, dried cherries or plums, and raisins.

2. Preheat the oven to 400°F and line two baking sheets with parchment paper. Place teaspoons of the mixture on the baking sheets, place the cookies in the oven, and bake for 5 to 10 minutes, until golden brown. Remove from the oven and let the cookies cool on the baking sheets for 5 minutes before transferring to wire racks to cool completely.

3. Fill a saucepan halfway with water and bring to a gentle simmer. Place the chocolate chips in a heatproof bowl, place it over the simmering water, and stir until melted. Spread the melted chocolate on the undersides of the Florentines and leave to set before serving.

Kipferl Biscuits

YIELD: 12 COOKIES | **ACTIVE TIME:** 40 MINUTES | **TOTAL TIME:** 2 HOURS

6.7 OZ. ALL-PURPOSE FLOUR, PLUS MORE AS NEEDED

1½ OZ. UNSWEETENED COCOA POWDER

½ TEASPOON INSTANT ESPRESSO POWDER

¼ TEASPOON FINE SEA SALT

½ LB. UNSALTED BUTTER, DIVIDED INTO TABLESPOONS AND SOFTENED

3 OZ. CONFECTIONERS' SUGAR, SIFTED

2½ OZ. FINE ALMOND FLOUR

1 TEASPOON PURE VANILLA EXTRACT

½ CUP WHITE CHOCOLATE CHIPS

1. Place all of the ingredients, except for the white chocolate chips, in the work bowl of a stand mixer fitted with the paddle attachment and beat at medium speed until the mixture comes together as a soft dough. Flatten the dough into a disc, cover it with plastic wrap, and refrigerate for 1 hour.

2. Preheat the oven to 350°F and line two large baking sheets with parchment paper. Remove the dough from the fridge and let it stand at room temperature for 5 minutes. Place the dough on a flour-dusted work surface, roll it into a ¾-inch-thick log, cut it into 2-inch-long pieces, and roll them to form into cylinders with your hands, while tapering and curling the ends to create crescent shapes. Place them on the baking sheets.

3. Place in the oven and bake for about 15 minutes, until set and firm. Remove from the oven and transfer the cookies to wire racks to cool.

4. Fill a small saucepan halfway with water and bring it to a gentle simmer. Place the white chocolate chips in a heatproof bowl, place it over the simmering water, and stir until melted. Drizzle the melted white chocolate over the cooled biscuits and let it set before serving.

Pfeffernüsse

YIELD: 24 COOKIES | **ACTIVE TIME:** 30 MINUTES | **TOTAL TIME:** 2 HOURS

11.2 OZ. ALL-PURPOSE FLOUR, SIFTED

½ TEASPOON FINE SEA SALT

½ TEASPOON BLACK PEPPER

½ TEASPOON CINNAMON

¼ TEASPOON BAKING SODA

¼ TEASPOON ALLSPICE

¼ TEASPOON FRESHLY GRATED NUTMEG

PINCH OF GROUND CLOVES

4 OZ. UNSALTED BUTTER, SOFTENED

7 OZ. LIGHT BROWN SUGAR

3 TABLESPOONS MOLASSES, WARMED

1 LARGE EGG

2¼ CUPS CONFECTIONERS' SUGAR

1. Place the flour, salt, pepper, cinnamon, baking soda, allspice, nutmeg, and cloves in a large mixing bowl and whisk to combine. Place the butter, brown sugar, and molasses in the work bowl of a stand mixer fitted with the paddle attachment and beat at medium speed until pale and fluffy, scraping down the sides of the bowl as needed. Add the egg and beat to incorporate. With the mixer running on low speed, gradually add the dry mixture to the wet mixture and beat until the mixture comes together as a dough. Cover the dough in plastic wrap and refrigerate for 1 hour.

2. Preheat the oven to 350°F and line two baking sheets with parchment paper. Form tablespoons of the dough into rounded rectangles and place them on the baking sheets. Place the cookies in the oven and bake for 12 to 14 minutes, until the cookies are firm. Remove from the oven and transfer to wire racks to cool briefly.

3. Place the confectioners' sugar in a bowl and toss the warm cookies in it until completely coated. Place the cookies back on the wire racks to cool completely.

Gluten-Free Ginger Cookies

YIELD: 18 COOKIES | **ACTIVE TIME:** 15 MINUTES | **TOTAL TIME:** 1 HOUR

¼ CUP UNSALTED BUTTER, SOFTENED

⅓ CUP SUGAR

1 LARGE EGG YOLK

1 TEASPOON PURE VANILLA EXTRACT

1⅓ CUPS GLUTEN-FREE ALL-PURPOSE FLOUR

2 TEASPOONS GLUTEN-FREE BAKING POWDER

1 TEASPOON GROUND GINGER

½ TEASPOON CINNAMON

¼ TEASPOON FINE SEA SALT

2 TABLESPOONS CANDIED GINGER, CHOPPED

2 TABLESPOONS MILK

1. Preheat the oven to 375°F. Line two baking sheets with parchment paper. In the work bowl of a stand mixer fitted with the paddle attachment, cream the butter and sugar on medium speed until the mixture is very light and fluffy, about 5 minutes. Add the egg yolk and vanilla and beat until incorporated. Add the flour, baking powder, ginger, cinnamon, salt, candied ginger, and milk and beat the mixture until it comes together as a soft dough.

2. Roll tablespoons of the dough into balls and arrange them on the baking sheets, making sure to leave enough space between them. Flatten slightly, place in the oven, and bake until golden brown and cracked, 10 to 12 minutes. Remove from the oven and let the cookies cool on the baking sheets for 5 minutes before transferring to cooling racks to cool completely.

Gluten-Free Hazelnut & Almond Cookies

YIELD: 24 COOKIES | **ACTIVE TIME:** 15 MINUTES | **TOTAL TIME:** 1 HOUR

1 CUP ALMOND FLOUR

1 CUP HAZELNUT FLOUR

⅓ CUP UNSALTED BUTTER, SOFTENED

⅓ CUP BROWN SUGAR

½ TEASPOON PURE VANILLA EXTRACT

¼ TEASPOON FINE SEA SALT

1 SMALL EGG WHITE, LIGHTLY BEATEN

24 HAZELNUTS

1. Preheat the oven to 350°F. Line two baking sheets with parchment paper. In a mixing bowl, combine the flours, butter, brown sugar, vanilla, salt, and egg white and work the mixture until it comes together as a rough dough.

2. Roll tablespoons of the dough into balls and arrange on the baking sheets, making sure to leave enough space between them. Flatten them slightly and make a slight indent in each one. Place a hazelnut in each indentation, place in the oven, and bake until golden brown, 10 to 12 minutes. Remove from the oven and let the cookies cool on the sheets for a few minutes before transferring to a wire rack to cool completely.

Gluten-Free Honey & Lavender Biscuits

YIELD: 20 COOKIES | **ACTIVE TIME:** 15 MINUTES | **TOTAL TIME:** 1 HOUR AND 30 MINUTES

4 OZ. UNSALTED BUTTER, SOFTENED

¾ CUP BROWN SUGAR

½ CUP ACACIA HONEY

1 LARGE EGG

½ TEASPOON PURE VANILLA EXTRACT

2½ CUPS GLUTEN-FREE ALL-PURPOSE FLOUR, PLUS MORE AS NEEDED

½ TEASPOON XANTHAN GUM

1 TEASPOON BAKING SODA

PINCH OF FINE SEA SALT

1 TABLESPOON DRIED LAVENDER BUDS

1. In the work bowl of a stand mixer fitted with the paddle attachment, cream the butter and brown sugar on medium speed until the mixture is very light and fluffy, about 5 minutes. Add the honey, egg, and vanilla and beat until incorporated, scraping down the work bowl as needed. Sift in the flour, xanthan gum, baking soda, and salt and beat until the mixture comes together as a rough dough. Add the dried lavender and fold to incorporate. Form the dough into a disk, cover in plastic wrap, and chill in the refrigerator for 30 minutes.

2. Preheat the oven to 350°F. Line two baking sheets with parchment paper. Roll out the dough on a flour-dusted work surface to ¼ inch thick. Cut into rounds and arrange them on the baking sheets, making sure to leave enough space between them.

3. Place them in the oven and bake until golden brown and set, 10 to 12 minutes. Remove from the oven and let the cookies cool on the sheets for a few minutes. Transfer them to a wire rack and let them cool completely.

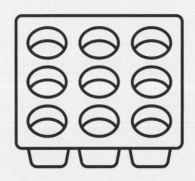

Gluten-Free Macaroons

YIELD: 24 COOKIES | **ACTIVE TIME:** 15 MINUTES | **TOTAL TIME:** 1 HOUR AND 30 MINUTES

2½ CUPS UNSWEETENED SHREDDED COCONUT

1½ TABLESPOONS POTATO STARCH

½ CUP SUGAR

¼ TEASPOON FINE SEA SALT

4 LARGE EGG WHITES

1 TEASPOON PURE VANILLA EXTRACT

1. Combine the shredded coconut, potato starch, sugar, and salt in a large mixing bowl and work the mixture until thoroughly combined, breaking up any chunks of potato starch.

2. Place the egg whites and vanilla in a separate bowl and beat until frothy. Pour the egg white mixture into the coconut mixture and stir until combined. Let the mixture sit for 20 to 30 minutes.

3. Preheat the oven to 325°F and line a baking sheet with a Silpat mat. Drop tablespoons of the dough onto the baking sheet, making sure to leave space between them. Use moist fingers to shape the macaroons into domes.

4. Place the cookies in the oven and bake until golden brown, 20 to 25 minutes. Remove from the oven and let the cookies cool on the baking sheet, as they will crumble if you try to move them too early.

Gluten-Free Peanut Butter Cookies

YIELD: 24 TO 36 COOKIES | **ACTIVE TIME:** 20 MINUTES | **TOTAL TIME:** 35 MINUTES

1 CUP BROWN RICE FLOUR

¼ CUP TAPIOCA FLOUR

¼ CUP CORNSTARCH

1¼ TEASPOONS GLUTEN-FREE BAKING POWDER

½ TEASPOON XANTHAN GUM

½ TEASPOON KOSHER SALT

4 OZ. UNSALTED BUTTER, SOFTENED

1 CUP CREAMY PEANUT BUTTER

½ CUP SUGAR

½ CUP FIRMLY PACKED DARK BROWN SUGAR

1 LARGE EGG

1 LARGE EGG YOLK

½ TEASPOON PURE VANILLA EXTRACT

1. Preheat the oven to 375°F and line two baking sheets with parchment paper. Place the rice flour, tapioca flour, cornstarch, baking powder, xanthan gum, and salt in a mixing bowl and whisk to combine.Place the butter, peanut butter, and sugars in a mixing bowl and beat at medium speed with a handheld mixer fitted with the paddle attachment until pale and fluffy, scraping down the sides of the bowl as needed. Add the egg, egg yolk, and vanilla, reduce the speed to low, and beat to incorporate. Gradually add the dry mixture to the wet mixture and beat at low speed until a stiff dough forms.

2. Form tablespoons of the dough into balls and place them on the baking sheets. Flatten the balls with the tines of a fork, making a crosshatch pattern on the top. Bake for 8 to 10 minutes, until golden brown. Remove from the oven and let the cookies cool on the baking sheets for 5 minutes before transferring them to wire racks to cool completely.

Snowballs

YIELD: 36 COOKIES | **ACTIVE TIME:** 20 MINUTES | **TOTAL TIME:** 1 HOUR

1½ OZ. CREAM CHEESE, SOFTENED

ZEST AND JUICE OF 1 LIME

6 OZ. CONFECTIONERS' SUGAR

12½ OZ. ALL-PURPOSE FLOUR

6 OZ. CASTER (SUPERFINE) SUGAR

¼ TEASPOON FINE SEA SALT

½ LB. UNSALTED BUTTER, DIVIDED INTO TABLESPOONS AND SOFTENED

2 TEASPOONS PURE VANILLA EXTRACT

1½ CUPS SWEETENED SHREDDED COCONUT, FINELY CHOPPED

1. Preheat the oven to 350°F and line two baking sheets with parchment paper. Place 1 tablespoon of the cream cheese and the lime juice in a mixing bowl and stir until the mixture is smooth. Add the confectioners' sugar and whisk until the mixture is smooth and thin, adding lime juice as needed until the glaze reaches the desired consistency. Set the glaze aside.

2. Place the flour, caster sugar, salt, and lime zest in a separate mixing bowl and whisk to combine. Add the butter one piece at a time and use a pastry blender to work the mixture until it is a coarse meal. Add the vanilla and remaining cream cheese and work the mixture until it is a smooth dough.

3. Form the mixture into balls and place them on the baking sheets. Place in the oven and bake until the cookies are a light brown, about 15 minutes. Remove from the oven and let cool to room temperature. Brush the glaze over the cookies and sprinkle the coconut on top. Let the glaze set before serving.

Bourbon Balls

YIELD: 24 COOKIES | **ACTIVE TIME:** 15 MINUTES | **TOTAL TIME:** 3 HOURS

½ LB. UNSALTED BUTTER, SOFTENED

2 LBS. CONFECTIONERS' SUGAR

½ CUP BOURBON

½ TEASPOON FINE SEA SALT

MELTED CHOCOLATE, COCOA POWDER, CONFECTIONERS' SUGAR, OR SHREDDED COCONUT, FOR COATING

1. Combine the butter and 1 pound of the confectioners' sugar in a mixing bowl and beat at low speed with a handheld mixer. Increase the speed to high and beat until light and fluffy. Add the remaining sugar, bourbon, and salt and beat for 2 minutes. Transfer the mixture to the refrigerator and chill until firm, about 2 hours.

2. Line baking sheets with parchment paper and form tablespoons of the butter-and-bourbon mixture into balls. Coat the balls in melted chocolate, cocoa powder, confectioners' sugar, and/or shredded coconut and then transfer the sheets to the refrigerator. Chill for 45 minutes before serving.

Mocha Balls

YIELD: 24 BALLS | **ACTIVE TIME:** 20 MINUTES | **TOTAL TIME:** 1 HOUR

2 TABLESPOONS ESPRESSO POWDER

2 TABLESPOONS BOILING WATER

4 OZ. UNSALTED BUTTER, CUT INTO SMALL PIECES AND SOFTENED

2.3 OZ. SUGAR

1 LARGE EGG, AT ROOM TEMPERATURE

½ TEASPOON PURE VANILLA EXTRACT

3¾ OZ. UNSWEETENED COCOA POWDER

6.7 OZ. ALL-PURPOSE FLOUR

PINCH OF FINE SEA SALT

1. Preheat the oven to 350°F.

2. Place the espresso powder and water in a small bowl and stir until the powder has dissolved. Set aside and let cool.

3. Place the butter and sugar in the work bowl of a stand mixer fitted with the paddle attachment and beat at medium speed until light and fluffy. Add the egg and vanilla, beat until well combined, and then add ¾ oz. of the cocoa powder and the espresso mixture. Beat until combined, scraping down the bowl as necessary. Reduce the speed to low, add the flour and salt, and beat until the mixture comes together as a dough.

4. Form tablespoons of the dough into balls and place them on parchment-lined baking sheets. Place in the oven and bake until firm, about 15 minutes.

5. Sift the remaining cocoa powder into a shallow bowl and use a spatula to transfer a few cookies at a time into the bowl. Roll the cookies around until well coated and then transfer them to wire racks to cool completely.

Oatmeal Raisin Cookies

YIELD: 16 COOKIES | **ACTIVE TIME:** 20 MINUTES | **TOTAL TIME:** 1 HOUR

2 OZ. UNSALTED BUTTER

¼ TEASPOON CINNAMON

5.3 OZ. DARK BROWN SUGAR

3½ OZ. SUGAR

½ CUP CANOLA OIL

1 LARGE EGG

1 LARGE EGG YOLK

1 TEASPOON PURE VANILLA EXTRACT

5 OZ. ALL-PURPOSE FLOUR

½ TEASPOON BAKING SODA

¾ TEASPOON FINE SEA SALT

3 CUPS ROLLED OATS

½ CUP RAISINS

1. Preheat the oven to 350°F.

2. Place the butter in a skillet and warm over medium-high heat until it is a dark golden brown and has a nutty aroma. Transfer to a mixing bowl and whisk in the cinnamon, brown sugar, sugar, and canola oil. When the mixture is combined, add the egg, egg yolk, and vanilla and whisk until incorporated.

3. Place the flour, baking soda, and salt in a separate mixing bowl and whisk to combine. Add this mixture to the wet mixture and stir until well combined. Add the oats and raisins and fold the mixture until they are evenly distributed throughout.

4. Form the dough into 16 balls and divide them between two parchment-lined baking sheets. Press down on the balls of dough to flatten them slightly. Place the sheets in the oven and bake the cookies until the edges start to brown, about 10 minutes. Remove from the oven and let cool on the sheets for 5 minutes. Transfer to a wire rack and let cool completely.

Orange & Rosemary Shortbread

YIELD: 24 COOKIES | **ACTIVE TIME:** 20 MINUTES | **TOTAL TIME:** 2 HOURS

1 LB. UNSALTED BUTTER, SOFTENED

1¾ OZ. SUGAR

¼ CUP FRESH ORANGE JUICE

1 TABLESPOON ORANGE ZEST

2 TEASPOONS FRESH ROSEMARY, FINELY CHOPPED

22½ OZ. ALL-PURPOSE FLOUR

CONFECTIONERS' SUGAR, FOR DUSTING

1. Preheat the oven to 350°F and line two baking sheets with parchment paper.

2. Place all of the ingredients, except the flour and confectioners' sugar, in the work bowl of a stand mixer fitted with the paddle attachment and beat at low speed until the mixture is smooth and creamy.

3. Slowly add the flour and beat until a crumbly dough forms. Press the dough into a rectangle that is approximately ½ inch thick. Cover with plastic wrap and place the dough in the refrigerator for 1 hour.

4. Cut rounds out of the dough and place them on the baking sheets. Dust the cookies with confectioners' sugar, place in the oven, and bake until the edges start to brown, about 15 minutes. Remove and let cool before serving.

Gluten-Free Pumpkin & Cranberry Cookies

YIELD: 18 COOKIES | **ACTIVE TIME:** 15 MINUTES | **TOTAL TIME:** 1 HOUR

1 CUP GLUTEN-FREE ALL-PURPOSE FLOUR

1 TABLESPOON GROUND FLAXSEED MEAL

½ CUP BROWN SUGAR

¼ CUP SUGAR

1 TEASPOON CINNAMON

¼ TEASPOON FINE SEA SALT

½ TEASPOON BAKING SODA

½ CUP PUMPKIN PUREE

¼ CUP COCONUT OIL, MELTED

1 TEASPOON PURE VANILLA EXTRACT

½ CUP DRIED CRANBERRIES

1. Preheat the oven to 350°F. Line two baking sheets with parchment paper. In a large mixing bowl, combine the flour, flaxseed meal, sugars, cinnamon, salt, and baking soda. Add the pumpkin puree, coconut oil, and vanilla and stir until the mixture comes together as a smooth dough. Fold in the cranberries.

2. Drop tablespoons of the cookie dough on the baking sheets, making sure to leave enough space between them. Place in the oven and bake until set and golden brown, 10 to 12 minutes. Remove and let cool on the baking sheets for a few minutes before transferring to cooling racks to cool completely.

Baklava

YIELD: 48 PIECES | **ACTIVE TIME:** 30 MINUTES | **TOTAL TIME:** 1 HOUR

3½ CUPS WALNUTS, TOASTED

17½ OZ. SUGAR

1 TEASPOON CINNAMON

¼ TEASPOON GROUND CLOVES

1 LB. FROZEN PHYLLO DOUGH, THAWED

1½ CUPS UNSALTED BUTTER, MELTED

1½ CUPS WATER

½ CUP HONEY

½ LEMON, SLICED THIN

1 CINNAMON STICK

PISTACHIOS, CHOPPED, FOR GARNISH (OPTIONAL)

1. Place the walnuts, ½ cup of the sugar, the cinnamon and cloves in a food processor. Pulse until very fine and set the mixture aside.

2. Preheat the oven to 375°F and coat a 18 x 13–inch baking sheet with nonstick cooking spray. Place the phyllo sheets on a plate and cover with plastic wrap or a damp paper towel to keep them from drying out. Place 1 sheet of phyllo on the baking sheet and brush with some of the melted butter. Repeat with 7 more sheets and spread one-third of the walnut mixture on top. Place 4 more sheets of phyllo dough on top, brushing each with butter. Spread half of the remaining walnut mixture on top, and then repeat. Top the last of the walnut mixture with the remaining sheets of phyllo dough, brushing each one with butter. Trim the edges to make a neat rectangle.

3. Cut the pastry into squares or triangles, taking care not to cut through the bottom crust. Place in the oven and bake for 25 to 30 minutes, until the top layer of phyllo is brown.

4. While the pastry is cooking, combine the remaining sugar, water, honey, lemon, and cinnamon stick in a saucepan. Bring to a boil over medium heat while stirring occasionally. Reduce the heat to low and simmer for 5 minutes. Strain the syrup and keep it hot while the pastry finishes baking.

5. Remove the baking sheet from the oven and pour the hot syrup over the pastry. Place the pan on a wire rack, allow to cool to room temperature, and then cut through the bottom crust. If desired, garnish with pistachios before serving.

Classic Gingerbread Cookies

YIELD: 24 COOKIES | **ACTIVE TIME:** 20 MINUTES | **TOTAL TIME:** 2 HOURS

6 OZ. UNSALTED BUTTER, SOFTENED

3½ OZ. LIGHT BROWN SUGAR

⅔ CUP MOLASSES

1 LARGE EGG, AT ROOM TEMPERATURE

1 TEASPOON BAKING SODA

1 TEASPOON GROUND GINGER

1 TEASPOON APPLE PIE SPICE

½ TEASPOON FINE SEA SALT

½ TEASPOON PURE VANILLA EXTRACT

¼ TEASPOON FRESHLY GROUND BLACK PEPPER

3 CUPS ALL-PURPOSE FLOUR, PLUS MORE AS NEEDED

ROYAL ICING (SEE PAGE 504)

CANDIES, FOR DECORATION (OPTIONAL)

1. Place the butter and brown sugar in the work bowl of a stand mixer fitted with the paddle attachment and beat at low speed until combined. Increase the speed to high and beat until the mixture is light and fluffy. Add the molasses, egg, baking soda, ginger, apple pie spice, salt, vanilla, and pepper and beat for 1 minute. Slowly add the flour to the mixture and beat until it is a stiff dough.

2. Divide the dough in half and wrap each half in plastic wrap. Flatten each piece into a disc and refrigerate for 1 hour. The dough will keep in the refrigerator for up to 2 days.

3. Preheat the oven to 350°F and line two baking sheets with parchment paper. Place the dough on a flour-dusted work surface and roll to a thickness of ¼ inch. Dip cookie cutters in flour and cut the dough into the desired shapes. Transfer the cookies to the baking sheets and bake until firm, about 10 minutes.

4. Remove the cookies from the oven, let rest for 2 minutes, and then set on wire racks to cool completely. Decorate with the Royal Icing and candies (if desired).

Gingerbread Madeleines

YIELD: 16 MADELEINES | **ACTIVE TIME:** 25 MINUTES | **TOTAL TIME:** 3 HOURS

2½ OZ. UNSALTED BUTTER, PLUS MORE AS NEEDED

3½ OZ. BROWN SUGAR

2 EGGS

1-INCH PIECE OF FRESH GINGER, PEELED AND GRATED

1¼ TEASPOONS PURE VANILLA EXTRACT

1½ TABLESPOONS MOLASSES

⅓ CUP WHOLE MILK

2½ OZ. ALL-PURPOSE FLOUR

2 OZ. CAKE FLOUR

¼ TEASPOON BAKING POWDER

1½ TEASPOONS FINE SEA SALT

¼ TEASPOON GROUND CLOVES

¼ TEASPOON FRESHLY GRATED NUTMEG

1 TEASPOON CINNAMON

1. Place the butter in a small saucepan and cook over medium heat until lightly brown. Remove from heat and let cool to room temperature.

2. Place the butter and brown sugar in the work bowl of a stand mixer fitted with the whisk attachment. Beat on high until light and frothy. Reduce the speed to low, add the eggs one at a time, and beat until incorporated. Add the ginger, vanilla, molasses, and milk and beat until incorporated.

3. Sift the flours and baking powder into a bowl. Add the salt, cloves, nutmeg, and cinnamon and stir to combine.

4. Gradually add the dry mixture to the wet mixture and beat until the dry mixture has been thoroughly incorporated. Transfer the dough to the refrigerator and chill for 2 hours.

5. Preheat the oven to 375°F and brush each shell-shaped depression in the madeleine pan with butter. Place the pan in the freezer for at least 10 minutes.

6. Remove the pan from the freezer and the batter from the refrigerator. Fill each "shell" two-thirds of the way with batter, place the pan in the oven, and bake until a toothpick inserted into the center of a cookie comes out clean, about 12 minutes. Remove from the oven and place the cookies on a wire rack to cool slightly. Serve warm or at room temperature.

Polvorones

YIELD: 36 COOKIES | **ACTIVE TIME:** 20 MINUTES | **TOTAL TIME:** 1 HOUR

½ LB. UNSALTED BUTTER, SOFTENED

7 OZ. CONFECTIONERS' SUGAR

4 OZ. CAKE FLOUR, PLUS MORE AS NEEDED

5 OZ. SELF-RISING FLOUR

1 CUP ALMONDS, BLANCHED AND MINCED

½ TEASPOON PURE VANILLA EXTRACT

WARM WATER (110°F), AS NEEDED

1. Preheat the oven to 350°F and line two baking sheets with parchment paper. Place the butter and 5 oz. of the confectioners' sugar in the work bowl of a stand mixer fitted with the paddle attachment and beat at medium speed until light and fluffy. Add the flours, almonds, and vanilla and beat until the dough is just combined and very stiff. Add a few drops of water, if necessary, to make it pliable.

2. Remove tablespoons of the dough and roll them into balls. Place the balls on the baking sheets and flatten them slightly with the bottom of a glass that has been dipped in flour. Place in the oven and bake until lightly browned, about 10 minutes. Remove from oven.

3. Sift the remaining confectioners' sugar into a shallow bowl and use a spatula to transfer the cookies to the bowl. Roll the cookies in the sugar until they are evenly coated and then transfer them to wire racks to cool completely.

Salted Caramel Macaroons

YIELD: 16 MACAROONS | **ACTIVE TIME:** 20 MINUTES | **TOTAL TIME:** 2 HOURS

6 TABLESPOONS UNSALTED BUTTER

3 TABLESPOONS WHOLE MILK

¾ LB. SOFT CARAMELS

1 TEASPOON FINE SEA SALT

4 CUPS SWEETENED SHREDDED COCONUT

4 OZ. DARK CHOCOLATE CHIPS

1. Place the butter, milk, caramels, and salt in a small saucepan and cook over medium heat. Once the caramels and butter have melted, add the coconut and stir until it is coated.

2. Line a baking sheet with parchment paper and scoop tablespoons of the caramel-and-coconut mixture onto the sheet. Let stand for 1 hour.

3. Fill a small saucepan halfway with water and bring it to a gentle simmer. Place the chocolate chips in a heatproof bowl, place it over the simmering water, and stir until melted.

4. Dip half of the cooled macaroons into the melted chocolate and place them back on the baking sheet. Once all the macaroons have been dipped, drizzle the remaining chocolate over the top. Place in the refrigerator and chill until the chocolate has hardened, about 30 minutes.

Chrusciki

YIELD: 20 COOKIES | **ACTIVE TIME:** 25 MINUTES | **TOTAL TIME:** 1 HOUR AND 30 MINUTES

3 LARGE EGGS, AT ROOM TEMPERATURE

¼ CUP WHOLE MILK

5.2 OZ. SUGAR

4 OZ. UNSALTED BUTTER

1 TEASPOON BAKING SODA

1 TEASPOON PURE VANILLA EXTRACT

½ TEASPOON FINE SEA SALT

½ TEASPOON FRESHLY GRATED NUTMEG

17½ OZ. ALL-PURPOSE FLOUR, PLUS MORE AS NEEDED

CANOLA OIL, AS NEEDED

1 CUP CONFECTIONERS' SUGAR, FOR DUSTING

1. Place the eggs, milk, sugar, and butter in a mixing bowl and whisk until well combined. Whisk in the baking soda, vanilla, salt, and nutmeg, and then add the flour. Mix until a soft dough forms, cover the bowl tightly with plastic wrap, and chill in the refrigerator for 1 hour. The dough will keep in the refrigerator for up to 3 days.

2. Dust a work surface with flour and roll out the dough to ¼ inch thick. Cut into 1-inch-wide strips and then cut the strips on a diagonal every 3 inches to form diamond-shaped cookies.

3. Add canola oil to a Dutch oven until it is 1½ inches deep. Heat to 375°F and add the cookies a few at a time, using a slotted spoon to turn them as they brown. When the cookies are browned all over, remove, set to drain on paper towels, and sprinkle with the confectioners' sugar. Serve immediately.

Vegan Apricot Bars

YIELD: 48 BARS | **ACTIVE TIME:** 15 MINUTES | **TOTAL TIME:** 40 MINUTES

1½ CUPS SWEETENED SHREDDED COCONUT

1 CUP WHOLE WHEAT PASTRY FLOUR

½ CUP ALL-PURPOSE FLOUR

1 CUP FIRMLY PACKED LIGHT BROWN SUGAR

¼ TEASPOON KOSHER SALT

¾ CUP VEGETABLE SHORTENING

1 CUP ROLLED OATS

¾ CUP APRICOT JAM

¾ CUP ALMONDS

1. Preheat the oven to 375°F and grease a 13 x 9–inch baking pan with nonstick cooking spray. Place half of the coconut on a baking sheet and toast it in the oven for 6 to 8 minutes, until it starts to brown. Remove from the oven and let cool.

2. Place the flours, brown sugar, and salt in a food processor and blitz to combine. Add the shortening and blitz until the mixture is coarse crumbs. Transfer the mixture to a mixing bowl, add the toasted coconut and oats, and use your hands to knead the mixture until a smooth dough forms.

3. Reserve ¾ cup dough and press the remaining dough into the bottom of the baking pan. Spread the jam over the dough, crumble the reserved dough on top of the jam, and sprinkle the remaining coconut over everything. Arrange the almonds on top in a decorative pattern.

4. Bake for about 20 minutes, until the top is golden brown. Remove from the oven and let cool in the pan before cutting into bars.

Vegan Chili, Lime & Chocolate Cookies

YIELD: 12 COOKIES | **ACTIVE TIME:** 15 MINUTES | **TOTAL TIME:** 1 HOUR

2 TABLESPOONS GROUND FLAXSEED

⅓ CUP REAL MAPLE SYRUP

1 TEASPOON PURE VANILLA EXTRACT

1 (14 OZ.) CAN OF BLACK BEANS, DRAINED AND RINSED

2 TABLESPOONS COCONUT OIL

⅓ CUP COCOA POWDER

¼ TEASPOON FINE SEA SALT

¼ TEASPOON CAYENNE PEPPER

½ CUP CHOPPED DARK CHOCOLATE (70 PERCENT)

ZEST OF 1 LIME

1. Preheat the oven to 375°F. Line a large baking sheet with parchment paper. Combine the flaxseed, maple syrup, and vanilla in a mixing bowl. Place the black beans, coconut oil, cocoa powder, salt, and cayenne in a food processor and blitz until well combined. Add the maple syrup mixture and pulse until the mixture is a wet dough that can hold its shape.

2. Transfer to a mixing bowl and stir in the chocolate and lime zest. Drop tablespoons of the dough onto the baking sheet, making sure to leave enough space between them. Flatten slightly, place in the oven, and bake until just firm, 10 to 15 minutes. Remove from the oven and let cool on the baking sheets for a few minutes before transferring to a cooling rack to cool completely.

Vegan Crinkle Cookies

YIELD: 36 COOKIES | **ACTIVE TIME:** 20 MINUTES | **TOTAL TIME:** 45 MINUTES

2 TABLESPOONS INSTANT COFFEE GROUNDS

2 TABLESPOONS BOILING WATER

½ CUP VEGETABLE SHORTENING

2 CUPS CONFECTIONERS' SUGAR

¼ CUP SILKEN TOFU

½ TEASPOON PURE VANILLA EXTRACT

¼ CUP UNSWEETENED COCOA POWDER

⅔ CUP ALL-PURPOSE FLOUR

⅔ CUP WHOLE WHEAT PASTRY FLOUR

PINCH OF KOSHER SALT

1. Preheat the oven to 350°F and line two baking sheets with parchment paper. Place the instant coffee and boiling water in a small bowl and stir to dissolve the coffee. Let cool. Place the shortening and ½ cup of the confectioners' sugar in a mixing bowl. Beat at medium speed with a handheld mixer until light and fluffy. Add the tofu and vanilla and beat until incorporated. Add the cocoa powder and instant coffee and beat until thoroughly incorporated. Gradually add the flours and salt and beat at low speed until the dough just holds together.

2. Form tablespoons of the dough into balls and place them on the baking sheets. Bake for 15 to 18 minutes, until firm and starting to crack. Remove from the oven and let the cookies cool on the baking sheets for 2 minutes. Sift the remaining confectioners' sugar into a shallow dish and roll the cookies in the sugar until coated. Transfer the cookies to wire racks to cool completely.

Scottish Shortbread

YIELD: 24 COOKIES | **ACTIVE TIME:** 20 MINUTES | **TOTAL TIME:** 2 HOURS AND 30 MINUTES

10 OZ. UNSALTED BUTTER

3½ OZ. PLUS 2 TABLESPOONS SUGAR

12½ OZ. ALL-PURPOSE FLOUR

1 TEASPOON FINE SEA SALT

1. Preheat the oven to 325°F. Grate the butter into a bowl and place it in the freezer for 30 minutes.

2. Place the 3½ oz. of sugar, the flour, salt, and frozen butter in the work bowl of a stand mixer fitted with the paddle attachment and beat slowly until it is fine like sand. Be careful not to overwork the mixture.

3. Press the mixture into a square 8-inch baking pan and bake for 1 hour and 15 minutes.

4. Remove from the oven and sprinkle the remaining sugar over the top. Let cool and then cut the shortbread into bars or circles.

Vegan Double Chocolate Cookies

YIELD: 12 COOKIES | **ACTIVE TIME:** 15 MINUTES | **TOTAL TIME:** 1 HOUR

½ CUP VEGAN BUTTER

½ CUP SUGAR

½ CUP BROWN SUGAR

1 TEASPOON PURE VANILLA
EXTRACT

1 CUP ALL-PURPOSE FLOUR,
PLUS MORE AS NEEDED

⅔ CUP COCOA POWDER

1 TEASPOON BAKING SODA

¼ TEASPOON FINE SEA SALT

1 TABLESPOON SOY MILK

1. Preheat the oven to 350°F. Line two baking sheets with parchment paper. In the work bowl of a stand mixer fitted with the paddle attachment, cream the butter, sugar, brown sugar, and vanilla on medium speed until the mixture is very light and fluffy, about 5 minutes.

2. Sift the flour, cocoa powder, baking soda, and salt into a separate mixing bowl. Gradually add the flour mixture to the creamed butter and beat until incorporated. Add the soy milk and beat until the mixture comes together as a thick dough.

3. Form the mixture into 12 balls and arrange them on the baking sheets, making sure to leave enough space between. Flatten slightly, place in the oven, and bake until set and cracked on top, about 15 minutes. Remove from the oven, place the baking sheets on wire racks, and let the cookies cool on the sheets.

Vegan Fig & Walnut Bars

YIELD: 12 BARS | **ACTIVE TIME:** 15 MINUTES | **TOTAL TIME:** 1 HOUR AND 20 MINUTES

4 CUPS ROLLED OATS

⅔ CUP ALL-PURPOSE FLOUR

1 CUP WALNUT HALVES,
CHOPPED

1 CUP DRIED FIGS, CHOPPED

¾ CUP VEGAN BUTTER

⅔ CUP REAL MAPLE SYRUP

1 CUP BROWN SUGAR

1 TEASPOON PURE VANILLA
EXTRACT

1. Preheat the oven to 350°F. Line a square 9-inch baking pan with parchment paper. In a large mixing bowl, combine the oats, flour, walnuts, and figs. Place the vegan butter, maple syrup, sugar, and vanilla in a saucepan and cook over medium heat, stirring until the butter has melted and the sugar has dissolved.

2. Pour the butter mixture over the oat mixture and stir until the mixture is thoroughly combined. Transfer the mixture into the pan and press down until it is packed firmly in an even layer.

3. Place in the oven and bake until set and golden brown on top, 25 to 35 minutes. Remove from the oven and let the bars cool in the pan for 10 minutes. Slice and let the bars cool completely in the pan before enjoying.

Peanut Butter & Jam Thumbprints

YIELD: 24 COOKIES | **ACTIVE TIME:** 20 MINUTES | **TOTAL TIME:** 1 HOUR

5.3 OZ. LIGHT BROWN SUGAR

4 OZ. UNSALTED BUTTER, SOFTENED

1 CUP CREAMY PEANUT BUTTER

1 LARGE EGG, AT ROOM TEMPERATURE

½ TEASPOON PURE VANILLA EXTRACT

1 TEASPOON BAKING SODA

⅛ TEASPOON FINE SEA SALT

1 CUP ALL-PURPOSE FLOUR

1½ CUPS SEEDLESS RASPBERRY JAM

1. Preheat the oven to 375°F and line two baking sheets with parchment paper. Place the brown sugar, butter, and peanut butter in the work bowl of a stand mixer fitted with the paddle attachment and beat at low speed until combined. Increase the speed to high and beat until the mixture is light and fluffy.

2. Add the egg, vanilla, baking soda, and salt and beat for 1 minute. Slowly add the flour and beat until the mixture comes together as a soft dough.

3. Remove tablespoons of the dough and roll them into balls. Place the balls on the baking sheets, 1½ inches apart. Use your index finger to make a large depression in the center of each ball. Place the cookies in the oven and bake for 10 to 12 minutes, until the edges are brown. Remove, let cool for 2 minutes, and then transfer to wire racks to cool completely.

4. While the cookies are cooling, place the raspberry jam in a saucepan and cook over medium heat. Bring to a boil, while stirring frequently, and cook until the jam has been reduced by one-quarter. Spoon a teaspoon of the jam into each cookie and allow it to set.

Meyer Lemon Crinkle Cookies

YIELD: 24 COOKIES | **ACTIVE TIME:** 45 MINUTES | **TOTAL TIME:** 2 HOURS AND 30 MINUTES

½ LB. UNSALTED BUTTER, SOFTENED

1 LB. SUGAR

ZEST AND JUICE OF 2 MEYER LEMONS

2 EGGS

2 DROPS OF LEMON YELLOW GEL FOOD COLORING

15 OZ. ALL-PURPOSE FLOUR

½ TEASPOON BAKING POWDER

¼ TEASPOON BAKING SODA

½ TEASPOON FINE SEA SALT

2 CUPS CONFECTIONERS' SUGAR, FOR COATING

1. Line two baking sheets with parchment paper. In the work bowl of a stand mixer fitted with the paddle attachment, cream the butter, sugar, and lemon zest on medium speed until the mixture is very light and fluffy, about 5 minutes. Scrape down the work bowl and then beat the mixture for another 5 minutes.

2. Add the eggs one at a time and beat until incorporated, again scraping the work bowl as needed. When both eggs have been incorporated, scrape down the work bowl, add the lemon juice and food coloring, and beat for another minute. Add the flour, baking powder, baking soda, and salt and beat until the mixture comes together as a smooth dough.

3. Drop 2-oz. portions of the dough on the baking sheets, making sure to leave enough space between them. Place the baking sheets in the refrigerator and let the dough firm up for 1 hour.

4. Preheat the oven to 350°F. Place the confectioners' sugar in a mixing bowl, toss the cookie dough balls in the sugar until completely coated, and then place them back on the baking sheet.

5. Place the cookies in the oven and bake until a cake tester comes out clean after being inserted, 12 to 14 minutes.

6. Remove the cookies from the oven, transfer them to a cooling rack, and let them cool for 20 to 30 minutes before enjoying.

Raspberry Pie Bars

YIELD: 12 TO 24 BARS | **ACTIVE TIME:** 15 MINUTES | **TOTAL TIME:** 1 HOUR AND 30 MINUTES

2 BALLS OF PERFECT PIECRUST DOUGH (SEE PAGE 496)

3.2 OZ. ALL-PURPOSE FLOUR, PLUS MORE AS NEEDED

7 CUPS FRESH RASPBERRIES

14 OZ. SUGAR, PLUS MORE FOR TOPPING

2 TABLESPOONS FRESH LEMON JUICE

PINCH OF FINE SEA SALT

1 EGG, BEATEN

1. Preheat the oven to 350°F and coat a rimmed 15 x 10-inch baking sheet with nonstick cooking spray. Roll out one of the balls of dough on a lightly floured work surface so that it fits the baking sheet. Place it in the pan, press down to ensure that it is even, and prick it with a fork. Roll out the other crust so that it is slightly larger than the sheet.

2. Place the raspberries, sugar, flour, lemon juice, and salt in a mixing bowl and stir until well combined. Spread this mixture evenly across the crust in the baking sheet.

3. Place the top crust over the filling and trim away any excess. Brush the top crust with the egg and sprinkle additional sugar on top.

4. Place the bars in the oven and bake until golden brown, about 40 minutes. Remove from the oven and let cool before slicing.

Chewy Peanut Butter & Oat Bars

YIELD: 12 BARS | **ACTIVE TIME:** 15 MINUTES | **TOTAL TIME:** 45 MINUTES

¾ CUP WHOLE MILK

7 OZ. SUGAR

¼ TEASPOON FINE SEA SALT

4 OZ. DARK CHOCOLATE, CHOPPED

1 TEASPOON PURE VANILLA EXTRACT

½ CUP CREAMY PEANUT BUTTER

1 CUP ROLLED OATS

1. Place the milk, sugar, and salt in a small saucepan and whisk to combine. Cook over medium heat until the mixture comes to a boil and thickens, approximately 10 minutes. Remove the pan from heat.

2. Fill a small saucepan halfway with water and bring it to a gentle simmer. Place the chocolate in a heatproof bowl, place it over the simmering water, and stir until melted.

3. Add the vanilla, one-quarter of the melted chocolate, and the peanut butter to the pan and mix until well combined. Fold in the oats and stir until they are completely coated.

4. Line a square 8-inch cake pan with parchment paper and pour the contents of the saucepan into it. Press into an even layer, spread the remaining melted chocolate over the top, and let sit for 30 minutes. Cut into little bars and serve immediately, or store in the refrigerator until ready to serve.

Marble Brownies

YIELD: 16 BROWNIES | **ACTIVE TIME:** 15 MINUTES | **TOTAL TIME:** 1 HOUR AND 15 MINUTES

2½ OZ. ALL-PURPOSE FLOUR, PLUS MORE AS NEEDED

4 OZ. UNSALTED BUTTER

4 OZ. MILK CHOCOLATE CHIPS

3 LARGE EGGS, AT ROOM TEMPERATURE

7 OZ. SUGAR

PINCH OF FINE SEA SALT

1 CUP CREAM CHEESE, SOFTENED

½ TEASPOON PURE VANILLA EXTRACT

1. Preheat the oven to 350°F. Coat a square 8-inch cake pan with nonstick cooking spray and dust it with flour, knocking out any excess.

2. Fill a small saucepan halfway with water and bring it to a gentle simmer. Place the butter and chocolate chips in a heatproof bowl, place it over the simmering water, and stir until the mixture is melted and smooth. Remove the mixture from heat and let it cool for 5 minutes.

3. Place 2 of the eggs and three-quarters of the sugar in the work bowl of a stand mixer fitted with the paddle attachment and beat on medium speed for 1 minute. Add the chocolate-and-butter mixture, beat for 1 minute, and then add the flour and salt. Beat until just combined and then pour into the prepared pan.

4. In a separate bowl, combine the cream cheese, remaining sugar, remaining egg, and vanilla. Beat with a handheld mixer on medium speed until light and fluffy. Spread on top of the batter and use a fork to stir the layers together. Place in the oven and bake for 35 minutes, until the top is springy to the touch. Remove, allow the brownies to cool in the pan, and then cut into bars.

Dark Chocolate & Stout Brownies

YIELD: 16 BROWNIES | **ACTIVE TIME:** 15 MINUTES | **TOTAL TIME:** 1 HOUR AND 15 MINUTES

12 OZ. GUINNESS OR OTHER STOUT

½ LB. UNSALTED BUTTER

¾ LB. DARK CHOCOLATE CHIPS

10½ OZ. SUGAR

3 LARGE EGGS

1 TEASPOON PURE VANILLA EXTRACT

3¾ OZ. ALL-PURPOSE FLOUR

1¼ TEASPOONS FINE SEA SALT

COCOA POWDER, FOR TOPPING

1. Preheat the oven to 350°F and coat a square 8-inch cake pan with nonstick cooking spray. Place the stout in a medium saucepan and bring to a boil. Cook until it has reduced by half. Remove the pan from heat and let cool.

2. Fill a small saucepan halfway with water and bring it to a gentle simmer. Place the butter and chocolate chips in a heatproof bowl, place it over the simmering water, and stir until the mixture is melted and smooth. Remove the mixture from heat and let it cool for 5 minutes.

3. Place the sugar, eggs, and vanilla in a large bowl and stir until combined. Slowly whisk in the chocolate-and-butter mixture and then whisk in the stout.

4. Fold in the flour and salt. Pour the batter into the greased pan, place it in the oven, and bake for 35 to 40 minutes, until the surface begins to crack and a cake tester inserted into the center comes out with a few moist crumbs attached. Remove the pan from the oven, place on a wire rack, and let cool for at least 20 minutes. When cool, sprinkle cocoa powder over the top and cut the brownies into squares.

Lemon & Almond Biscotti

YIELD: 24 BISCOTTI | **ACTIVE TIME:** 1 HOUR | **TOTAL TIME:** 4 HOURS AND 30 MINUTES

½ LB. UNSALTED BUTTER, SOFTENED

ZEST OF 1 LEMON

7 OZ. SUGAR

¾ TEASPOON PURE VANILLA EXTRACT

2 EGGS

10 OZ. ALL-PURPOSE FLOUR

½ TEASPOON BAKING SODA

½ TEASPOON BAKING POWDER

½ TEASPOON FINE SEA SALT

½ LB. SLIVERED ALMONDS, TOASTED

1. Line a baking sheet with parchment paper. In the work bowl of a stand mixer fitted with the paddle attachment, cream the butter, lemon zest, sugar, and vanilla extract on medium until the mixture is very light and fluffy, about 5 minutes. Scrape down the work bowl and then beat the mixture for another 5 minutes.

2. Add the eggs one at a time and beat on low until incorporated, again scraping the work bowl as needed. When both eggs have been incorporated, scrape down the work bowl and beat on medium for 1 minute.

3. Add the remaining ingredients, reduce the speed to low, and beat until the mixture comes together as a dough.

4. Place the dough on the baking sheet and form it into a log that is the length of the pan and anywhere from 3 to 4 inches wide. Place the dough in the refrigerator for 1 hour.

5. Preheat the oven to 350°F.

6. Place the biscotti dough in the oven and bake until golden brown and a cake tester comes out clean when inserted into the center, 25 to 30 minutes. Remove the biscotti from the oven, transfer it to a cooling rack, and let it cool completely before chilling in the refrigerator for 2 hours.

7. Preheat the oven to 250°F. Cut the biscotti to the desired size, place them on their sides, place in the oven, and bake for 10 minutes. Remove from the oven, turn them over, and bake for another 6 minutes. Remove from the oven and let them cool completely before enjoying.

Vegan Lavender Biscuits

YIELD: 24 COOKIES | **ACTIVE TIME:** 15 MINUTES | **TOTAL TIME:** 1 HOUR

2 CUPS ALMOND FLOUR

⅓ CUP COCONUT SUGAR, PLUS MORE FOR TOPPING

1 TEASPOON BAKING POWDER

¼ TEASPOON FINE SEA SALT

¼ CUP AQUAFABA

½ CUP FRESH LAVENDER BUDS

1. Preheat the oven to 350°F. Line two baking sheets with parchment paper. Combine the almond flour, coconut sugar, baking powder, and salt in a mixing bowl. Gradually add the aquafaba and stir until the mixture comes together as a dough. Add the lavender and fold to incorporate.

2. Form teaspoons of the dough into balls and arrange them on the baking sheets, making sure to leave space between them. Flatten slightly, place the cookies in the oven, and bake until golden brown and set at the edges, 12 to 15 minutes. Remove from the oven, sprinkle additional coconut sugar over them, and let the cookies cool on the baking sheets for a few minutes before transferring to wire racks to cool completely.

Vegan Madeleines

YIELD: 12 COOKIES | **ACTIVE TIME:** 15 MINUTES | **TOTAL TIME:** 2 HOURS

½ CUP VEGAN BUTTER

⅓ CUP ALL-PURPOSE FLOUR, PLUS MORE AS NEEDED

½ CUP ALMOND FLOUR

¾ CUP CONFECTIONERS' SUGAR

⅓ CUP AQUAFABA

1. Melt the vegan butter in a saucepan. Remove from heat and let cool.

2. Combine the flour, almond flour, and confectioners' sugar in a bowl. Add the aquafaba and stir until incorporated. Stir in the melted butter and work the mixture until it is a smooth batter. Cover the bowl with plastic wrap and chill in the refrigerator for 1 hour.

3. Preheat the oven to 325°F. Coat a madeleine pan with nonstick cooking spray and dust the wells with flour. Spoon the batter into the wells, place the pan in the oven, and bake until dry to the touch and set, 10 to 12 minutes. Insert a knife into the center; if it comes out clean, the madeleines are ready. Gently turn the madeleines out onto a cooling rack and enjoy warm or at room temperature.

Vegan Pumpkin & Chocolate Chip Cookies

YIELD: 24 COOKIES | **ACTIVE TIME:** 15 MINUTES | **TOTAL TIME:** 1 HOUR

2⅓ CUPS SPELT FLOUR

1 TABLESPOON FLAXSEED MEAL

1 TEASPOON BAKING SODA

1 TEASPOON CINNAMON

½ TEASPOON GROUND GINGER

½ TEASPOON FINE SEA SALT

¼ TEASPOON FRESHLY GRATED NUTMEG

¼ TEASPOON CARDAMOM

1 CUP PUMPKIN PUREE

½ CUP VEGAN BUTTER, MELTED

¼ CUP REAL MAPLE SYRUP

⅓ CUP COCONUT SUGAR

1 TABLESPOON UNSALTED CREAMY ALMOND BUTTER

1 CUP VEGAN CHOCOLATE CHIPS

1. Preheat the oven to 350°F. Line two baking sheets with parchment paper. In a large bowl, combine the flour, flaxseed meal, baking soda, cinnamon, ginger, salt, nutmeg, and cardamom.

2. In the work bowl of a stand mixer fitted with the paddle attachment, combine the pumpkin puree, vegan butter, maple syrup, coconut sugar, and almond butter and beat until smooth. Add the wet mixture to the dry mixture and stir until the mixture just comes together as a dough. Add the chocolate chips and fold to incorporate.

3. Drop 2-tablespoon portions of the dough on the baking sheets, making sure to leave enough space between them. Flatten the cookies, place them in the oven, and bake until firm with lightly browned edges, about 10 minutes. Remove from the oven and let the cookies rest on the baking sheets for a few minutes before transferring them to a cooling rack to cool completely.

Red Velvet Crinkle Cookies

YIELD: 24 COOKIES | **ACTIVE TIME:** 45 MINUTES | **TOTAL TIME:** 2 HOURS AND 30 MINUTES

9 OZ. ALL-PURPOSE FLOUR

2 TABLESPOONS COCOA POWDER

1½ TEASPOONS BAKING POWDER

½ TEASPOON KOSHER SALT

4 OZ. UNSALTED BUTTER, SOFTENED

4 OZ. SUGAR

5 OZ. LIGHT BROWN SUGAR

2 EGGS

2 TEASPOONS PURE VANILLA EXTRACT

2 DROPS OF RED GEL FOOD COLORING

2 CUPS CONFECTIONERS' SUGAR, FOR COATING

1. Line two baking sheets with parchment paper. In a mixing bowl, whisk the flour, cocoa powder, baking powder, and salt together. Set the mixture aside.

2. In the work bowl of a stand mixer fitted with the paddle attachment, cream the butter, sugar, and brown sugar on medium speed until the mixture is very light and fluffy, about 5 minutes. Scrape down the work bowl and then beat the mixture for another 5 minutes.

3. Add the eggs one at a time and beat until incorporated, again scraping the work bowl as needed. When both eggs have been incorporated, scrape down the work bowl, add the vanilla and food coloring, and beat for another minute. Add the dry mixture and beat until the mixture comes together as a smooth dough.

4. Drop 2-oz. portions of the dough on the baking sheets, making sure to leave enough space between them. Place the baking sheets in the refrigerator and let the dough firm up for 1 hour.

5. Preheat the oven to 350°F. Place the confectioners' sugar in a mixing bowl, toss the cookie dough balls in the sugar until completely coated, and then place them back on the baking sheets.

6. Place the cookies in the oven and bake until a cake tester comes out clean after being inserted, 12 to 14 minutes.

7. Remove the cookies from the oven, transfer them to a cooling rack, and let them cool for 20 to 30 minutes before enjoying.

Vegan Sesame & Pistachio Cookies

YIELD: 30 COOKIES | **ACTIVE TIME:** 15 MINUTES | **TOTAL TIME:** 2 HOURS

1 CUP VEGAN BUTTER, SOFTENED

1¼ CUPS CONFECTIONERS' SUGAR

2 TABLESPOONS FLAXSEED MEAL

6 TABLESPOONS WATER

2 TEASPOONS PURE VANILLA EXTRACT

2 TEASPOONS WHITE VINEGAR

3 CUPS ALL-PURPOSE FLOUR

1 TEASPOON BAKING POWDER

PINCH OF FINE SEA SALT

1 CUP SESAME SEEDS

3 TABLESPOONS AGAVE NECTAR

1 CUP SHELLED PISTACHIOS, MINCED

1. In the work bowl of a stand mixer fitted with the paddle attachment, cream the vegan butter and sugar on medium speed until the mixture is very light and fluffy, about 5 minutes. Add the flaxseed meal and water and beat until incorporated. Add the vanilla and vinegar and beat for another 30 seconds.

2. Combine the flour, baking powder, and salt in a separate mixing bowl. Gradually add the dry mixture to the wet mixture and beat until incorporated. Cover the bowl with plastic wrap and refrigerate for 1 hour.

3. Preheat the oven to 350°F. Line two baking sheets with parchment paper. Combine the sesame seeds and agave nectar in one bowl. Place the pistachios in another bowl. Form the dough into 1½-inch balls, roll them in the pistachios, and flatten them slightly. Press the tops of the cookies into the sesame seed mixture and then arrange the cookies on the baking sheets, making sure to leave enough space between them.

4. Place the cookies in the oven and bake until the bottoms are golden brown, 15 to 20 minutes. Remove from the oven and let the cookies cool on the baking sheets for a few minutes before transferring them to a cooling rack to cool completely.

Orange & Pistachio Biscotti

YIELD: 24 BISCOTTI | **ACTIVE TIME:** 1 HOUR | **TOTAL TIME:** 4 HOURS AND 30 MINUTES

4 OZ. UNSALTED BUTTER, SOFTENED

ZEST OF 1 ORANGE

7 OZ. SUGAR

¾ TEASPOON PURE VANILLA EXTRACT

2 EGGS

10 OZ. ALL-PURPOSE FLOUR

½ TEASPOON BAKING SODA

½ TEASPOON BAKING POWDER

½ TEASPOON FINE SEA SALT

4 OZ. SHELLED PISTACHIOS, TOASTED

1 CUP DRIED CRANBERRIES

1. Line a baking sheet with parchment paper. In the work bowl of a stand mixer fitted with the paddle attachment, cream the butter, orange zest, sugar, and vanilla extract on medium until the mixture is very light and fluffy, about 5 minutes. Scrape down the work bowl and then beat the mixture for another 5 minutes.

2. Add the eggs one at a time and beat on low until incorporated, again scraping the work bowl as needed. When both eggs have been incorporated, scrape down the work bowl and beat on medium for 1 minute.

3. Add the remaining ingredients, reduce the speed to low, and beat until the mixture comes together as a dough.

4. Place the dough on the baking sheet and form it into a log that is the length of the pan and anywhere from 3 to 4 inches wide. Place the dough in the refrigerator for 1 hour.

5. Preheat the oven to 350°F.

6. Place the biscotti dough in the oven and bake until golden brown and a cake tester comes out clean when inserted into the center, 25 to 30 minutes. Remove the biscotti from the oven, transfer it to a cooling rack, and let it cool completely before chilling in the refrigerator for 2 hours.

7. Preheat the oven to 250°F. Cut the biscotti to the desired size, place them on their sides, place in the oven, and bake for 10 minutes. Remove from the oven, turn them over, and bake for another 6 minutes. Remove from the oven and let them cool completely before enjoying.

Oreo Cookies

YIELD: 20 COOKIES | **ACTIVE TIME:** 30 MINUTES | **TOTAL TIME:** 2 HOURS AND 15 MINUTES

½ LB. UNSALTED BUTTER, SOFTENED

1 LB. SUGAR

2 EGGS

¾ TEASPOON PURE VANILLA EXTRACT

9½ OZ. ALL-PURPOSE FLOUR

4½ OZ. COCOA POWDER

1½ TEASPOONS BAKING SODA

½ TEASPOON BAKING POWDER

¾ TEASPOON KOSHER SALT

1 CUP BUTTERFLUFF FILLING (SEE PAGE 517)

1. Line two baking sheets with parchment paper. In the work bowl of a stand mixer fitted with the paddle attachment, cream the butter and sugar on medium until the mixture is light and fluffy, about 5 minutes. Scrape down the work bowl with a rubber spatula and beat the mixture for another 5 minutes.

2. Reduce the speed to low, add the eggs one at a time, and beat until incorporated, again scraping the work bowl as needed. When both eggs have been incorporated, scrape down the work bowl, add the vanilla, and beat for another minute.

3. Add the flour, cocoa powder, baking soda, baking powder, and salt and beat on low until the dough comes together.

4. Drop 1-oz. portions of the dough on the baking sheets, making sure to leave enough space between them. Place the baking sheets in the refrigerator and let the dough firm up for 1 hour.

5. Preheat the oven to 350°F.

6. Place the cookies in the oven and bake until they are starting to firm up, about 8 minutes.

7. Remove the cookies from the oven, transfer them to a cooling rack, and let them cool for 20 to 30 minutes

8. Place the filling in a piping bag and cut a ½-inch hole in the bag. Pipe about 1 tablespoon of filling on half of the cookies. Use the other halves to assemble the sandwich and enjoy.

Vegan Snickerdoodles

YIELD: 30 COOKIES | **ACTIVE TIME:** 15 MINUTES | **TOTAL TIME:** 40 MINUTES

1 CUP VEGETABLE SHORTENING

1¼ CUPS PLUS 6 TABLESPOONS SUGAR

2 TABLESPOONS OAT MILK

1 TEASPOON PURE VANILLA EXTRACT

1 CUP ALL-PURPOSE FLOUR

⅔ CUP WHOLE WHEAT PASTRY FLOUR

2 TABLESPOONS CORNSTARCH

1 TEASPOON BAKING POWDER

¼ TEASPOON KOSHER SALT

1 TEASPOON CINNAMON

¼ TEASPOON GRATED NUTMEG

1. Preheat the oven to 350°F and line two baking sheets with parchment paper. Place the shortening, 1¼ cups sugar, the oat milk, and vanilla in a mixing bowl and beat at medium speed with a handheld mixer fitted with the paddle attachment until light and fluffy, scraping down the sides of the bowl as needed. Reduce the speed to low and incorporate the flours, cornstarch, baking powder, and salt. Beat until the dough just holds together.

2. Place the remaining sugar, the cinnamon, and nutmeg in a small bowl, and stir to combine. Form tablespoons of the dough into balls, roll them in the sugar mixture until coated, and place them on the baking sheets.

3. Bake for 12 to 14 minutes, until the edges start to brown. Remove from the oven and let the cookies cool on the baking sheets for 2 minutes before transferring them to wire racks to cool completely.

Vegan Spritz Cookies

YIELD: 96 COOKIES | **ACTIVE TIME:** 25 MINUTES | **TOTAL TIME:** 2 HOURS

1 TABLESPOON EGG REPLACER

¼ CUP COLD WATER

1 CUP VEGETABLE SHORTENING

⅔ CUP SUGAR

1 TEASPOON PURE VANILLA EXTRACT

¼ TEASPOON KOSHER SALT

2½ CUPS ALL-PURPOSE FLOUR

COLORED SUGARS, FOR DECORATION

PREFERRED CANDIES, FOR DECORATION

1. Place the egg replacer and water in a cup and whisk to combine. Place the shortening and sugar in a mixing bowl and beat at medium speed with a handheld mixer fitted with the paddle attachment until pale and fluffy, scraping down the sides of the bowl as needed. Add the egg replacer mixture, vanilla, and salt and beat until thoroughly incorporated. Gradually add the flour and beat until a soft dough forms. Divide the dough in half, cover each half in plastic wrap, and refrigerate for 1 hour.

2. Preheat the oven to 350°F and line two baking sheets with parchment paper. Shape handfuls of the dough into logs, place them in a cookie press, and press them onto the baking sheets. Decorate the cookies with the colored sugars and candies as desired.

3. Place the cookies in the oven and bake until the edges are brown, 12 to 15 minutes. Remove the cookies from the oven and let them cool on the baking sheets for 2 minutes before transferring them to wire racks to cool completely.

Vegan Vanilla & Matcha Cookies

YIELD: 40 COOKIES | **ACTIVE TIME:** 15 MINUTES | **TOTAL TIME:** 1 HOUR AND 30 MINUTES

1 CUP VEGAN BUTTER,
SOFTENED

½ CUP SUGAR

1 TEASPOON PURE VANILLA
EXTRACT

2⅔ CUPS ALL-PURPOSE
FLOUR, PLUS MORE AS
NEEDED

2 PINCHES OF FINE SEA SALT

1 TABLESPOON MATCHA
POWDER

1. In the work bowl of a stand mixer fitted with the paddle attachment, cream the vegan butter and sugar on medium speed until the mixture is very light and fluffy, about 5 minutes. Add the vanilla and beat until incorporated. Gradually add the flour, salt, and matcha powder and beat the mixture until it just comes together as a dough. Turn the dough out onto a flour-dusted work surface and gently roll into a log. Cover in plastic wrap and refrigerate for 30 minutes.

2. Preheat the oven to 350°F. Line two large baking sheets with parchment paper. Cut the log into ⅓-inch-thick slices and arrange them on the baking sheets, making sure to leave enough space in between.

3. Place the cookies in the oven and bake until they are golden brown around the edges, 10 to 12 minutes. Remove from the oven and let the cookies cool on the sheets for a few minutes before transferring to cooling racks to cool completely.

Matcha Rice Krispies Treats

YIELD: 12 BARS | **ACTIVE TIME:** 15 MINUTES | **TOTAL TIME:** 1 HOUR AND 15 MINUTES

¾ LB. MARSHMALLOW CREME

4½ OZ. UNSALTED BUTTER

2 TABLESPOONS MATCHA POWDER

¾ TEASPOON FINE SEA SALT

9 CUPS RICE KRISPIES

¾ TEASPOON PURE VANILLA EXTRACT

2½ CUPS WHITE CHOCOLATE CHIPS

1. Line a 13 x 9–inch baking pan with parchment paper and coat it with nonstick cooking spray.

2. Fill a small saucepan halfway with water and bring it to a simmer. Place the marshmallow creme, butter, matcha powder, and salt in a heatproof mixing bowl, place it over the simmering water, and stir the mixture with a rubber spatula until the butter has melted and the mixture is thoroughly combined. Remove the bowl from heat, add the cereal, and fold until combined. Add the vanilla and white chocolate chips and fold until evenly distributed.

3. Transfer the mixture to the baking pan and spread it with a rubber spatula. Place another piece of parchment over the mixture and pack it down with your hand until it is flat and even. Remove the top piece of parchment.

4. Place the pan in the refrigerator for 1 hour.

5. Run a knife along the edge of the pan and turn the mixture out onto a cutting board. Cut into squares and enjoy.

Spritz Cookies

YIELD: 24 COOKIES | **ACTIVE TIME:** 20 MINUTES | **TOTAL TIME:** 2 HOURS

4 OZ. UNSALTED BUTTER

1½ CUPS CONFECTIONERS' SUGAR

2 EGG WHITES

1 TEASPOON PURE VANILLA EXTRACT

1 TEASPOON ALMOND EXTRACT

2 CUPS ALL-PURPOSE FLOUR

½ TEASPOON KOSHER SALT

1 EGG, BEATEN

1 CUP RASPBERRY JAM (SEE PAGE 533)

1. In the work bowl of a stand mixer fitted with the paddle attachment, cream the butter and confectioners' sugar on medium until the mixture is very light and fluffy, about 5 minutes. Scrape down the work bowl and beat for another 5 minutes.

2. Reduce the speed to low, add the egg whites, vanilla, and almond extract gradually, and beat until incorporated. Scrape down the work bowl and beat on medium for 1 minute.

3. Add the flour and salt and beat on low until the mixture comes together as a smooth dough. Transfer it to a piping bag fit with a star tip. Pipe 2-inch-wide roses onto parchment-lined baking sheets, making sure to leave ½ inch between each cookie. Place the baking sheets in the refrigerator for 1 hour.

4. Preheat the oven to 350°F.

5. Gently brush all of the cookies with the egg.

6. Place the jam in a piping bag and cut a ½-inch slit in it. Pipe ½ teaspoon of jam in the center of each cookie.

7. Place the cookies in the oven and bake until the edges are a light golden brown, 15 to 20 minutes.

8. Remove from the oven, transfer the cookies to a wire rack, and let them cool completely before enjoying.

Peanut Butter & Chocolate Chip Cookies

YIELD: 24 COOKIES | **ACTIVE TIME:** 30 MINUTES | **TOTAL TIME:** 2 HOURS

4 OZ. UNSALTED BUTTER, SOFTENED

4 OZ. SMOOTH PEANUT BUTTER

½ LB. SUGAR

½ LB. DARK BROWN SUGAR

1½ TEASPOONS KOSHER SALT

1 TEASPOON BAKING SODA

2 EGGS

1½ TEASPOONS PURE VANILLA EXTRACT

14½ OZ. ALL-PURPOSE FLOUR

14 OZ. SEMISWEET CHOCOLATE CHIPS

1. Line two baking sheets with parchment paper. In the work bowl of a stand mixer fitted with the paddle attachment, cream the butter, peanut butter, sugar, dark brown sugar, salt, and baking soda on medium speed until the mixture is very light and fluffy, about 5 minutes. Scrape down the work bowl and then beat the mixture for another 5 minutes.

2. Add the eggs one at a time and beat until incorporated, again scraping the work bowl as needed. When both eggs have been incorporated, scrape down the work bowl, add the vanilla, and beat for another minute. Add the flour and chocolate chips and beat until the mixture comes together as a dough.

3. Drop 2-oz. portions of the dough on the baking sheets, making sure to leave enough space between them. Place the baking sheets in the refrigerator and let the dough firm up for 1 hour.

4. Preheat the oven to 350°F.

5. Place the cookies in the oven and bake until they are lightly golden brown around their edges, 10 to 12 minutes. Do not let the cookies become fully brown or they will end up being too crispy.

6. Remove the cookies from the oven, transfer them to a cooling rack, and let them cool for 20 to 30 minutes before enjoying.

Flourless Fudge Brownies

YIELD: 12 BROWNIES | **ACTIVE TIME:** 30 MINUTES | **TOTAL TIME:** 2 HOURS AND 45 MINUTES

1 LB. DARK CHOCOLATE (55 TO 65 PERCENT)

½ LB. UNSALTED BUTTER

¾ LB. SUGAR

4 OZ. LIGHT BROWN SUGAR

¼ CUP COCOA POWDER

¾ TEASPOON KOSHER SALT

6 EGGS

1½ TEASPOONS PURE VANILLA EXTRACT

1. Preheat the oven to 350°F. Line a 13 x 9–inch baking pan with parchment paper and coat it with nonstick cooking spray.

2. Fill a small saucepan halfway with water and bring it to a simmer. Place the dark chocolate and butter in a heatproof bowl, place it over the simmering water, and stir until they have melted and been combined. Remove from heat and set aside.

3. In a separate mixing bowl, whisk the sugar, brown sugar, cocoa powder, and salt together, making sure to break up any clumps. Whisk in the eggs, vanilla, and melted chocolate mixture. Pour the batter into the baking pan and use a rubber spatula to even out the top. Lightly tap the baking pan on the counter and remove any air bubbles.

4. Place the brownies in the oven and bake until a cake tester comes out clean, 30 to 40 minutes.

5. Remove from the oven, transfer the brownies to a cooling rack, and let them cool completely. Once they are cool, transfer to the refrigerator and chill for 1 hour.

6. Run a paring knife along the sides of the pan, cut the brownies into squares, and enjoy.

Praline Bars

YIELD: 12 BARS | **ACTIVE TIME:** 30 MINUTES | **TOTAL TIME:** 1 HOUR AND 30 MINUTES

FOR THE CRUST

9 OZ. UNSALTED BUTTER

4 CUPS GRAHAM CRACKER CRUMBS

3 TABLESPOONS SUGAR

¼ CUP PLUS 1 TABLESPOON ALL-PURPOSE FLOUR

FOR THE FILLING

4½ CUPS DARK BROWN SUGAR

6 EGGS

1 CUP GRAHAM CRACKER CRUMBS

1½ TEASPOONS KOSHER SALT

¾ TEASPOON BAKING POWDER

1 TABLESPOON PURE VANILLA EXTRACT

1½ CUPS PECANS, CHOPPED

1. Preheat the oven to 350°F. Line a 13 x 9–inch baking pan with parchment paper and coat it with nonstick cooking spray. To begin preparations for the crust, melt the butter in a small saucepan over medium-low heat. Set the butter aside.

2. In a mixing bowl, combine the graham cracker crumbs, sugar, and flour. Add the melted butter and fold to incorporate. Place the mixture in the baking pan and press down on it so that it is flat and even. Set aside.

3. To prepare the filling, whisk the dark brown sugar and eggs together in a mixing bowl until there are no clumps left, about 2 minutes. Add the graham cracker crumbs, salt, baking powder, and vanilla and whisk until thoroughly incorporated. Pour the filling over the crust and evenly distribute the pecans on top, pressing down so they adhere.

4. Place in the oven and bake until the top is golden brown, 25 to 30 minutes. Remove from the oven, transfer to a cooling rack, and let cool. When cool, cut into bars and enjoy.

Rice Krispies Treats

YIELD: 12 BARS | **ACTIVE TIME:** 30 MINUTES | **TOTAL TIME:** 1 HOUR AND 30 MINUTES

¾ LB. MARSHMALLOW CREME

4½ OZ. UNSALTED BUTTER

¾ TEASPOON FINE SEA SALT

9 CUPS CRISPY RICE CEREAL

¾ TEASPOON PURE VANILLA EXTRACT

2½ CUPS CHOCOLATE CHIPS OR M&M'S (OPTIONAL)

1. Line a 13 x 9–inch baking pan with parchment paper and coat with nonstick cooking spray.

2. Fill a small saucepan halfway with water and bring it to a simmer. Place the marshmallow creme, butter, and salt in a heatproof mixing bowl over the simmering water and stir the mixture with a rubber spatula until the butter has melted and the mixture is thoroughly combined. Remove the bowl from heat, add the cereal and vanilla, and fold until combined. If desired, add the chocolate chips or M&M's and fold until evenly distributed.

3. Transfer the mixture to the baking pan and spread it with a rubber spatula. Place another piece of parchment over the mixture and pack it down with your hand until it is flat and even. Remove the top piece of parchment.

4. Place the pan in the refrigerator for 1 hour.

5. Run a knife along the edge of the pan and turn the mixture out onto a cutting board. Cut into squares and enjoy.

Mexican Chocolate Crinkle Cookies

YIELD: 20 COOKIES | **ACTIVE TIME:** 30 MINUTES | **TOTAL TIME:** 2 HOURS

9 OZ. MEXICAN CHOCOLATE

4½ OZ. UNSALTED BUTTER, SOFTENED

7 OZ. DARK BROWN SUGAR

¾ TEASPOON PURE VANILLA EXTRACT

2 EGGS

7 OZ. ALL-PURPOSE FLOUR

2½ OZ. COCOA POWDER

2 TEASPOONS BAKING POWDER

½ TEASPOON CINNAMON

¼ TEASPOON ANCHO CHILE POWDER

1 TEASPOON KOSHER SALT

2 CUPS CONFECTIONERS' SUGAR, FOR COATING

1. Line two baking sheets with parchment paper. Fill a small saucepan halfway with water and bring it to a simmer. Place the chocolate in a heatproof bowl, place it over the simmering water, and stir until melted. Remove from heat and set aside.

2. In the work bowl of a stand mixer fitted with the paddle attachment, cream the butter, brown sugar, and vanilla on medium speed until the mixture is very light and fluffy, about 5 minutes. Scrape down the work bowl and then beat the mixture for another 5 minutes.

3. Reduce the speed to low, add the melted chocolate, and beat until incorporated.

4. Add the eggs one at a time and beat until incorporated, again scraping the work bowl as needed. When both eggs have been incorporated, scrape down the work bowl. Set the speed to medium and beat for 1 minute.

5. Add the flour, cocoa powder, baking powder, cinnamon, ancho chile powder, and salt, reduce the speed to low, and beat until the mixture comes together as a dough.

6. Drop 2-oz. portions of the dough on the baking sheets, making sure to leave enough space between them. Place the baking sheets in the refrigerator and let the dough firm up for 1 hour.

7. Preheat the oven to 350°F. Place the confectioners' sugar in a mixing bowl, toss the cookie dough balls in the sugar until completely coated, and then place them back on the baking sheets.

8. Place the cookies in the oven and bake until a cake tester comes out clean after being inserted, 12 to 14 minutes.

9. Remove the cookies from the oven, transfer them to a cooling rack, and let them cool for 20 to 30 minutes before enjoying.

White Chocolate Chip & Macadamia Cookies

YIELD: 24 COOKIES | **ACTIVE TIME:** 20 MINUTES | **TOTAL TIME:** 2 HOURS

½ LB. UNSALTED BUTTER, SOFTENED

½ LB. SUGAR

½ LB. DARK BROWN SUGAR

1½ TEASPOONS KOSHER SALT

1 TEASPOON BAKING SODA

2 EGGS

1½ TEASPOONS PURE VANILLA EXTRACT

14½ OZ. ALL-PURPOSE FLOUR

7 OZ. MACADAMIA NUTS, TOASTED

7 OZ. WHITE CHOCOLATE CHIPS

1. Line two baking sheets with parchment paper. In the work bowl of a stand mixer fitted with the paddle attachment, cream the butter, sugar, dark brown sugar, salt, and baking soda on medium speed until the mixture is very light and fluffy, about 5 minutes. Scrape down the work bowl and then beat the mixture for another 5 minutes.

2. Reduce the speed to low, add the eggs one at a time, and beat until incorporated, again scraping the work bowl as needed. When both eggs have been incorporated, scrape down the work bowl, add the vanilla, raise the speed to medium, and beat for 1 minute.

3. Add the flour, macadamia nuts, and white chocolate chips, reduce the speed to low, and beat until the dough comes together.

4. Drop 2-oz. portions of the dough on the baking sheets, making sure to leave enough space between them. Place the baking sheets in the refrigerator and let the dough firm up for 1 hour.

5. Preheat the oven to 350°F.

6. Place the cookies in the oven and bake until lightly golden brown around their edges, 10 to 12 minutes. Remove the cookies from the oven, transfer them to a cooling rack, and let them cool for 20 to 30 minutes before enjoying.

Chewy Ginger Cookies

YIELD: 24 COOKIES | **ACTIVE TIME:** 30 MINUTES | **TOTAL TIME:** 2 HOURS

6½ OZ. UNSALTED BUTTER, SOFTENED

18 OZ. SUGAR

6½ OZ. MOLASSES

2 EGGS

1½ TABLESPOONS WHITE VINEGAR

23 OZ. ALL-PURPOSE FLOUR

2 TEASPOONS BAKING SODA

2 TEASPOONS GROUND GINGER

1 TEASPOON CINNAMON

½ TEASPOON FRESHLY GRATED NUTMEG

½ TEASPOON KOSHER SALT

1. Line two baking sheets with parchment paper. In the work bowl of a stand mixer fitted with the paddle attachment, cream the butter and sugar on medium speed until the mixture is very light and fluffy, about 5 minutes. Scrape down the work bowl and then beat the mixture for another 5 minutes.

2. Reduce the speed to low, add the molasses, and beat to incorporate. Add the eggs one at a time and beat until incorporated, again scraping the work bowl as needed. When both eggs have been incorporated, scrape down the work bowl, add the vinegar, raise the speed to medium, and beat for 1 minute.

3. Add the flour, baking soda, ginger, cinnamon, nutmeg, and salt, reduce the speed to low, and beat until the dough comes together.

4. Drop 2-oz. portions of the dough on the baking sheets, making sure to leave enough space between them. Place the baking sheets in the refrigerator and let the dough firm up for 1 hour.

5. Preheat the oven to 350°F.

6. Place the cookies in the oven and bake until lightly golden brown around their edges, 10 to 12 minutes. Do not allow the cookies to become fully brown or they will come out too crispy.

7. Remove the cookies from the oven, transfer them to a cooling rack, and let them cool for 20 to 30 minutes before enjoying.

Alfajores

YIELD: 36 COOKIES | **ACTIVE TIME:** 1 HOUR | **TOTAL TIME:** 3 HOURS

8.9 OZ. UNSALTED BUTTER, SOFTENED

5.4 OZ. SUGAR

½ TEASPOON KOSHER SALT

1 TABLESPOON PURE VANILLA EXTRACT

ZEST OF 1 LEMON

4 EGG YOLKS

10.7 OZ. CORNSTARCH

7.1 OZ. ALL-PURPOSE FLOUR, PLUS MORE AS NEEDED

1 TEASPOON BAKING SODA

¾ LB. DULCE DE LECHE

1 CUP CONFECTIONERS' SUGAR, FOR DUSTING

1. In the work bowl of a stand mixer fitted with the paddle attachment, cream the butter, sugar, salt, vanilla, and lemon zest on medium speed until the mixture is very light and fluffy, about 5 minutes. Scrape down the work bowl and then beat the mixture for another 5 minutes.

2. Reduce the speed to low, add the egg yolks, and beat until incorporated. Scrape down the work bowl and beat the mixture for 1 minute on medium.

3. Add the cornstarch, flour, and baking soda, reduce the speed to low, and beat until the dough comes together. Form the dough into a ball and then flatten it into a disc. Envelop the dough in plastic wrap and refrigerate for 2 hours.

4. Preheat the oven to 350°F and line two baking sheets with parchment paper.

5. Remove the dough from the refrigerator and let it sit on the counter for 5 minutes.

6. Place the dough on a flour-dusted work surface and roll it out until it is approximately ¼ inch thick. Use a 2-inch ring cutter to cut cookies out of the dough and place them on the baking sheets. Form any scraps into a ball, roll it out, and cut into cookies. If the dough becomes too sticky or warm, place it back in the refrigerator for 15 minutes to firm up.

7. Place the cookies in the oven and bake until lightly golden brown at their edges, about 8 minutes. Remove from the oven, transfer to a wire rack, and let cool for 10 minutes.

8. Place about a teaspoon of dulce de leche on half of the cookies and use the other cookies to assemble the sandwiches. Dust with the confectioners' sugar and enjoy.

Vanilla Tuiles

YIELD: 24 COOKIES | **ACTIVE TIME:** 45 MINUTES | **TOTAL TIME:** 3 HOURS

3½ OZ. ALL-PURPOSE FLOUR

5 EGG WHITES

4½ OZ. CONFECTIONERS' SUGAR

½ TEASPOON PURE VANILLA EXTRACT

5.3 OZ. UNSALTED BUTTER

1. Sift the flour into a small bowl and set it aside.

2. In a medium bowl, whisk the egg whites, confectioners' sugar, and vanilla together. Set the mixture aside.

3. In a small saucepan, melt the butter over low heat. Stir it into the egg white mixture, add the sifted flour, and whisk until the mixture is a smooth batter. Cover the bowl with plastic wrap and place in the refrigerator for 2 hours.

4. Preheat the oven to 400°F.

5. Line an 18 x 13–inch baking sheet with a Silpat mat. Place 2-teaspoon portions of the batter about 5 inches apart from one another. Use a small, offset spatula to spread the batter into 4-inch circles. Tap the pan lightly on the counter to remove any air bubbles and level the circles.

6. Place the tuiles in the oven and bake until the edges begin to color, 4 to 5 minutes. Remove from the oven. Working quickly, carefully remove the tuiles with the offset spatula and transfer them immediately to a cooling rack.

7. Repeat until all of the batter has been used.

Chocolate Tuiles

YIELD: 24 COOKIES | **ACTIVE TIME:** 45 MINUTES | **TOTAL TIME:** 3 HOURS

2½ OZ. ALL-PURPOSE FLOUR

2 TABLESPOONS COCOA POWDER

5 EGG WHITES

4½ OZ. CONFECTIONERS' SUGAR

½ TEASPOON PURE VANILLA EXTRACT

5.3 OZ. UNSALTED BUTTER

1. Sift the flour and cocoa powder into a small bowl and set the mixture aside.

2. In a medium bowl, whisk the egg whites, confectioners' sugar, and vanilla together. Set the mixture aside.

3. In a small saucepan, melt the butter over low heat. Stir it into the egg white mixture, add the flour mixture, and whisk until the mixture is a smooth batter. Cover the bowl with plastic wrap and place in the refrigerator for 2 hours.

4. Preheat the oven to 400°F.

5. Line an 18 x 13–inch baking sheet with a Silpat mat. Place 2-teaspoon portions of the batter about 5 inches apart from one another. Use a small, offset spatula to spread the batter into 4-inch circles. Tap the pan lightly on the counter to remove any air bubbles and level the circles.

6. Place the tuiles in the oven and bake until the edges begin to curl up, 4 to 5 minutes. Remove from the oven. Working quickly, carefully remove the tuiles with the offset spatula and transfer them immediately to a cooling rack.

7. Repeat until all of the batter has been used.

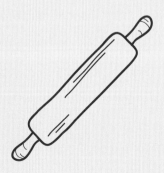

Double Shot Cookies

YIELD: 18 COOKIES | **ACTIVE TIME:** 30 MINUTES | **TOTAL TIME:** 2 HOURS

7.7 OZ. DARK CHOCOLATE
(55 TO 65 PERCENT)

1.1 OZ. UNSALTED BUTTER,
SOFTENED

2 EGGS

3.6 OZ. SUGAR

¾ TEASPOON PURE VANILLA
EXTRACT

1¼ OZ. ALL-PURPOSE FLOUR

¼ TEASPOON BAKING
POWDER

¼ TEASPOON KOSHER SALT

¼ CUP ESPRESSO POWDER

6 OZ. CHOCOLATE CHIPS

1. Line two baking sheets with parchment paper. Fill a small saucepan halfway with water and bring it to a simmer. Place the dark chocolate and butter in a heatproof bowl, place it over the simmering water, and stir until they have melted and been combined. Remove from heat and whisk in the eggs, sugar, and vanilla.

2. Add the flour, baking powder, salt, and espresso powder and whisk until the dough comes together. Add the chocolate chips and fold until evenly distributed.

3. Drop 2-oz. portions of the dough on the baking sheets, making sure to leave enough space between them. Place the baking sheets in the refrigerator and let the dough firm up for 1 hour.

4. Preheat the oven to 350°F.

5. Place the cookies in the oven and bake until a cake tester comes out clean after being inserted, 12 to 14 minutes.

6. Remove the cookies from the oven, transfer them to a cooling rack, and let them cool for 20 to 30 minutes before enjoying.

Fig Newtons

YIELD: 60 COOKIES | **ACTIVE TIME:** 1 HOUR | **TOTAL TIME:** 2 HOURS AND 30 MINUTES

10 OZ. UNSALTED BUTTER, SOFTENED

½ LB. LIGHT BROWN SUGAR

2 OZ. HONEY

ZEST OF 1 ORANGE

6 EGG YOLKS

1 OZ. ORANGE JUICE

21 OZ. ALL-PURPOSE FLOUR, PLUS MORE AS NEEDED

1¼ TEASPOONS BAKING SODA

½ TEASPOON CINNAMON

½ TEASPOON KOSHER SALT

6 CUPS FIG PRESERVES OR JAM

1. In the work bowl of a stand mixer fitted with the paddle attachment, cream the butter, brown sugar, honey, and orange zest on medium speed until the mixture is very light and fluffy, about 5 minutes. Scrape down the work bowl and then add the egg yolks and orange juice. Beat until combined, add the flour, baking soda, cinnamon, and salt, and beat until the dough comes together.

2. Place the dough on a flour-dusted work surface and divide it into two 6-inch squares. Envelop each piece of dough in plastic wrap and chill in the refrigerator for an hour.

3. Preheat the oven to 350°F and line two baking sheets with parchment paper. Place one piece of dough on a flour-dusted work surface and roll out until it is a 15-inch square. Cut the dough into 3-inch-wide strips.

4. Place the preserves or jam in a piping bag and cut a 1-inch hole in it. Pipe a strip of filling down the center of each strip, leaving 1 inch on either side.

5. Gently fold the dough over the filling so that it is sealed. Flip the strips over so that the seams are facing down. Transfer to the baking sheets, place back in the refrigerator, and let them chill for 10 minutes.

6. Cut the strips into 2-inch squares and place them back on the baking sheets, leaving 1 inch between.

7. Place the cookies in the oven and bake until golden brown, 10 to 12 minutes. Remove from the oven, transfer them to a wire rack to cool, and repeat with the other piece of dough.

Kudos Bars

YIELD: 12 BARS | **ACTIVE TIME:** 30 MINUTES | **TOTAL TIME:** 2 HOURS AND 30 MINUTES

6 CUPS CRISPY RICE CEREAL

3 CUPS ROLLED OATS

4 CUPS CHOCOLATE CHIPS

1 CUP DARK BROWN SUGAR

6 OZ. UNSALTED BUTTER

¾ CUP HONEY

¼ CUP LIGHT CORN SYRUP

4 TEASPOONS KOSHER SALT

2 TABLESPOONS PURE VANILLA EXTRACT

2 CUPS CHOCOLATE GANACHE (SEE PAGE 523), WARM

1. Line a 13 x 9–inch baking pan with parchment paper and coat it with nonstick cooking spray. Place the cereal, oats, and 2 cups of the chocolate chips in a mixing bowl and stir to combine. Set the mixture aside.

2. In a medium saucepan, combine the brown sugar, butter, honey, corn syrup, and salt. Bring to a boil over medium heat and cook for another 2 minutes. Remove the pan from heat, whisk in the vanilla, and then pour it over the cereal mixture. Stir with a rubber spatula until combined.

3. Transfer the mixture to the baking pan and press down on it until it is flat and even. Sprinkle the remaining chocolate chips over the mixture and gently press them down into it. Place the baking pan in the refrigerator for 2 hours.

4. Remove from the refrigerator and cut the mixture into bars.

5. Drizzle the ganache over the bars and enjoy.

Lemon Bars

YIELD: 12 BARS | **ACTIVE TIME:** 40 MINUTES | **TOTAL TIME:** 5 HOURS

FOR THE CRUST

10 OZ. ALL-PURPOSE FLOUR

4 OZ. SUGAR

¼ TEASPOON KOSHER SALT

½ LB. UNSALTED BUTTER, SOFTENED

FOR THE FILLING

1 LB. SUGAR

¾ CUP ALL-PURPOSE FLOUR

ZEST OF 2 LEMONS

¼ TEASPOON KOSHER SALT

5 EGGS

1 CUP FRESH LEMON JUICE

1 CUP CONFECTIONERS' SUGAR, FOR DUSTING

1. Preheat the oven to 325°F. Line a 13 x 9–inch baking pan with parchment paper and coat it with nonstick cooking spray. To prepare the crust, place all of the ingredients in a mixing bowl and work the mixture with your hands until combined, soft, and crumbly.

2. Firmly press the crust into the baking pan, making sure it is flat and even. Place in the oven and bake until the crust begins to brown at the edges, about 20 minutes. Remove from the oven and place it on a cooling rack.

3. To prepare the filling, place the sugar, flour, lemon zest, and salt in a mixing bowl and whisk until combined. Add the eggs and lemon juice, whisk until incorporated, and spread the mixture over the baked crust.

4. Place in the oven and bake until the center is set, 20 to 25 minutes.

5. Remove from the oven, transfer to a cooling rack, and let cool for 2 hours.

6. Transfer to the refrigerator and chill for 2 hours. Cut the bars, dust them with the confectioners' sugar, and store in the refrigerator until ready to serve.

Butterscotch, Toffee & Pecan Cookies

YIELD: 20 COOKIES | **ACTIVE TIME:** 40 MINUTES | **TOTAL TIME:** 2 HOURS

½ LB. PECANS

½ LB. UNSALTED BUTTER, SOFTENED

3½ OZ. SUGAR

6½ OZ. LIGHT BROWN SUGAR

2 EGGS

¾ LB. ALL-PURPOSE FLOUR

½ TEASPOON BAKING SODA

½ TEASPOON KOSHER SALT

4 OZ. TOFFEE BITS

10 OZ. BUTTERSCOTCH CHIPS

1. Preheat the oven to 350°F and line two baking sheets with parchment paper.

2. Place the pecans on a separate baking sheet, place them in the oven, and bake until toasted and fragrant, about 10 minutes. Remove from the oven and let cool for 15 minutes. Chop the toasted pecans and let them cool. Turn the oven off.

3. In the work bowl of a stand mixer fitted with the paddle attachment, cream the butter, sugar, and brown sugar on medium speed until the mixture is very light and fluffy, about 5 minutes. Scrape down the work bowl and then beat the mixture for another 5 minutes.

4. Reduce the speed to low, add the eggs one at a time, and beat until incorporated, again scraping the work bowl as needed. When both eggs have been incorporated, scrape down the work bowl and then beat for another minute on medium. Add the flour, baking soda, salt, toffee bits, butterscotch chips, and pecans and beat until the mixture comes together as a dough.

5. Drop 2-oz. portions of the dough on the baking sheets, making sure to leave enough space between them. Place the baking sheets in the refrigerator and let the dough firm up for 1 hour.

6. Preheat the oven to 350°F.

7. Place the cookies in the oven and bake until their edges are a light golden brown, 10 to 12 minutes.

8. Remove the cookies from the oven, transfer them to a cooling rack, and let them cool for 20 to 30 minutes before enjoying.

Peppermint Bars

YIELD: 12 BARS | **ACTIVE TIME:** 1 HOUR | **TOTAL TIME:** 3 HOURS AND 30 MINUTES

FOR THE CRUST

½ LB. DARK CHOCOLATE (55 TO 65 PERCENT)

4 OZ. UNSALTED BUTTER

6 OZ. SUGAR

2 OZ. LIGHT BROWN SUGAR

2 TABLESPOONS COCOA POWDER

¼ TEASPOON KOSHER SALT

3 EGGS

¾ TEASPOON PURE VANILLA EXTRACT

FOR THE TOPPING

28½ OZ. CONFECTIONERS' SUGAR

6 TABLESPOONS UNSALTED BUTTER, SOFTENED

½ CUP HEAVY CREAM

2 CUPS PEPPERMINT CANDY PIECES, PLUS MORE FOR GARNISH

2 CUPS CHOCOLATE GANACHE (SEE PAGE 523), WARM

1. Preheat the oven to 350°F. Line a 13 x 9–inch baking pan with parchment paper and coat it with nonstick cooking spray. To begin preparations for the crust, fill a small saucepan halfway with water and bring it to a simmer. Place the chocolate and butter in a heatproof bowl, place it over the simmering water, and stir until they are melted and combined. Remove from heat and set aside.

2. In a mixing bowl, whisk the sugar, brown sugar, cocoa powder, and salt together, making sure to break up any clumps. Add the eggs and vanilla, whisk to incorporate, and then add the melted chocolate mixture. Whisk to incorporate, pour the batter into the baking pan, and even the surface with a rubber spatula. Lightly tap the baking pan on the counter to settle the batter and remove any air bubbles.

3. Place in the oven and bake until a cake tester comes out clean, 20 to 30 minutes. Remove from the oven and transfer the pan to a cooling rack.

4. To prepare the topping, place the confectioners' sugar, butter, and heavy cream in the work bowl of a stand mixer fitted with the paddle attachment and cream on low until the mixture comes together. Raise the speed to medium and beat until light and fluffy. Add the peppermint candies and beat until just incorporated.

5. Spread the mixture over the baked crust, using an offset spatula to even it out. Transfer the pan to the refrigerator and chill until the topping is set, about 2 hours.

6. Run a sharp knife along the edge of the pan and carefully remove the bars. Place them on a cutting board and cut. Drizzle the ganache over the bars, sprinkle the additional peppermint candies on top, and store in the refrigerator until ready to serve.

CAKES

Triple Chocolate Cake

YIELD: 1 CAKE | **ACTIVE TIME:** 1 HOUR | **TOTAL TIME:** 3 HOURS AND 30 MINUTES

FOR THE CAKES

20 OZ. SUGAR

13 OZ. ALL-PURPOSE FLOUR

4 OZ. COCOA POWDER

1 TABLESPOON BAKING SODA

1½ TEASPOONS BAKING POWDER

1½ TEASPOONS KOSHER SALT

1½ CUPS SOUR CREAM

¾ CUP CANOLA OIL

3 EGGS

1½ CUPS BREWED COFFEE, HOT

FOR THE FILLING

BUTTERFLUFF FILLING (SEE PAGE 517)

¼ CUP COCOA POWDER

FOR THE FROSTING

ITALIAN BUTTERCREAM (SEE PAGE 509)

1 CUP COCOA POWDER

FOR TOPPING

CHOCOLATE GANACHE (SEE PAGE 523), WARM

CHOCOLATE, SHAVED

1. Preheat the oven to 350°F. Line three round 8-inch cake pans with parchment paper and coat them with nonstick cooking spray.

2. To begin preparations for the cakes, sift the sugar, flour, the cocoa powder, baking soda, baking powder, and salt into a medium bowl. Set the mixture aside.

3. In the work bowl of a stand mixer fitted with the whisk attachment, combine the sour cream, canola oil, and eggs on medium speed.

4. Reduce the speed to low, add the dry mixture, and whisk until combined. Scrape the sides of the bowl with a rubber spatula as needed. Add the hot coffee and whisk until thoroughly incorporated.

5. Pour 1½ cups of batter into each cake pan. Bang the pans on the countertop to spread the batter and to remove any possible air bubbles.

6. Place the cakes in the oven and bake until a cake tester inserted into the center of each cake comes out clean, 25 to 30 minutes.

7. Remove from the oven and place the cakes on a cooling rack. Let them cool completely.

8. To prepare the filling, place 2 cups of the butterfluff and the cocoa powder in a small bowl and whisk to combine.

9. To prepare the frosting, place the buttercream and cocoa powder in another mixing bowl and whisk until combined. Set the mixtures aside.

10. Trim a thin layer off the top of each cake to create a flat surface. Transfer 2 cups of the frosting to a piping bag and cut a ½-inch slit in it.

11. Place one cake on a cake stand and pipe one ring of frosting around the edge. Place 1 cup of the filling in the center and level it with an offset spatula. Place the second cake on top and repeat the process with the frosting and filling. Place the last cake on top, place 1½ cups of the frosting on the cake, and frost the top and sides of the cake using an offset spatula. Refrigerate the cake for at least 1 hour.

12. Carefully spoon some the ganache over the edge of the cake so that it drips down. Spread any remaining ganache over the center of the cake.

13. Place the cake in the refrigerator for 30 minutes so that the ganache hardens. To serve, sprinkle the curls of chocolate over the top and slice.

Triple Chocolate Cake
PAGES 134–135

Spiced Honey Cake

YIELD: 8 SERVINGS | **ACTIVE TIME:** 20 MINUTES | **TOTAL TIME:** 1 HOUR AND 20 MINUTES

2 CUPS GLUTEN-FREE ALL-PURPOSE BAKING FLOUR

1½ TEASPOONS BAKING POWDER

½ TEASPOON BAKING SODA

½ TEASPOON SEA SALT

1½ TEASPOONS CINNAMON

½ TEASPOON GROUND GINGER

⅛ TEASPOON FRESHLY GRATED NUTMEG

⅔ CUP SUGAR

¼ CUP PACKED LIGHT BROWN SUGAR

½ CUP AVOCADO OIL

½ CUP HONEY

1 LARGE EGG

1 LARGE EGG YOLK

SEEDS FROM ½ VANILLA BEAN

½ CUP FRESH ORANGE JUICE

½ CUP BUTTERMILK

1. Preheat the oven to 350°F. Coat a 9-inch cake pan with nonstick cooking spray and line the bottom with a circle of parchment paper.

2. Place the flour, baking powder, baking soda, salt, cinnamon, ginger, and nutmeg in a mixing bowl and stir to combine.

3. Combine the sugar, brown sugar, avocado oil, honey, egg, and egg yolk in the work bowl of a stand mixer fitted with the paddle attachment. Add the vanilla seeds and beat the mixture until it is pale and thick, about 4 minutes. Reduce the speed to medium-low and gradually pour in the orange juice and buttermilk. Beat until frothy, about 2 minutes. Reduce speed to low and gradually incorporate the dry mixture. Beat until the mixture comes together as a thin, pancake-like batter.

4. Pour the batter into the prepared pan and bake until the cake is golden brown and the center springs back when gently pressed (a cake tester inserted will not come out clean), 45 to 55 minutes.

5. Remove the cake from the oven, place the pan on a wire rack, and let the cake cool for 20 minutes. Run a knife around the edge of the cake to loosen it and invert it onto the rack. Let the cake cool completely before enjoying.

Sumac, Spelt & Apple Cake

YIELD: 4 SERVINGS | **ACTIVE TIME:** 20 MINUTES | **TOTAL TIME:** 1 HOUR AND 20 MINUTES

FOR THE APPLESAUCE

2 LARGE GRANNY SMITH APPLES, PEELED, CORED, AND CHOPPED

1 TABLESPOON FRESH LEMON JUICE

½ CUP WATER

FOR THE CAKE

1⅔ CUPS SPELT FLOUR

½ CUP GROUND ALMONDS

1 TABLESPOON SUMAC, PLUS MORE FOR TOPPING

1 TEASPOON BAKING POWDER

1 TEASPOON BAKING SODA

¼ CUP AVOCADO OIL

½ CUP PLUS 2 TABLESPOONS SUGAR

3 GOLDEN APPLES, PEELED, CORED, AND FINELY DICED

FOR THE ICING

½ CUP CONFECTIONERS' SUGAR, PLUS MORE AS NEEDED

1 TABLESPOON FRESH LEMON JUICE, PLUS MORE AS NEEDED

1. To prepare the applesauce, place all of the ingredients in a saucepan and bring to a simmer. Cook until the apples are completely tender, 10 to 12 minutes. Remove the pan from heat and mash the apples until smooth. Set the applesauce aside.

2. Preheat the oven to 350°F. Coat a 1-pound loaf pan with cooking spray and line it with parchment paper. To begin preparations for the cake, place the flour, ground almonds, sumac, baking powder, and baking soda in a mixing bowl and stir to combine.

3. Place the avocado oil, sugar, and 1½ cups of the applesauce in a separate bowl and stir to combine. Add the wet mixture to the dry mixture and gently stir until the mixture comes together as a thick batter, making sure there are no clumps of flour. Stir in the apples.

4. Pour the batter into the loaf pan, place it in the oven, and bake until a cake tester inserted into the center of the cake comes out clean, 45 to 50 minutes.

5. Remove the cake from the oven and let it cool completely in the pan.

6. Place the confectioners' sugar and lemon juice in a mixing bowl and whisk the mixture until it is thick enough to coat the back of a wooden spoon. If it's too thin, add more sugar; if it's too thick, add more lemon juice.

7. Drizzle the icing over the cake, top with additional sumac, and enjoy.

Keto Lava Cakes

YIELD: 4 SERVINGS | **ACTIVE TIME:** 10 MINUTES | **TOTAL TIME:** 25 MINUTES

CANOLA OIL, AS NEEDED

¼ CUP HEAVY CREAM

4 LARGE EGGS

½ TEASPOON KOSHER SALT

1 TEASPOON BAKING POWDER

1 TEASPOON PURE VANILLA EXTRACT

½ CUP UNSWEETENED COCOA POWDER

½ CUP GRANULATED ERYTHRITOL OR PREFERRED KETO-FRIENDLY SWEETENER

1. Preheat the oven to 350°F and coat four ramekins with canola oil. Place the cream, eggs, salt, baking powder, and vanilla in a bowl and whisk until combined. Stir in the cocoa powder and erythritol and divide the mixture among 4 ramekins.

2. Place the ramekins in the oven and bake until the cakes are just set, 10 to 12 minutes. Place a plate over the top of each ramekin, invert it, and tap on the counter to release the cake. Enjoy immediately.

Nutritional Info Per Serving: Calories: 152; Fat: 11.8 g; Net Carbs: 3.5 g; Protein: 8.7 g

Keto Vanilla Cake

YIELD: 1 SERVING | **ACTIVE TIME:** 5 MINUTES | **TOTAL TIME:** 10 MINUTES

FOR THE CAKE

1 OZ. COCONUT FLOUR

2 TABLESPOONS UNSALTED BUTTER

2 TEASPOONS COCONUT MILK

½ TEASPOON PURE VANILLA EXTRACT

¼ TEASPOON BAKING POWDER

1 EGG

STEVIA OR PREFERRED KETO-FRIENDLY SWEETENER, TO TASTE

PINCH OF KOSHER SALT

FOR THE GANACHE

1½ TEASPOONS UNSALTED BUTTER OR COCOA BUTTER

1½ TEASPOONS NATURAL, NO SUGAR ADDED PEANUT BUTTER

½ TEASPOON UNSWEETENED COCOA POWDER

STEVIA OR PREFERRED KETO-FRIENDLY SWEETENER, TO TASTE

½ TEASPOON COCONUT MILK

1. To prepare the cake, combine all of the ingredients in a large mug, place the mug in the microwave, and microwave on high for 1½ minutes. Remove the mug from the microwave, turn the mug over, and tap it until the cake falls out.

2. To prepare the ganache, place the butter and peanut butter in a microwave-safe bowl and microwave on medium for 30 seconds. Remove and stir to combine. Add the cocoa powder, sweetener, and coconut milk and stir until thoroughly combined. Drizzle half of the ganache over the cake and enjoy.

Nutritional Info Per Serving of Cake: Calories: 218; Fat: 17 g; Net Carbs: 3 g; Protein: 5 g. **Per Serving of Ganache (1 Serving = ½ Ganache):** Calories: 156; Fat: 21 g; Net Carbs: 1 g; Protein: 3 g

Keto No-Bake Blueberry Cheesecake

YIELD: 12 SERVINGS | **ACTIVE TIME:** 15 MINUTES | **TOTAL TIME:** 5 HOURS

3¾ OZ. RAW CASHEWS

2 OZ. UNSWEETENED SHREDDED COCONUT

2 TABLESPOONS COCONUT OIL

7 OZ. BLUEBERRIES

2 TABLESPOONS BEET JUICE

¼ CUP STEVIA OR PREFERRED KETO-FRIENDLY SWEETENER

1 TABLESPOON WATER

1 (14 OZ.) CAN OF COCONUT MILK, CHILLED

2 CUPS FULL-FAT GREEK YOGURT

8½ OZ. FIRM SILKEN TOFU

1. Line a springform pan with parchment paper and coat the paper with nonstick cooking spray. Place 1 cup of the cashews, the coconut, and coconut oil in a food processor and pulse until the mixture is coarse crumbs. Press the mixture into the base of the springform pan and chill it in the refrigerator.

2. Place three-quarters of the blueberries, the beet juice, sweetener, and water in a saucepan, cover the pan, and cook over medium heat until the berries are soft and juicy, about 6 to 8 minutes. Transfer the mixture to a blender and puree until smooth.

3. Strain the puree through a fine sieve into a mixing bowl. Place the coconut milk, yogurt, and tofu in a separate mixing bowl and whisk until the mixture is smooth. Scrape both mixtures on top of the base in the springform pan and gently stir with a rubber spatula until the mixture is swirled. Chill the cheesecake in the refrigerator for 4 hours.

4. Crush the remaining cashews. Sprinkle them and the remaining blueberries over the cheesecake and enjoy.

Nutritional Info Per Serving: Calories: 213; Fat: 16.6 g; Net Carbs: 8.7 g; Protein: 6.1 g

Classic Cheesecake

YIELD: 1 CHEESECAKE | **ACTIVE TIME:** 30 MINUTES | **TOTAL TIME:** 8 HOURS

2 LBS. CREAM CHEESE, SOFTENED

⅔ CUP SUGAR

¼ TEASPOON KOSHER SALT

4 EGGS

1 TABLESPOON PURE VANILLA EXTRACT

1 GRAHAM CRACKER CRUST (SEE PAGE 496), IN A 9-INCH SPRINGFORM PAN

SUMMER BERRY COMPOTE (SEE PAGE 531), FOR SERVING

1. Preheat the oven to 350°F. Bring 8 cups of water to a boil in a small saucepan.

2. In the work bowl of a stand mixer fitted with the paddle attachment, cream the cream cheese, sugar, and salt on high until the mixture is fluffy, about 10 minutes. Scrape down the sides of the work bowl as needed.

3. Reduce the speed of the mixer to medium and incorporate one egg at a time, scraping down the work bowl as needed. Add the vanilla and beat until incorporated.

4. Pour the mixture into the Graham Cracker Crust, place the cheesecake in a large baking pan with high sides, and gently pour the boiling water into the baking pan until it reaches halfway up the sides of the springform pan.

5. Cover the baking pan with aluminum foil, place it in the oven, and bake until the cheesecake is set and only slightly jiggly in the center, 50 minutes to 1 hour.

6. Turn off the oven and leave the oven door cracked. Allow the cheesecake to rest in the cooling oven for 45 minutes.

7. Remove the cheesecake from the oven and transfer it to a cooling rack. Let it sit at room temperature for 1 hour.

8. Transfer the cheesecake to the refrigerator and let it cool for at least 4 hours before serving and slicing. To serve, top each slice with a heaping spoonful of compote.

Classic Cheesecake
SEE PAGE 143

Lemon Polenta Cake

YIELD: 1 CAKE | **ACTIVE TIME:** 15 MINUTES | **TOTAL TIME:** 1 HOUR AND 30 MINUTES

7 OZ. COCONUT OIL OR
UNSALTED BUTTER

7 OZ. SUGAR

7 OZ. ALMOND FLOUR

3½ OZ. POLENTA

1½ TEASPOONS BAKING
POWDER

3 EGGS

ZEST OF 2 LEMONS

1. Preheat the oven to 325°F.

2. Beat together the coconut oil or butter and sugar until fluffy.

3. In a separate bowl, combine the dry ingredients and add the mixture to the sugar mixture, alternating with the eggs.

4. Add the lemon zest to the mixture.

5. Cut a circle of parchment paper to the size of an 8- or 9-inch springform pan. Spray the pan with nonstick cooking spray and place the parchment paper on the bottom.

6. Pour the batter into the pan and bake for 50 minutes, turning the pan halfway through. Bake until a cake tester inserted into the center comes out clean. Remove and let it cool before serving.

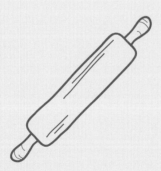

Coconut Cake

YIELD: 1 CAKE | **ACTIVE TIME:** 1 HOUR | **TOTAL TIME:** 3 HOURS

FOR THE CAKES

½ LB. CAKE FLOUR

2¼ TEASPOONS BAKING POWDER

½ TEASPOON KOSHER SALT

6 OZ. UNSALTED BUTTER, SOFTENED

11 OZ. SUGAR

3 EGGS

1 TEASPOON PURE VANILLA EXTRACT

2 TEASPOONS COCONUT EXTRACT

1 CUP COCONUT MILK

½ CUP SWEETENED SHREDDED COCONUT

FOR THE FROSTING

AMERICAN BUTTERCREAM (SEE PAGE 509)

1 TEASPOON COCONUT EXTRACT

2 CUPS SWEETENED SHREDDED COCONUT

1. Preheat the oven to 350°F. Line three round 8-inch cake pans with parchment paper and coat them with nonstick cooking spray.

2. To begin preparations for the cakes, place the flour, baking powder, and salt in a mixing bowl and whisk to combine. Set the mixture aside.

3. In the work bowl of a stand mixer fitted with the paddle attachment, cream the butter and sugar on medium for 5 minutes.

4. Reduce the speed to low and incorporate the eggs one at a time, scraping down the work bowl as needed.

5. Add the dry mixture, beat until combined, and then add the remaining ingredients. Beat until incorporated.

6. Pour 1½ cups of batter into each cake pan. Bang the pans on the countertop to spread the batter and to remove any possible air bubbles.

7. Place the cakes in the oven and bake until they are lightly golden brown and baked through, 20 to 25 minutes. Insert a cake tester in the center of each cake to check for doneness.

8. Remove from the oven and place the cakes on a cooling rack. Let them cool completely.

9. To begin preparations for the frosting, place the buttercream and coconut extract in a mixing bowl and whisk until combined. Set the frosting aside.

10. Trim a thin layer off the top of each cake to create a flat surface.

11. Place one cake on a cake stand. Place 1 cup of the buttercream in the center and level it with an offset spatula. Place the second cake on top and repeat the process with the buttercream. Place the last cake on top and spread 1 cup of the buttercream over the entire cake using an offset spatula. Sprinkle the coconut over the top and side of the cake.

12. Refrigerate the cake for at least 1 hour before slicing and serving.

Key Lime Pie Cupcakes

YIELD: 24 CUPCAKES | **ACTIVE TIME:** 1 HOUR | **TOTAL TIME:** 24 HOURS

FOR THE FILLING

1 CUP CREAM CHEESE, SOFTENED

1 (14 OZ.) CAN OF SWEETENED CONDENSED MILK

⅔ CUP FRESH LIME JUICE

FOR THE CRUST

2 (4.8 OZ.) PACKAGES OF GRAHAM CRACKERS

2 TABLESPOONS SUGAR

½ LB. UNSALTED BUTTER, MELTED

FOR THE CUPCAKES

12½ OZ. ALL-PURPOSE FLOUR

5 TEASPOONS BAKING POWDER

1 TEASPOON FINE SEA SALT

10½ OZ. SUGAR

4 OZ. UNSALTED BUTTER, SOFTENED

4 EGGS

½ CUP VEGETABLE OIL

½ CUP SOUR CREAM

⅔ CUP WHOLE MILK, AT ROOM TEMPERATURE

⅔ CUP FRESH LIME JUICE, AT ROOM TEMPERATURE

1. Preheat the oven to 325°F. Prepare the filling at least a day in advance so that it has time to harden in the refrigerator. To do this, beat the softened cream cheese in a large bowl until smooth, add the sweetened condensed milk, and then slowly add the lime juice to avoid splattering.

2. To prepare the crust, place the graham crackers in a large resealable bag and crush them with a rolling pin until very finely ground. Place the crumbs in a large bowl and add the sugar, mixing to incorporate. Next, add the melted butter and mix until you've achieved a graham cracker paste. Line a large, 24-well muffin tin with cupcake liners and divide the graham cracker paste evenly among the liners. Press the graham cracker crumbs down in each well to form a crust.

3. To prepare the cupcakes, combine the flour, baking powder, and salt in a medium bowl. Whisk together for 20 seconds with a fork. In a large bowl, add the sugar and softened butter. Beat on low with a stand or handheld mixer, adding the eggs, vegetable oil, and sour cream. Once smooth, alternate adding the flour mixture with the milk and lime juice until the flour and liquid have all been incorporated. Using an ice cream scoop, fill each muffin tin well nearly completely full and bake until they are cooked through, 15 to 17 minutes.

4. Remove the cupcakes from the oven and let them cool for 15 minutes before removing them from the muffin tin. Please note that the center of the cupcakes will seem uncooked and won't be firm to the touch; this is normal. Once the cupcake centers are removed in the next step, you will be left with a perfectly baked cupcake. If you were to bake the cupcakes until the centers were firm, the outer part that remains would be too dry.

5. Remove the centers of the cooled cupcakes with a cupcake corer (or a spoon, but you'll get a cleaner core with the corer) and fill them with the cream cheese filling, either placing the filling in a pastry bag fit with a plain tip or a large resealable bag with a hole cut in one of the bottom corners. Enjoy immediately.

Lemon Poppy Seed Cake

YIELD: 1 CAKE | **ACTIVE TIME:** 30 MINUTES | **TOTAL TIME:** 24 HOURS

⅔ CUP POPPY SEEDS, PLUS MORE FOR TOPPING

1 CUP FULL-FAT GREEK YOGURT

3 CUPS ALL-PURPOSE FLOUR, PLUS MORE AS NEEDED

1 TABLESPOON BAKING POWDER

1½ TEASPOONS FINE SEA SALT

1⅓ CUPS SUGAR

5 EGGS

1 CUP EXTRA-VIRGIN OLIVE OIL

ZEST AND JUICE OF 2 LEMONS

LEMON GLAZE (SEE PAGE 533)

1. Place the poppy seeds and yogurt in a small bowl and stir to combine. Place the mixture in the refrigerator and let it chill overnight.

2. Preheat the oven to 350°F. Coat a 6-quart Bundt pan with nonstick cooking spray and sprinkle some flour over it, knocking out any excess flour. Sift the flour, baking powder, and salt into a small bowl and set the mixture aside.

3. Place the sugar, eggs, and olive oil in the work bowl of a stand mixer fitted with the whisk attachment and whip the mixture until it is pale yellow, frothy, and comes off a rubber spatula in ribbons, about 5 minutes, scraping down the work bowl as necessary.

4. Add the poppy seed yogurt and whip until it has been incorporated. Add the dry mixture and gently fold until incorporated. Add the lemon zest and lemon juice and stir until incorporated.

5. Pour the batter into the Bundt pan, place it in the oven, and bake until a toothpick inserted into the cake's center comes out clean, about 40 minutes, rotating the pan halfway through.

6. Remove the cake from the oven and let it cool completely.

7. Invert the cake onto a platter. Pour the glaze over the cake, let it set for a few minutes, and sprinkle additional poppy seeds over the top.

Chocolate Souffles

YIELD: 6 SOUFFLES | **ACTIVE TIME:** 30 MINUTES | **TOTAL TIME:** 1 HOUR

9 OZ. SUGAR, PLUS MORE AS NEEDED

20 OZ. DARK CHOCOLATE (55 TO 65 PERCENT)

4 OZ. UNSALTED BUTTER

19 OZ. WATER, PLUS MORE AS NEEDED

2 OZ. HEAVY CREAM

11 EGGS, SEPARATED

1½ OZ. SOUR CREAM

½ TEASPOON CREAM OF TARTAR

1. Preheat the oven to 375°F. Coat the insides of six 8-oz. ramekins with nonstick cooking spray. Place 2 tablespoons of sugar in each ramekin and spread it to evenly coat the insides of the dishes. Knock out any excess sugar and set the ramekins aside.

2. Place the dark chocolate and butter in a large, heatproof bowl. Add 2 inches of water to a small saucepan and bring it to a simmer. Place the bowl on top and melt the butter and chocolate together over the double boiler.

3. In a medium saucepan, bring the water and heavy cream to a simmer. Remove the chocolate mixture from the double boiler and whisk it into the water-and-cream mixture. Remove the saucepan from heat.

4. Place the egg yolks and the sour cream in a mixing bowl and whisk until combined. Gradually incorporate the cream-and-chocolate mixture, while whisking constantly. Set the mixture aside.

5. In the work bowl of a stand mixer fitted with the whisk attachment, whip the egg whites and cream of tartar on high until the mixture holds stiff peaks. Reduce the speed to medium and gradually incorporate the 9 oz. of sugar. Once all of the sugar has been incorporated, raise the speed back to high and whip until it is a glossy, stiff meringue.

6. Working in three increments, add the meringue to the chocolate base, folding gently with a rubber spatula.

7. Spoon the souffle base to the rims of the ramekins. Gently tap the bottoms of the ramekins with the palm of your hand to remove any air, but not so hard as to deflate the meringue.

8. Place in the oven and bake until the souffles have risen significantly and set on the outside, but are still jiggly at the center, 25 to 27 minutes. Remove from the oven and serve immediately.

Strawberry Rhubarb Ricotta Cakes

YIELD: 4 SMALL CAKES | **ACTIVE TIME:** 30 MINUTES | **TOTAL TIME:** 1 HOUR AND 15 MINUTES

4 OZ. UNSALTED BUTTER, SOFTENED

3½ OZ. SUGAR

2 EGGS

¼ TEASPOON PURE VANILLA EXTRACT

ZEST OF 1 LEMON

¾ CUP RICOTTA CHEESE

3¾ OZ. ALL-PURPOSE FLOUR

1 TEASPOON BAKING POWDER

½ TEASPOON KOSHER SALT

½ CUP MINCED STRAWBERRIES, PLUS MORE FOR GARNISH

½ CUP RHUBARB JAM (SEE PAGE 522)

ITALIAN MERINGUE (SEE PAGE 508)

1. Preheat the oven to 350°F and coat a 9 x 5–inch loaf pan with nonstick cooking spray. To prepare the cakes, place the butter and sugar in the work bowl of a stand mixer fitted with the paddle attachment and beat on high until the mixture is smooth and a pale yellow. Reduce the speed to medium, add the eggs one at a time, and beat until incorporated. Add the vanilla, lemon zest, and ricotta and beat until the mixture is smooth.

2. Place the flour, baking powder, and salt in a mixing bowl and whisk to combine. Reduce the speed of the mixer to low, add the dry mixture to the wet mixture, and beat until incorporated. Scrape the mixing bowl as needed while mixing the batter.

3. Add the strawberries and fold to incorporate. Place the batter in the loaf pan, place it in the oven, and bake until a cake tester inserted into the center comes out clean, about 35 minutes. Remove from the oven and let the cake cool to room temperature in the pan.

4. Remove the cooled cake from the pan and cut it into 8 equal pieces. Spread some of the jam over four of the pieces. Cover the jam with some of the meringue and then place the unadorned pieces of cake on top. Spread more meringue on top, garnish with additional strawberries, and serve.

Molten Lava Cakes

YIELD: 6 SMALL CAKES | **ACTIVE TIME:** 20 MINUTES | **TOTAL TIME:** 40 MINUTES

1 CUP COCOA POWDER, PLUS MORE AS NEEDED

3 OZ. ALL-PURPOSE FLOUR

¼ TEASPOON KOSHER SALT

½ LB. DARK CHOCOLATE (55 TO 65 PERCENT)

4 OZ. UNSALTED BUTTER

3 EGGS

3 EGG YOLKS

4 OZ. SUGAR

CONFECTIONERS' SUGAR, FOR DUSTING

1. Preheat the oven to 425°F. Spray six 6-oz. ramekins with nonstick cooking spray and coat each one with cocoa powder. Tap out any excess cocoa powder and set the ramekins aside.

2. Sift the flour and salt into a small bowl and set the mixture aside.

3. Fill a small saucepan halfway with water and bring it to a gentle simmer. Place the chocolate and butter in a heatproof mixing bowl and place it over the simmering water. Stir occasionally until the mixture is melted and completely smooth. Remove from heat and set it aside.

4. In another mixing bowl, whisk together the eggs, egg yolks, and sugar. Add the chocolate mixture and whisk until combined. Add the dry mixture and whisk until a smooth batter forms.

5. Pour approximately ½ cup of batter into each of the ramekins. Place them in the oven and bake until the cakes look firm and are crested slightly at the top, 12 to 15 minutes. Remove from the oven and let them cool for 1 minute.

6. Invert each cake onto a plate (be careful, as the ramekins will be very hot). Dust the cakes with confectioners' sugar and serve.

Coffee Cake

YIELD: 1 CAKE | **ACTIVE TIME:** 20 MINUTES | **TOTAL TIME:** 2 HOURS AND 30 MINUTES

1 LB. ALL-PURPOSE FLOUR

1 TEASPOON BAKING POWDER

1½ TEASPOONS BAKING SODA

½ TEASPOON KOSHER SALT

½ LB. UNSALTED BUTTER, SOFTENED

11 OZ. SUGAR

4 EGGS

2 CUPS SOUR CREAM

COFFEE CAKE TOPPING (SEE PAGE 536)

CONFECTIONERS' SUGAR, FOR DUSTING

1. Preheat the oven to 350°F. Coat a round 9-inch cake pan with nonstick cooking spray.

2. Place the flour, baking powder, baking soda, and salt in a mixing bowl and whisk to combine.

3. In the work bowl of a stand mixer fitted with the paddle attachment, cream the butter and sugar on medium until it is light and fluffy, about 5 minutes.

4. Reduce the speed to low and incorporate the eggs one at a time, scraping down the work bowl as needed. Add the sour cream, raise the speed to medium, and beat to incorporate. Add the dry mixture, reduce the speed to low, and beat until the mixture is a smooth batter.

5. Pour half of the batter into the cake pan and spread it into an even layer. Sprinkle 1 cup of the topping over the batter. Pour the remaining batter over the topping and spread it into an even layer. Sprinkle the remaining topping over the top of the cake.

6. Place the cake in the oven and bake until a cake tester inserted into the center comes out clean, 45 to 55 minutes.

7. Remove from the oven and place the pan on a wire rack to cool for 1 hour. Remove the cake from the pan, dust the top with confectioners' sugar, and enjoy.

Lemon & Yogurt Pound Cake

YIELD: 1 CAKE | **ACTIVE TIME:** 20 MINUTES | **TOTAL TIME:** 2 HOURS

½ LB. ALL-PURPOSE FLOUR

1½ TEASPOONS BAKING POWDER

¾ TEASPOON KOSHER SALT

10 OZ. SUGAR

3 EGGS

5 OZ. CANOLA OIL

ZEST AND JUICE OF 2 LEMONS

1½ TEASPOONS PURE VANILLA EXTRACT

7 OZ. FULL-FAT YOGURT

LEMON SYRUP (SEE PAGE 538)

1. Preheat the oven to 350°F. Coat an 9 x 5–inch loaf pan with nonstick cooking spray.

2. Place the flour, baking powder, salt, and 5 oz. of the sugar in a mixing bowl and whisk to combine. Set aside.

3. In the work bowl of a stand mixer fitted with the paddle attachment, beat the eggs, canola oil, remaining sugar, lemon zest, lemon juice, and vanilla on medium for 5 minutes. Add the dry mixture, reduce the speed to low, and beat until the mixture comes together as a smooth batter. Add the yogurt and beat to incorporate.

4. Pour the batter into the prepared loaf pan, place it in the oven, and bake until a cake tester inserted into the center of the cake comes out clean, 60 to 70 minutes.

5. Remove the pan from the oven and place it on a wire rack to cool. Generously brush the cake with the syrup and let it cool completely before serving.

Orange & Cardamom Coffee Cake

YIELD: 1 CAKE | **ACTIVE TIME:** 20 MINUTES | **TOTAL TIME:** 2 HOURS AND 30 MINUTES

1 LB. ALL-PURPOSE FLOUR

1 TEASPOON BAKING POWDER

1½ TEASPOONS BAKING SODA

2 TEASPOONS CARDAMOM

½ TEASPOON CINNAMON

½ TEASPOON KOSHER SALT

½ LB. UNSALTED BUTTER, SOFTENED

11 OZ. SUGAR

ZEST OF 2 ORANGES

4 EGGS

2 CUPS SOUR CREAM

COFFEE CAKE TOPPING (SEE PAGE 536)

CONFECTIONERS' SUGAR, FOR DUSTING

1. Preheat the oven to 350°F. Coat a round 9-inch cake pan with nonstick cooking spray.

2. Place the flour, baking powder, baking soda, cardamom, cinnamon, and salt in a mixing bowl and whisk to combine.

3. In the work bowl of a stand mixer fitted with the paddle attachment, cream the butter, sugar, and orange zest on medium until it is light and fluffy, about 5 minutes.

4. Reduce the speed to low and incorporate the eggs one at a time, scraping down the work bowl as needed. Add the sour cream, raise the speed to medium, and beat to incorporate. Add the dry mixture, reduce the speed to low, and beat until the mixture is a smooth batter.

5. Pour half of the batter into the cake pan and spread it into an even layer. Sprinkle 1 cup of the topping over the batter. Pour the remaining batter over the topping and spread it into an even layer. Sprinkle the remaining topping over the top of the cake.

6. Place the cake in the oven and bake until a cake tester inserted into the center comes out clean, 45 to 55 minutes.

7. Remove from the oven and place the pan on a wire rack to cool for 1 hour. Remove the cake from the pan, dust the top with confectioners' sugar, and enjoy.

Conchas

YIELD: 42 CONCHAS | **ACTIVE TIME:** 1 HOUR AND 30 MINUTES | **TOTAL TIME:** 13 HOURS

FOR THE DOUGH

2 CUPS WARMED MILK (90°F)

2 CUPS SUGAR

2 OZ. ACTIVE DRY YEAST

1½ LBS. EGGS

SEEDS OF 1 VANILLA BEAN

45 OZ. ALL-PURPOSE FLOUR, PLUS MORE AS NEEDED

½ OZ. FINE SEA SALT

⅛ TEASPOON (SCANT) CARDAMOM

1 LB. UNSALTED BUTTER, SOFTENED

FOR THE TOPPING

6 OZ. ALL-PURPOSE FLOUR

6 OZ. CONFECTIONERS' SUGAR

4.8 OZ. UNSALTED BUTTER, SOFTENED

1. To begin preparations for the dough, place the milk, sugar, and yeast in the work bowl of a stand mixer fitted with the dough hook attachment and stir gently to combine. Let the mixture sit until it is foamy, about 10 minutes.

2. Add the eggs and stir gently to incorporate. Add the vanilla, flour, salt, and cardamom and work the mixture until it comes together as a scraggly dough.

3. Knead the dough on medium for about 3 minutes. Add the butter in four increments and work the mixture for 2 minutes after each addition, scraping down the work bowl as needed.

4. Increase the mixer's speed and knead the dough until it can be lifted cleanly out of the bowl, about 10 minutes.

5. Place the dough on a flour-dusted work surface and lightly flour your hands and the top of the dough. Fold the edges of the dough toward the middle and gently press them into the dough. Carefully turn the dough over and use your palms to shape the dough to form a tight ball. Carefully pick up the dough and place it in a mixing bowl. Let it rise in a naturally warm place until it has doubled in size, about 1 hour.

6. Place the dough on a flour-dusted work surface and press down gently to deflate the dough with your hands. Fold in the edges toward the middle and press them in. Carefully flip the dough over and tighten the dough into a ball with a smooth, taut surface.

7. Place the dough back in the mixing bowl, cover it with plastic wrap, and chill in the refrigerator for 8 hours.

8. Divide the dough into 2½-oz. portions and form them into balls. Place the balls on parchment-lined baking sheets, cover them with kitchen towels, and let them rise at room temperature for 2 hours.

9. To begin preparations for the topping, place all of the ingredients in the work bowl of a stand mixer fitted with the paddle attachment and beat until the mixture comes together as a smooth dough.

10. Divide the topping into ⅓-oz. portions. Line a tortilla press with plastic, place a piece of the topping mixture on top, and top with another piece of plastic. Flatten the mixture, place it on one of the proofed conchas, and make small cuts in the topping that are the same shape as the top of an oyster shell. Repeat with the remaining topping mixture and let the conchas rest for 10 minutes.

11. Place in the oven and bake for 10 minutes. Rotate the pans, lower the oven's temperature to 300°F, and bake for an additional 2 minutes. Remove and let them cool before enjoying.

Conchas
SEE PAGE 161

Dark Chocolate Entremet

YIELD: 1 CAKE | **ACTIVE TIME:** 3 HOURS | **TOTAL TIME:** 15 HOURS

FOR THE CAKE

1 OZ. ALL-PURPOSE FLOUR

1 TABLESPOON COCOA POWDER

2 OZ. ALMOND FLOUR

2.4 OZ. CONFECTIONERS' SUGAR

3 EGG WHITES

¼ TEASPOON KOSHER SALT

2 TABLESPOONS SUGAR

FOR THE GELEE

2 SHEETS OF SILVER GELATIN

¼ CUP WATER

7 OZ. PASSION FRUIT PUREE

3 TABLESPOONS SUGAR

FOR THE MOUSSE

2 SHEETS OF SILVER GELATIN

1 LB. DARK CHOCOLATE (55 TO 65 PERCENT)

14 OZ. PLUS ½ CUP HEAVY CREAM

½ CUP MILK

2 EGG YOLKS

2 TABLESPOONS SUGAR

FOR THE GLAZE

5 SHEETS OF SILVER GELATIN

9 OZ. SUGAR

5 OZ. WATER

3 OZ. COCOA POWDER

3 OZ. SOUR CREAM

2 OZ. DARK CHOCOLATE

1. Preheat the oven to 350°F. Coat a round 6-inch cake pan with nonstick cooking spray.

2. To begin preparations for the cake, sift the flour, cocoa powder, almond flour, and confectioners' sugar into a medium bowl. Set the mixture aside.

3. In the work bowl of a stand mixer fitted with the whisk attachment, whip the egg whites and salt on high until soft peaks begin to form. Reduce the speed to low and gradually incorporate the sugar. Raise the speed to high and whip the mixture until it holds stiff peaks.

4. Fold the meringue into the dry mixture until fully incorporated and then pour the batter into the prepared cake pan.

5. Place the cake in the oven and bake until set and a cake tester comes out clean after being inserted, 10 to 12 minutes. Remove the cake from the oven and set it on a wire rack to cool completely. Once cool, remove the cake from the pan and set aside.

6. To begin preparations for the gelee, place the gelatin sheets in a small bowl, and add 1 cup of ice and enough cold water to cover the sheets. Place the water, passion fruit puree, and sugar in a small saucepan and bring to a simmer over medium heat.

7. Prepare a 6-inch ring mold by wrapping plastic wrap tightly over the bottom. Set the ring mold on a small baking sheet.

8. Remove the pan from heat. Remove the gelatin from the ice bath and squeeze out as much water as possible. Whisk the gelatin into the passion fruit mixture until fully dissolved. Let the gelee cool to room temperature and then pour it into the ring mold. Place the cake ring in the freezer for at least 4 hours to fully freeze.

9. To begin preparations for the mousse, place the gelatin sheets in a small bowl, and add 1 cup of ice and enough cold water to cover the sheets.

10. Prepare an 8-inch ring mold by wrapping plastic wrap tightly over the bottom. Set the ring mold on a small baking sheet.

11. Fill a small saucepan halfway with water and bring it to a gentle simmer. Place the dark chocolate in a heatproof bowl, place the bowl over the simmering water, and stir with a rubber spatula until the chocolate has melted. Remove the chocolate from heat and set it aside.

12. In the work bowl of a stand mixer fitted with the whisk attachment, whip 14 oz. of the heavy cream on high until soft peaks form. Place the whipped cream in the refrigerator.

13. In a small saucepan, combine the milk and remaining heavy cream and bring to a boil over medium heat.

14. Place the egg yolks and sugar in a small bowl and whisk to combine. Gradually add the heated milk mixture into the egg-and-sugar mixture while whisking constantly. When fully incorporated, transfer the tempered mixture back into the saucepan.

15. Cook the mixture over medium heat, whisking until the mixture has thickened slightly and reads 175°F on an instant-read thermometer. Remove the pan from heat, remove the gelatin from the ice bath, and squeeze out as much water as possible. Whisk the gelatin into the warm mousse until fully dissolved.

16. Pour the mixture over the melted chocolate and stir to combine.

17. Remove the whipped cream from the refrigerator and, working in two increments, fold it into the mixture.

18. Pour 2 cups of the mousse into the 8-inch ring mold. Spread it into an even layer with an offset spatula.

19. Remove the passion fruit gelee from the freezer, carefully remove the plastic wrap, and remove the gelee from the cake ring. Place the gelee in the center of the mousse and press down.

20. Add more of the mousse until it reaches about ½ inch from the top of the ring mold.

21. Place the chocolate cake in the mousse, top side down, and push down gently until the cake and mousse are level with each other.

22. Transfer the entremet to the freezer and chill for at least 4 hours.

23. To begin preparations for the glaze, place the gelatin sheets in a small bowl, and add 1 cup of ice and enough cold water to cover the sheets.

Continued . . .

24. In a medium saucepan, combine the sugar, water, cocoa powder, and sour cream and warm over low heat, stirring continuously until the mixture begins to steam. Take care to not let the mixture come to a boil, as it can burn easily.

25. Remove the pan from heat, remove the gelatin from the ice bath, and squeeze out as much water as possible. Whisk the gelatin into the warm mixture until fully dissolved.

26. Add the dark chocolate and stir until the mixture is smooth. Let the glaze cool to 95°F.

27. Remove the entremet from the freezer and peel off the plastic wrap from the bottom. Using a kitchen torch, lightly heat the sides of the ring mold to loosen the entremet.

28. Place a wire rack on a piece of parchment paper. Flip the entremet over so that the cake is bottom side up.

29. Pour the glaze carefully and evenly over the top in a circular motion, starting from the center and working out toward the edge. Allow the glaze to fall over the side and cover the entirety of the cake. Use an offset spatula to spread the glaze as needed. If there are any air bubbles, carefully go over them with a kitchen torch, as a smooth, shiny finish is a key piece of a successful entremet.

30. Using a spatula, transfer the glazed cake to a serving tray and refrigerate for 4 hours to allow the glaze to set and the center of the cake to thaw. When ready to serve, use a hot knife to cut the cake.

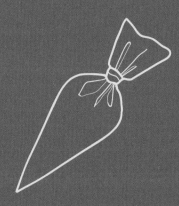

King Cake

YIELD: 1 CAKE | **ACTIVE TIME:** 40 MINUTES | **TOTAL TIME:** 4 HOURS

⅓ CUP WHOLE MILK

1¾ TEASPOONS ACTIVE DRY YEAST

15 OZ. ALL-PURPOSE FLOUR, PLUS MORE AS NEEDED

⅓ CUP CONFECTIONERS' SUGAR

¼ TEASPOON FRESHLY GRATED NUTMEG

1 TEASPOON LEMON ZEST

2 EGGS

1 EGG YOLK

1 TEASPOON ORANGE BLOSSOM WATER

3 OZ. UNSALTED BUTTER, CUT INTO SMALL PIECES

1 TEASPOON FINE SEA SALT

5 TABLESPOONS WARM WATER (110°F)

3 TABLESPOONS SUGAR

YELLOW, PURPLE, AND GREEN FOOD COLORING (OPTIONAL)

CANDIED FRUIT, ROUGHLY CHOPPED, FOR TOPPING

1. Place the milk in a saucepan and heat to 100°F. Add the yeast, gently stir, and let the mixture rest for 5 minutes.

2. Place the mixture in a large mixing bowl. Add the flour, confectioners' sugar, nutmeg, lemon zest, one of the eggs, the egg yolk, and orange blossom water and beat until combined.

3. Transfer the dough to the work bowl of a stand mixer fitted with the dough hook attachment. Work the dough and gradually incorporate the butter. When all of the butter has been incorporated, add the salt and work the mixture until it is very smooth. This should take about 20 minutes. Place the dough in a naturally warm spot and let it rise until it has doubled in size, about 1 to 1½ hours.

4. Transfer the dough to flour-dusted work surface and shape it into a ball. Place the ball in a 13 x 9–inch baking pan lined with parchment paper and flatten it slightly. Make a small hole in the center of the dough and use your hands to gradually enlarge the hole and create a crown. Cover and let stand for 1 hour.

5. Preheat the oven to 320°F. Place the remaining egg and 1 tablespoon of the warm water in a measuring cup and beat to combine. Brush the crown with the egg wash. Place in the oven and bake until the crown is golden brown and a cake tester comes out clean, about 30 minutes.

6. Place the sugar and the remaining warm water in a mixing bowl and stir until the sugar has dissolved. Add the food coloring, if desired, and stir to combine. Brush the hot crown with the glaze and decorate with the chopped candied fruit.

Carrot Cake

YIELD: 1 CAKE | **ACTIVE TIME:** 30 MINUTES | **TOTAL TIME:** 2 HOURS

9 OZ. ALL-PURPOSE FLOUR

2 TEASPOONS BAKING SODA

1 TABLESPOON CINNAMON

1½ TEASPOONS GROUND GINGER

1 TEASPOON KOSHER SALT

14 OZ. SUGAR

1¼ CUPS CANOLA OIL

4 EGGS

3 LARGE CARROTS, PEELED AND GRATED

½ CUP SWEETENED SHREDDED COCONUT

CREAM CHEESE FROSTING (SEE PAGE 510)

1. Preheat the oven to 350°F. Line three round 8-inch cake pans with parchment paper and coat them with nonstick cooking spray.

2. Place the flour, baking soda, cinnamon, ginger, and salt in a mixing bowl and whisk to combine. Set the mixture aside.

3. In the work bowl of a stand mixer fitted with the whisk attachment, combine the sugar, canola oil, eggs, carrots, and coconut and whip on medium for 5 minutes.

4. Reduce the speed to low, add the dry mixture, and whisk until combined. Scrape down the sides of the work bowl with a rubber spatula as needed.

5. Pour 1½ cups of batter into each cake pan. Bang the pans on the countertop to spread the batter and to remove any possible air bubbles.

6. Place the cakes in the oven and bake until they are lightly golden brown and baked through, 22 to 26 minutes. Insert a cake tester in the center of each cake to check for doneness.

7. Remove from the oven and place the cakes on a cooling rack. Let them cool completely.

8. Trim a thin layer off the top of each cake to create a flat surface.

9. Place one cake on a cake stand. Place 1 cup of the frosting in the center and level it with an offset spatula. Place the second cake on top and repeat the process with the frosting. Place the last cake on top, place 2 cups of the frosting on the cake, and frost the top and sides of the cake using an offset spatula. Refrigerate the cake for at least 1 hour before enjoying.

Carrot Cake
SEE PAGE 169

Date & Toffee Pudding Cakes

YIELD: 8 SMALL CAKES | **ACTIVE TIME:** 45 MINUTES | **TOTAL TIME:** 1 HOUR AND 30 MINUTES

¾ CUP PLUS 1 TABLESPOON WARM WATER (110°F)

½ TEASPOON BAKING SODA

½ LB. PITTED DATES, CHOPPED

6¼ OZ. ALL-PURPOSE FLOUR

½ TEASPOON BAKING POWDER

¾ TEASPOON FINE SEA SALT

12¼ OZ. DARK BROWN SUGAR

2 LARGE EGGS

4 OZ. UNSALTED BUTTER, HALF MELTED, HALF SOFTENED

1½ TABLESPOONS PURE VANILLA EXTRACT

1 CUP HEAVY CREAM

DASH OF FRESH LEMON JUICE

1. Place ¾ cup of the warm water, the baking soda, and half of the dates in a large mason jar and soak for 5 minutes. The liquid should cover the dates.

2. Preheat the oven to 350°F and coat eight 4-oz. ramekins with nonstick cooking spray. Bring water to boil in a small saucepan.

3. Place the flour, baking powder, and ½ teaspoon of the salt in a large bowl and whisk to combine.

4. Place ¾ cup of the brown sugar and the remaining dates in a blender or food processor and blitz until the mixture is fine. Drain the soaked dates, reserve the liquid, and set them aside. Add the reserved liquid to the blender with the eggs, melted butter, and vanilla and puree until smooth. Add the puree and soaked dates to the flour mixture and fold to combine.

5. Fill each ramekin two-thirds of the way with the batter, place the filled ramekins in a large roasting pan, and pour the boiling water in the roasting pan so that it goes halfway up each ramekin.

6. Cover tightly with aluminum foil and place the pan in the oven. Bake until each cake is puffy and the surfaces are spongy but firm, about 40 minutes. Remove the ramekins from the roasting pan and let them cool on a wire rack for 10 minutes.

7. Place the remaining butter in a saucepan and warm over medium-high heat. When the butter is melted, add the remaining brown sugar and salt and whisk until smooth. Cook, while stirring occasionally, until the brown sugar has dissolved. Slowly add the cream, while stirring constantly, until it has all been incorporated and the mixture is smooth. Reduce the heat to low and simmer until the mixture starts to bubble. Remove from heat and stir in the lemon juice.

8. To serve, invert each cake into a bowl or onto a dish, and spoon a generous amount of the sauce over each.

Black Forest Cake

YIELD: 1 CAKE | **ACTIVE TIME:** 1 HOUR | **TOTAL TIME:** 3 HOURS AND 30 MINUTES

20 OZ. SUGAR

13 OZ. ALL-PURPOSE FLOUR

4 OZ. COCOA POWDER

1 TABLESPOON BAKING SODA

1½ TEASPOONS BAKING POWDER

1½ TEASPOONS KOSHER SALT

1½ CUPS SOUR CREAM

¾ CUP CANOLA OIL

3 EGGS

1½ CUPS BREWED COFFEE, HOT

2 BATCHES OF CHANTILLY CREAM (SEE PAGE 518)

2 CUPS CHERRY JAM

CHOCOLATE GANACHE (SEE PAGE 523), MADE WITH DARK CHOCOLATE, WARM

DARK CHOCOLATE, SHAVED, FOR GARNISH

2 CUPS FRESH RED CHERRIES, FOR GARNISH

1. Preheat the oven to 350°F. Line three round 8-inch cake pans with parchment paper and coat them with nonstick cooking spray.

2. In a medium bowl, sift the sugar, flour, cocoa powder, baking soda, baking powder, and salt into a mixing bowl and set it aside.

3. In the work bowl of a stand mixer fitted with the whisk attachment, combine the sour cream, canola oil, and eggs on medium speed. Reduce the speed to low, add the dry mixture, and beat until combined. Scrape the sides of the work bowl with a rubber spatula as needed.

4. With the mixer running on low, gradually add the hot coffee and beat until fully incorporated. Pour 1½ cups of batter into each cake pan. Bang the pans on the counter to distribute the batter evenly and remove any air bubbles.

5. Place the cakes in the oven and bake until browned and cooked through, 25 to 30 minutes. Insert a cake tester in the center of each cake to check for doneness. Remove the cakes from the oven, transfer them to a cooling rack, and let them cool completely.

6. Trim a thin layer off the top of each cake to create a flat surface. Transfer 2 cups of the Chantilly Cream into a piping bag and cut a ½-inch slit in the bag.

7. Place one cake on a cake stand and pipe one ring of cream around the edge. Place 1 cup of the cherry jam in the center and level it with an offset spatula. Place the second cake on top and repeat the process with the Chantilly Cream and cherry jam. Place the last cake on top and spread 1½ cups of the Chantilly Cream over the entire cake using an offset spatula. Refrigerate the cake for at least 1 hour.

8. Carefully spoon some the ganache over the edge of the cake so that it drips down. Spread any remaining ganache over the center of the cake.

9. Place the cake in the refrigerator for 30 minutes so that the ganache hardens.

10. Garnish the cake with the shaved chocolate and fresh cherries before slicing and serving.

Red Velvet Cake

YIELD: 1 CAKE | **ACTIVE TIME:** 1 HOUR | **TOTAL TIME:** 3 HOURS

12¾ OZ. CAKE FLOUR

1 OZ. COCOA POWDER

½ TEASPOON KOSHER SALT

1 TEASPOON BAKING SODA

13.4 OZ. UNSALTED BUTTER, SOFTENED

14½ OZ. SUGAR

6 EGGS

1 TEASPOON WHITE VINEGAR

2½ OZ. BUTTERMILK

1 TEASPOON PURE VANILLA EXTRACT

2 TEASPOONS RED FOOD COLORING

CREAM CHEESE FROSTING (SEE PAGE 510)

1. Preheat the oven to 350°F. Line three round 8-inch cake pans with parchment paper and spray with nonstick cooking spray.

2. In a medium bowl, whisk together the cake flour, cocoa powder, salt, and baking soda. Set the mixture aside.

3. In the work bowl of a stand mixer fitted with the paddle attachment, cream the butter and sugar on high speed until the mixture is creamy and fluffy, about 5 minutes. Reduce the speed to low, add the eggs two at a time, and beat until incorporated, scraping down the sides of the bowl with a rubber spatula between additions. Add the vinegar, beat until incorporated, and then add the dry mixture. Beat until thoroughly incorporated, add the buttermilk, vanilla extract, and food coloring, and beat until they have been combined.

4. Pour 1½ cups of batter into each cake pan and bang the pans on the counter to distribute the batter evenly and remove any air bubbles.

5. Place the cakes in the oven and bake until set and cooked through, 26 to 28 minutes. Insert a cake tester in the center of each cake to check for doneness. Remove the cakes from the oven, transfer to a cooling rack, and let them cool completely.

6. Trim a thin layer off the top of each cake to create a flat surface.

7. Place one cake on a cake stand, place 1 cup of the frosting in the center, and level it with an offset spatula. Place the second cake on top and repeat the process with the frosting. Place the last cake on top and spread 2 cups of the frosting over the entire cake using an offset spatula. Refrigerate the cake for at least 1 hour before slicing and serving.

Elderflower Souffles

3½ OZ. SUGAR, PLUS MORE
AS NEEDED

2 TABLESPOONS
CORNSTARCH

¼ CUP COLD WATER

10½ OZ. MILK

ZEST OF ½ LEMON

2 OZ. ELDERFLOWER
LIQUEUR

4 EGG WHITES

¼ TEASPOON CREAM OF
TARTAR

1. Preheat the oven to 375°F. Coat four 8-oz. ramekins with nonstick cooking spray. Place 2 tablespoons of sugar in each ramekin and spread it to evenly coat the insides of the dishes. Knock out any excess sugar and set the ramekins aside.

2. In a small bowl, whisk together the cornstarch and cold water. Set the mixture aside.

3. Bring the milk and lemon zest to a boil over medium heat in a medium saucepan. Gradually pour in the cornstarch mixture while continually whisking. Continue to whisk until the mixture has thickened and has boiled for 30 seconds. Immediately remove the pan from heat and whisk in the elderflower liqueur.

4. Transfer the souffle base to a medium bowl. Take plastic wrap and place it directly on the mixture so that no air can get to it. This will prevent a skin from forming. Place the bowl in the refrigerator until it reaches room temperature, about 1 hour.

5. In the work bowl of a stand mixer fitted with the whisk attachment, whip the egg whites and cream of tartar on high until the mixture holds stiff peaks. Reduce the speed to medium and gradually incorporate the sugar. Once all of the sugar has been incorporated, raise the speed back to high and whip until it is a glossy, stiff meringue.

6. Working in three increments, add the meringue to the souffle base, folding gently with a rubber spatula.

7. Spoon the souffle base to the rims of the ramekins. Gently tap the bottoms of the ramekins with the palm of your hand to remove any air, but not so hard as to deflate the meringue.

8. Place in the oven and bake until the souffles have risen significantly and set on the outside, but are still jiggly at the center, 22 to 25 minutes. Remove from the oven and serve immediately.

Red Velvet Cake
SEE PAGE 176

Lavender & Lemon Cupcakes

YIELD: 24 CUPCAKES | **ACTIVE TIME:** 30 MINUTES | **TOTAL TIME:** 1 HOUR AND 30 MINUTES

14 OZ. ALL-PURPOSE FLOUR

1 TABLESPOON PLUS
2 TEASPOONS BAKING
POWDER

½ TEASPOON KOSHER SALT

1 TABLESPOON DRIED
LAVENDER, GROUND

½ LB. UNSALTED BUTTER,
SOFTENED

15 OZ. SUGAR

ZEST OF 2 LEMONS

7 EGG WHITES

¾ CUP MILK

AMERICAN BUTTERCREAM
(SEE PAGE 509)

2 DROPS OF VIOLET GEL
FOOD COLORING

DRIED LAVENDER BUDS, FOR
GARNISH

1. Preheat the oven to 350°F. Line a 24-well cupcake pan with liners.

2. In a medium bowl, whisk together the flour, baking powder, salt, and lavender. Set the mixture aside.

3. In the work bowl of a stand mixer fitted with the paddle attachment, cream the butter, sugar, and lemon zest on high until the mixture is light and fluffy, about 5 minutes. Reduce the speed to low and gradually incorporate the egg whites, scraping the sides of the bowl with a rubber spatula as needed. Add the dry mixture and beat until incorporated.

4. Add the milk and beat until the mixture is a smooth batter. Pour approximately ¼ cup of batter into each cupcake liner, place the cupcakes in the oven, and bake until they are lightly golden brown and baked through, 15 to 18 minutes. Insert a cake tester in the center of each cupcake to check for doneness.

5. Remove the cupcakes from the oven and transfer them to a cooling rack. Let them cool completely.

6. Place the buttercream and violet gel food coloring in the work bowl of a stand mixer fitted with the paddle attachment and beat until combined. Place the frosting in a piping bag fitted with a plain piping tip and frost the cupcakes. Place the cupcakes in the refrigerator and let the frosting set before garnishing with the dried lavender buds and enjoying.

Lemon Tea Cake

YIELD: 1 CAKE | **ACTIVE TIME:** 30 MINUTES | **TOTAL TIME:** 1 HOUR AND 30 MINUTES

5⅓ OZ. SUGAR

ZEST OF 2 LEMONS

6 TABLESPOONS UNSALTED BUTTER, CUT INTO SMALL PIECES

2 EGGS

5 OZ. ALL-PURPOSE FLOUR

1 TEASPOON BAKING POWDER

½ CUP WHOLE MILK

CONFECTIONERS' SUGAR, FOR DUSTING

1. Preheat the oven to 350°F and coat a round 9-inch cake pan with nonstick cooking spray. In a large bowl, combine the sugar and lemon zest. Add the butter and beat until the mixture is light and fluffy. Add the eggs one at a time, stirring to incorporate thoroughly before adding the next one.

2. Place the flour and baking powder in a measuring cup and stir to combine. Alternate adding the flour mixture and milk to the butter-and-sugar mixture, stirring after each addition until incorporated.

3. Transfer the batter to the cake pan, place it in the oven, and bake for about 30 to 35 minutes, until the top is golden brown and a cake tester inserted into the middle comes out clean. Remove and let cool before dusting with confectioners' sugar and cutting into wedges.

Coconut Tres Leches Cake

YIELD: 1 CAKE | **ACTIVE TIME:** 1 HOUR | **TOTAL TIME:** 4 HOURS

FOR THE SPONGE CAKE

16 EGGS, YOLKS AND WHITES SEPARATED

28.2 OZ. SUGAR

28.9 OZ. ALL-PURPOSE FLOUR, SIFTED

⅔ TEASPOON FINE SEA SALT

¼ CUP BAKING POWDER

4.6 OZ. WATER

5 TEASPOONS PURE VANILLA EXTRACT

FRESH BERRIES, FOR SERVING

FOR THE SOAKING LIQUID

2 (14 OZ.) CANS OF SWEETENED CONDENSED MILK

2 (12 OZ.) CANS OF EVAPORATED MILK

½ CUP HEAVY CREAM

1¾ CUPS COCONUT MILK

½ CUP SUGAR

1. Preheat the oven to 325°F. Coat a baking pan with nonstick cooking spray. To begin preparations for the sponge cake, place the egg whites and sugar in the work bowl of a stand mixer fitted with the whisk attachment and whip to full volume.

2. Combine the flour, salt, and baking powder in a separate bowl.

3. Incorporate the egg yolks into the meringue one at a time. Add one-third of the meringue into the dry mixture along with the water and vanilla and beat until incorporated. Add another one-third of the meringue and fold to combine. Add the remaining one-third and carefully fold until incorporated.

4. Transfer the batter into the baking pan and gently spread until it is even. Place in the oven and bake until a knife inserted into the center comes out clean, about 40 minutes.

5. While the cake is in the oven, prepare the soaking liquid. Place all of the ingredients in a saucepan and warm it over medium heat, stirring to combine. When the mixture starts to steam and all of the sugar has dissolved, remove the pan from heat.

6. Pour the soaking liquid over the cake and chill it in the refrigerator for 2 hours.

7. To serve, top slices with berries and enjoy.

Orange Meringue Cheesecake

YIELD: 1 CHEESECAKE | **ACTIVE TIME:** 30 MINUTES | **TOTAL TIME:** 2 HOURS

3 OZ. HEAVY CREAM

1½ CUPS CREAM CHEESE, SOFTENED

2 OZ. SUGAR

ZEST AND JUICE OF 1 ORANGE

1½ TEASPOONS CONFECTIONERS' SUGAR

2 TABLESPOONS SOUR CREAM

1 TEASPOON FRESH LEMON JUICE

1 TEASPOON PURE VANILLA EXTRACT

1 GRAHAM CRACKER CRUST (SEE PAGE 496), IN A 9-INCH PAN

SWISS MERINGUE (SEE PAGE 508)

1. In the work bowl of a stand mixer fitted with the whisk attachment, whip the heavy cream until it forms soft peaks. Transfer the whipped cream to a bowl and store it in the refrigerator.

2. Wipe out the work bowl of the stand mixer and fit it with the paddle attachment. Place the cream cheese, sugar, and orange zest in the work bowl and beat on high until the mixture is fluffy, about 10 minutes. Scrape down the sides of the work bowl as needed.

3. Add the confectioners' sugar, sour cream, orange juice, lemon juice, and vanilla and beat until incorporated.

4. Remove the bowl from the stand mixer. Add the whipped cream and fold gently until thoroughly incorporated.

5. Pour the mixture into the Graham Cracker Crust and place the cheesecake in the refrigerator to chill for 1 hour.

6. Remove the cheesecake from the refrigerator and spread 1 cup of the Swiss Meringue over the top. Use a kitchen torch to lightly torch the meringue.

7. Place the cheesecake in the refrigerator and chill for 30 minutes before slicing and serving.

Cookies 'N' Cream Cheesecake

YIELD: 1 CHEESECAKE | **ACTIVE TIME:** 30 MINUTES | **TOTAL TIME:** 8 HOURS

FOR THE CRUST

24 OREO COOKIES (SEE PAGE 105 FOR HOMEMADE)

3 OZ. UNSALTED BUTTER, MELTED

FOR THE FILLING

15 OREO COOKIES

2 LBS. CREAM CHEESE, SOFTENED

⅔ CUP SUGAR

¼ TEASPOON KOSHER SALT

4 EGGS

1 TEASPOON PURE VANILLA EXTRACT

CHANTILLY CREAM (SEE PAGE 518), FOR SERVING

1. Preheat the oven to 350°F. To begin preparations for the crust, place the cookies in a food processor and pulse until finely ground. Transfer to a medium bowl and combine with the melted butter.

2. Transfer the mixture to a 9-inch pie plate and press it into the bottom and side in an even layer. Use the bottom of a dry measuring cup to help flatten the bottom of the crust. Use a paring knife to trim away any excess crust and create a flat and smooth edge.

3. Place the pie plate on a baking sheet and bake until it is firm, 8 to 10 minutes. Remove from the oven, transfer the crust to a cooling rack, and let it cool for at least 2 hours.

4. Preheat the oven to 350°F. To begin preparations for the filling, place the cookies in a food processor and pulse until finely ground. Set the filling aside.

5. Bring 8 cups of water to a boil in a small saucepan.

6. In the work bowl of a stand mixer fitted with the paddle attachment, cream the cream cheese, sugar, and salt on high until the mixture is fluffy, about 10 minutes. Scrape down the sides of the work bowl as needed.

7. Reduce the speed of the mixer to medium and incorporate one egg at a time, scraping down the work bowl as needed. Add the vanilla and beat until incorporated. Remove the work bowl from the mixer and fold in the cookie crumbs.

8. Pour the mixture into the crust, place the cheesecake in a large baking pan with high sides, and gently pour the boiling water into the baking pan until it reaches halfway up the sides of the pie plate.

9. Cover the baking pan with aluminum foil, place it in the oven, and bake until the cheesecake is set and only slightly jiggly in the center, 50 minutes to 1 hour.

10. Turn off the oven and leave the oven door cracked. Allow the cheesecake to rest in the cooling oven for 45 minutes.

11. Remove the cheesecake from the oven and transfer it to a cooling rack. Let it sit at room temperature for 1 hour.

12. Refrigerate the cheesecake for at least 4 hours before serving and slicing. To serve, top each slice with a heaping spoonful of Chantilly Cream.

Gluten-Free Vanilla Cake

YIELD: 1 CAKE | **ACTIVE TIME:** 15 MINUTES | **TOTAL TIME:** 1 HOUR AND 30 MINUTES

8½ OZ. GLUTEN-FREE FLOUR, PLUS MORE AS NEEDED

6 OZ. UNSALTED BUTTER, SOFTENED

9.6 OZ. SUGAR

2 EGGS, AT ROOM TEMPERATURE

1 TEASPOON PURE VANILLA EXTRACT

1 TEASPOON XANTHAN GUM

2 TEASPOONS BAKING SODA

½ TEASPOON FINE SEA SALT

1 CUP BUTTERMILK

CONFECTIONERS' SUGAR, FOR DUSTING

1. Preheat the oven to 350°F. Liberally coat a Bundt pan with nonstick cooking spray and then lightly dust it with flour, making sure to knock out the excess.

2. Place the butter and sugar in the mixing bowl of a stand mixer fitted with the paddle attachment and beat on medium until the mixture is light and fluffy. Add the eggs one at a time, beating until each one is incorporated before adding the next. Scrape down the bowl after incorporating each egg. Add the vanilla and beat to incorporate.

3. Place the flour, xanthan gum, baking soda, and salt in a separate mixing bowl and whisk to combine.

4. Divide the flour mixture and the buttermilk into three portions and alternate adding them to the butter-and-sugar mixture. Incorporate each portion completely before adding the next.

5. Transfer the batter to the prepared Bundt pan and ensure that it is spread evenly. Place in the oven and bake until a toothpick inserted into the center comes out with just a few crumbs, about 45 minutes.

6. Remove from the oven and let cool in the pan for 30 minutes. Invert the cake onto a wire rack and let cool completely before dusting with confectioners' sugar.

Butterscotch Souffles

YIELD: 4 SOUFFLES | **ACTIVE TIME:** 30 MINUTES | **TOTAL TIME:** 2 HOURS

3 OZ. SUGAR, PLUS MORE AS NEEDED

2 TABLESPOONS CORNSTARCH

1 EGG

10½ OZ. MILK

3 OZ. DARK BROWN SUGAR

1 OZ. UNSALTED BUTTER

½ TEASPOON PURE VANILLA EXTRACT

4 EGG WHITES

¼ TEASPOON CREAM OF TARTAR

1. Preheat the oven to 375°F. Coat four 8-oz. ramekins with nonstick cooking spray. Place 2 tablespoons of sugar in each ramekin and spread it to evenly coat the insides of the dishes. Knock out any excess sugar and set the ramekins aside.

2. In a medium bowl, whisk together the cornstarch and egg. Set the mixture aside.

3. Bring the milk, dark brown sugar, and butter to a boil over medium heat in a medium saucepan.

4. Gradually add the heated milk mixture into the egg-and-cornstarch mixture while whisking constantly. When fully incorporated, transfer the tempered mixture back into the saucepan.

5. Cook the mixture over medium heat, whisking until the mixture has thickened. Immediately remove the saucepan from heat and whisk in the vanilla.

6. Take plastic wrap and place it directly on the mixture so that no air can get to it. This will prevent a skin from forming. Place the bowl in the refrigerator until it reaches room temperature, about 1 hour.

7. In the work bowl of a stand mixer fitted with the whisk attachment, whip the egg whites and cream of tartar on high until the mixture holds stiff peaks. Reduce the speed to medium and gradually incorporate the sugar. Once all of the sugar has been incorporated, raise the speed back to high and whip until it is a glossy, stiff meringue.

8. Working in three increments, add the meringue to the souffle base, folding gently with a rubber spatula.

9. Spoon the souffle base to the rims of the ramekins. Gently tap the bottoms of the ramekins with the palm of your hand to remove any air, but not so hard as to deflate the meringue.

10. Place in the oven and bake until the souffles have risen significantly and set on the outside, but are still jiggly at the center, 22 to 25 minutes. Remove from the oven and serve immediately.

Angel Food Cake

YIELD: 1 CAKE | **ACTIVE TIME:** 30 MINUTES | **TOTAL TIME:** 2 HOURS

1 CUP CAKE FLOUR

1½ CUPS SUGAR

12 EGG WHITES, AT ROOM TEMPERATURE

¼ TEASPOON KOSHER SALT

1 TEASPOON PURE VANILLA EXTRACT

CONFECTIONERS' SUGAR, FOR DUSTING

STRAWBERRY PRESERVES (SEE PAGE 536), FOR SERVING

1. Preheat the oven to 325°F. Coat a 10-inch Bundt pan with nonstick cooking spray.

2. Sift the cake flour and ½ cup of the sugar into a medium bowl.

3. In the work bowl of a stand mixer fitted with the whisk attachment, whip the egg whites and salt on high until soft peaks begin to form. Reduce the speed to low and add the remaining sugar a few tablespoons at a time until all of it has been incorporated. Add the vanilla, raise the speed back to high, and whisk the mixture until it holds stiff peaks.

4. Remove the work bowl from the mixer and gently fold in the dry mixture. Pour the batter into the prepared Bundt pan.

5. Place in the oven and bake until the cakes are lightly golden brown and baked through, 45 to 55 minutes. Insert a cake tester in the center of the cake to check for doneness.

6. Remove the cake from the oven and transfer it to a cooling rack. Let it cool for 30 minutes.

7. Invert the cake onto a cake stand or serving tray, dust the top with confectioners' sugar, and serve with the preserves.

Hostess Cupcakes

YIELD: 24 CUPCAKES | **ACTIVE TIME:** 40 MINUTES | **TOTAL TIME:** 2 HOURS

20 OZ. SUGAR

13 OZ. ALL-PURPOSE FLOUR

4 OZ. COCOA POWDER

1 TABLESPOON BAKING SODA

1½ TEASPOONS BAKING POWDER

1½ TEASPOONS KOSHER SALT

1½ CUPS SOUR CREAM

¾ CUP CANOLA OIL

3 EGGS

1½ CUPS BREWED COFFEE, HOT

BUTTERFLUFF FILLING (SEE PAGE 517)

CHOCOLATE GANACHE (SEE PAGE 523), WARM

1. Preheat the oven to 350°F. Line a 24-well cupcake pan with liners.

2. In a medium bowl, whisk together the sugar, flour, cocoa powder, baking soda, baking powder, and salt. Sift the mixture into a separate bowl and set it aside.

3. In the work bowl of a stand mixer fitted with the whisk attachment, combine the sour cream, canola oil, and eggs on medium speed.

4. Reduce the speed to low, add the dry mixture, and beat until incorporated, scraping the sides of the bowl with a rubber spatula as needed. Gradually add the hot coffee and beat until thoroughly incorporated. Pour about ¼ cup of batter into each cupcake liner.

5. Place the cupcakes in the oven and bake until browned and baked through, 18 to 22 minutes. Insert a cake tester in the center of each cupcake to check for doneness. Remove from the oven and place the cupcakes on a cooling rack until completely cool.

6. Using a cupcake corer or a sharp paring knife, carefully remove the center of each cupcake. Place 2 cups of the Butterfluff Filling in a piping bag and fill the centers of the cupcakes with it.

7. While the ganache is warm, dip the tops of the cupcakes in the ganache and place them on a flat baking sheet. Refrigerate the cupcakes for 20 minutes so that the chocolate will set.

8. Place 1 cup of the Butterfluff Filling in a piping bag fit with a thin, plain tip and pipe decorative curls on top of each cupcake. Allow the curls to set for 10 minutes before serving.

Blueberry & Lemon Cheesecake

YIELD: 1 CHEESECAKE | **ACTIVE TIME:** 1 HOUR | **TOTAL TIME:** 8 HOURS

2 PINTS OF BLUEBERRIES

1 TABLESPOON WATER

2 TABLESPOONS SUGAR

2 LBS. CREAM CHEESE, SOFTENED

⅔ CUP SUGAR

¼ TEASPOON KOSHER SALT

4 EGGS

1 TEASPOON PURE VANILLA EXTRACT

2 TABLESPOONS FRESH LEMON JUICE

1 GRAHAM CRACKER CRUST (SEE PAGE 496), IN A 9-INCH SPRINGFORM PAN

1. Preheat the oven to 350°F. Bring 8 cups of water to a boil in a medium saucepan.

2. In a small saucepan, cook the blueberries, water, and sugar over medium heat until the blueberries burst and start to become fragrant, about 5 minutes. Remove the pan from heat.

3. In the work bowl of a stand mixer fitted with the paddle attachment, cream the cream cheese, sugar, and salt on high until the mixture is soft and airy, about 10 minutes. Scrape down the sides of the bowl with a rubber spatula as needed.

4. Reduce the speed of the mixer to medium and incorporate the eggs one at a time, scraping the bowl as needed. Add the vanilla extract and mix until incorporated.

5. Divide the mixture between two mixing bowls. Add the blueberry mixture to one bowl and whisk to combine. Whisk the lemon juice into the mixture in the other bowl.

6. Starting with the lemon mixture, add 1 cup to the crust. Add 1 cup of the blueberry mixture, and then alternate between the mixtures until all of them have been used.

7. If desired, use a paring knife to gently swirl the blueberry and lemon mixtures together, making sure not to overmix.

8. Place the cheesecake in a large baking pan with high sides. Gently pour the boiling water into the pan until it reaches halfway up the sides of the cheesecake pan. Cover the baking pan with aluminum foil and place it in the oven. Bake until the cheesecake is set and only slightly jiggly in the center, 50 minutes to 1 hour.

9. Turn off the oven and leave the oven door cracked. Allow the cheesecake to rest in the cooling oven for 45 minutes.

10. Remove the cheesecake from the oven and transfer the springform pan to a cooling rack. Let it sit at room temperature for 1 hour.

11. Transfer the cheesecake to the refrigerator and let it cool for at least 4 hours before slicing and serving.

Chocolate Beet Cake

YIELD: 1 CAKE | **ACTIVE TIME:** 45 MINUTES | **TOTAL TIME:** 3 HOURS AND 15 MINUTES

2 MEDIUM RED BEETS, RINSED

4½ OZ. ALL-PURPOSE FLOUR

3 TABLESPOONS COCOA POWDER

1¼ TEASPOONS BAKING POWDER

¼ TEASPOON KOSHER SALT

7 OZ. DARK CHOCOLATE (55 TO 65 PERCENT)

7 OZ. UNSALTED BUTTER

¼ CUP MILK

5 EGGS

7 OZ. SUGAR

1 CUP CHOCOLATE GANACHE (SEE PAGE 523), WARM

FRESH BLACKBERRIES, FOR GARNISH

1. Preheat the oven to 350°F. Coat a round 9-inch cake pan with nonstick cooking spray.

2. Place the beets in a large saucepan, cover them with water, and bring it to a boil. Cook the beets until they are very tender when poked with a knife, about 1 hour. Drain and let the beets cool. When cool enough to handle, place the beets under cold running water and rub off their skins. Cut the beets into 1-inch chunks, place them in a food processor, and puree. Set the beets aside.

3. Whisk the flour, cocoa powder, baking powder, and salt together in a small bowl. Set the mixture aside.

4. Bring a small saucepan filled halfway with water to a gentle simmer. Add the chocolate and butter to a heatproof mixing bowl and set it over the simmering water until it melts, stirring occasionally. Remove from heat and set the mixture aside.

5. Place the milk in a clean saucepan, warm it over medium-low heat until it starts to steam, and pour it into the chocolate mixture. Stir to combine, add the eggs and sugar, and whisk until incorporated. Add the beet puree, stir to incorporate, and add the dry mixture. Whisk until the mixture comes together as a smooth batter.

6. Pour the batter into the prepared cake pan, place it in the oven, and bake until baked through, 40 to 45 minutes. Insert a cake tester in the center of the cake to check for doneness. Remove from the oven, transfer the cake to a cooling rack, and let it cool completely.

7. Carefully remove the cake from the pan and transfer to a serving plate.

8. Spread the warm ganache over the top of the cake, garnish with blackberries, and serve.

Cherry & Amaretto Souffles

YIELD: 6 SOUFFLES | **ACTIVE TIME:** 30 MINUTES | **TOTAL TIME:** 2 HOURS

½ LB. SUGAR, PLUS MORE AS NEEDED

5 TABLESPOONS CORNSTARCH

½ CUP COLD WATER

10 OZ. MORELLO CHERRIES, PUREED

10 OZ. MILK

2 OZ. AMARETTO

8 EGG WHITES

½ TEASPOON CREAM OF TARTAR

1. Preheat the oven to 375°F. Coat six 8-oz. ramekins with nonstick cooking spray. Place 2 tablespoons of sugar in each ramekin and spread it to evenly coat the insides of the dishes. Knock out any excess sugar and set the ramekins aside.

2. In a small bowl, whisk together the cornstarch and cold water. Set the mixture aside.

3. Bring the cherry puree and milk to a boil over medium heat in a medium saucepan. Gradually pour in the cornstarch slurry while continually whisking. Continue to whisk until the mixture has thickened and has boiled for 30 seconds. Immediately remove the pan from heat and whisk in the Amaretto.

4. Transfer the cherry mixture to a medium bowl. Cover with plastic wrap, placing it directly on the mixture so that no air can get to it. This will prevent a skin from forming. Place the bowl in the refrigerator until it reaches room temperature, about 1 hour.

5. In the work bowl of a stand mixer fitted with a whisk attachment, whip the egg whites and cream of tartar on high until the mixture holds stiff peaks. Reduce the speed to medium and gradually incorporate the sugar. Once all of the sugar has been added, raise the speed back to high and whip until it is a glossy, stiff meringue.

6. Working in three increments, add the meringue to the cherry base, folding gently with a rubber spatula.

7. Spoon the souffle base to the rims of the ramekins. Gently tap the bottoms of the ramekins with the palm of your hand to remove any air, but not so hard as to deflate the meringue.

8. Place in the oven and bake until the souffles have risen significantly and set on the outside, but are still jiggly at the center, 25 to 27 minutes. Remove from the oven and serve immediately.

Lemon Ricotta Cheesecake

YIELD: 1 CHEESECAKE | **ACTIVE TIME:** 1 HOUR | **TOTAL TIME:** 8 HOURS

½ LB. WHOLE MILK RICOTTA CHEESE

½ LB. CREAM CHEESE, SOFTENED

6 OZ. SUGAR

ZEST AND JUICE OF 1 LEMON

1 EGG

¼ TEASPOON PURE VANILLA EXTRACT

1 TABLESPOON PLUS 1½ TEASPOONS CORNSTARCH

1½ TABLESPOONS ALL-PURPOSE FLOUR

1 OZ. UNSALTED BUTTER, MELTED

1 CUP SOUR CREAM

1 GRAHAM CRACKER CRUST (SEE PAGE 496), IN A 9-INCH SPRINGFORM PAN

CHANTILLY CREAM (SEE PAGE 518)

1. Preheat the oven to 350°F. Bring 8 cups of water to a boil in a medium saucepan.

2. In the work bowl of a stand mixer fitted with the paddle attachment, cream the ricotta, cream cheese, sugar, and lemon zest on high until the mixture is soft and airy, about 10 minutes. Scrape down the work bowl with a rubber spatula as needed. Reduce the speed of the mixer to medium and incorporate the egg, scraping the bowl as needed. Add the lemon juice and mix until incorporated. Add the cornstarch and flour and beat until incorporated. Reduce the speed to low, add the butter and sour cream, and beat until the mixture is very smooth.

3. Pour the mixture into the crust, place the cheesecake in a large baking pan with high sides, and gently pour the boiling water into the baking pan until it reaches halfway up the side of the springform pan.

4. Cover the baking pan with aluminum foil, place it in the oven, and bake until the cheesecake is set and only slightly jiggly in the center, 50 minutes to 1 hour.

5. Turn off the oven and leave the oven door cracked. Allow the cheesecake to rest in the cooling oven for 45 minutes.

6. Remove the cheesecake from the oven and transfer to a cooling rack. Let it sit at room temperature for 1 hour.

7. Transfer the cheesecake to the refrigerator and let it cool for at least 4 hours before serving and slicing. To serve, top each slice with a dollop of Chantilly Cream.

Vanilla Cake

YIELD: 1 CAKE | **ACTIVE TIME:** 1 HOUR | **TOTAL TIME:** 3 HOURS AND 30 MINUTES

13 OZ. CAKE FLOUR

2 TEASPOONS BAKING POWDER

¼ TEASPOON KOSHER SALT

½ LB. UNSALTED BUTTER, SOFTENED

½ CUP CANOLA OIL

3 CUPS SUGAR

5 EGGS

½ CUP MILK

½ CUP BUTTERMILK

1 TABLESPOON PURE VANILLA EXTRACT

ITALIAN BUTTERCREAM (SEE PAGE 509)

BUTTERFLUFF FILLING (SEE PAGE 517)

1. Preheat the oven to 350°F. Line three round 8-inch cake pans with parchment paper and coat them with nonstick cooking spray.

2. In a medium bowl, whisk together the cake flour, baking powder, and salt. Sift this mixture into another mixing bowl and set it aside.

3. In the work bowl of a stand mixer fitted with the paddle attachment, cream the butter, canola oil, and sugar until the mixture is smooth and creamy, about 5 minutes.

4. Incorporate the eggs one at a time, scraping down the sides of the work bowl with a rubber spatula as needed.

5. Reduce the speed to low, add the dry mixture, and beat until combined.

6. Gradually add the milk, buttermilk, and vanilla extract. When they have been thoroughly incorporated, pour 1½ cups of batter into each cake pan. Bang the pans on the countertop to spread the batter evenly and to dissolve any air bubbles.

7. Place the cakes in the oven and bake until lightly golden brown and baked through, 25 to 30 minutes. Insert a cake tester in the center of each cake to check for doneness.

8. Remove from the oven and place the cakes on a cooling rack. Let them cool completely.

9. Trim a thin layer off the top of each cake to create a flat surface. Transfer 2 cups of the buttercream to a piping bag and cut a ½-inch slit in it.

10. Place one cake on a cake stand and pipe one ring of buttercream around the edge. Place 1 cup of the Butterfluff Filling in the center and level it with an offset spatula. Place the second cake on top and repeat the process with the buttercream and filling. Place the last cake on top. Pipe the remaining buttercream onto the cake and frost the top and sides of the cake using an offset spatula. Refrigerate the cake for at least 1 hour before slicing and serving.

Cheesecake with Citrus & Brie

YIELD: 1 CHEESECAKE | **ACTIVE TIME:** 1 HOUR | **TOTAL TIME:** 8 HOURS

1½ LBS. CREAM CHEESE, SOFTENED

½ LB. TRIPLE-CREAM BRIE CHEESE, RIND REMOVED

⅔ CUP SUGAR

¼ TEASPOON KOSHER SALT

ZEST OF 1 ORANGE

4 EGGS

1 TABLESPOON PURE VANILLA EXTRACT

2 TABLESPOONS GRAND MARNIER

1 GRAHAM CRACKER CRUST (SEE PAGE 496), IN A 9-INCH SPRINGFORM PAN

STRAWBERRY PRESERVES (SEE PAGE 536)

1. Preheat the oven to 350°F. Bring 8 cups of water to a boil in a small saucepan.

2. In the work bowl of a stand mixer fitted with the paddle attachment, cream the cream cheese, Brie, sugar, salt, and orange zest on high until the mixture is fluffy, about 10 minutes. Scrape down the sides of the work bowl as needed.

3. Reduce the speed of the mixer to medium and incorporate one egg at a time, scraping the bowl as needed. Add the vanilla and Grand Marnier and mix until incorporated.

4. Pour the mixture into the crust, place the cheesecake in a large baking pan with high sides, and gently pour the boiling water into the baking pan until it reaches halfway up the sides of the springform pan.

5. Cover the baking pan with aluminum foil, place it in the oven, and bake until the cheesecake is set and only slightly jiggly in the center, 50 minutes to 1 hour.

6. Turn off the oven and leave the oven door cracked. Allow the cheesecake to rest in the cooling oven for 45 minutes.

7. Remove the cheesecake from the oven and transfer to a cooling rack. Let it sit at room temperature for 1 hour.

8. Transfer the cheesecake to the refrigerator and let it cool for at least 4 hours before serving and slicing. To serve, top each slice with a heaping spoonful of Strawberry Preserves.

Mango Shortcake

YIELD: 1 CAKE | **ACTIVE TIME:** 1 HOUR AND 30 MINUTES | **TOTAL TIME:** 8 HOURS

FOR THE CAKE

½ CUP CAKE FLOUR

¾ CUP SUGAR

6 EGG WHITES, AT ROOM TEMPERATURE

⅛ TEASPOON KOSHER SALT

½ TEASPOON PURE VANILLA EXTRACT

FOR THE MANGO MOUSSE

4 SHEETS OF SILVER GELATIN

1¼ CUPS MANGO PUREE

2½ OZ. CONFECTIONERS' SUGAR

ZEST OF 1 LIME

1¼ CUPS HEAVY CREAM

FOR THE MANGO GELEE

4 SHEETS OF SILVER GELATIN

½ CUP WATER

1¼ CUPS MANGO PUREE

2 TABLESPOONS SUGAR

1. Preheat the oven to 325°F. Coat a 13 x 9–inch baking pan with nonstick cooking spray.

2. To begin preparations for the cake, sift the flour and ¼ cup of the sugar into a mixing bowl. Set the mixture aside.

3. In the work bowl of a stand mixer fitted with the whisk attachment, whip the egg whites and salt on high until soft peaks begin to form. Reduce the speed to low and add the remaining sugar a few tablespoons at a time. When all of the sugar has been incorporated, add the vanilla, raise the speed back to high, and whip until the mixture holds stiff peaks.

4. Remove the work bowl from the mixer and gently fold in the dry mixture. Pour the batter into the prepared pan, place it in the oven, and bake until the cake is lightly golden brown and baked through, 20 to 25 minutes. Insert a cake tester in the center of the cake to check for doneness. Remove the cake from the oven, transfer it to a cooling rack, and let it cool completely.

5. While the cake is cooling, began preparations for the mango mousse. Place the gelatin sheets in a small bowl, and add 1 cup of ice and enough cold water to cover the sheets. In a small saucepan, bring the mango puree, confectioners' sugar, and lime zest to a simmer over medium heat. Immediately remove the pan from heat. Remove the gelatin from the ice bath and squeeze out as much water as possible. Whisk the gelatin into the mango mixture until fully dissolved. Let the mixture cool to room temperature.

6. Place the heavy cream in the work bowl of a stand mixer fitted with the paddle attachment and whip on high until soft peaks form. Fold the whipped cream into the mousse base.

7. Pour the mousse over the angel cake and use a rubber spatula to spread it evenly. Place the cake in the refrigerator for 4 hours.

8. To prepare the mango gelee, place the gelatin sheets in a small bowl, and add 1 cup of ice and enough cold water to cover the sheets. Place the water, mango puree, and sugar in a small saucepan and bring to a simmer over medium heat.

9. Remove the pan from heat. Remove the gelatin from the ice bath and squeeze out as much water as possible. Whisk the gelatin into the mango mixture until fully dissolved. Let the gelee cool to room temperature.

10. Pour the gelee over the mousse layer and place the cake in the refrigerator for 2 hours.

11. To serve, run a paring knife or spatula along the edge of the pan and cut the shortcake into bars.

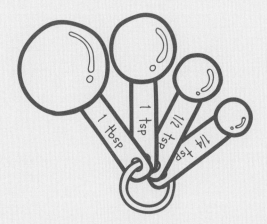

Gluten-Free Almond Torte

YIELD: 1 CAKE | **ACTIVE TIME:** 40 MINUTES | **TOTAL TIME:** 2 HOURS

2½ OZ. GLUTEN-FREE FLOUR

¼ TEASPOON XANTHAN GUM

¾ TEASPOON BAKING POWDER

¼ TEASPOON KOSHER SALT

4 OZ. ALMOND PASTE

4 OZ. UNSALTED BUTTER, SOFTENED

4.7 OZ. SUGAR

¼ TEASPOON PURE VANILLA EXTRACT

¼ TEASPOON ALMOND EXTRACT

3 EGGS

½ CUP SLIVERED ALMONDS

ALMOND SYRUP (SEE PAGE 522)

CONFECTIONERS' SUGAR, FOR DUSTING

1. Preheat the oven to 375°F. Line a round 9-inch cake pan with parchment paper and coat it with nonstick cooking spray.

2. In a medium bowl, whisk together the flour, xanthan gum, baking powder, and salt. Set the mixture aside.

3. In the work bowl of a stand mixer fitted with the paddle attachment, cream the almond paste, butter, sugar, vanilla, and almond extract on high until the mixture is smooth and fluffy, about 10 minutes. Reduce the speed to low and incorporate the eggs one at a time. Scrape down the sides of the bowl with a rubber spatula between each addition. Add the dry mixture, beat until combined, and raise the speed to high. Beat the mixture for 2 minutes to thicken it.

4. Pour the batter into the prepared cake pan. Bang the pan on the countertop to evenly distribute the batter and remove any air bubbles. Sprinkle the slivered almonds over the batter and place it in the oven.

5. Bake the cake until lightly golden brown and baked through, 20 to 25 minutes. Insert a cake tester in the center of the cake to check for doneness. Remove from the oven, transfer the cake to a cooling rack, and let it cool completely.

6. Gently brush the syrup over the torte and dust with confectioners' sugar before slicing and serving.

Flourless Chocolate Torte

YIELD: 1 CAKE | **ACTIVE TIME:** 30 MINUTES | **TOTAL TIME:** 3 HOURS AND 30 MINUTES

9 OZ. DARK CHOCOLATE (55 TO 65 PERCENT)

4 OZ. UNSALTED BUTTER

¼ CUP WATER, PLUS MORE AS NEEDED

PINCH OF KOSHER SALT

3 OZ. SUGAR

3 EGGS

½ TEASPOON PURE VANILLA EXTRACT

CONFECTIONERS' SUGAR, FOR DUSTING

FRESH RASPBERRIES, FOR GARNISH

1. Preheat the oven to 375°F. Line a round 9-inch cake pan with parchment paper and coat it with nonstick cooking spray.

2. Fill a small saucepan halfway with water and bring it to a gentle simmer. In a heatproof medium bowl, combine the chocolate and butter. Place the bowl over the simmering water and stir the mixture with a rubber spatula until it has melted. Remove the mixture from heat and set it aside.

3. In another small saucepan, bring the water, salt, and sugar to a boil over medium heat. Pour the mixture into the melted chocolate and whisk to combine. Incorporate the eggs and vanilla and then pour the batter into the prepared cake pan.

4. Place the cake in the oven and bake until set and the internal temperature reaches 200°F, 25 to 30 minutes. Remove the cake from the oven and let it cool on a wire rack for 30 minutes.

5. Place the torte in the refrigerator for 2 hours.

6. Run a paring knife along the edge of the pan and invert the torte onto a serving plate. Dust the top of the torte with confectioners' sugar and garnish with fresh raspberries.

Opera Torte

YIELD: 1 CAKE | **ACTIVE TIME:** 3 HOURS | **TOTAL TIME:** 3 HOURS AND 45 MINUTES

FOR THE JOCONDE

5 OZ. FINE ALMOND FLOUR

5 OZ. CONFECTIONERS' SUGAR

1 OZ. ALL-PURPOSE FLOUR

5 EGGS

5 EGG WHITES

¼ TEASPOON KOSHER SALT

2 TABLESPOONS SUGAR

FOR THE COFFEE SYRUP

½ CUP WATER

½ CUP SUGAR

1 TABLESPOON GROUND ESPRESSO

FOR THE HAZELNUT & PRALINE CRUNCH

4 OZ. DARK CHOCOLATE (55 TO 65 PERCENT)

4 OZ. PRALINE PASTE

3 OZ. FEUILLETINE FLAKES

FOR THE MOCHA CREAM

1 CUP SUGAR

¼ CUP WATER

6 EGG YOLKS

3 TABLESPOONS ESPRESSO POWDER

½ LB. UNSALTED BUTTER, SOFTENED

FOR TOPPING

CHOCOLATE GANACHE (SEE PAGE 523), AT ROOM TEMPERATURE

---

1. Preheat the oven to 400°F. Coat two 13 x 9–inch baking pans with nonstick cooking spray.

2. To begin preparations for the joconde, sift the almond flour, confectioners' sugar, and all-purpose flour into a large bowl. Add the eggs and whisk until combined. Set the mixture aside.

3. In the work bowl of a stand mixer fitted with the whisk attachment, whip the egg whites and salt on high until soft peaks begin to form. Reduce the speed to low and gradually incorporate the sugar. Raise the speed back to high and continue to whip until stiff peaks form. Add the meringue to the dry mixture and fold until thoroughly incorporated. Divide the batter between the two prepared pans, place them in the oven, and bake until they are set and lightly browned, 8 to 10 minutes. Remove from the oven, transfer to a cooling rack, and let them cool completely.

4. To prepare the coffee syrup, place the water, sugar, and espresso in a small saucepan and bring to a simmer over medium heat while stirring frequently to dissolve the sugar and espresso. Remove from heat and let the syrup cool completely.

5. To prepare the hazelnut and praline crunch, bring a small saucepan filled halfway with water to a gentle simmer. Place the chocolate in a small heatproof bowl, place it over the simmering water, and stir until the chocolate has melted. Remove from heat stir in the praline paste and the feuilletine flakes, and spread the mixture over the two joconde. Place the cakes in the refrigerator.

6. To begin preparations for the mocha cream, place the sugar and water in a small saucepan over high heat. Cook until the mixture reaches 245°F on a candy thermometer.

7. While the sugar and water are heating up, place the egg yolks and espresso powder in the work bowl of a stand mixer fitted with the whisk attachment and whip the mixture on high.

8. When the syrup reaches the correct temperature, gradually add it to the egg yolk mixture. Continue to whip on high until the mixture cools slightly. Reduce the speed to low and gradually add the softened butter. When all of the butter has been incorporated, raise the speed back to high and whip the mixture until smooth and fluffy. Set the mocha cream aside.

9. Remove both cakes from the refrigerator and carefully remove them from the pans. Place one cake on a serving tray with the coated layer facing down. Brush the cake with some of the coffee syrup and spread half of the mocha cream over the top. Lay the second cake on top so that the mocha and hazelnut layers are touching. Brush the top of this cake with the remaining coffee syrup and then spread the remaining mocha cream over the cake.

10. Place the cake in the refrigerator for 30 minutes. Spread the Chocolate Ganache over the cake and let it sit for 10 minutes. To serve, use a hot knife to cut the cake into rectangles.

    Note: Feuilletine flakes are a crispy confection made from thin, sweetened crepes. They can be found at many baking shops, and are also available online.

Opera Torte
SEE PAGES 204–205

Tres Leches Cake

YIELD: 1 CAKE | **ACTIVE TIME:** 45 MINUTES | **TOTAL TIME:** 3 HOURS

14 OZ. ALL-PURPOSE FLOUR

1 TEASPOON BAKING POWDER

½ TEASPOON KOSHER SALT

½ LB. UNSALTED BUTTER, SOFTENED

1 LB. SUGAR

ZEST OF 1 ORANGE

10 EGGS

1½ TEASPOONS PURE VANILLA EXTRACT

1 (12 OZ.) CAN OF EVAPORATED MILK

1 (14 OZ.) CAN OF SWEETENED CONDENSED MILK

½ CUP MILK

½ CUP HEAVY CREAM

CHANTILLY CREAM (SEE PAGE 518)

FRESH STRAWBERRIES, SLICED, FOR SERVING

1. Preheat the oven to 350°F. Line a 13 x 9–inch baking pan with parchment paper and coat it with nonstick cooking spray.

2. Sift the flour, baking powder, and salt into a medium bowl and set the mixture aside.

3. In the work bowl of a stand mixer fitted with the paddle attachment, cream the butter, sugar, and orange zest on medium speed until the mixture is smooth and creamy, about 5 minutes.

4. Incorporate the eggs two at a time, scraping down the sides of the work bowl with a rubber spatula between each addition.

5. Reduce the speed of the mixer to low, add the dry mixture, and beat until combined. Incorporate the vanilla and then pour the batter into the prepared pan. Gently tap the pan on the countertop to evenly distribute the batter and remove any air bubbles.

6. Place the cake in the oven and bake until golden brown and cooked through, 30 to 35 minutes. Insert a cake tester in the center of the cake to check for doneness. Remove the cake from the oven and transfer to a cooling rack. Let cool for 1 hour.

7. While the cake is cooling, combine the evaporated milk, sweetened condensed milk, milk, and heavy cream in a small bowl.

8. Once the cake has cooled for 1 hour, poke holes in it using a fork. Slowly pour the milk mixture over the entire top of the cake. Refrigerate the cake for at least 1 hour, allowing the cake to soak up the milk.

9. Spread the Chantilly Cream over the top of the cake, slice it into squares, and serve with sliced strawberries.

Eggnog Cupcakes

YIELD: 24 CUPCAKES | **ACTIVE TIME:** 30 MINUTES | **TOTAL TIME:** 1 HOUR AND 30 MINUTES

FOR THE CUPCAKES

11.4 OZ. ALL-PURPOSE FLOUR

9½ OZ. SUGAR

1¾ TEASPOONS BAKING POWDER

½ TEASPOON KOSHER SALT

½ LB. UNSALTED BUTTER, SOFTENED

4 EGG WHITES

½ TEASPOON PURE VANILLA EXTRACT

2¾ TEASPOONS FRESHLY GRATED NUTMEG

1 CUP HEAVY CREAM

⅓ CUP MILK

FOR THE FROSTING

AMERICAN BUTTERCREAM (SEE PAGE 509)

1 TABLESPOON FRESHLY GRATED NUTMEG, PLUS MORE FOR TOPPING

1. Preheat the oven to 350°F. Line a 24-well cupcake pan with liners.

2. To begin preparations for the cupcakes, whisk together the flour, sugar, baking powder, and salt in a medium bowl. Set the mixture aside.

3. In the work bowl of a stand mixer fitted with the paddle attachment, combine the butter, egg whites, vanilla, and nutmeg on medium speed. The batter will look separated and broken. Reduce the speed to low, add the dry mixture, and beat until incorporated, scraping the sides of the bowl with a rubber spatula as needed.

4. Gradually add the heavy cream and milk until the mixture comes together as a smooth cake batter. Pour approximately ¼ cup of the batter into each cupcake liner.

5. Place in the oven and bake until the cupcakes are lightly golden brown and baked through, 16 to 20 minutes. Insert a cake tester in the center of each cupcake to check for doneness.

6. Remove from the oven and place the cupcakes on a cooling rack.

7. To prepare the frosting, place the buttercream in the work bowl of a stand mixer fitted with the paddle attachment and add the nutmeg. Beat on medium speed until combined. Spoon the frosting into a piping bag fitted with a plain piping tip, frost the cupcakes, and top each one with a little more nutmeg.

Raspberry Chiffon Cake

YIELD: 1 CAKE | **ACTIVE TIME:** 30 MINUTES | **TOTAL TIME:** 2 HOURS AND 30 MINUTES

6 OZ. CAKE FLOUR

10 OZ. SUGAR

½ TEASPOON KOSHER SALT

1½ TEASPOONS BAKING POWDER

¼ CUP CANOLA OIL

2 EGGS

¾ CUP PUREED RASPBERRIES

1½ TEASPOONS PURE VANILLA EXTRACT

6 EGG WHITES

¼ TEASPOON CREAM OF TARTAR

CONFECTIONERS' SUGAR, FOR DUSTING

CHANTILLY CREAM (SEE PAGE 518), FOR SERVING

FRESH RASPBERRIES, FOR SERVING

1. Preheat the oven to 325°F. Place a 10-inch tube pan with a removable bottom near your workspace. Do not grease the pan!

2. Sift the cake flour, 6 oz. of the sugar, the salt, and baking powder into a small bowl. Set the mixture aside.

3. In a medium bowl, whisk together the canola oil, eggs, raspberry puree, and vanilla. Add the dry mixture and whisk until thoroughly incorporated.

4. In the work bowl of a stand mixer fitted with the whisk attachment, whip the egg whites and cream of tartar on high until soft peaks begin to form. Decrease the speed to low and add the remaining sugar a few tablespoons at a time. When all of the sugar has been incorporated, raise the speed back to high and whip until the mixture holds stiff peaks.

5. Remove the work bowl from the mixer and gently fold half of the meringue into the cake batter base. Add the remaining meringue and fold the mixture until no white streaks remain. Pour the batter into the tube pan, place it in the oven, and bake until the cake is lightly golden brown and baked through, about 1 hour. Insert a cake tester in the center of the cake to check for doneness.

6. Remove the cake from the oven and let it cool completely.

7. Run a long metal spatula around the inside of the tube pan and center. Turn the cake out onto a serving platter, dust the top with confectioners' sugar, and serve with the Chantilly Cream and fresh raspberries.

Olive Oil Cake

YIELD: 1 CAKE | **ACTIVE TIME:** 30 MINUTES | **TOTAL TIME:** 1 HOUR AND 30 MINUTES

ZEST AND JUICE OF 3 LEMONS

½ CUP PLUS 7 OZ. SUGAR

7 OZ. ALL-PURPOSE FLOUR

1 TEASPOON BAKING SODA

1 TEASPOON BAKING POWDER

½ TEASPOON KOSHER SALT

¾ CUP FULL-FAT PLAIN YOGURT

¾ CUP EXTRA-VIRGIN OLIVE OIL

3 EGGS

CONFECTIONERS' SUGAR, FOR DUSTING

1. Preheat the oven to 325°F. Coat a round 9-inch cake pan with nonstick cooking spray.

2. Place the lemon juice and ½ cup sugar in a small saucepan and bring the mixture to a boil, stirring to dissolve the sugar. Remove from heat and let the mixture cool.

3. Sift the flour, baking soda, and baking powder into a small bowl and set the mixture aside.

4. In a medium bowl, whisk the lemon zest, remaining sugar, the salt, yogurt, olive oil, and eggs until the mixture is smooth and combined. Add the dry mixture and whisk until a smooth batter forms.

5. Pour the batter into the prepared cake pan, place it in the oven, and bake until the cake is lightly golden brown and baked through, 45 minutes to 1 hour. Insert a cake tester in the center of the cake to check for doneness.

6. Remove the cake from the oven, transfer to a cooling rack, and gently pour the lemon syrup over the hot cake. Let the cake cool completely.

7. Carefully remove the cake from the pan, transfer to a serving plate, dust with confectioners' sugar, and serve.

Brown Butter Cake

YIELD: 1 CAKE | **ACTIVE TIME:** 1 HOUR | **TOTAL TIME:** 3 HOURS AND 30 MINUTES

1½ LBS. ALL-PURPOSE FLOUR

1 TABLESPOON BAKING POWDER

2 TEASPOONS KOSHER SALT

1 LB. BROWN BUTTER (SEE PAGE 523)

1 LB. SUGAR

8 EGGS

AMERICAN BUTTERCREAM (SEE PAGE 509)

CARAMEL SAUCE (SEE PAGE 529)

1. Preheat the oven to 350°F. Line three round 8-inch cake pans with parchment paper and coat them with nonstick cooking spray.

2. Sift the flour, baking powder, and salt into a medium bowl and set the mixture aside.

3. In the work bowl of a stand mixer fitted with the paddle attachment, cream the Brown Butter and sugar on high until the mixture is smooth and creamy, about 5 minutes.

4. Incorporate the eggs two at a time, scraping down the sides of the work bowl with a rubber spatula between each addition. Reduce the speed to low, add the dry mixture, and beat until combined.

5. Pour 1½ cups of batter into each cake pan. Bang the pans on the countertop to evenly distribute the batter and remove any air bubbles.

6. Place the cakes in the oven and bake until they are lightly golden brown and baked through, 35 to 40 minutes. Insert a cake tester in the center of each cake to check for doneness. Remove from the oven, transfer to a cooling rack, and let the cakes cool completely.

7. While the cakes cool, place the buttercream and 1 cup of the caramel in the work bowl of a stand mixer fitted with the paddle attachment and beat on medium speed until combined. Set the frosting aside.

8. Trim a thin layer off the top of each cake to create a flat surface. Place one cake on a cake stand and pipe one ring of cream around the edge. Place 1 cup of the frosting in the center and level it with an offset spatula. Place the second cake on top and repeat the process with the frosting. Place the last cake on top and spread 1½ cups of the frosting over the entire cake using an offset spatula.

9. Gently spoon some of the remaining caramel over the edge of the cake and let it drip down the side. Spread ½ cup of the caramel over the top of the cake.

10. Place the cake in the refrigerator for 1 hour before slicing and serving.

Autumn Spice Cake

YIELD: 1 CAKE | **ACTIVE TIME:** 1 HOUR | **TOTAL TIME:** 3 HOURS AND 30 MINUTES

FOR THE CAKE

14 OZ. ALL-PURPOSE FLOUR

2 TEASPOONS BAKING SODA

1 TABLESPOON BAKING POWDER

2 TEASPOONS CINNAMON

2 TEASPOONS GROUND CLOVES

2 TEASPOONS FRESHLY GRATED NUTMEG

1 TEASPOON GROUND GINGER

1 TEASPOON KOSHER SALT

8 EGGS

¾ LB. SUGAR

3 OZ. LIGHT BROWN SUGAR

¾ LB. PUMPKIN PUREE

1 CUP CANOLA OIL

2 TEASPOONS PURE VANILLA EXTRACT

4 OZ. BUTTERMILK

¾ LB. UNSALTED BUTTER, MELTED

FOR THE FROSTING

BUTTERFLUFF FILLING (SEE PAGE 517)

1 TABLESPOON MAPLE EXTRACT

2 TABLESPOONS CINNAMON, PLUS MORE FOR DUSTING

ITALIAN BUTTERCREAM (SEE PAGE 509)

1. Preheat the oven to 350°F. Line three round 8-inch cake pans with parchment paper and coat them with nonstick cooking spray.

2. To begin preparations for the cakes, sift the flour, baking soda, baking powder, cinnamon, cloves, nutmeg, ginger, and salt into a mixing bowl. Set the mixture aside.

3. In the work bowl of a stand mixer fitted with the whisk attachment, beat the eggs, sugar, brown sugar, pumpkin puree, canola oil, and vanilla on medium until combined. Add the buttermilk and melted butter and beat until incorporated.

4. Reduce the speed to low, add the dry mixture, and whisk until a smooth batter forms. Pour 1½ cups of batter into each cake pan. Bang the pans on the counter to evenly distribute the batter and remove any air bubbles.

5. Place the cakes in the oven and bake until lightly golden brown and baked through, 35 to 45 minutes. Insert a cake tester in the center of each cake to check for doneness. Remove from the oven, transfer the cakes to a cooling rack, and let them cool completely.

6. To prepare the frosting, combine the butterfluff and maple extract in a mixing bowl. In a separate bowl, whisk the cinnamon and buttercream together. Set the mixtures aside.

7. Trim a thin layer off the top of each cake to create a flat surface. Place 2 cups of the cinnamon buttercream in a piping bag and cut a ½-inch slit in it. Place one cake on a cake stand and pipe one ring of cream around the edge. Place 1 cup of the maple butterfluff in the center and level it with an offset spatula. Place the second cake on top and repeat the process with the cinnamon buttercream and maple butterfluff. Place the last cake on top and spread 1½ cups of the cinnamon buttercream over the entire cake. Dust the top of the cake with additional cinnamon and refrigerate for 1 hour before slicing and serving.

Chocolate Cake Roll

YIELD: 10 TO 12 SERVINGS | **ACTIVE TIME:** 45 MINUTES | **TOTAL TIME:** 3 HOURS

7½ OZ. ALL-PURPOSE FLOUR

1.8 OZ. COCOA POWDER, PLUS MORE AS NEEDED

¾ LB. SUGAR

1½ TEASPOONS KOSHER SALT

¾ TEASPOON BAKING POWDER

5 OZ. CANOLA OIL

5 EGGS

5 OZ. WATER

7 EGG WHITES

½ TEASPOON CREAM OF TARTAR

BUTTERFLUFF FILLING (SEE PAGE 517)

CHOCOLATE GANACHE (SEE PAGE 523), WARM

1. Preheat the oven to 350°F. Line an 18 x 13–inch baking sheet with parchment paper and coat it with nonstick cooking spray.

2. Sift the flour, cocoa powder, 7 oz. of the sugar, the salt, and baking powder into a small bowl. Set the mixture aside.

3. In a medium bowl, whisk the canola oil, eggs, and water until combined. Add the dry mixture and whisk until combined.

4. In the work bowl of a stand mixer fitted with the whisk attachment, whip the egg whites and cream of tartar on high until soft peaks begin to form. Reduce the speed to low and add the remaining sugar a few tablespoons at a time. When all of the sugar has been incorporated, raise the speed back to high and whip until the mixture holds stiff peaks.

5. Remove the work bowl from the mixer. Gently fold half of the meringue into the cake batter. Add the remaining meringue and fold until no white streaks remain. Spread the cake batter over the baking sheet, place it in the oven, and bake until the center of the cake springs back when poked with a finger and a cake tester comes out clean, 10 to 12 minutes. Remove the cake from the oven and immediately dust the top with cocoa powder. Turn the sponge cake onto a fresh piece of parchment paper. Peel the parchment away from the bottom side of the cake. Place a fresh piece of parchment on the bottom of the cake and turn it over so that the dusted side of the cake is facing up.

6. Using a rolling pin, gently roll up the cake into a tight roll, starting with the narrow end. Let the cake cool to room temperature while coiled around the rolling pin.

7. Gently unroll the cake and spread the filling evenly over the top, leaving an approximately ½-inch border around the edges. Carefully roll the cake back up with your hands (do not use the rolling pin). Place the cake roll on a cooling rack that has parchment paper beneath it.

8. Pour the ganache over the cake roll. Refrigerate for at least 1 hour to let the chocolate set before slicing and serving.

Strawberry Shortcake

YIELD: 1 CAKE | **ACTIVE TIME:** 45 MINUTES | **TOTAL TIME:** 2 HOURS AND 30 MINUTES

4 OZ. CAKE FLOUR

3½ OZ. PLUS 7 OZ. SUGAR

12 EGG WHITES, AT ROOM TEMPERATURE

¼ TEASPOON KOSHER SALT

1 TEASPOON PURE VANILLA EXTRACT

CHANTILLY CREAM (SEE PAGE 518)

3 CUPS HALVED STRAWBERRIES

STRAWBERRY PRESERVES (SEE PAGE 536), FOR GARNISH

1. Preheat the oven to 350°F. Line three round 8-inch cake pans with parchment paper and coat them with nonstick cooking spray.

2. Sift the flour and 3½ oz. of sugar into a mixing bowl. Set the mixture aside.

3. In the work bowl of a stand mixer fitted with the whisk attachment, whip the egg whites and salt on high until the mixture begins to form soft peaks.

4. Reduce the speed to low and incorporate the remaining 7 oz. of sugar a few tablespoons at a time. Add the vanilla, raise the speed to high, and whip the mixture until it holds stiff peaks.

5. Remove the bowl from the mixer and gently fold in the dry mixture.

6. Divide the batter among the cake pans. Bang the pans on the countertop to spread the batter and remove any possible air bubbles.

7. Place the cakes in the oven and bake until they are lightly golden brown and baked through, 15 to 20 minutes. Insert a cake tester in the center of each cake to check for doneness.

8. Remove from the oven and place the cakes on a cooling rack. Let them cool completely and then remove them from the pans.

9. Trim a thin layer off the top of each cake to create a flat surface.

10. Place one cake on a cake stand. Place 1 cup of the Chantilly Cream in the center and spread it to within ½ inch of the cake's edge. Arrange 1 cup of the strawberries on top in an even layer. Place the second cake on top and repeat the process with the cream and strawberries. Place the last cake on top and spread 1 cup of the cream over the top.

11. Refrigerate the cake for at least 1 hour before slicing and serving. Garnish each slice with preserves and the remaining strawberries.

Chocolate Cake Roll
SEE PAGE 214

PIES, TARTS
& GALETTES

Apple Pie

YIELD: 1 PIE | **ACTIVE TIME:** 30 MINUTES | **TOTAL TIME:** 1 HOUR AND 45 MINUTES

2 PERFECT PIECRUSTS (SEE PAGE 496), ROLLED OUT

3 HONEYCRISP APPLES, PEELED, CORED, AND SLICED

3 GRANNY SMITH APPLES, PEELED, CORED, AND SLICED

½ CUP SUGAR

¼ CUP LIGHT BROWN SUGAR

1½ TABLESPOONS CORNSTARCH

1 TEASPOON CINNAMON

½ TEASPOON FRESHLY GRATED NUTMEG

¼ TEASPOON CARDAMOM

ZEST AND JUICE OF 1 LEMON

¼ TEASPOON KOSHER SALT

1 EGG, BEATEN

SANDING SUGAR, FOR TOPPING

1. Preheat the oven to 375°F. Coat a 9-inch pie pan with nonstick cooking spray and place one of the crusts in it.

2. Place the apples, sugar, brown sugar, cornstarch, cinnamon, nutmeg, cardamom, lemon juice, lemon zest, and salt in a mixing bowl and toss until the apples are evenly coated.

3. Fill the crust with the apple filling, lay the other crust over the top, and crimp the edge to seal. Brush the top crust with the egg and sprinkle sanding sugar over it. Cut several slits in the top crust.

4. Place the pie in the oven and bake until the filling is bubbly and has thickened, about 50 minutes. Remove from the oven and let the pie cool completely before serving.

Banana Cream Pie

YIELD: 1 PIE | **ACTIVE TIME:** 30 MINUTES | **TOTAL TIME:** 2 HOURS AND 30 MINUTES

2 BANANAS, PEELED AND SLICED

1½ CUPS MILK

1 CUP HEAVY CREAM

¾ TEASPOON PURE VANILLA EXTRACT

4 OZ. SUGAR

½ TEASPOON KOSHER SALT

¼ CUP CORNSTARCH

4 EGG WHITES

1 OZ. UNSALTED BUTTER, SOFTENED

1 GRAHAM CRACKER CRUST (SEE PAGE 496)

CHANTILLY CREAM (SEE PAGE 518)

1. Place the bananas, milk, heavy cream, and vanilla in a blender and puree until smooth.

2. Place the puree in a medium saucepan and bring to a boil over medium heat. Remove the pan from heat once it comes to a boil.

3. While the puree is coming to a boil, place the sugar, salt, cornstarch, and egg whites in a small bowl and whisk for 2 minutes.

4. While whisking constantly, incorporate small amounts of the puree into the egg white mixture. When half of the puree has been incorporated, add the tempered mixture to the saucepan and place it over medium heat. While whisking continually, cook until the mixture thickens and begins to bubble. Remove the pan from heat, add the butter, and whisk until incorporated.

5. Strain the custard through a fine-mesh strainer and into a small bowl. Pour the strained custard into the crust and place plastic wrap directly onto the custard to prevent a skin from forming. Place the pie in the refrigerator for 2 hours.

6. Spread the Chantilly Cream over the filling, slice the pie, and enjoy.

Apple Pie
SEE PAGE 220

Blueberry Pie

YIELD: 1 PIE | **ACTIVE TIME:** 30 MINUTES | **TOTAL TIME:** 1 HOUR AND 30 MINUTES

6 CUPS FRESH BLUEBERRIES

1 CUP SUGAR, PLUS MORE
FOR TOPPING

2 TABLESPOONS
CORNSTARCH

½ TEASPOON FRESHLY
GRATED NUTMEG

1 TABLESPOON FRESH
LEMON JUICE

1 TEASPOON LEMON ZEST

¼ TEASPOON FINE SEA SALT

2 PERFECT PIECRUSTS (SEE
PAGE 496), ROLLED OUT

1 EGG WHITE

1. Preheat the oven to 350°F. Coat a 9-inch pie plate with nonstick cooking spray. Place the blueberries, sugar, cornstarch, nutmeg, lemon juice, lemon zest, and salt in a large mixing bowl and stir to combine.

2. Place one of the crusts in the pie plate and fill it with the blueberry mixture. Place the other crust over the mixture and crimp the edge to seal.

3. Brush the top crust with the egg white and then sprinkle additional sugar over it. Cut a few slits in the middle, place the pie in the oven, and bake until the top crust is golden brown and the filling is bubbling, about 40 minutes.

4. Remove the pie from the oven and let it cool before serving.

Cherry Pie

YIELD: 1 PIE | **ACTIVE TIME:** 30 MINUTES | **TOTAL TIME:** 1 HOUR AND 45 MINUTES

4 CUPS RAINIER CHERRIES, PITTED

2 CUPS SUGAR

2 TABLESPOONS FRESH LEMON JUICE

3 TABLESPOONS CORNSTARCH

1 TABLESPOON WATER

¼ TEASPOON ALMOND EXTRACT

2 PERFECT PIECRUSTS (SEE PAGE 496), ROLLED OUT

1 EGG, BEATEN

1. Preheat the oven to 350°F. Coat a 9-inch pie plate with nonstick cooking spray. Place the cherries, sugar, and lemon juice in a saucepan and cook, stirring occasionally, over medium heat until the mixture is syrupy.

2. Combine the cornstarch and water in a small bowl and then stir this mixture into the saucepan. Reduce the heat to low and cook, while stirring, until the mixture is thick and syrupy. Remove from heat, stir in the almond extract, and let the filling cool.

3. When the cherry mixture has cooled, place the bottom crust in the pie plate and pour the filling into the crust. Top with the other crust, make a few slits in the top, and brush the top crust with the beaten egg.

4. Place the pie in the oven and bake until the top crust is golden brown and the filling is bubbly, about 45 minutes. Remove and let cool before serving.

Classic Fruit Tart

YIELD: 1 TART | **ACTIVE TIME:** 15 MINUTES | **TOTAL TIME:** 30 MINUTES

2 CUPS PASTRY CREAM (SEE PAGE 512)

1 PÂTÉ SUCRÉE (SEE PAGE 502), BLIND BAKED IN A 9-INCH TART PAN

2 CUPS HULLED AND SLICED STRAWBERRIES

2 CUPS BLACKBERRIES, SLICED LENGTHWISE

1 CUP RASPBERRIES

APRICOT GLAZE (SEE PAGE 537)

1. Spread the Pastry Cream over the bottom of the tart shell. Arrange the strawberries around the outside edge of the shell. Arrange the blackberries in a ring just inside the strawberries and then pile the raspberries in the center.

2. Gently brush the fresh fruit with the glaze. Place the fruit tart in the refrigerator and let it chill for 15 minutes before slicing and serving.

Linzer Tart

YIELD: 1 TART | **ACTIVE TIME:** 30 MINUTES | **TOTAL TIME:** 2 HOURS AND 45 MINUTES

3.3 OZ. FINE ALMOND FLOUR

7 OZ. SUGAR

6 OZ. UNSALTED BUTTER, SOFTENED

1 TEASPOON LEMON ZEST

3 EGGS

6¼ OZ. ALL-PURPOSE FLOUR, PLUS MORE AS NEEDED

½ TEASPOON CINNAMON

¼ TEASPOON GROUND CLOVES

1 TABLESPOON UNSWEETENED COCOA POWDER

¼ TEASPOON KOSHER SALT

1½ CUPS RASPBERRY JAM (SEE PAGE 533)

1. Preheat the oven to 250°F. Place the almond flour on a baking sheet, place it in the oven, and toast for 5 minutes. Remove the almond flour from the oven and set it aside.

2. In the work bowl of a stand mixer fitted with the paddle attachment, combine the sugar, butter, and lemon zest and beat on medium until the mixture is pale and fluffy.

3. Incorporate two of the eggs one at a time, scraping down the work bowl as needed.

4. Place the flour, almond flour, cinnamon, cloves, cocoa powder, and salt in a separate bowl and whisk to combine. Gradually add this mixture to the wet mixture and beat until the mixture comes together as a dough. Divide the dough in half, cover each piece with plastic wrap, and refrigerate it for 1 hour.

5. Preheat the oven to 350°F and coat a 9-inch tart pan with nonstick cooking spray. Place the pieces of dough on a flour-dusted work surface and roll them out to fit the tart pan. Place one piece of dough in the pan and then cut the other piece of dough into ¾-inch-wide strips.

6. Fill the crust in the pan with the jam. Lay some of the strips over the tart and trim any excess. To make a lattice crust, lift every other strip and fold back so you can place another strip across those strips that remain flat. Lay the folded strips back down over the cross-strip. Fold back the strips that you laid the cross-strip on top of and repeat until the lattice covers the surface of the tart. Beat the remaining egg until scrambled and brush the strips with it, taking care not to get any egg on the filling.

7. Place the tart in the oven and bake for about 45 minutes, until the lattice crust is golden brown. Remove from the oven and let it cool before serving.

Linzer Tart
SEE PAGE 229

Golden Peach Pie

YIELD: 1 PIE | **ACTIVE TIME:** 30 MINUTES | **TOTAL TIME:** 6 HOURS

2 PERFECT PIECRUSTS (SEE PAGE 496), ROLLED OUT

8 RIPE PEACHES, PITTED AND SLICED

1 CUP LIGHT BROWN SUGAR

2 TABLESPOONS CORNSTARCH

½ TEASPOON CINNAMON

½ TEASPOON GROUND GINGER

¼ TEASPOON FRESHLY GRATED NUTMEG

ZEST AND JUICE OF 1 LEMON

¼ TEASPOON KOSHER SALT

1 EGG, BEATEN

SANDING SUGAR, FOR TOPPING

1. Preheat the oven to 375°F. Coat a 9-inch pie plate with nonstick cooking spray and place one of the crusts in it.

2. Place the peaches, brown sugar, cornstarch, cinnamon, ginger, nutmeg, lemon zest, lemon juice, and salt in a mixing bowl and toss until the peaches are evenly coated.

3. Using a pizza cutter or a chef's knife, cut the other crust into 14 to 16 strips that are about ½ inch wide. Lay half of the strips over the filling and trim any excess. To make a lattice crust, lift every other strip and fold back so you can place another strip across those strips that remain flat. Lay the folded strips back down over the cross-strip. Fold back the strips that you laid the cross-strip on top of and repeat until the lattice covers the surface of the pie.

4. Brush the strips with the egg, taking care not to get any egg on the filling. Sprinkle sanding sugar over the pie, place it in the oven, and bake until the filling has thickened and starts to bubble, 75 to 90 minutes.

5. Remove the pie from the oven, place it on a wire rack, and let it cool for 4 hours before serving.

Wild Blueberry Tart

YIELD: 1 TART | **ACTIVE TIME:** 30 MINUTES | **TOTAL TIME:** 5 HOURS

1 PÂTÉ SUCRÉE (SEE PAGE 502)

ALL-PURPOSE FLOUR, AS NEEDED

2 PINTS OF FRESH BLUEBERRIES

2 EGGS

3 OZ. HEAVY CREAM

ZEST OF ½ LEMON

PINCH OF KOSHER SALT

1. Line a fluted 9-inch tart pan with nonstick cooking spray. Remove the dough from the refrigerator and let it rest at room temperature for 30 minutes.

2. Place the dough on a flour-dusted work surface and roll it out to 12 inches. Carefully transfer the dough to the tart pan and press it firmly against the bottom and side, taking care not to tear the dough. Use a paring knife to trim away any excess dough. Cover the pan with plastic wrap and refrigerate for 30 minutes.

3. Preheat the oven to 350°F.

4. Remove the pan from the refrigerator and poke holes all over the bottom of the dough with a fork. Place a sheet of aluminum foil directly on the dough and fill it with your preferred weight.

5. Place the pan in the oven and bake the crust for 15 minutes. Remove it from the oven, remove the weight and aluminum foil, and return the crust to the oven. Bake until the center of the crust just begins to color. Remove the crust from the oven, place the pan on a wire rack, and let it cool completely.

6. Place half of the blueberries in a blender and puree until smooth. Transfer the puree to a small bowl, add the eggs, heavy cream, lemon zest, and salt and stir until combined.

7. Pour the mixture into the prepared tart shell and sprinkle the remaining blueberries over the top.

8. Place the tart in the oven and bake until the custard has puffed up around on the edges and the center has set, 20 to 25 minutes.

9. Remove the tart from the oven and place it on a cooling rack. Let it cool at room temperature for 1 hour and then transfer the tart to the refrigerator for 2 hours before slicing and serving.

Lemon Meringue Pie

YIELD: 1 PIE | **ACTIVE TIME:** 30 MINUTES | **TOTAL TIME:** 1 HOUR AND 30 MINUTES

¼ CUP CORNSTARCH

¼ CUP ALL-PURPOSE FLOUR

1¾ CUPS SUGAR

¼ TEASPOON FINE SEA SALT

2 CUPS WATER

4 EGG YOLKS, LIGHTLY BEATEN

½ CUP FRESH LEMON JUICE

1½ TABLESPOONS LEMON ZEST

1 OZ. UNSALTED BUTTER

1 PERFECT PIECRUST (SEE PAGE 496), BLIND BAKED IN A 9-INCH PIE PLATE

SWISS MERINGUE (SEE PAGE 508)

1. Place the cornstarch, flour, sugar, and salt in a saucepan and stir until well combined. Add the water in a slow stream and stir until incorporated. Cook the mixture over medium heat, stirring occasionally, until it is thick, about 20 minutes. Remove from heat.

2. While whisking constantly, add ¼ cup of the mixture in the saucepan into the beaten egg yolks. Stir the tempered eggs into the saucepan and place it over medium-low heat.

3. Add the lemon juice, lemon zest, and butter and stir constantly until the mixture is thick enough to coat the back of a wooden spoon. Remove the mixture from heat and let it cool completely. Preheat the oven to 400°F.

4. Add the cooled filling to the baked piecrust and use a rubber spatula to smooth the top.

5. Spread the meringue over the filling and use a large spoon or a spatula to create swirled peaks. Place in the oven and bake until the peaks of meringue are light brown, about 6 minutes. Remove from the oven and let the pie cool completely before serving.

Keto Coffee & Chocolate Tarts

YIELD: 3 SERVINGS | **ACTIVE TIME:** 5 MINUTES | **TOTAL TIME:** 1 HOUR AND 20 MINUTES

1½ OZ. ALMOND FLOUR

1 TEASPOON UNSWEETENED COCOA POWDER

STEVIA OR PREFERRED KETO-FRIENDLY SWEETENER, TO TASTE

1 TEASPOON PURE VANILLA EXTRACT

2 TABLESPOONS SALTED BUTTER, MELTED

1 TEASPOON INSTANT ESPRESSO POWDER

2 TABLESPOONS HOT WATER (125°F)

5.3 OZ. MASCARPONE CHEESE

3½ OZ. HEAVY CREAM

1 OZ. DARK CHOCOLATE (85 PERCENT)

COARSE SEA SALT, FOR TOPPING

1. Preheat the oven to 350°F. Place the almond flour, cocoa powder, sweetener, vanilla, and butter in a mixing bowl and stir until the mixture has the consistency of wet sand.

2. Divide the mixture among three ramekins and press it into their bases until it is smooth and even. Place the ramekins in the oven and bake the bases for 10 minutes. Remove the bases from the oven and let them cool slightly.

3. Dissolve the instant espresso powder in the hot water and let it cool.

4. Place the mascarpone cheese, more sweetener, and the espresso in a bowl and beat until the mixture is nice and fluffy. Pour the mascarpone mixture over the cooled tart bases and refrigerate the tarts for 10 minutes.

5. Place the heavy cream in a microwave-safe bowl and microwave on medium for 30 seconds. Add the chocolate and more sweetener and stir until you have a creamy ganache. Pour the ganache over the tarts and refrigerate for 1 hour.

6. Sprinkle sea salt over the tarts and enjoy.

Nutritional Info Per Serving: Calories: 490; Fat: 49 g; Net Carbs: 3 g; Protein: 8 g

Rhubarb, Brown Sugar & Fennel Pie

YIELD: 8 SERVINGS | **ACTIVE TIME:** 25 MINUTES | **TOTAL TIME:** 1 HOUR AND 45 MINUTES

2 PERFECT PIECRUSTS (SEE PAGE 496), ROLLED OUT

3 CUPS SLICED RHUBARB

1 FENNEL BULB, TRIMMED AND CHOPPED

⅔ CUP PACKED LIGHT BROWN SUGAR

JUICE OF 1 ORANGE

1 TEASPOON PURE VANILLA EXTRACT

2 TABLESPOONS PASTIS (OPTIONAL)

¼ CUP WATER

2 TABLESPOONS CORNSTARCH

2 TABLESPOONS MILK

1 TO 2 TEASPOONS FENNEL SEEDS

1. Coat a 9-inch pie plate with nonstick cooking spray and place one of the piecrusts in it.

2. Place the rhubarb, chopped fennel, brown sugar, orange juice, vanilla, pastis (if using), and water in a saucepan, partially cover the pan, and cook over medium heat until the rhubarb is very tender and juicy, 12 to 15 minutes. Remove the pan from heat, stir the cornstarch into the mixture, and let the mixture cool. Preheat the oven to 350°F.

3. Evenly distribute the rhubarb mixture in the piecrust, top with the remaining piecrust, and crimp the edge to seal. Cut four or five slits in the top crust, brush it with the milk, and sprinkle the fennel seeds over the top.

4. Place the pie in the oven and bake for about 45 minutes, until the top crust is golden brown and the filling is bubbling. Remove the pie from the oven and let it cool before enjoying.

Carrot & White Chocolate Pie

YIELD: 8 SERVINGS | **ACTIVE TIME:** 20 MINUTES | **TOTAL TIME:** 2 HOURS AND 15 MINUTES

6 CUPS PEELED AND CHOPPED CARROTS

4 TABLESPOONS UNSALTED BUTTER, DIVIDED INTO TABLESPOONS

2 TEASPOONS PURE VANILLA EXTRACT

¾ CUP WHITE CHOCOLATE CHIPS

2 TEASPOONS GROUND GINGER

1 LARGE EGG

3 LARGE EGG YOLKS

1¼ CUPS PACKED LIGHT BROWN SUGAR

1¼ CUPS SOUR CREAM

1 GRAHAM CRACKER CRUST (SEE PAGE 496)

1. Preheat the oven to 400°F. Place the carrots, butter, and vanilla in a large mixing bowl and stir to combine. Place the mixture on a large, rimmed baking sheet and roast, removing to toss two or three times, until the carrots are fork-tender, about 1 hour.

2. Remove the baking sheet from the oven and place the carrots in a food processor. Pulse until minced, add the white chocolate chips, and pulse until they have melted. Add the ginger, egg, egg yolks, light brown sugar, and sour cream and puree until smooth, scraping down the work bowl as needed. Reduce the oven's temperature to 325°F.

3. Evenly distribute the filling in the piecrust, place the pie in the oven, and bake for about 50 minutes, until the filling is set and dry to the touch. Remove from the oven and let cool before enjoying.

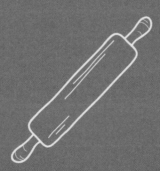

Lemony Rice Pudding Pie

YIELD: 1 PIE | **ACTIVE TIME:** 20 MINUTES | **TOTAL TIME:** 2 HOURS AND 30 MINUTES

3 CUPS MEYER LEMON CURD (SEE PAGE 369)

2 CUPS WHOLE MILK

1 TEASPOON PURE VANILLA EXTRACT

1½ CUPS LEFTOVER RICE

1 GRAHAM CRACKER CRUST (SEE PAGE 496)

CHANTILLY CREAM (SEE PAGE 518), FOR SERVING

CINNAMON, FOR DUSTING (OPTIONAL)

1. Place the Meyer Lemon Curd and milk in a large mixing bowl and whisk to combine. Add the vanilla and cooked rice and fold to combine.

2. Evenly distribute the filling in the piecrust, smoothing the top with a rubber spatula. Cover the pie with plastic wrap and place in the refrigerator for 2 hours.

3. Preheat the oven's broiler to high. Remove the pie from the refrigerator and place it underneath the broiler. Broil until the top starts to brown, about 5 minutes. Remove the pie from the oven and let it cool. Top each slice with Chantilly Cream and, if desired, cinnamon.

Whoopie Pies

YIELD: 20 WHOOPIE PIES | **ACTIVE TIME:** 30 MINUTES | **TOTAL TIME:** 1 HOUR

9 OZ. ALL-PURPOSE FLOUR

1½ OZ. COCOA POWDER

1½ TEASPOONS BAKING SODA

½ TEASPOON KOSHER SALT

4 OZ. UNSALTED BUTTER, SOFTENED

½ LB. SUGAR

1 EGG

1 TEASPOON PURE VANILLA EXTRACT

1 CUP BUTTERMILK

2 CUPS BUTTERFLUFF FILLING (SEE PAGE 517)

1. Preheat the oven to 350°F and line two baking sheets with parchment paper. Sift the flour, cocoa powder, baking soda, and salt into a mixing bowl. Set the mixture aside.

2. In the work bowl of a stand mixer fitted with the paddle attachment, cream the butter and sugar on medium until the mixture is very light and fluffy, about 5 minutes. Scrape down the work bowl with a rubber spatula and then beat the mixture for another 5 minutes.

3. Reduce the speed to low, add the egg, and beat until incorporated. Scrape down the work bowl, raise the speed to medium, and beat the mixture for 1 minute.

4. Reduce the speed to low, add the vanilla and the dry mixture, and beat until it comes together as a smooth batter. Add the buttermilk in a slow stream and beat to incorporate.

5. Scoop 2-oz. portions of the batter onto the baking sheets, making sure to leave 2 inches between each portion. Tap the bottom of the baking sheets gently on the counter to remove any air bubbles and let the portions spread out slightly.

6. Place in the oven and bake until a cake tester inserted into the centers of the whoopie pies comes out clean, 10 to 12 minutes.

7. Remove the whoopie pies from the oven and let them cool completely on the baking sheets.

8. Carefully remove the whoopie pies from the parchment paper. Scoop about 2 oz. of the Butterfluff Filling on half of the whoopie pies and then create sandwiches by topping with the remaining half.

Nutty Caramel & Cranberry Pie

YIELD: 1 PIE | **ACTIVE TIME:** 45 MINUTES | **TOTAL TIME:** 3 HOURS

1 PERFECT PIECRUST (SEE PAGE 496), ROLLED OUT

1 CUP SLIVERED ALMONDS

1 CUP CASHEWS, CHOPPED

1⅓ CUPS SUGAR

½ CUP WATER

6 TABLESPOONS UNSALTED BUTTER

1 TEASPOON PURE VANILLA EXTRACT

¼ TEASPOON KOSHER SALT

1½ CUPS FRESH CRANBERRIES

1. Preheat the oven to 375°F. Coat a 9-inch pie pan with nonstick cooking spray and place the piecrust in it.

2. Place the almonds and cashews on a parchment-lined baking sheet, place them in the oven, and toast until they are fragrant and starting to brown, 8 to 10 minutes. Remove from the oven and let them cool. Leave the oven on.

3. In a medium saucepan, bring the sugar and water to a boil over high heat. Cook, swirling the pan occasionally, until the mixture is a deep amber color. Remove the pan from heat.

4. Whisk in the butter, vanilla, and salt and let the caramel cool.

5. Place the toasted nuts and cranberries in a mixing bowl and toss to combine. Place the mixture in the piecrust and pour the caramel over it until the crust is filled. Save any remaining caramel for another preparation.

6. Place the pie in the oven and bake until the filling is set at the edge and the center barely jiggles when you shake the pie plate, about 1 hour. Remove from the oven and let the pie cool completely before slicing and serving.

Raspberry Cream Pie

YIELD: 1 PIE | **ACTIVE TIME:** 15 MINUTES | **TOTAL TIME:** 4 HOURS AND 30 MINUTES

½ LB. CREAM CHEESE, SOFTENED

1⅔ CUPS SWEETENED CONDENSED MILK

1½ CUPS CHANTILLY CREAM (SEE PAGE 518)

1 TEASPOON PURE VANILLA EXTRACT

1⅓ CUPS RASPBERRIES

1 COOKIE CRUST (SEE PAGE 497)

1. Place the cream cheese in the work bowl of a stand mixer fitted with the paddle attachment and beat until smooth and creamy.

2. Add the condensed milk and beat the mixture until it is smooth and thick, about 5 minutes. Remove the bowl from the stand mixer, add the Chantilly Cream, vanilla, and raspberries, and fold to incorporate.

3. Spoon the filling into the crust and use a rubber spatula to even out the top. Cover with plastic wrap and freeze until set, about 4 hours.

4. To serve, remove the pie from the freezer and let it sit at room temperature for 10 minutes before slicing.

Pear & Frangipane Tart

YIELD: 1 TART | **ACTIVE TIME:** 30 MINUTES | **TOTAL TIME:** 2 HOURS AND 15 MINUTES

6 CUPS WATER

2 CUPS SUGAR

2 CINNAMON STICKS

1 STAR ANISE POD

1 TABLESPOON PURE VANILLA EXTRACT

ZEST AND JUICE OF 1 LEMON

3 ANJOU PEARS

2 CUPS FRANGIPANE (SEE PAGE 504)

1 PÂTÉ SUCRÉE (SEE PAGE 502), BLIND BAKED IN A 9-INCH TART PAN

CONFECTIONERS' SUGAR, FOR DUSTING

1. Preheat the oven to 375°F. In a medium saucepan, combine the water, sugar, cinnamon sticks, star anise, vanilla, lemon juice, and lemon zest and bring the mixture to a simmer over medium heat.

2. Peel the pears and slice them in half lengthwise. Core the pears and gently lay them in the simmering poaching liquid. Let them simmer until tender, about 15 minutes. Transfer the poached pears to a paper towel–lined plate and let them cool to room temperature. When the pears are cool enough to handle, slice them into ⅛-inch-wide strips. Set the pears aside.

3. Spread the Frangipane evenly over the bottom of the tart shell and arrange the pears over it, making sure the thinnest parts are pointing toward the center. Place the tart in the oven and bake until the Frangipane has risen up around the pears and is golden brown. Remove from the oven and let the tart cool for 1 hour before dusting with confectioners' sugar and slicing.

Grasshopper Pie

YIELD: 1 PIE | **ACTIVE TIME:** 20 MINUTES | **TOTAL TIME:** 4 HOURS AND 45 MINUTES

½ CUP WHOLE MILK

32 LARGE MARSHMALLOWS

¼ CUP GREEN CRÈME DE MENTHE

¼ CUP WHITE CRÈME DE CACAO

1½ CUPS CHANTILLY CREAM (SEE PAGE 518)

2 DROPS OF GREEN GEL FOOD COLORING

1 COOKIE CRUST (SEE PAGE 497)

1. Place the milk and marshmallows in a large saucepan and cook over low heat, stirring frequently, until the marshmallows have melted. Place the pan in the refrigerator and chill for 20 minutes, stirring occasionally.

2. Stir the crème de menthe and crème de cacao into the mixture. Fold the marshmallow mixture into the Chantilly Cream and then stir in the green food coloring.

3. Place the filling in the crust and smooth the top with a rubber spatula. Place in the refrigerator and chill for 4 hours before serving.

White Chocolate Pie

YIELD: 1 PIE | **ACTIVE TIME:** 15 MINUTES | **TOTAL TIME:** 1 HOUR AND 30 MINUTES

¾ LB. WHITE CHOCOLATE CHIPS

4 OZ. UNSALTED BUTTER, CUT INTO SMALL PIECES

2 EGGS

1 CUP HEAVY CREAM

½ CUP SUGAR

1 TEASPOON PURE VANILLA EXTRACT

PINCH OF FINE SEA SALT

1 PÂTÉ SUCRÉE (SEE PAGE 502), BLIND BAKED

WHITE CHOCOLATE, SHAVED, FOR TOPPING

¼ CUP HULLED AND SLICED STRAWBERRIES, FOR TOPPING

1. Preheat the oven to 350°F. Fill a small saucepan halfway with water and bring it to a simmer. Place the white chocolate chips and butter in a large heatproof bowl, place it over the simmering water, and stir occasionally until the mixture is melted and combined. Remove from heat and set aside.

2. In a mixing bowl, whisk together the eggs, cream, sugar, vanilla, and salt. While whisking constantly, gradually add the white chocolate mixture. Pour the filling into the crust and gently tap the pie plate to evenly distribute the filling.

3. Place the pie in the oven and bake until the filling is set around the edges but still soft in the center, 15 to 20 minutes. Remove from the oven and let cool completely before topping with the white chocolate shavings and strawberries.

Sweet Potato Pie

YIELD: 1 PIE | **ACTIVE TIME:** 20 MINUTES | **TOTAL TIME:** 4 HOURS AND 30 MINUTES

15 OZ. SWEET POTATO PUREE

2 EGGS

½ CUP HEAVY CREAM

1 CUP DARK BROWN SUGAR

1 TEASPOON CINNAMON

½ TEASPOON FRESHLY GRATED NUTMEG

¼ TEASPOON GROUND GINGER

½ TEASPOON PURE VANILLA EXTRACT

¼ TEASPOON KOSHER SALT

1 PERFECT PIECRUST (SEE PAGE 496), BLIND BAKED

WHIPPED CREAM, FOR SERVING

1. Preheat the oven to 350°F. Place the sweet potato puree, eggs, heavy cream, brown sugar, cinnamon, nutmeg, ginger, vanilla, and salt in a mixing bowl and whisk until smooth.

2. Pour the filling into the crust, place the pie in the oven, and bake until the filling is just set, about 30 minutes.

3. Remove the pie from the oven, place it on a cooling rack, and let it sit for 30 minutes.

4. Place the pie in the refrigerator and chill for 3 hours.

5. To serve, top each slice with a dollop of whipped cream.

Buttermilk Pie

YIELD: 1 PIE | **ACTIVE TIME:** 10 MINUTES | **TOTAL TIME:** 1 HOUR AND 30 MINUTES

3 LARGE EGGS

1 CUP WHITE SUGAR

¼ CUP HONEY

3 TABLESPOONS ALL-PURPOSE FLOUR

4 OZ. UNSALTED BUTTER, MELTED AND SLIGHTLY COOLED

1¼ CUPS BUTTERMILK

1 TEASPOON PURE VANILLA EXTRACT

1 TABLESPOON FRESH LEMON JUICE

1 TEASPOON LEMON ZEST

¼ TEASPOON KOSHER SALT

1 PERFECT PIECRUST (SEE PAGE 496), BLIND BAKED

1. Preheat the oven to 350°F. Place all of the ingredients, except for the piecrust, in the work bowl of a stand mixer fitted with the paddle attachment and beat on medium until the mixture is fluffy and thoroughly combined, about 3 to 4 minutes.

2. Pour the mixture into the piecrust, place the pie in the oven, and bake for about 45 minutes, until the filling is set and starting to brown. Remove from the oven and let cool slightly before serving.

Raspberry Pie

YIELD: 1 PIE | **ACTIVE TIME:** 15 MINUTES | **TOTAL TIME:** 1 HOUR AND 30 MINUTES

2 PERFECT PIECRUSTS (SEE PAGE 496), ROLLED OUT

7 CUPS FRESH RASPBERRIES

2 CUPS SUGAR, PLUS MORE FOR TOPPING

⅔ CUP ALL-PURPOSE FLOUR

2 TABLESPOONS FRESH LEMON JUICE

PINCH OF KOSHER SALT

1 EGG, BEATEN

1. Preheat the oven to 350°F. Coat a 9-inch pie plate with nonstick cooking spray and place one of the crusts in it.

2. Place the raspberries, sugar, flour, lemon juice, and salt in a mixing bowl and stir until well combined. Evenly distribute this mixture in the crust in the pie plate.

3. Place the top crust over the filling, trim away any excess, and crimp the edge to seal. Brush the top crust with the egg, make four to five slits in it, and sprinkle additional sugar on top.

4. Place the pie in the oven and bake until golden brown, about 45 minutes. Remove from the oven and let cool before serving.

Apple Pie with Quark

YIELD: 1 PIE | **ACTIVE TIME:** 20 MINUTES | **TOTAL TIME:** 1 HOUR AND 30 MINUTES

1 PERFECT PIECRUST (SEE PAGE 496), ROLLED OUT

½ CUP SUGAR

4 OZ. UNSALTED BUTTER, SOFTENED

3 LARGE EGGS, LIGHTLY BEATEN

2 CUPS QUARK CHEESE

1 TEASPOON PURE VANILLA EXTRACT

1 TEASPOON LEMON ZEST

1 TEASPOON FRESH LEMON JUICE

½ CUP ALL-PURPOSE FLOUR

1 TEASPOON BAKING POWDER

¼ TEASPOON KOSHER SALT

3 LARGE BRAEBURN APPLES, PEELED, CORES REMOVED, SLICED

1. Preheat the oven to 350°F, coat a 9-inch pie plate with nonstick cooking spray, and place the piecrust in it. Place the sugar, butter, eggs, quark, vanilla, lemon zest, and lemon juice in a food processor and puree until smooth, scraping the work bowl as needed.

2. Sift the flour, baking powder, and salt into a mixing bowl. Add the mixture to the food processor and pulse until incorporated. Evenly distribute the mixture in the crust and arrange the apples in the mixture.

3. Place the pie in the oven and bake until the filling is set and golden brown, about 40 minutes. Remove from the oven and let cool before serving.

Chocolate & Bourbon Pecan Pie

YIELD: 1 PIE | **ACTIVE TIME:** 30 MINUTES | **TOTAL TIME:** 3 HOURS

1 PERFECT PIECRUST (SEE PAGE 496), ROLLED OUT

½ LB. LARGE PECAN HALVES

3 EGGS

6 OZ. DARK BROWN SUGAR

1 CUP LIGHT CORN SYRUP

1 TEASPOON PURE VANILLA EXTRACT

½ TEASPOON KOSHER SALT

2 TABLESPOONS BOURBON

5 OZ. SEMISWEET CHOCOLATE CHIPS

1. Preheat the oven to 375°F. Coat a 9-inch pie plate with nonstick cooking spray and place the piecrust in it. Trim away any excess and crimp the edge.

2. Place the pecans on a parchment-lined baking sheet, place them in the oven, and toast until fragrant, 8 to 10 minutes. Remove the pecans from the oven and let them cool.

3. Place the eggs, dark brown sugar, corn syrup, vanilla, salt, and bourbon in a mixing bowl and whisk until combined.

4. Cover the bottom of the piecrust with the semisweet chocolate chips. Arrange the toasted pecans on top of the chocolate chips and then pour the filling into the crust.

5. Place the pie in the oven and bake until the center of the pie is set, 55 to 60 minutes.

6. Remove the pie from the oven, place it on a cooling rack, and let it cool for 1 to 2 hours before slicing and serving.

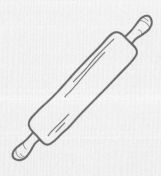

Shoofly Pie

YIELD: 1 PIE | **ACTIVE TIME:** 15 MINUTES | **TOTAL TIME:** 1 HOUR AND 15 MINUTES

1 PÂTÉ SUCRÉE (SEE PAGE 502), ROLLED OUT

1 CUP MOLASSES

1 TEASPOON BAKING SODA

¾ CUP BOILING WATER

1½ CUPS ALL-PURPOSE FLOUR

½ CUP PACKED DARK BROWN SUGAR

½ TEASPOON CINNAMON

PINCH OF FRESHLY GRATED NUTMEG

PINCH OF FINE SEA SALT

4 OZ. UNSALTED BUTTER, CHILLED AND DIVIDED INTO TABLESPOONS

1. Preheat the oven to 350°F. Coat a 9-inch pie plate with nonstick cooking spray and place the rolled-out dough in it. Place the molasses, baking soda, and boiling water in a large mixing bowl and stir to combine. Evenly distribute the mixture in the piecrust.

2. Place the flour, brown sugar, cinnamon, nutmeg, and salt in a large mixing bowl and stir to combine. Add the butter and work the mixture with your hands until it is sticking together in clumps. Distribute the mixture over the pie.

3. Place the pie in the oven and bake until the crust is golden brown and the topping is dry to the touch, about 45 minutes. Remove from the oven and let cool before serving.

Shoofly Pie
SEE PAGE 255

Crack Pie

YIELD: 1 PIE | **ACTIVE TIME:** 45 MINUTES | **TOTAL TIME:** 24 HOURS

FOR THE CRUST

4 OZ. UNSALTED BUTTER, SOFTENED

2.7 OZ. LIGHT BROWN SUGAR

2 TABLESPOONS SUGAR

1 LARGE EGG, AT ROOM TEMPERATURE

¾ CUP PLUS 2 TABLESPOONS OATS

2½ OZ. ALL-PURPOSE FLOUR

⅛ TEASPOON BAKING POWDER

⅛ TEASPOON BAKING SODA

¼ TEASPOON FINE SEA SALT

FOR THE FILLING

¾ CUP SUGAR

½ CUP PACKED LIGHT BROWN SUGAR

1 TABLESPOON NONFAT MILK POWDER

¼ TEASPOON KOSHER SALT

4 OZ. UNSALTED BUTTER, MELTED AND SLIGHTLY COOLED

½ CUP HEAVY CREAM

4 LARGE EGG YOLKS

1 TEASPOON PURE VANILLA EXTRACT

¼ CUP CONFECTIONERS' SUGAR, FOR TOPPING

1. Preheat the oven to 350°F and line a 13 x 9-inch baking sheet with parchment paper. To begin preparations for the crust, place 5 tablespoons of the butter, ¼ cup of the brown sugar, and the sugar in the work bowl of a stand mixer fitted with the paddle attachment and beat on medium speed until pale and fluffy.

2. Add the egg, beat to incorporate, and then stir in the ¾ cup of oats, the flour, baking powder, baking soda, and salt. Press the mixture into the baking sheet, place it in the oven, and bake for 16 to 18 minutes, until it is dry to the touch. Remove and let cool completely.

3. When the crust has cooled, break it up into pieces, place them in a food processor, and pulse until they are fine crumbs. Add the remaining butter, brown sugar, and oats and pulse until incorporated. Coat a 9-inch pie plate with nonstick cooking spray and press the mixture into it. Place the crust in the refrigerator.

4. To begin preparations for the filling, place the sugars, milk powder, and salt in the work bowl of a stand mixer fitted with the paddle attachment and stir to combine. Add the melted butter and beat on medium speed until pale and fluffy. Add the cream, egg yolks, and vanilla and beat until the mixture is thoroughly combined.

5. Pour the filling into the piecrust and tap the pie plate to distribute it evenly. Place the pie in the oven and bake for 30 minutes. Reduce the oven temperature to 325°F and bake for another 20 minutes, until the filling is set and the center wobbles slightly when poked. Remove from the oven, let cool completely, cover with plastic wrap, and chill overnight. When ready to serve, sprinkle the confectioners' sugar over the top.

Mississippi Mud Pie

YIELD: 1 PIE | **ACTIVE TIME:** 15 MINUTES | **TOTAL TIME:** 1 HOUR AND 45 MINUTES

6 OZ. UNSALTED BUTTER

1 CUP PACKED DARK BROWN SUGAR

4 LARGE EGGS, LIGHTLY BEATEN

¼ CUP COCOA POWDER

1¼ CUPS BITTERSWEET CHOCOLATE CHIPS, MELTED AND SLIGHTLY COOLED

2 TEASPOONS ESPRESSO POWDER

1¼ CUPS HEAVY CREAM

1 COCOA CRUST (SEE PAGE 500)

CHANTILLY CREAM (SEE PAGE 518), FOR TOPPING

DARK CHOCOLATE, SHAVED, FOR TOPPING

1. Preheat the oven to 350°F. Place the butter and brown sugar in the work bowl of a stand mixer fitted with the paddle attachment and beat on medium until pale and fluffy, about 5 minutes. Add the eggs and cocoa powder, beat to incorporate, and then fold in the chocolate chips and espresso powder. Add the cream and beat until incorporated.

2. Evenly distribute the mixture in the piecrust, place the pie in the oven, and bake until the filling is set, about 35 minutes. Remove from the oven and let the pie cool completely. Top with the Chantilly Cream and shaved chocolate before serving.

Funfetti Whoopie Pies

YIELD: 20 WHOOPIE PIES | **ACTIVE TIME:** 30 MINUTES | **TOTAL TIME:** 1 HOUR AND 45 MINUTES

¾ LB. ALL-PURPOSE FLOUR

1 TEASPOON BAKING SODA

¾ TEASPOON BAKING POWDER

¾ TEASPOON KOSHER SALT

4 OZ. UNSALTED BUTTER, SOFTENED

9 OZ. SUGAR

1 EGG

1½ TEASPOONS PURE VANILLA EXTRACT

⅔ CUP BUTTERMILK

½ CUP RAINBOW SPRINKLES

2 CUPS BUTTERFLUFF FILLING (SEE PAGE 517)

1. Preheat the oven to 350°F and line two baking sheets with parchment paper. Sift the flour, baking soda, baking powder, and salt into a mixing bowl and set the mixture aside.

2. In the work bowl of a stand mixer fitted with the paddle attachment, cream the butter and sugar on medium speed until the mixture is very light and fluffy, about 5 minutes. Scrape down the work bowl and then beat the mixture for another 5 minutes.

3. Add the egg, reduce the speed to low, and beat until incorporated, again scraping the work bowl as needed. Add the vanilla and beat to incorporate it.

4. Add the dry mixture and beat on low until the batter comes together. Gradually add in the buttermilk and beat until incorporated. When all of the buttermilk has been combined, add the sprinkles and fold the mixture until they are evenly distributed.

5. Drop 2-oz. portions of the dough on the baking sheets, making sure to leave 2 inches of space between them.

6. Place in the oven and bake until a cake tester inserted into the centers of the whoopie pies comes out clean, about 12 minutes. Remove from the oven and let the whoopie pies cool completely.

7. Spread the filling on half of the whoopie pies and use the other halves to assemble the whoopie pies.

Plum Tart with Hazelnut Crumble

YIELD: 1 TART | **ACTIVE TIME:** 20 MINUTES | **TOTAL TIME:** 1 HOUR AND 30 MINUTES

FOR THE TART

1 OZ. UNSALTED BUTTER

10 RIPE PLUMS, PITTED AND HALVED

½ CUP SUGAR

¼ CUP WATER

2 TABLESPOONS CORNSTARCH

1 TABLESPOON FRESH LEMON JUICE

1 PÂTÉ SUCRÉE (SEE PAGE 502), BLIND BAKED IN A 9-INCH TART PAN

FOR THE CRUMBLE

¼ CUP LIGHT BROWN SUGAR

¼ CUP SUGAR

½ CUP ALL-PURPOSE FLOUR

⅓ CUP ALMOND MEAL

3 TABLESPOONS UNSALTED BUTTER

¼ TEASPOON CINNAMON

¼ TEASPOON KOSHER SALT

⅓ CUP BLANCHED HAZELNUTS, CHOPPED

1. Preheat the oven to 350°F. To begin preparations for the tart, place the butter in a saucepan and melt over medium heat. Add the plums, sugar, and water and cook, stirring occasionally, until the plums start to break down, 7 to 10 minutes.

2. Remove from heat and stir in the cornstarch and lemon juice. Evenly distribute the mixture in the tart shell, making sure the plums are cut side up.

3. To prepare the crumble, place all of the ingredients, except for the hazelnuts, in a food processor and pulse until the mixture is a coarse meal. Spread the mixture over the pie and sprinkle the hazelnuts on top.

4. Place in the oven and bake until the crumble is golden brown, about 40 minutes. Remove from the oven and let cool before serving.

Nectarine Pie

YIELD: 1 PIE | **ACTIVE TIME:** 30 MINUTES | **TOTAL TIME:** 1 HOUR AND 45 MINUTES

2 PERFECT PIECRUSTS (SEE PAGE 496), ROLLED OUT

7 NECTARINES, PITTED AND SLICED

½ CUP SUGAR

½ CUP LIGHT BROWN SUGAR

3 TABLESPOONS CORNSTARCH

¼ TEASPOON CINNAMON

¼ TEASPOON FRESHLY GRATED NUTMEG

ZEST AND JUICE OF 1 LEMON

¼ TEASPOON KOSHER SALT

1 EGG, BEATEN

COARSE SUGAR, FOR TOPPING

1. Preheat the oven to 375°F. Coat a 9-inch pie pan with nonstick cooking spray and place one of the crusts in it.

2. Place the nectarines, sugar, brown sugar, cornstarch, cinnamon, nutmeg, lemon juice, lemon zest, and salt in a mixing bowl and toss until the nectarines are evenly coated.

3. Fill the crust with the nectarine mixture, lay the other crust over the top, and crimp the edge to seal. Brush the top crust with the egg and sprinkle the coarse sugar over it. Cut several slits in the top crust.

4. Place the pie in the oven and bake until the filling is bubbly and has thickened, about 50 minutes. Remove from the oven and let the pie cool completely before serving.

Strawberry Rhubarb Pie

YIELD: 1 PIE | **ACTIVE TIME:** 30 MINUTES | **TOTAL TIME:** 1 HOUR AND 45 MINUTES

2 PERFECT PIECRUSTS (SEE PAGE 496), ROLLED OUT

3 CUPS STRAWBERRIES, HULLED AND QUARTERED

3 CUPS CHOPPED RHUBARB

1 CUP SUGAR

2 TABLESPOONS CORNSTARCH

¼ TEASPOON CARDAMOM

ZEST OF 2 ORANGES

¼ TEASPOON KOSHER SALT

1 EGG, BEATEN

COARSE SUGAR, FOR TOPPING

1. Preheat the oven to 375°F. Coat a 9-inch pie pan with nonstick cooking spray and place one of the crusts in it.

2. Place the strawberries, rhubarb, sugar, cornstarch, cardamom, orange zest, and salt in a mixing bowl and toss until the strawberries and rhubarb are evenly coated.

3. Fill the crust with the strawberry mixture, lay the other crust over the top, and crimp the edge to seal. Brush the top crust with the egg and sprinkle the coarse sugar over it. Cut several slits in the top crust.

4. Place the pie in the oven and bake until the filling is bubbly and has thickened, about 50 minutes. Remove from the oven and let the pie cool completely before serving.

Key Lime Pie

1 (14 OZ.) CAN OF SWEETENED CONDENSED MILK

4 EGG YOLKS

½ CUP FRESH KEY LIME JUICE

¼ TEASPOON KOSHER SALT

½ TEASPOON PURE VANILLA EXTRACT

1 GRAHAM CRACKER CRUST (SEE PAGE 496)

SWISS MERINGUE (SEE PAGE 508)

1. Preheat the oven to 350°F. In a mixing bowl, whisk together the condensed milk, egg yolks, key lime juice, salt, and vanilla extract. When the mixture is smooth, pour it into the crust.

2. Place the pie in the oven and bake until the filling is just set, about 16 minutes. Remove from the oven and let the pie cool at room temperature for 30 minutes before transferring it to the refrigerator. Chill the pie for 3 hours.

3. Place the meringue in a piping bag fit with a star tip. Pipe the meringue around the border of the pie and lightly brown it with a kitchen torch. Slice and serve.

Sour Cherry Crumble Pie

YIELD: 1 PIE | **ACTIVE TIME:** 30 MINUTES | **TOTAL TIME:** 1 HOUR AND 45 MINUTES

1 PERFECT PIECRUST (SEE PAGE 496), ROLLED OUT

6 CUPS MORELLO CHERRIES, PITTED AND HALVED

½ CUP SUGAR

3 TABLESPOONS CORNSTARCH

¼ TEASPOON GROUND GINGER

ZEST AND JUICE OF 1 LEMON

¼ TEASPOON KOSHER SALT

STREUSEL TOPPING (SEE PAGE 541)

1. Preheat the oven to 375°F. Coat a 9-inch pie pan with nonstick cooking spray and place the crust in it.

2. Place the cherries, sugar, cornstarch, ginger, lemon juice, lemon zest, and salt in a mixing bowl and toss until the cherries are evenly coated.

3. Fill the crust with the cherry mixture and sprinkle the topping over it.

4. Place the pie in the oven and bake until the filling is bubbly and has thickened, about 50 minutes. Remove from the oven and let the pie cool completely before serving.

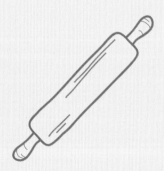

Black & Blue Galette

YIELD: 1 GALETTE | **ACTIVE TIME:** 20 MINUTES | **TOTAL TIME:** 1 HOUR AND 30 MINUTES

1 BALL OF PERFECT PIECRUST DOUGH (SEE PAGE 496)

ALL-PURPOSE FLOUR, AS NEEDED

1½ CUPS FRESH BLUEBERRIES

1½ CUPS FRESH BLACKBERRIES

½ CUP LIGHT BROWN SUGAR

JUICE OF ½ LEMON

3 TABLESPOONS CORNSTARCH

PINCH OF FINE SEA SALT

1 EGG, BEATEN

1 TABLESPOON SUGAR

1. Preheat the oven to 400°F. Place the ball of dough on a flour-dusted work surface, roll it out to 9 inches, and then place it on a parchment-lined baking sheet.

2. Place the berries, brown sugar, lemon juice, cornstarch, and salt in a large mixing bowl and stir until the berries are evenly coated.

3. Spread the berry mixture over the dough, making sure to leave a 1½-inch border. Fold the crust over the filling, brush the folded-over crust with the beaten egg, and sprinkle the sugar over it.

4. Place the galette in the oven and bake until the crust is golden brown and the filling is bubbly, about 35 to 40 minutes. Remove from the oven and let cool before serving.

Squash Whoopie Pies

YIELD: 12 WHOOPIE PIES | **ACTIVE TIME:** 20 MINUTES | **TOTAL TIME:** 1 HOUR

1⅓ CUPS ALL-PURPOSE FLOUR

1 TEASPOON CINNAMON

1 TEASPOON GROUND GINGER

¼ TEASPOON GROUND CLOVES

½ TEASPOON FRESHLY GRATED NUTMEG

½ TEASPOON BAKING SODA

½ TEASPOON BAKING POWDER

1 TEASPOON KOSHER SALT

1 CUP PACKED LIGHT BROWN SUGAR

2 TABLESPOONS REAL MAPLE SYRUP

1 CUP PUREED BUTTERNUT OR ACORN SQUASH

1 EGG

1 CUP EXTRA-VIRGIN OLIVE OIL

1⅓ CUPS CONFECTIONERS' SUGAR

4 TABLESPOONS UNSALTED BUTTER

½ LB. CREAM CHEESE, SOFTENED

1-INCH PIECE OF FRESH GINGER, PEELED AND GRATED

½ TEASPOON PURE VANILLA EXTRACT

1. Preheat the oven to 350°F. Sift the flour, cinnamon, ginger, cloves, nutmeg, baking soda, baking powder, and salt into a mixing bowl.

2. Place the brown sugar, maple syrup, pureed squash, egg, and olive oil in a separate mixing bowl and stir until combined. Sift the dry mixture into the squash mixture and stir until it has been incorporated.

3. Use an ice cream scoop to place dollops of the batter onto parchment-lined baking sheets. Make sure to leave plenty of space between the scoops. Place the sheets in the oven and bake until the whoopie pies are golden brown, about 10 to 15 minutes. Remove and let cool.

4. While the whoopie pies are cooling, place the remaining ingredients in a bowl and beat with a handheld mixer until the mixture is fluffy.

5. When the whoopie pies have cooled completely, spread the filling on one of the whoopie pies. Top with another half and repeat until all of the whoopie pies and filling have been used.

Pumpkin Pie

YIELD: 1 PIE | **ACTIVE TIME:** 30 MINUTES | **TOTAL TIME:** 5 HOURS

1 (14 OZ.) CAN OF PUMPKIN PUREE

1 (12 OZ.) CAN OF EVAPORATED MILK

2 EGGS

6 OZ. LIGHT BROWN SUGAR

1 TEASPOON CINNAMON

1 TEASPOON GROUND GINGER

½ TEASPOON FRESHLY GRATED NUTMEG

¼ TEASPOON GROUND CLOVES

½ TEASPOON KOSHER SALT

1 PERFECT PIECRUST (SEE PAGE 496), BLIND BAKED

CHANTILLY CREAM (SEE PAGE 518), FOR SERVING

1. Preheat the oven to 350°F. In a mixing bowl, whisk together the pumpkin puree, evaporated milk, eggs, brown sugar, cinnamon, ginger, nutmeg, cloves, and salt. When the mixture is smooth, pour it into the crust.

2. Place the pie in the oven and bake until the filling is just set, about 40 minutes. Remove from the oven and let the pie cool at room temperature for 30 minutes before transferring it to the refrigerator. Chill the pie for 3 hours.

3. Slice the pie, top each piece with a dollop of whipped cream, and serve.

Pear Galette with Maple Caramel

YIELD: 1 GALETTE | **ACTIVE TIME:** 30 MINUTES | **TOTAL TIME:** 1 HOUR AND 45 MINUTES

FOR THE DOUGH

7½ OZ. ALL-PURPOSE FLOUR, PLUS MORE AS NEEDED

1 TEASPOON CINNAMON

¼ TEASPOON FRESHLY GRATED NUTMEG

¼ TEASPOON GROUND CLOVES

1½ TEASPOONS FINE SEA SALT

2 TEASPOONS BROWN SUGAR

1 CUP UNSALTED BUTTER

½ CUP ICE WATER

1 EGG YOLK, BEATEN

FOR THE FILLING

¼ CUP SUGAR

2 TEASPOONS CINNAMON

3 ANJOU PEARS, CORED AND CUT INTO ¼-INCH SLICES

1½ TABLESPOONS LEMON ZEST

½-INCH PIECE OF FRESH GINGER, PEELED AND GRATED

1 OZ. UNSALTED BUTTER, CUT INTO SMALL PIECES

FOR THE MAPLE CARAMEL

½ CUP UNSALTED BUTTER

1 CUP DARK BROWN SUGAR

½ TEASPOON FINE SEA SALT

½ CUP MAPLE SYRUP

1. To prepare the dough, place the flour, cinnamon, nutmeg, cloves, salt, and brown sugar in a bowl and whisk to combine. Divide the butter into tablespoons and place them in the freezer for 15 minutes.

2. Place the flour mixture and frozen pieces of butter in a food processor and blitz until combined. Gradually add the water and blitz until the dough just holds together. Remove from the food processor, place on a lightly floured work surface, and knead until all of the ingredients are thoroughly incorporated. Place in the refrigerator for 20 minutes before rolling out.

3. Preheat the oven to 400°F and prepare the filling. Place the sugar and cinnamon in a bowl, stir to combine, and set aside. Place the pears, lemon zest, ginger, and butter in a separate bowl and gently toss, being careful not to break the slices of pear.

4. Place the dough on a lightly floured work surface and roll out into a 12-inch circle that is approximately ¼ inch thick. Place it on a parchment-lined baking sheet and then place the pear slices on the dough in layers, making sure to leave a 1½-inch border. Sprinkle each layer with the sugar-and-cinnamon mixture before adding the next layer.

5. Fold the edge of the dough over the filling and crimp. Brush the crust with the egg yolk and sprinkle with the sugar-and-cinnamon mixture. Place the galette in the oven and bake until the crust is golden brown and the pears are tender, about 25 minutes.

6. While the galette is baking, prepare the maple caramel. Place the butter in a saucepan and melt over medium heat. Add the brown sugar and salt and cook, stirring constantly, until the sugar is dissolved, about 5 minutes. Add the maple syrup and cook until the mixture is smooth and thick. Remove from heat.

7. Remove the galette from the oven, drizzle the maple caramel over the top, and let cool for 5 to 10 minutes before serving.

Tarte Tatin

YIELD: 1 TART | **ACTIVE TIME:** 30 MINUTES | **TOTAL TIME:** 24 TO 48 HOURS

6 TO 8 BRAEBURN OR HONEYCRISP APPLES, PEELED, CORED, AND QUARTERED

6.3 OZ. ALL-PURPOSE FLOUR, PLUS MORE AS NEEDED

1 OZ. CONFECTIONERS' SUGAR

½ TEASPOON FINE SEA SALT

4 OZ. UNSALTED BUTTER, CHILLED

1 EGG, BEATEN

3 OZ. SALTED BUTTER, SOFTENED

⅔ CUP SUGAR

1. Place the apples in a mixing bowl and let them sit in the refrigerator for 24 to 48 hours. This will allow them to dry out.

2. Whisk together the flour, confectioners' sugar, and salt in a large bowl. Add the unsalted butter and use your fingers or a pastry blender to work the mixture until it is a collection of coarse clumps. Add the egg and work the mixture until the dough just holds together. Shape it into a ball, cover it with plastic wrap, flatten into a 4-inch disc, and refrigerate for 1 hour. If preparing ahead of time, the dough will keep in the refrigerator overnight.

3. Preheat the oven to 375°F. Coat a 10-inch cast-iron skillet with the salted butter. When the butter is melted, remove the skillet from heat and sprinkle the sugar evenly over the butter. Place the apple slices in a circular pattern, starting at the center of the pan and working out to the edge. The pieces should overlap and face the same direction.

4. Place the dough on a flour-dusted work surface and roll it out to ⅛ inch thick. Use the roller to carefully roll up the dough. Place it over the apples and tuck it in around the edges.

5. Place the skillet over low heat and gradually raise it until the juices in the pan are a deep amber color, about 7 minutes.

6. Place the skillet in the oven and bake until the crust is golden brown and firm, 35 to 40 minutes.

7. Remove the tart from the oven, allow to cool for about 5 minutes, and then run a knife around the edges to loosen the tart. Using oven mitts, carefully invert the tart onto a large plate. Place any apples that are stuck to the skillet back on the tart and enjoy.

Graceland Pie

YIELD: 1 PIE | **ACTIVE TIME:** 30 MINUTES | **TOTAL TIME:** 1 HOUR

¾ CUP SUGAR

⅓ CUP ALL-PURPOSE FLOUR

¼ TEASPOON FINE SEA SALT

2 CUPS WHOLE MILK

3 EGG YOLKS, BEATEN

1 OZ. UNSALTED BUTTER

1¼ TEASPOONS PURE VANILLA EXTRACT

4 BANANAS, SLICED

CREAMY NATURAL PEANUT BUTTER, WARM

1 GRAHAM CRACKER CRUST (SEE PAGE 496), MADE WITH CHOCOLATE GRAHAM CRACKERS

CHANTILLY CREAM (SEE PAGE 518)

DEHYDRATED BANANA CHIPS, FOR GARNISH

¼ CUP CRISPY, CHOPPED BACON, FOR GARNISH (OPTIONAL)

1. Place the sugar, flour, and salt in a saucepan and whisk to combine. Whisk the milk into the mixture and bring to a simmer, while stirring constantly, over medium heat. Simmer, while stirring, for 2 minutes and then remove the pan from heat.

2. While whisking constantly, stir a small amount of the warmed mixture into the beaten egg yolks. Add the tempered egg yolks to the saucepan, place the pan back over medium heat, and cook until the mixture thickens and starts bubbling, while whisking constantly. Remove from heat, add the butter and vanilla, and stir until combined. Add half of the sliced bananas, stir to coat, and let the mixture cool.

3. While the mixture is cooling, place the peanut butter in a saucepan and warm over medium heat until it starts to melt.

4. Place the remaining bananas in the piecrust and then pour the cooled banana cream over the bananas. Cover with the Chantilly Cream, drizzle the peanut butter over it, and arrange the dehydrated banana chips and bacon pieces (if desired) on top.

Mixed Berry Pie

YIELD: 1 PIE | **ACTIVE TIME:** 30 MINUTES | **TOTAL TIME:** 1 HOUR AND 30 MINUTES

1½ CUPS FRESH BLUEBERRIES

1 CUP FRESH BLACKBERRIES

1 CUP FRESH RASPBERRIES

1½ CUPS FRESH STRAWBERRIES, HULLED AND HALVED

1 TABLESPOON FRESH LEMON JUICE

½ CUP LIGHT BROWN SUGAR

2 TABLESPOONS CORNSTARCH

½ CUP UNSWEETENED RASPBERRY PRESERVES

2 PERFECT PIECRUSTS (SEE PAGE 496)

ALL-PURPOSE FLOUR, AS NEEDED

1 EGG, BEATEN

1. Preheat the oven to 375°F and coat a 9-inch pie plate with nonstick cooking spray.

2. Place all of the berries, lemon juice, brown sugar, and cornstarch in a large bowl and toss to combine. Transfer the fruit to a large saucepan and cook over medium heat until the berries start to break down, 7 to 10 minutes. Stir in the preserves, remove the pan from heat, and set the mixture aside.

3. Place the balls of dough on a flour-dusted work surface and roll them out to fit the pie plate. Transfer one of the crusts to the pie plate and fill it with the berry mixture.

4. Cut the other crust into 1-inch-wide strips. Lay some of the strips over the pie and trim the strips so that they fit. To make a lattice crust, lift every other strip and fold them back so you can place another strip across those strips that remain flat. Lay the folded strips back down over the cross-strip. Fold back the strips that you laid the cross-strip on top of and repeat until the lattice covers the surface of the pie. Brush the strips with the beaten egg, taking care not to get any egg on the filling.

5. Place the pie in the oven and bake for 45 minutes, until the crust is golden brown and the filling is bubbling. Remove from the oven and let cool before serving.

Roasted Strawberry Handpies

YIELD: 8 HANDPIES | **ACTIVE TIME:** 40 MINUTES | **TOTAL TIME:** 2 HOURS

3 QUARTS OF FRESH STRAWBERRIES, HULLED AND SLICED

1 CUP SUGAR

2 TEASPOONS FRESH LEMON JUICE

1 TABLESPOON CORNSTARCH

½ TABLESPOON WATER

1 BALL OF PERFECT PIECRUST DOUGH (SEE PAGE 496)

2 EGGS, BEATEN

1½ CUPS SIFTED CONFECTIONERS' SUGAR

3 TABLESPOONS WHOLE MILK

1 TEASPOON CINNAMON

1. Preheat the oven to 400°F. Place the strawberries on a baking sheet, place it in the oven, and roast until they start to darken and release their juice, about 20 to 30 minutes. If you prefer, you can bake them for up to an hour. Cooking the strawberries for longer will caramelize the sugars and lend them an even richer flavor. Reduce the oven's temperature to 350°F.

2. Remove the strawberries from the oven and place them in a saucepan with the sugar and lemon juice. Bring to a simmer over medium heat and cook for 20 minutes, until the mixture has thickened slightly.

3. Place the cornstarch and water in a small cup and stir until there are no lumps in the mixture. Add to the saucepan and stir until the mixture is syrupy. Remove the pan from heat.

4. Divide the ball of piecrust dough into two pieces, roll them out into squares that are about ⅛ inch thick, and then cut each square into quarters. Spoon some of the strawberry mixture into the center of each quarter.

5. Take a bottom corner of each pie and fold to the opposite top corner. Press down to ensure that none of the mixture leaks out and then use a fork to seal the edge. Place the pies on a baking sheet and brush them with the beaten eggs. Place in the oven and bake until golden brown, about 20 to 30 minutes.

6. While the pies are cooking, place the confectioners' sugar, milk, and cinnamon in a bowl and stir until well combined.

7. Remove the pies from the oven, brush them with the sugar-and-cinnamon glaze, and allow to cool before serving.

Plum Galette

YIELD: 1 GALETTE | **ACTIVE TIME:** 20 MINUTES | **TOTAL TIME:** 1 HOUR

1 BALL OF PERFECT PIECRUST DOUGH (SEE PAGE 496)

ALL-PURPOSE FLOUR, AS NEEDED

5 PLUMS, PITS REMOVED, SLICED

½ CUP PLUS 1 TABLESPOON SUGAR

JUICE OF ½ LEMON

3 TABLESPOONS CORNSTARCH

PINCH OF FINE SEA SALT

2 TABLESPOONS BLACKBERRY JAM

1 EGG, BEATEN

1. Preheat the oven to 400°F. Place the ball of dough on a flour-dusted work surface, roll it out to 9 inches, and place it on a parchment-lined baking sheet.

2. Place the plums, the ½ cup of sugar, the lemon juice, cornstarch, and salt in a mixing bowl and stir until the plums are evenly coated.

3. Spread the jam over the crust, making sure to leave a 1½-inch border. Distribute the plum mixture on top of the jam and fold the crust over it. Brush the folded-over crust with the beaten egg and sprinkle it with the remaining sugar.

4. Put the galette in the oven and bake until the crust is golden brown and the filling is bubbly, about 35 to 40 minutes. Remove from the oven and allow to cool before serving.

Pecan Pie

YIELD: 1 PIE | **ACTIVE TIME:** 20 MINUTES | **TOTAL TIME:** 1 HOUR AND 30 MINUTES

1 CUP LIGHT CORN SYRUP

1 CUP PACKED DARK BROWN SUGAR

3 EGGS, LIGHTLY BEATEN

6 TABLESPOONS UNSALTED BUTTER, MELTED

½ TEASPOON FINE SEA SALT

1 CUP PECAN HALVES

1 PERFECT PIECRUST (SEE PAGE 496)

ALL-PURPOSE FLOUR, AS NEEDED

1. Preheat the oven to 350°F. Coat a 9-inch pie plate with nonstick cooking spray. Place all of the ingredients, except for the piecrust and flour, in a large mixing bowl and stir to combine. Set the filling aside.

2. Roll out the piecrust on a flour-dusted work surface. Place the dough in the pie plate, trim the edges, and then crimp the crust. Place the crust in the refrigerator for 15 minutes.

3. Pour the filling into the crust. Place the pie in the oven and bake until the crust is golden brown and the filling is set, 45 to 50 minutes. Remove from the oven and let cool completely before serving.

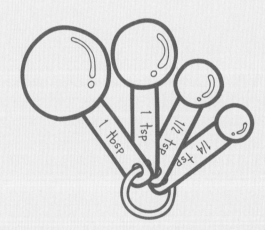

Boston Cream Pie

YIELD: 1 PIE | **ACTIVE TIME:** 45 MINUTES | **TOTAL TIME:** 2 HOURS AND 30 MINUTES

6½ OZ. ALL-PURPOSE FLOUR

1½ TEASPOONS BAKING POWDER

½ TEASPOON KOSHER SALT

3 EGGS

½ LB. SUGAR

½ CUP MILK

3 OZ. UNSALTED BUTTER

2 TEASPOONS PURE VANILLA EXTRACT

PASTRY CREAM (SEE PAGE 512)

½ CUP HEAVY CREAM

1 TABLESPOON LIGHT CORN SYRUP

4 OZ. DARK CHOCOLATE (55 TO 65 PERCENT)

1. Preheat the oven to 350°F. Line two round 9-inch cake pans with parchment paper and coat them with nonstick cooking spray.

2. Sift the flour, baking powder, and salt into a bowl. Set the mixture aside.

3. In the work bowl of a stand mixer fitted with the whisk attachment, whip the eggs and sugar on high until the mixture is pale and thick, about 5 minutes.

4. Reduce the speed to low, add the dry mixture, and beat until incorporated.

5. Combine the milk and butter in a small saucepan and warm over medium heat until the butter has melted. Whisk in the vanilla and remove the pan from heat. With the mixer running on low, add the milk mixture to the work bowl and beat the mixture until it comes together as a smooth batter.

6. Divide the batter between the cake pans. Bang the pans on the countertop to spread the batter and to remove any possible air bubbles.

7. Place the cakes in the oven and bake until they are lightly golden brown and baked through, 35 to 40 minutes. Insert a cake tester in the center of each cake to check for doneness.

8. Remove the cakes from the oven and place them on a cooling rack. Let them cool completely.

9. Trim a thin layer off the top of each cake to create a flat surface.

10. Place one cake on a cake stand. Place 1 cup of the Pastry Cream in the center and spread it with an offset spatula. Place the second cake on top.

11. Combine the heavy cream and corn syrup in a saucepan and bring it to a boil, stirring to dissolve the corn syrup. Remove the pan from heat and add the dark chocolate. Stir until the chocolate has melted and the mixture is smooth. Let the ganache cool for 10 minutes.

12. Pour the ganache over the cake and spread it to the edge, allowing some ganache to drip down the side. Let the cake rest for 20 minutes before slicing.

Chocolate Cream Pie

YIELD: 1 PIE | **ACTIVE TIME:** 10 MINUTES | **TOTAL TIME:** 1 HOUR AND 10 MINUTES

6 CUPS CHOCOLATE PUDDING (SEE PAGE 387)

1 PERFECT PIECRUST (SEE PAGE 496), BLIND BAKED

2 CUPS CHANTILLY CREAM (SEE PAGE 518)

CHOCOLATE SHAVINGS, RASPBERRIES, OR SLICED STRAWBERRIES, FOR GARNISH

1. Place the pudding in the piecrust, smooth the top with a rubber spatula, and cover with plastic wrap. Refrigerate for 1 hour.

2. When ready to serve, spread the Chantilly Cream on top of the filling in a thick layer. Garnish with the chocolate shavings, raspberries, or strawberries, if desired.

PASTRIES

Canelés

YIELD: 18 CANELÉS | **ACTIVE TIME:** 1 HOUR | **TOTAL TIME:** 48 HOURS

FOR THE PASTRIES

17.1 OZ. WHOLE MILK

1¾ OZ. CULTURED BUTTER, SOFTENED

1 VANILLA BEAN

3½ OZ. ALL-PURPOSE FLOUR

7 OZ. SUGAR

PINCH OF FINE SEA SALT

2 EGGS

2 EGG YOLKS

1¾ OZ. DARK RUM OR COGNAC

FOR THE MOLDS

1¾ OZ. BEESWAX

1¾ OZ. UNSALTED BUTTER

1. To begin preparations for the pastries, place the milk and butter in a saucepan. Scrape the vanilla bean's seeds into the saucepan, and add the pod as well. Place the pan over medium heat and bring the mixture to a simmer. Immediately remove the pan from heat and let it sit for 10 minutes.

2. In a large mixing bowl, whisk the flour, sugar, and salt together. Set the mixture aside. Place the eggs and egg yolks in a heatproof mixing bowl and whisk to combine, making sure not to add any air to the mixture.

3. While whisking, add the milk mixture in small increments. When all of the milk mixture has been thoroughly incorporated, whisk in the rum or Cognac.

4. Remove the vanilla bean pod and reserve. While whisking, add the tempered eggs to the dry mixture and whisk until just combined, taking care not to overwork the mixture. Strain the custard through a fine sieve. If the mixture is still warm, place the bowl in an ice bath until it has cooled to room temperature.

5. Add the vanilla bean pod to the custard, cover it with plastic wrap, and refrigerate for at least 24 hours; however, 48 hours is strongly recommended.

6. Preheat the oven to 500°F. To prepare the molds, grate the beeswax into a mason jar and add the butter. Place the jar in a saucepan filled with a few inches of water and bring the water to a simmer. When the beeswax mixture is melted and combined, pour it into one mold, immediately pour it back into the jar, and set the mold, right side up, on a wire rack to drain. When all of the molds have been coated, place them in the freezer for 15 minutes. Remove the custard from the refrigerator and let it come to room temperature.

7. Pour the custard into the molds so that they are filled about 85 percent of the way. Place the filled molds, upside down, on a baking sheet, place them in the oven, and bake for 10 minutes. Reduce the oven's temperature to 375°F and bake until they are a deep brown, about 40 minutes. Turn the canelès out onto a wire rack and let them cool completely before enjoying. Reheat the beeswax mixture and let the molds cool before refilling them with the remaining batter.

Sufganiyot

YIELD: 20 SUFGANIYOT | **ACTIVE TIME:** 45 MINUTES | **TOTAL TIME:** 3 HOURS

3½ TABLESPOONS UNSALTED BUTTER, CHOPPED, PLUS MORE AS NEEDED

3½ CUPS ALL-PURPOSE FLOUR, PLUS MORE AS NEEDED

½ TEASPOON FINE SEA SALT

¼ CUP SUGAR

1 TABLESPOON INSTANT YEAST

1 EGG

1¼ CUPS LUKEWARM MILK (85°F)

AVOCADO OIL, AS NEEDED

½ CUP STRAWBERRY JAM

¼ CUP CONFECTIONERS' SUGAR, FOR TOPPING

1. Coat a mixing bowl with some butter and set it aside. Sift the flour into the work bowl of a stand mixer fitted with the dough hook. Add the salt, sugar, and yeast and stir to incorporate.

2. Add the egg and butter to the mixture and mix to incorporate. Gradually add the milk and work the mixture until it comes together as a soft dough, 8 to 10 minutes.

3. Form the dough into a ball and place it in the buttered mixing bowl. Cover with a linen towel and let it rise until doubled in size, about 2 hours.

4. Line two baking sheets with parchment paper. Place the dough on a flour-dusted work surface and roll it out until it is about ¾ inch thick. Cut the dough into 2-inch circles, place them on the baking sheets, and cover with a linen towel. Let them rise for another 20 minutes.

5. Add avocado oil to a Dutch oven until it is about 2 inches deep and warm it to 325°F. Add the dough in batches of four and fry until golden brown, about 6 minutes, turning them over halfway through.

6. Drain the sufganiyot on a paper towel–lined plate. Fill a piping bag with the jam, and make a small slit on the top of each sufganiyah. Place the piping bag in the slit and fill until you see the filling coming back out. Sprinkle with the confectioners' sugar and enjoy.

Brioche Doughnuts

YIELD: 15 DOUGHNUTS | **ACTIVE TIME:** 1 HOUR | **TOTAL TIME:** 24 HOURS

1 CUP MILK

1 CUP WATER

2 TABLESPOONS ACTIVE DRY YEAST

4 OZ. SUGAR

¼ TEASPOON FRESHLY GRATED NUTMEG

1 EGG

1 EGG YOLK

28 OZ. BREAD FLOUR, PLUS MORE AS NEEDED

1 TEASPOON KOSHER SALT

3 OZ. UNSALTED BUTTER, SOFTENED

CANOLA OIL, AS NEEDED

HONEY GLAZE (SEE PAGE 519)

1. In the work bowl of a stand mixer, combine the milk, water, yeast, sugar, nutmeg, egg, and egg yolk.

2. Add the flour and salt, fit the mixer with the dough hook, and knead on low speed for 5 minutes.

3. Gradually add the butter and knead to incorporate. When all of the butter has been added, knead at low speed for 5 minutes.

4. Raise the speed to medium and knead until the dough starts to pull away from the sides of the bowl, about 6 minutes. Cover the bowl with plastic wrap and place it in the refrigerator overnight.

5. Add canola oil to a Dutch oven until it is about 2 inches deep and warm it to 350°F over medium heat. Set a cooling rack in a rimmed baking sheet beside the stove.

6. Remove the dough from the refrigerator and place it on a flour-dusted work surface. Roll the dough out until it is ½ inch thick. Cut out the doughnuts using a round 4-inch cookie cutter and then use a round 1-inch cookie cutter to cut out the centers. If you want to fill the doughnuts, leave the centers in the rounds.

7. Transfer the doughnuts to the wire rack and let them sit at room temperature for 10 minutes.

8. Working in batches, carefully place the doughnuts in the oil and fry, turning them once, until browned and cooked through, 2 to 4 minutes. Transfer the cooked doughnuts to the wire rack to drain and cool.

9. When the doughnuts have cooled, coat them in the glaze and enjoy.

Sfenj

YIELD: 15 SERVINGS | **ACTIVE TIME:** 40 MINUTES | **TOTAL TIME:** 3 HOURS

4 CUPS ALL-PURPOSE FLOUR

2 TEASPOONS INSTANT YEAST

1 TEASPOON FINE SEA SALT

1 TABLESPOON SUGAR

2 LARGE EGG YOLKS

1½ CUPS LUKEWARM WATER (90°F)

AVOCADO OIL, AS NEEDED

CONFECTIONERS' SUGAR OR HONEY, FOR TOPPING

1. Place the flour, yeast, salt, and sugar in a mixing bowl and stir to combine. Add the egg yolks and slowly drizzle in the water while mixing by hand.

2. Knead the mixture until it comes together as a sticky, smooth, and soft dough.

3. Spray the dough with nonstick cooking spray and cover the bowl with plastic wrap. Let the dough rise at room temperature for 2 hours.

4. Coat a large baking sheet with some avocado oil. Set it aside.

5. Divide the dough into 15 parts, roll each piece into a ball, and place it on the greased baking sheet. Cover the balls of dough with a slightly damp linen towel and let them rise for another 30 minutes.

6. Add avocado oil to a large, deep skillet until it is one-third to halfway full and warm it to 375°F.

7. Using your forefinger and thumb, make a hole in the center of the dough balls and gently slip them into the hot oil. Fry until lightly golden brown all over, turning the sfenj as necessary.

8. Top the fried sfenj with confectioners' sugar or honey and enjoy immediately.

Sfenj

SEE PAGE 297

Mille-Feuille

YIELD: 6 SERVINGS | **ACTIVE TIME:** 20 MINUTES | **TOTAL TIME:** 45 MINUTES

2 SHEETS OF FROZEN PUFF PASTRY, THAWED

CONFECTIONERS' SUGAR, FOR DUSTING

PASTRY CREAM (SEE PAGE 512)

ZEST OF 1 ORANGE

1 TABLESPOON GRAND MARNIER

1 PINT OF FRESH RASPBERRIES

1. Preheat the oven to 400°F and line two baking sheets with parchment paper. Roll out the sheets of puff pastry and place each one on a baking sheet. Dust the sheets generously with confectioners' sugar, place them in the oven, and bake for 12 to 15 minutes, until golden brown. Remove from the oven, transfer to a wire rack, and let cool.

2. Place the Pastry Cream in a bowl, add the orange zest and Grand Marnier, and fold to incorporate. Transfer the mixture into a piping bag fitted with a plain tip and place it in the refrigerator to chill while the puff pastry continues to cool.

3. Divide each sheet of the cooled puff pastry into 3 equal portions. Remove the piping bag from the refrigerator and place a thick layer of cream on one of the pieces of puff pastry. Dot the edges of the cream with the raspberries and press down on them gently. Fill the space between the raspberries with more of the cream and place another piece of puff pastry on top. Repeat the process with the cream and raspberries, and then place the last piece of puff pastry on top. Carefully cut into the desired number of portions and serve.

Beignets

YIELD: 15 BEIGNETS | **ACTIVE TIME:** 1 HOUR | **TOTAL TIME:** 24 HOURS

1½ CUPS MILK

2 EGGS

2 EGG YOLKS

½ CUP SUGAR

4 OZ. UNSALTED BUTTER, MELTED

2 TABLESPOONS ACTIVE DRY YEAST

25 OZ. ALL-PURPOSE FLOUR, PLUS MORE AS NEEDED

1¼ TEASPOONS KOSHER SALT

CANOLA OIL, AS NEEDED

1 CUP CONFECTIONERS' SUGAR, FOR DUSTING

1. In the work bowl of a stand mixer fitted with the paddle attachment, combine the milk, eggs, egg yolks, sugar, and butter and beat on medium speed for 2 minutes.

2. Add the yeast, flour, and salt and beat until the mixture comes together as a dough, about 5 minutes.

3. Coat a medium heatproof bowl with nonstick cooking spray, transfer the dough to the bowl, and cover with plastic wrap. Refrigerate overnight.

4. Add canola oil to a Dutch oven until it is about 2 inches deep and warm it to 350°F over medium heat. Set a paper towel–lined baking sheet beside the stove.

5. Remove the dough from the refrigerator and place it on a flour-dusted work surface. Roll the dough out until it is ½ inch thick. Cut the dough into 2-inch squares.

6. Working in batches, carefully slip the beignets into the canola oil and fry, turning them once, until browned and cooked through, 2 minutes. Transfer the cooked doughnuts to the baking sheet to drain and cool.

7. When the beignets have cooled, dust them generously with the confectioners' sugar and enjoy.

Eclairs

YIELD: 12 ECLAIRS | **ACTIVE TIME:** 40 MINUTES | **TOTAL TIME:** 1 HOUR AND 30 MINUTES

17 OZ. WATER

8½ OZ. UNSALTED BUTTER

1 TEASPOON FINE SEA SALT

2.4 OZ. SUGAR

12½ OZ. ALL-PURPOSE FLOUR

6 EGGS

PASTRY CREAM (SEE PAGE 512)

CHOCOLATE GANACHE (SEE PAGE 523), WARM

1. Preheat the oven to 425°F and line two baking sheets with parchment paper. In a medium saucepan, combine the water, butter, salt, and sugar and warm the mixture over medium heat until the butter is melted.

2. Add the flour to the pan and use a rubber spatula or wooden spoon to fold the mixture until it comes together as a thick, shiny dough, taking care not to let the dough burn.

3. Transfer the dough to the work bowl of a stand mixer fitted with the paddle attachment and beat on medium speed until the dough is no longer steaming and the bowl is just warm to the touch, at least 10 minutes.

4. Incorporate the eggs two at a time, scraping down the work bowl between each addition. Transfer the dough to a piping bag fit with a plain tip. Pipe 12 eclairs onto the baking sheets, leaving 1½ inches between them. They should be approximately 5 inches long.

5. Place the eclairs in the oven and bake for 10 minutes. Lower the oven's temperature to 325°F and bake until golden brown and a cake tester inserted into their centers comes out clean, 20 to 25 minutes. Remove from the oven and let them cool on a wire rack.

6. Fill a piping bag with the Pastry Cream and fit the piping bag with a plain tip.

7. Using a paring knife, cut 3 small slits on the undersides of the eclairs and fill them with the Pastry Cream.

8. Carefully dip the top halves of the eclairs in the ganache, or drizzle the ganache over the pastries. Allow the chocolate to set before serving.

Apple Dutch Baby

YIELD: 4 SERVINGS | **ACTIVE TIME:** 20 MINUTES | **TOTAL TIME:** 1 HOUR

4 TABLESPOONS UNSALTED BUTTER

2 FIRM AND TART APPLES, PEELED, CORES REMOVED, SLICED

¼ CUP PLUS 3 TABLESPOONS SUGAR

1 TABLESPOON CINNAMON

¾ CUP ALL-PURPOSE FLOUR

¼ TEASPOON FINE SEA SALT

¾ CUP MILK

4 EGGS

1 TEASPOON PURE VANILLA EXTRACT

CONFECTIONERS' SUGAR, FOR DUSTING

1. Preheat the oven to 425°F and place a rack in the middle position. Warm a cast-iron skillet over medium-high heat. Add the butter and apples to the pan and cook, stirring frequently, until the apples start to soften, 3 to 4 minutes. Add the ¼ cup of sugar and the cinnamon and cook, stirring occasionally, for another 3 or 4 minutes. Distribute the apple mixture evenly over the bottom of the skillet and remove it from heat.

2. In a large bowl, mix the remaining sugar, flour, and salt together. In a smaller bowl, whisk together the milk, eggs, and vanilla extract. Add the wet mixture to the dry mixture and stir until the mixture comes together as a smooth batter. Pour the batter over the apples.

3. Put the skillet in the oven and bake until the baby is puffy and golden brown, about 20 minutes. Remove the skillet from the oven and let it cool for a few minutes.

4. Run a knife along the edge of the skillet to loosen the baby, dust it with confectioners' sugar, and serve warm.

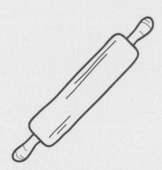

Eclairs
SEE PAGE 304

Croissant Dough

YIELD: DOUGH FOR 16 CROISSANTS | **ACTIVE TIME:** 2 HOURS | **TOTAL TIME:** 12 HOURS

FOR THE DOUGH

2 TABLESPOONS ACTIVE
DRY YEAST

1 CUP WATER

1 CUP MILK

2 OZ. SUGAR

29 OZ. ALL-PURPOSE FLOUR,
PLUS MORE AS NEEDED

1 TABLESPOON PLUS 1
TEASPOON KOSHER SALT

11 OZ. UNSALTED BUTTER,
SOFTENED

FOR THE BUTTER BLOCK

1 LB. UNSALTED BUTTER,
SOFTENED

¼ CUP ALL-PURPOSE FLOUR

1. To begin preparations for the dough, place the yeast, water, and milk in the work bowl of a stand mixer fitted with the dough hook, gently stir, and let the mixture sit until it starts to foam, about 10 minutes.

2. Add the sugar, flour, and salt and knead the mixture on low until it comes together as a dough, about 5 minutes. Add the butter, continue to knead on low for 2 minutes, and then raise the speed to medium. Knead until the dough is smooth and the butter has been entirely incorporated, 6 to 7 minutes.

3. Spray a mixing bowl with nonstick cooking spray. Transfer the dough to the bowl, cover it with plastic wrap, and chill it in the refrigerator for 3 hours.

4. While the croissant dough is resting, prepare the butter block. Fit the stand mixer with the paddle attachment, add the butter and flour, and beat the mixture until smooth. Transfer the mixture to a Silpat mat that is in a baking sheet. Use a small spatula to spread the mixture into a 7 x 10–inch rectangle. Place the baking sheet in the refrigerator for 30 minutes to 1 hour. You want the butter block to be firm but pliable. If the butter block is too firm for the following steps, let the butter sit at room temperature for a few minutes.

5. Remove the dough from the refrigerator, place it on a flour-dusted work surface, and roll it into a 10 x 20–inch rectangle.

6. Place the butter block in the center of the dough. Fold the dough over the butter block like a letter, folding a third of the dough from the left side of the dough and a third from the right so that they meet in the center. Pinch the seam to seal.

7. Turn the dough 90 degrees clockwise and flip it over so that the seam is facing down. Roll out the dough into a 10 x 20–inch rectangle. Make another letter fold of the dough, place the dough on the Silpat mat, and cover it with plastic wrap. Chill in the refrigerator for 1 hour.

8. Place the dough on a flour-dusted work surface, roll it into a 10 x 20–inch rectangle, and fold the dough like a letter, lengthwise. Pinch the seam to seal, turn the dough 90 degrees clockwise, and flip the dough over so that the seam is facing down. Place the dough back on the baking sheet, cover it in plastic wrap, and refrigerate for 1 hour.

9. Place the dough on a flour-dusted work surface, roll it into a 10 x 20–inch rectangle, and fold the dough like a letter, lengthwise. Pinch the seam to seal, turn the dough 90 degrees clockwise, and flip the dough over so that the seam is facing down. Place the dough back on the baking sheet, cover it in plastic wrap, and refrigerate for 4 hours. After this period of rest, the dough will be ready to make croissants with.

Almond Croissants

YIELD: 16 CROISSANTS | **ACTIVE TIME:** 30 MINUTES | **TOTAL TIME:** 2 HOURS

FRANGIPANE (SEE PAGE 504)

CROISSANT DOUGH (SEE PAGE 308)

ALL-PURPOSE FLOUR, AS NEEDED

1 EGG, BEATEN

2 CUPS SLICED ALMONDS

CONFECTIONERS' SUGAR, FOR DUSTING

1. Line two baking sheets with parchment paper. Place the Frangipane in a piping bag and set aside.

2. Place the dough on a flour-dusted work surface and roll it into an 8 x 20–inch rectangle. Using a pizza cutter or chef 's knife, cut the dough horizontally in the center so that you have two 4 x 20–inch rectangles. Cut each rectangle vertically into strips that are 5 inches wide.

3. Cut each rectangle diagonally, yielding 16 triangles. Gently roll out each triangle until it is 8 inches long.

4. Cut a hole in the piping bag and pipe about 3 tablespoons of Frangipane toward the wide side of each triangle. Spread the filling out a bit with an offset spatula.

5. Roll the croissants up tight, moving from the wide side of the triangle to the tip. Tuck the tip under each croissant. Place eight croissants on each of the baking sheets.

6. Cover the baking sheets with plastic wrap and let the croissants rest at room temperature for 1 hour.

7. Preheat the oven to 375°F.

8. Remove the plastic wrap and brush the croissants with the beaten egg. Sprinkle the almonds over the croissants and press them down gently so that they adhere.

9. Place the croissants in the oven and bake until they are golden brown, 20 to 22 minutes.

10. Remove the croissants from the oven and place them on wire racks. Let the croissants cool slightly before dusting them with confectioners' sugar and enjoying.

Sweet Empanadas

YIELD: 12 EMPANADAS | **ACTIVE TIME:** 30 MINUTES | **TOTAL TIME:** 2 HOURS

FOR THE DOUGH

4 CUPS SIFTED ALL-PURPOSE FLOUR, PLUS MORE AS NEEDED

3 TABLESPOONS PLUS 1 TEASPOON SUGAR

1 TEASPOON KOSHER SALT

¾ CUP SHORTENING

2 TABLESPOONS UNSALTED BUTTER, CHILLED

2 EGG YOLKS

1 CUP COLD WATER, PLUS MORE AS NEEDED

FOR THE FILLING

1 (14 OZ.) CAN OF PUMPKIN PUREE

½ CUP SUGAR

1 TEASPOON CINNAMON

1 EGG WHITE, BEATEN

1. To begin preparations for the dough, place the flour in a large mixing bowl and add the sugar, salt, shortening, and butter. Work the mixture with a pastry blender until it resembles coarse bread crumbs.

2. Combine the egg yolks and water in a separate mixing bowl and add to the flour mixture a little at a time until it comes together as a dough, whisking to incorporate. Knead the dough until it is smooth but slightly shaggy, adding more water or flour as needed. Cover the dough in plastic wrap and chill in the refrigerator for about 1 hour.

3. Preheat the oven to 350°F and line a baking sheet with parchment paper. Roll out the dough on a floured surface to about ¼ inch thick. Cut it into 5-inch circles.

4. To prepare the filling, place the pumpkin, sugar, and cinnamon in a mixing bowl and stir until combined.

5. Place about 2 tablespoons of the filling in the bottom-middle half of each circle, fold the circles into half-moons, and crimp the edge to seal.

6. Place the empanadas on the baking sheet, brush the tops with the egg white, and place them in the oven. Bake until golden brown, 20 to 25 minutes.

7. Remove the empanadas from the oven and briefly cool on wire racks before serving.

Almond Croissants
SEE PAGE 310

Apple Cider Doughnuts

YIELD: 12 DOUGHNUTS | **ACTIVE TIME:** 1 HOUR | **TOTAL TIME:** 24 HOURS

1¼ CUPS APPLE CIDER

2 EGGS

1 EGG YOLK

½ CUP UNSALTED BUTTER, MELTED

6 OZ. LIGHT BROWN SUGAR

2½ TEASPOONS BAKING POWDER

1 TEASPOON BAKING SODA

1 TEASPOON KOSHER SALT

½ TEASPOON PLUS 1 TABLESPOON CINNAMON

½ TEASPOON FRESHLY GRATED NUTMEG

½ TEASPOON CARDAMOM

½ TEASPOON ALLSPICE

19 OZ. ALL-PURPOSE FLOUR, PLUS MORE AS NEEDED

1.4 OZ. WHOLE WHEAT FLOUR

CANOLA OIL, AS NEEDED

2 CUPS SUGAR

1. In the work bowl of a stand mixer fitted with the paddle attachment, combine the apple cider, eggs, egg yolk, butter, and brown sugar and beat on medium speed for 2 minutes.

2. Add the baking powder, baking soda, salt, ½ teaspoon of the cinnamon, the nutmeg, cardamom, allspice, and flours and beat until the mixture comes together as a dough, about 5 minutes.

3. Coat a medium heatproof bowl with nonstick cooking spray, transfer the dough to the bowl, and cover with plastic wrap. Refrigerate overnight.

4. Add canola oil to a Dutch oven until it is about 2 inches deep and warm it to 350°F. Set a cooling rack in a rimmed baking sheet beside the stove.

5. Remove the dough from the refrigerator and place it on a flour-dusted work surface. Roll the dough out until it is ½ inch thick. Cut out the doughnuts using a round 4-inch cookie cutter and then use a round 1-inch cookie cutter to cut out the centers.

6. Transfer the doughnuts to the wire rack and let them sit at room temperature for 10 minutes.

7. Working in batches, carefully slip the doughnuts into the hot oil and fry, turning them once, until browned and cooked through, 2 to 4 minutes. Transfer the cooked doughnuts to the wire rack to drain and cool.

8. Place the sugar and remaining cinnamon in a small bowl and stir to combine.

9. When the doughnuts have cooled, toss them in the cinnamon sugar and serve.

Apple Strudel

YIELD: 6 SERVINGS | **ACTIVE TIME:** 25 MINUTES | **TOTAL TIME:** 1 HOUR AND 30 MINUTES

¾ LB. APPLES, PEELED, CORES REMOVED, CHOPPED

¼ TEASPOON LEMON ZEST

1 TEASPOON FRESH LEMON JUICE

1½ TABLESPOONS SUGAR

DASH OF CINNAMON

¼ TEASPOON GROUND GINGER

2 PINCHES OF FINE SEA SALT

4 TABLESPOONS UNSALTED BUTTER, MELTED

7 SHEETS OF FROZEN PHYLLO DOUGH, THAWED

1 TABLESPOON CONFECTIONERS' SUGAR, PLUS MORE FOR DUSTING

1. Preheat the oven to 350°F and line a baking sheet with parchment paper. Place the apples, lemon zest, lemon juice, sugar, cinnamon, ginger, and a pinch of salt in a large mixing bowl and toss until the apples are evenly coated. Place the mixture in a skillet and cook over medium heat until the apples begin to release their liquid. Remove the pan from heat and let it cool for 10 minutes before draining the mixture.

2. Place the melted butter in a bowl and stir in the remaining salt.

3. Brush a sheet of phyllo dough with some of the salted butter and lightly dust it with some of the confectioners' sugar. Repeat with the remaining sheets of phyllo dough, stacking them on top of one another after they have been dressed.

4. Place the apple mixture in the center of the phyllo sheets, leaving a 2-inch border of dough on the sides. Fold the border over the filling so that the edges overlap and gently press down to seal.

5. Place the strudel on the baking sheet, place it in the oven, and bake, rotating the sheet halfway through, until the strudel is golden brown, 30 to 40 minutes. Remove the strudel from the oven, transfer it to a cutting board, and let it cool slightly. Slice the strudel into the desired portions and dust with additional confectioners' sugar before serving.

Chocolate Cake Doughnuts

YIELD: 12 DOUGHNUTS | **ACTIVE TIME:** 1 HOUR | **TOTAL TIME:** 24 HOURS

6 OZ. SUGAR

2 TABLESPOONS UNSALTED BUTTER, SOFTENED

3 EGG YOLKS

10.8 OZ. SOUR CREAM

11.4 OZ. ALL-PURPOSE FLOUR, PLUS MORE AS NEEDED

2.9 OZ. COCOA POWDER

2 TEASPOONS BAKING POWDER

1 TABLESPOON KOSHER SALT

CANOLA OIL, AS NEEDED

CHOCOLATE GANACHE (SEE PAGE 523), WARM

1. In the work bowl of a stand mixer fitted with the paddle attachment, cream the sugar and butter on medium speed until light and fluffy, about 5 minutes.

2. Incorporate the egg yolks one at a time, scraping down the work bowl as needed. When all of the egg yolks have been incorporated, add the sour cream and beat until incorporated. Add the flour, cocoa powder, baking powder, and salt and beat until the mixture comes together as a dough.

3. Coat a medium heatproof bowl with nonstick cooking spray, transfer the dough to the bowl, and cover with plastic wrap. Refrigerate overnight.

4. Add canola oil to a Dutch oven until it is about 2 inches deep and warm it to 350°F. Set a cooling rack in a rimmed baking sheet beside the stove.

5. Remove the dough from the refrigerator and place it on a flour-dusted work surface. Roll the dough out until it is ½ inch thick. Cut out the doughnuts using a round 4-inch cookie cutter and then use a round 1-inch cookie cutter to cut out the centers.

6. Transfer the doughnuts to the wire rack and let them sit at room temperature for 10 minutes.

7. Working in batches, carefully slip the doughnuts into the hot oil and fry, turning them once, until browned and cooked through, about 4 minutes. A cake tester inserted into the sides of the doughnuts should come out clean. Transfer the cooked doughnuts to the wire rack to drain and cool.

8. When cool, dip the top half of the doughnuts in the ganache, place them on a piece of parchment paper, and let the chocolate set before enjoying.

Danish Dough

YIELD: DOUGH FOR 20 DANISHES | **ACTIVE TIME:** 2 HOURS | **TOTAL TIME:** 12 HOURS

FOR THE DOUGH

11 OZ. MILK

1 TABLESPOON ACTIVE DRY YEAST

2 EGGS

2 OZ. SUGAR

22 OZ. ALL-PURPOSE FLOUR, PLUS MORE AS NEEDED

1 TABLESPOON KOSHER SALT

FOR THE BUTTER BLOCK

1 LB. UNSALTED BUTTER, SOFTENED

¼ CUP ALL-PURPOSE FLOUR

1. To begin preparations for the dough, place the milk and yeast in the work bowl of a stand mixer fitted with the dough hook, gently stir, and let the mixture sit until it starts to foam, about 10 minutes.

2. Add the eggs, sugar, flour, and salt and knead the mixture on low until it comes together as a smooth dough, about 5 minutes.

3. Spray a mixing bowl with nonstick cooking spray. Transfer the dough to the bowl, cover it with plastic wrap, and chill it in the refrigerator for 3 hours.

4. While the dough is resting, prepare the butter block. Fit the stand mixer with the paddle attachment, add the butter and flour, and beat the mixture until smooth. Transfer the mixture to a Silpat mat that is in a baking sheet. Use a small spatula to spread the mixture into a 7 x 10–inch rectangle. Place the baking sheet in the refrigerator for 30 minutes to 1 hour. You want the butter block to be firm but pliable. If the butter block is too firm for the following steps, let the butter sit at room temperature for a few minutes.

5. Remove the dough from the refrigerator, place it on a flour-dusted work surface, and roll it into a 10 x 20–inch rectangle.

6. Place the butter block in the center of the dough. Fold the dough over the butter block like a letter, folding a third of the dough from the left side of the dough and a third from the right so that they meet in the center. Pinch the seam to seal.

7. Turn the dough 90 degrees clockwise and flip it over so that the seam is facing down. Roll out the dough into a 10 x 20–inch rectangle. Make another letter fold of the dough, place the dough on the Silpat mat, and cover it with plastic wrap. Chill it in the refrigerator for 1 hour.

8. Place the dough on a flour-dusted work surface, roll it into a 10 x 20–inch rectangle, and fold the dough like a letter, lengthwise. Pinch the seam to seal, turn the dough 90 degrees clockwise, and flip the dough over so that the seam is facing down. Place the dough back on the baking sheet, cover it in plastic wrap, and refrigerate for 1 hour.

9. Place the dough on a flour-dusted work surface, roll it into a 10 x 20–inch rectangle, and fold the dough like a letter, lengthwise. Pinch the seam to seal, turn the dough 90 degrees clockwise, and flip the dough over so that the seam is facing down. Place the dough back on the baking sheet, cover it in plastic wrap, and refrigerate for 4 hours. After this period of rest, the dough will be ready to make danish with.

Cinnamon Apple Danish

YIELD: 16 DANISH | **ACTIVE TIME:** 30 MINUTES | **TOTAL TIME:** 2 HOURS

4 GRANNY SMITH APPLES, PEELED, CORE REMOVED, SLICED

1 TABLESPOON LIGHT BROWN SUGAR

2 TEASPOONS CINNAMON

DANISH DOUGH (SEE OPPOSITE PAGE)

ALL-PURPOSE FLOUR, AS NEEDED

PASTRY CREAM (SEE PAGE 512)

1 EGG, BEATEN

APRICOT GLAZE (SEE PAGE 537)

1. Line two baking sheets with parchment paper. Place the apples in a small bowl with the brown sugar and cinnamon and toss to coat.

2. Place the dough on a flour-dusted work surface and roll it into a 12-inch square. Using a pizza cutter or chef's knife, slice the dough into sixteen 3-inch squares.

3. To make the classic, frame-shaped danish, fold the squares into triangles. Make two diagonal cuts about ¼ inch inside from the edge of the triangles' short sides.

4. Open the triangle, take one edge of the "frame," and fold it over to the cut on the opposite side. Repeat with the other edge of the frame.

5. Place eight danish on each baking sheet. Place 2 tablespoons of Pastry Cream in the center of each danish and top the cream with 4 to 5 slices of apple.

6. Cover the baking sheets with plastic wrap and let the danish rest at room temperature for 45 minutes.

7. Preheat the oven to 375°F.

8. Brush the danish with the beaten egg, place them in the oven, and bake until they are golden brown, 15 to 20 minutes.

9. Remove the danish from the oven and place them on wire racks to cool for 10 minutes. Brush the tops of the danish with the glaze and let it set before enjoying.

Pain au Chocolat

YIELD: 16 CROISSANTS | **ACTIVE TIME:** 30 MINUTES | **TOTAL TIME:** 2 HOURS

CROISSANT DOUGH (SEE PAGE 308)

ALL-PURPOSE FLOUR, AS NEEDED

2 CUPS DARK CHOCOLATE COINS (55 PERCENT), CHOPPED

1 EGG, BEATEN

CONFECTIONERS' SUGAR, FOR DUSTING

1. Line two baking sheets with parchment paper.

2. Place the dough on a flour-dusted work surface and roll it into an 8 x 20–inch rectangle. Using a pizza cutter or chef's knife, cut the dough horizontally in the center so that you have two 4 x 20–inch rectangles. Cut each rectangle vertically into strips that are 5 inches wide.

3. Cut each rectangle in half at its equator, yielding 16 rectangles. Gently roll out each rectangle until it is 8 inches long.

4. Place 2 tablespoons of chocolate on one end of each rectangle and roll the rectangles up tightly.

5. Place eight croissants on each of the baking sheets. Cover the baking sheets with plastic wrap and let the croissants rest at room temperature for 1 hour.

6. Preheat the oven to 375°F.

7. Remove the plastic wrap and brush the croissants with the beaten egg.

8. Place the croissants in the oven and bake until they are golden brown, 20 to 22 minutes.

9. Remove the croissants from the oven and place them on wire racks. Let the croissants cool slightly before dusting them with confectioners' sugar and enjoying.

Orejas

YIELD: 12 OREJAS | **ACTIVE TIME:** 15 MINUTES | **TOTAL TIME:** 1 HOUR

1 SHEET OF FROZEN PUFF PASTRY, THAWED

1 EGG WHITE, BEATEN

1 TEASPOON CINNAMON

½ CUP SUGAR

1. Preheat the oven to 425°F and line a baking sheet with parchment paper. Brush the puff pastry with some of the egg white.

2. Combine the cinnamon and sugar in a bowl and then sprinkle the mixture all over the puff pastry. Fold the short edges of the pastry inward until they meet in the middle. Brush lightly with the egg white and fold in half again until sealed together. Chill in the refrigerator for 15 to 20 minutes.

3. Cut the pastry into ½-inch-thick slices. Place the slices on the baking sheet, cut side up, so you can see the folds.

4. Place the orejas in the oven and bake until they are golden brown, 8 to 12 minutes. Remove from the oven and let them cool on wire racks before enjoying.

Buñuelos

YIELD: 12 PASTRIES | **ACTIVE TIME:** 20 MINUTES | **TOTAL TIME:** 1 HOUR

2 CUPS ALL-PURPOSE FLOUR, PLUS MORE AS NEEDED

1 TEASPOON BAKING POWDER

1 TABLESPOON SUGAR

½ TEASPOON KOSHER SALT

1 EGG

1 TABLESPOON UNSALTED BUTTER, MELTED AND COOLED

1 TEASPOON PURE VANILLA EXTRACT

WATER, AS NEEDED

CANOLA OIL, AS NEEDED

1. In a large mixing bowl, combine the flour, baking powder, sugar, and salt. Add the egg, melted butter, and vanilla and work the mixture until it resembles coarse bread crumbs.

2. Incorporate water 1 tablespoon at a time until the mixture comes together as a soft, smooth dough. Cover the mixing bowl with plastic wrap and let it rest for 30 minutes.

3. Divide the dough into 12 portions and roll them out as thin as possible, without breaking them, on a flour-dusted work surface.

4. Add canola oil to a Dutch oven until it is about 2 inches deep and warm it to 350°F. Working in batches to avoid crowding the pot, gently slip the buñuelos into the oil and fry until they are crispy and golden brown, about 2 minutes. Transfer to a paper towel–lined plate and let them drain before enjoying.

Churros

YIELD: 75 CHURROS | **ACTIVE TIME:** 25 MINUTES | **TOTAL TIME:** 30 MINUTES

CANOLA OIL, AS NEEDED

35¼ OZ. MILK

81.1 OZ. WATER

2.8 OZ. SUGAR, PLUS MORE TO TASTE

1.4 OZ. SALT

38.8 OZ. "00" FLOUR

38.8 OZ. ALL-PURPOSE FLOUR

32 EGGS

CINNAMON, TO TASTE

CHOCOLATE GANACHE (SEE PAGE 523), WARM, FOR SERVING

1. Add canola oil to a Dutch oven until it is about 2 inches deep and warm to 350°F. Place the milk, water, sugar, and salt in a large saucepan and bring it to a boil.

2. Gradually add the flours and cook, stirring constantly, until the mixture pulls away from the sides of the pan.

3. Place the mixture in the work bowl of a stand mixer fitted with the paddle attachment and beat until the dough is almost cool. Incorporate the eggs one at a time, scraping down the work bowl as needed.

4. Combine some cinnamon and sugar in a shallow dish and set the mixture aside. Place the dough in a piping bag fitted with a star tip. Pipe 6-inch lengths of dough into the oil and fry until they are golden brown. Place them on paper towel–lined plates to drain and cool slightly. Toss in cinnamon sugar and enjoy, or store the churros in the freezer.

5. To serve frozen churros, preheat the oven to 450°F. Remove the churros from the freezer and toss them in cinnamon sugar until they are coated. Place them in the oven and bake for 5 minutes. Remove them from the oven, toss them in cinnamon sugar again, and serve with the ganache.

Braided Blueberry & Cream Cheese Danish

YIELD: 2 LARGE DANISH | **ACTIVE TIME:** 30 MINUTES | **TOTAL TIME:** 2 HOURS AND 30 MINUTES

DANISH DOUGH (SEE PAGE 318)

ALL-PURPOSE FLOUR, AS NEEDED

CREAM CHEESE DANISH FILLING (SEE PAGE 537)

2 PINTS OF BLUEBERRIES

1 EGG, BEATEN

PEARL OR SANDING SUGAR, FOR TOPPING

1. Line two baking sheets with parchment paper. Remove the dough from the refrigerator and cut it in half. Cover one of the halves in plastic wrap and place it back in the refrigerator.

2. Place the dough on a flour-dusted work surface and roll it into an 8 x 12–inch rectangle. Transfer the dough to one of the baking sheets.

3. Spread 1 cup of the filling down the center of the dough, in a strip that is about 3 inches wide. Spread half of the blueberries over the filling.

4. Cut 10 slanting strips that are about 1 inch wide on each side of the filling. Fold the strips over each other, alternating between the sides. Fold the ends of the danish inward, so that they are under the braid.

5. Repeat the steps above with the second piece of dough.

6. Cover the baking sheets with plastic wrap and let the danish rest at room temperature for 45 minutes.

7. Place the danish in the refrigerator for 30 minutes. Preheat the oven to 375°F.

8. Gently brush the tops of the danish with the egg and sprinkle pearl sugar generously over them.

9. Place the danish in the oven and bake for 20 to 24 minutes or until they are golden brown.

10. Remove the danish from the oven and place them on a wire rack to cool for 10 minutes before slicing and serving.

Golden Peach & Almond Danish

YIELD: 16 DANISH | **ACTIVE TIME:** 30 MINUTES | **TOTAL TIME:** 2 HOURS

DANISH DOUGH (SEE PAGE 318)

ALL-PURPOSE FLOUR, AS NEEDED

FRANGIPANE (SEE PAGE 504)

4 GOLDEN PEACHES, PEELED, PITS REMOVED, SLICED

1 EGG, BEATEN

2 CUPS SLICED ALMONDS

APRICOT GLAZE (SEE PAGE 537)

1. Line two baking sheets with parchment paper. Place the dough on a flour-dusted work surface and roll it into a 12-inch square. Using a pizza cutter or chef's knife, slice the dough into sixteen 3-inch squares.

2. To make the square danish, fold the corners of the squares into the center and press down to seal. Place eight danish on each baking sheet.

3. Place 2 tablespoons of Frangipane in the center of each danish and top with 3 to 4 overlapping slices of peach.

4. Cover the baking sheets with plastic wrap and let the danish rest at room temperature for 45 minutes.

5. Preheat the oven to 375°F.

6. Brush the danish with the beaten egg, sprinkle the almonds over them, and gently press them down so that they adhere.

7. Place the danish in the oven and bake until they are golden brown, 15 to 20 minutes.

8. Remove the danish from the oven and place them on a wire rack to cool for 10 minutes. Brush the tops of the danish with the glaze and let it set before enjoying.

Raspberry Danish

YIELD: 16 DANISH | **ACTIVE TIME:** 30 MINUTES | **TOTAL TIME:** 2 HOURS

DANISH DOUGH (SEE PAGE 318)

ALL-PURPOSE FLOUR, AS NEEDED

RASPBERRY JAM (SEE PAGE 533)

1 EGG, BEATEN

VANILLA GLAZE (SEE PAGE 519)

1. Line two baking sheets with parchment paper. Place the dough on a flour-dusted work surface and roll it into a 12-inch square. Using a pizza cutter or chef's knife, slice the dough into sixteen 3-inch squares.

2. To make pinwheeled-shaped danish, make four cuts of equal length, starting from the corners and moving toward the center. Make sure to not cut all the way through the center. Make two diagonal cuts about ¼ inch inside from the edges of the triangles' short sides.

3. Fold the point of every other half toward the center and press down to seal. Place eight danish on each baking sheet. Place 1 tablespoon of jam in the center of each danish.

4. Cover the baking sheets with plastic wrap and let the danish rest at room temperature for 45 minutes.

5. Preheat the oven to 375°F.

6. Brush the danish with the beaten egg, place them in the oven, and bake until they are golden brown, 15 to 20 minutes.

7. Remove the danish from the oven and place them on wire racks to cool for 10 minutes. Brush the tops of the danish with the glaze and let it set before enjoying.

Paris-Brest

YIELD: 6 PASTRIES | **ACTIVE TIME:** 50 MINUTES | **TOTAL TIME:** 2 HOURS

17 OZ. WATER

8½ OZ. UNSALTED BUTTER

1 TEASPOON FINE SEA SALT

2.4 OZ. SUGAR

12½ OZ. ALL-PURPOSE FLOUR

7 EGGS

1 CUP SLIVERED ALMONDS

HAZELNUT MOUSSELINE (SEE PAGE 524)

CONFECTIONERS' SUGAR, FOR DUSTING

1. Preheat the oven to 425°F and line two baking sheets with parchment paper. In a medium saucepan, combine the water, butter, salt, and sugar and warm the mixture over medium heat until the butter is melted.

2. Add the flour to the pan and use a rubber spatula or wooden spoon to fold the mixture until it comes together as a thick, shiny dough, taking care not to let the dough burn.

3. Transfer the dough to the work bowl of a stand mixer fitted with the paddle attachment and beat on medium speed until the dough is no longer steaming and the bowl is just warm to the touch, at least 10 minutes.

4. Incorporate six of the eggs two at a time, scraping down the work bowl between each addition. Transfer the dough to a piping bag fit with an #867 tip (this will be called a "French Star Tip" on occasion).

5. Pipe a 5-inch ring of dough onto a baking sheet and then pipe another ring inside the first ring. Pipe another ring atop the seam between the first two rings. Repeat until all of the dough has been used.

6. In a small bowl, whisk the remaining egg and brush the tops of the dough with it. Arrange the almonds on top and gently press down to ensure they adhere.

7. Place the pastries in the oven and bake for 10 minutes. Lower the oven's temperature to 300°F and bake until golden brown and a cake tester inserted into each one comes out clean, 30 to 35 minutes. Remove from the oven and let them cool on a wire rack.

8. Place the mousseline in a piping bag fit with a plain tip. Using a serrated knife, slice the pastries in half along their equators. Pipe rosettes of the mousseline around the inside. Place the top half of the pastries on top, dust them with confectioners' sugar, and enjoy.

Paris-Brest
SEE PAGE 327

Apple Turnovers

YIELD: 4 SERVINGS | **ACTIVE TIME:** 25 MINUTES | **TOTAL TIME:** 1 HOUR AND 15 MINUTES

2 APPLES, PEELED, CORES REMOVED, CHOPPED

¾ CUP SUGAR

1 TABLESPOON FRESH LEMON JUICE

PINCH OF FINE SEA SALT

¼ CUP APPLESAUCE

1 SHEET OF FROZEN PUFF PASTRY, THAWED

ALL-PURPOSE FLOUR, AS NEEDED

1 TEASPOON CINNAMON

SANDING SUGAR, FOR TOPPING

1. Preheat the oven to 375°F and line a baking sheet with parchment paper. Place the apples, 10 tablespoons of the sugar, the lemon juice, and salt in a food processor and pulse until the apples are minced. Strain the juice into a bowl through a fine sieve, reserve the juice, and place the solids in another small bowl. Stir in the applesauce and let the mixture sit for 5 minutes.

2. Place the sheet of puff pastry on a flour-dusted work surface and cut it into quarters. Place 2 tablespoons of the apple mixture in the middle of each quarter and brush the edges with some of the reserved liquid. Fold a bottom corner of each quarter to the opposing top corner and crimp to seal. Place the sealed pastries on a platter and chill them in the refrigerator for 10 minutes.

3. Place the remaining sugar and the cinnamon in a small bowl and stir to combine.

4. Place the turnovers on the baking sheet and brush the tops with some of the reserved liquid. Sprinkle the cinnamon-and-sugar mixture over the turnovers, place the sheet in the oven, and bake, rotating the baking sheet halfway through, until the turnovers are golden brown, about 25 minutes.

5. Remove the turnovers from the oven, transfer them to wire racks, sprinkle sanding sugar over the top, and let the turnovers cool before enjoying.

Cinnamon Twists

YIELD: 24 TWISTS | **ACTIVE TIME:** 15 MINUTES | **TOTAL TIME:** 30 MINUTES

2 SHEETS OF FROZEN PUFF PASTRY, THAWED

1 CUP SUGAR

3½ TABLESPOONS CINNAMON

1 TEASPOON FRESHLY GRATED NUTMEG

1 EGG

1 CUP CARAMEL SAUCE (SEE PAGE 529), WARMED, FOR SERVING

1. Preheat the oven to 375°F, line a baking sheet with parchment paper, and roll out the sheets of puff pastry. Combine the sugar, cinnamon, and nutmeg in a mixing bowl. Beat the egg in a separate bowl.

2. Lightly brush the top of each pastry sheet with the egg and then sprinkle the sugar-and-spice mixture evenly across both sheets of puff pastry.

3. Cut the pastries into long strips and twist them. Place the strips on the baking sheet and bake until golden brown, 10 to 15 minutes. Remove from the oven, flip each pastry over, and bake for an additional 2 to 3 minutes.

4. Remove the twists from the oven and let cool until just slightly warm. Serve with the Caramel Sauce on the side.

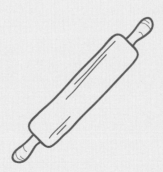

Red Velvet Doughnuts

YIELD: 12 DOUGHNUTS | **ACTIVE TIME:** 1 HOUR | **TOTAL TIME:** 24 HOURS

6 OZ. SUGAR

1 OZ. UNSALTED BUTTER, SOFTENED

3 EGG YOLKS

10.8 OZ. SOUR CREAM

12.9 OZ. ALL-PURPOSE FLOUR, PLUS MORE AS NEEDED

1½ OZ. COCOA POWDER

2 TEASPOONS BAKING POWDER

1 TABLESPOON KOSHER SALT

4 DROPS OF RED GEL FOOD COLORING

CANOLA OIL, AS NEEDED

CREAM CHEESE FROSTING (SEE PAGE 510)

1. In the work bowl of a stand mixer fitted with the paddle attachment, cream the sugar and butter on medium speed until light and fluffy, about 5 minutes.

2. Incorporate the egg yolks one at a time, scraping down the work bowl as needed. When all of the egg yolks have been incorporated, add the sour cream and beat until incorporated. Add the flour, cocoa powder, baking powder, salt, and food coloring and beat until the mixture comes together as a dough.

3. Coat a medium heatproof bowl with nonstick cooking spray, transfer the dough to the bowl, and cover with plastic wrap. Refrigerate overnight.

4. Add canola oil to a Dutch oven until it is about 2 inches deep and warm it to 350°F. Set a cooling rack in a rimmed baking sheet beside the stove.

5. Remove the dough from the refrigerator and place it on a flour-dusted work surface. Roll the dough out until it is ½ inch thick. Cut out the doughnuts using a round 4-inch cookie cutter and then use a round 1-inch cookie cutter to cut out the centers.

6. Transfer the doughnuts to the wire rack and let them sit at room temperature for 10 minutes.

7. Working in batches, carefully slip the doughnuts into the hot oil and fry, turning them once, until browned and cooked through, about 4 minutes. A cake tester inserted into the sides of the doughnuts should come out clean. Transfer the cooked doughnuts to the wire rack to drain and cool.

8. When cool, spread the frosting over the doughnuts and enjoy.

French Crullers

YIELD: 12 CRULLERS | **ACTIVE TIME:** 1 HOUR | **TOTAL TIME:** 1 HOUR AND 30 MINUTES

17 OZ. WATER

8½ OZ. UNSALTED BUTTER

1 TEASPOON FINE SEA SALT

2.4 OZ. SUGAR

12½ OZ. ALL-PURPOSE FLOUR

6 EGGS

CANOLA OIL, AS NEEDED

HONEY GLAZE (SEE PAGE 519)

1. In a medium saucepan, combine the water, butter, salt, and sugar and warm the mixture over medium heat until the butter has melted.

2. Add the flour to the pan and use a rubber spatula or wooden spoon to fold the mixture until it comes together as a thick, shiny dough, taking care not to let the dough burn.

3. Transfer the dough to the work bowl of a stand mixer fitted with the paddle attachment and beat on medium speed until the dough is no longer steaming and the bowl is just warm to the touch, at least 10 minutes.

4. Incorporate the eggs two at a time, scraping down the work bowl between each addition. Transfer the dough to a piping bag fit with a star tip.

5. Cut parchment paper into a dozen 4-inch squares, place them on a baking sheet, and coat them with nonstick cooking spray. Pipe 4-inch circles of dough onto the parchment and place the baking sheet in the refrigerator for 30 minutes.

6. Add canola oil to a Dutch oven until it is about 2 inches deep and warm it to 350°F. Set a cooling rack in a rimmed baking sheet beside the stove.

7. Working in batches, carefully lower the circles of dough, with the parchment attached, into the hot oil. Cook for 2 minutes, turn them over, and use tongs to remove the parchment paper. Cook until the crullers are a deep golden brown and then transfer them to the wire rack to drain and cool.

8. When the crullers are cool, dip them in the glaze and enjoy.

Cannoli

YIELD: 10 CANNOLI | **ACTIVE TIME:** 45 MINUTES | **TOTAL TIME:** 4 HOURS

¾ LB. WHOLE-MILK RICOTTA CHEESE

¾ LB. MASCARPONE CHEESE

4 OZ. CHOCOLATE, GRATED

¾ CUP CONFECTIONERS' SUGAR, PLUS MORE FOR DUSTING

1½ TEASPOONS PURE VANILLA EXTRACT

PINCH OF FINE SEA SALT

10 CANNOLI SHELLS

1. Line a colander with three pieces of cheesecloth and place it in the sink. Place the ricotta in the colander, form the cheesecloth into a pouch, and twist to remove as much liquid as possible from the ricotta. Keep the pouch taut and twisted, place it in a baking dish, and place a cast-iron skillet on top. Weigh the skillet down with two large, heavy cans and place in the refrigerator for 1 hour.

2. Discard the drained liquid and transfer the ricotta to a mixing bowl. Add the mascarpone, half of the grated chocolate, the confectioners' sugar, vanilla, and salt and stir until well combined. Cover the bowl and refrigerate for at least 1 hour. The mixture will keep in the refrigerator for up to 24 hours.

3. Line an 18 x 13–inch baking sheet with parchment paper. Fill a small saucepan halfway with water and bring it to a gentle simmer. Place the remaining chocolate in a heatproof mixing bowl, place it over the simmering water, and stir until it is melted.

4. Dip the ends of the cannoli shells in the melted chocolate, let the excess drip off, and transfer them to the baking sheet. Let the shells sit until the chocolate is firm, about 1 hour.

5. Place the cannoli filling in a piping bag and cut a ½-inch slit in it. Pipe the filling into the shells, working from both ends to ensure they are filled evenly. When all of the cannoli have been filled, dust them with confectioners' sugar and enjoy.

Sopaipillas

YIELD: 24 SOPAIPILLAS | **ACTIVE TIME:** 35 MINUTES | **TOTAL TIME:** 1 HOUR

3 CUPS SELF-RISING FLOUR

1½ TEASPOONS BAKING POWDER

1 TEASPOON FINE SEA SALT

1 TEASPOON SUGAR

1 CUP WARM WATER (105°F)

CANOLA OIL, AS NEEDED

CONFECTIONERS' SUGAR, FOR DUSTING

CINNAMON, FOR DUSTING

HONEY, FOR SERVING

1. In the bowl of a stand mixer fitted with the whisk attachment, combine the flour, baking powder, salt, and sugar. Turn the mixer on low speed and slowly drizzle in the warm water. Beat until the mixture comes together as a soft, smooth dough. Cover the bowl with a kitchen towel and let the dough rest for 20 minutes.

2. Add canola oil to a Dutch oven until it is about 2 inches deep and warm it to 325°F. Line a baking sheet with paper towels and place it beside the stove.

3. Divide the dough in half and pat each piece into a rectangle. Cut each rectangle into 12 squares and roll each square to ⅛ inch thick.

4. Working in batches of three, place the sopaipillas in the oil and use a pair of tongs to gently submerge them until puffy and golden brown, about 1 minute. Transfer the fried pastries to the baking sheet to drain and cool. When all of the sopaipillas have been fried, dust them with confectioners' sugar and cinnamon and serve with honey.

Blueberry Varenyky

YIELD: 36 VARENYKY | **ACTIVE TIME:** 1 HOUR | **TOTAL TIME:** 1 HOUR AND 30 MINUTES

3½ CUPS FRESH BLUEBERRIES

1 TABLESPOON SUGAR

ZEST OF 1 LEMON

3 CUPS ALL-PURPOSE FLOUR, PLUS MORE AS NEEDED

½ TEASPOON FINE SEA SALT, PLUS MORE TO TASTE

4½ OZ. UNSALTED BUTTER

⅔ CUP SOUR CREAM, AT ROOM TEMPERATURE

1 LARGE EGG, BEATEN

WATER, AS NEEDED

1 TABLESPOON CANOLA OIL

CONFECTIONERS' SUGAR, FOR DUSTING

1. Place two-thirds of the blueberries in a medium saucepan. Add the sugar and lemon zest and cook over medium heat, stirring occasionally, until the blueberries burst and release their juice, about 4 minutes. Reduce the heat to low and simmer until the mixture is very thick, about 18 minutes. Stir in the remaining blueberries, remove the pan from heat, and let the mixture cool completely.

2. Place the flour and salt in the work bowl of a stand mixer fitted with the paddle attachment. Add half of the butter and the sour cream and beat on medium speed until the mixture comes together as a crumbly dough, about 5 minutes.

3. Place the egg in a measuring cup and add enough water for the mixture to measure ¾ cup. Beat until combined and pour into the work bowl. Beat on medium speed until the dough holds together and is no longer sticky. If the dough is sticky, incorporate more flour, 1 teaspoon at a time.

4. Place the dough on a flour-dusted work surface and roll it out to ⅛ inch thick. Use a cookie cutter to cut as many 3-inch rounds from the dough as possible. Place the rounds on a parchment-lined baking sheet and lightly dust them with flour. When you have as many as you can fit in a single layer, cover with another piece of parchment.

5. To fill the varenyky, place a round in a slightly cupped hand and hold it so that it takes the shape of a taco. Place 1 teaspoon of the filling in the center. Using your thumb and index finger, firmly pinch the edges together to form a tight seal. You'll want this seal, or seam, to be approximately ¼ inch wide. Pat the sealed varenyky gently to evenly distribute the filling. Check for holes (patch any with a little bit of dough) and make sure the seal is tight. Reserve any leftover filling.

6. Bring a large pot of salted water to a boil. Once it's boiling, add the oil and stir. Working in batches, add the varenyky to the water and stir for 1 minute to keep them from sticking to the bottom. After the dumplings float to the surface, cook for another 3 minutes.

7. While the first batch of varenyky boils, melt the remaining butter in a skillet over low heat. Remove the varenyky from the water using a large slotted spoon and let them drain for a few seconds over the pot. Transfer to a warmed platter, top them with some of the melted butter, and gently toss to coat. Tent the platter loosely with aluminum foil to keep the dumplings warm while you cook the remaining varenyky.

8. To serve, dust the varenyky with confectioners' sugar and top with any remaining filling.

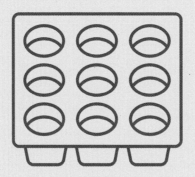

PUDDINGS
& CUSTARDS

Yogurt Mousse with Blueberry Compote & Granola

YIELD: 4 SERVINGS | **ACTIVE TIME:** 40 MINUTES | **TOTAL TIME:** 1 HOUR

2 SHEETS OF GELATIN

2 TABLESPOONS FRESH LEMON JUICE

⅓ CUP SUGAR

SEEDS AND POD OF ½ VANILLA BEAN

1 CUP HEAVY CREAM

1 CUP FULL-FAT GREEK YOGURT

BLUEBERRY COMPOTE (SEE PAGE 535)

GRANOLA (SEE PAGE 534)

1. Place the sheets of gelatin in a bowl, cover them with cold water, and let them sit.

2. Place the lemon juice, sugar, and vanilla seeds and pod in a saucepan and bring to a simmer. Remove the pan from heat.

3. Remove the sheets of gelatin from the water and squeeze them to remove excess moisture. Add them to the warm syrup and stir until they have dissolved.

4. Strain the gelatin into a bowl and let it cool until it is just slightly warm.

5. Place the cream in the work bowl of a stand mixer fitted with the whisk attachment and whip until it holds soft peaks. Set the whipped cream aside.

6. Add the yogurt to the gelatin and gently fold to combine. Add the whipped cream and fold to combine.

7. To serve, spoon the mousse into a serving dish and top each portion with some of the compote and Granola.

Goat Cheese & Honey Panna Cotta

YIELD: 4 SERVINGS | **ACTIVE TIME:** 30 MINUTES | **TOTAL TIME:** 5 HOURS

2 TABLESPOONS WATER

1 ENVELOPE OF UNFLAVORED GELATIN

2½ CUPS HEAVY CREAM

4 OZ. CREAMY GOAT CHEESE

½ CUP HONEY, PLUS MORE FOR GARNISH

FRESH BERRIES, FOR GARNISH

1. Place the water in a small saucepan and warm it over medium heat. Sprinkle the gelatin over the water and stir until thoroughly combined. The mixture will very quickly become a paste—remove the pan from heat as soon as it does and set it aside.

2. Place the cream in another small saucepan and warm it over medium heat. Stir in the goat cheese and cook until it has dissolved. Add the honey and cook until it has been incorporated.

3. Place the gelatin over low heat and gradually add the cream mixture, stirring continually. When all of the cream mixture has been incorporated, raise the heat to medium and cook the mixture until it has thickened, about 10 minutes, stirring frequently.

4. Remove the pan from heat and pour the mixture into 4-oz. ramekins or mason jars. Place them in the refrigerator and chill until they have set, 4 to 5 hours.

5. To serve, garnish each portion with fresh berries and honey.

Fermented Banana Fritters

YIELD: 2 SERVINGS | **ACTIVE TIME:** 25 MINUTES | **TOTAL TIME:** 4 TO 5 DAYS

2 BANANAS

1 TEASPOON ACTIVE DRY YEAST

2 CUPS WATER, PLUS MORE AS NEEDED

½ CUP ALL-PURPOSE FLOUR

1 TEASPOON BAKING POWDER

2 TABLESPOONS SUGAR

1 TABLESPOON CINNAMON

CANOLA OIL, AS NEEDED

2 TABLESPOONS PEANUT BUTTER

1. Peel the bananas, slice them into ½-inch-thick rounds, and place them in a mason jar. Add the yeast and then cover the bananas with the water. It is important that the bananas are completely covered, so add more water as necessary. Cover the jar and place it in a cupboard, keeping it at roughly 70°F, for 4 to 5 days, until the bananas start to smell a little like alcohol, though not funky. Any bananas at the top that brown should be thrown away.

2. Place the bananas in a mixing bowl and mash them. Add the flour and baking powder and stir until well combined.

3. Place the sugar and cinnamon in a bowl and stir to combine.

4. Add canola oil to a medium saucepan until it is about 1 inch deep and warm it to 325°F. Scoop tablespoons of the batter and fry until they are puffy and golden brown on one side, 1½ to 2 minutes. Turn the fritters over and cook until they are puffy and golden brown all over.

5. Remove the fritters from the hot oil, place them in the cinnamon sugar, and toss to coat.

6. Place the peanut butter in a microwave-safe bowl and microwave on medium in 10-second increments, until it has liquefied.

7. To serve, spread the melted peanut butter on a small plate and pile the fritters on top.

Cherry Clafoutis

YIELD: 6 SERVINGS | **ACTIVE TIME:** 20 MINUTES | **TOTAL TIME:** 45 MINUTES

½ CUP UNSALTED BUTTER, MELTED

1 CUP PLUS 2 TEASPOONS SUGAR

⅔ CUP ALL-PURPOSE FLOUR

½ TEASPOON FINE SEA SALT

1 TEASPOON PURE VANILLA EXTRACT

3 EGGS, BEATEN

1 CUP WHOLE MILK

3 CUPS CHERRIES, PITTED

CONFECTIONERS' SUGAR, FOR TOPPING

1. Preheat the oven to 400°F. Place three-quarters of the butter, ½ cup of the sugar, the flour, salt, vanilla, eggs, and milk in a large mixing bowl and stir until the mixture is well combined and smooth. Set the batter aside.

2. Grease a cast-iron skillet with the remaining butter and put the skillet in the oven to warm up.

3. When the skillet is warm, remove from the oven, place ½ cup of the sugar in the skillet, and shake to distribute it evenly. Distribute the cherries in the skillet and then pour in the batter. Sprinkle the remaining sugar on top, place the skillet in the oven, and bake until the custard is golden brown and set in the middle, about 30 minutes.

4. Remove from the oven, sprinkle confectioners' sugar over the clafoutis, and serve immediately.

Vanilla Panna Cotta

YIELD: 4 SERVINGS | **ACTIVE TIME:** 30 MINUTES | **TOTAL TIME:** 4 HOURS AND 45 MINUTES

3½ SHEETS OF SILVER GELATIN

13 OZ. HEAVY CREAM

13 OZ. MILK

3½ OZ. SUGAR

SEEDS AND POD OF ½ VANILLA BEAN

1. Place the gelatin sheets in a small bowl. Add 1 cup of ice and water until the sheets are submerged. Let the mixture rest.

2. Combine the heavy cream, milk, sugar, and the vanilla seeds and pod in a saucepan and bring to a simmer. Cook for 15 minutes and then remove the pan from heat. Remove the vanilla bean pod and discard.

3. Remove the bloomed gelatin from the ice water. Squeeze to remove as much water from the sheets as possible, add them to the warm mixture, and whisk until they have completely dissolved.

4. Strain the mixture into a bowl through a fine-mesh sieve and divide it among four 8-oz. ramekins, leaving about ½ inch of space at the top. Carefully transfer the ramekins to the refrigerator and chill until the panna cottas are fully set, about 4 hours.

Lemon Rice Pudding with Roasted Vanilla Cherries & Lemon Crème

YIELD: 4 SERVINGS | **ACTIVE TIME:** 45 MINUTES | **TOTAL TIME:** 2 HOURS

SEEDS OF 1 VANILLA BEAN

4 CUPS WHOLE MILK

½ CUP SUGAR

ZEST OF 1 LEMON

1 CUP RICE

ROASTED VANILLA CHERRIES (SEE PAGE 534)

LEMON CRÈME (SEE PAGE 535)

1. Place all of the ingredients, except for the cherries and crème, in a saucepan and bring the mixture to a simmer over medium-low heat. Cook, stirring frequently, until the rice is cooked through and the mixture has thickened to the consistency of yogurt, 20 to 30 minutes. Remove the pan from heat and let the mixture cool.

2. To serve, divide the rice pudding among the serving bowls and top each portion with some of the roasted cherries and Lemon Crème.

Crème Brûlée

YIELD: 4 SERVINGS | **ACTIVE TIME:** 1 HOUR | **TOTAL TIME:** 10 HOURS

12 EGG YOLKS

14 OZ. HEAVY CREAM

4 OZ. MILK

3 OZ. PLUS 2 OZ. SUGAR

¼ TEASPOON KOSHER SALT

¾ TEASPOON PURE VANILLA EXTRACT

1. Place the egg yolks in a mixing bowl and set aside.

2. Place the heavy cream, milk, 3 oz. of sugar, and the salt in a saucepan and bring to a boil over medium heat. Remove the pan from heat and stir in the vanilla.

3. While whisking, gradually add the hot milk mixture to the egg yolks. When all of the milk has been incorporated, place plastic wrap directly on the surface of the custard, place it in the refrigerator, and chill it for at least 4 hours. Crème brûlée is best when cooked chilled.

4. Preheat the oven to 325°F. Bring 8 cups of water to a boil and then set aside.

5. Fill four 8-oz. ramekins three-quarters of the way with custard. Place the ramekins in a 13 x 9–inch baking dish and pour the boiling water into the pan until it reaches halfway up the sides of the ramekins. Place the pan in the oven and bake until the custards are set at their edges and jiggle slightly at their centers, 30 to 40 minutes. Remove the custards from the oven and carefully transfer the ramekins to a wire rack. Let them cool for 1 hour.

6. Place the ramekins in the refrigerator and chill them for 4 hours.

7. Divide the remaining 2 oz. of sugar among the ramekins and spread evenly on top. Use a kitchen torch to caramelize the sugar and serve.

Classic Malabi

YIELD: 6 SERVINGS | **ACTIVE TIME:** 30 MINUTES | **TOTAL TIME:** 4 HOURS AND 30 MINUTES

FOR THE PUDDING

4 CUPS MILK

⅔ CUP CORNSTARCH

1 TEASPOON ROSE WATER

1 CUP HEAVY CREAM

½ CUP SUGAR

½ CUP ROASTED PEANUTS OR PISTACHIOS, FOR GARNISH

SHREDDED COCONUT, FOR GARNISH

FOR THE SYRUP

½ CUP WATER

½ CUP SUGAR

1 TEASPOON ROSE WATER

2 DROPS OF RED FOOD COLORING

1. To begin preparations for the pudding, place 1 cup of the milk in a bowl, add the cornstarch and rose water, and stir until the mixture is smooth. Set aside.

2. Place the remaining milk, heavy cream, and sugar in a saucepan. Bring to a simmer, stirring constantly, reduce the heat to low, and stir in the cornstarch mixture.

3. Cook, stirring constantly, until the mixture starts to thicken, 3 to 4 minutes. Pour the pudding into ramekins or small mason jars, place plastic wrap directly on the surface to prevent a skin from forming, and let the pudding cool completely. When it has cooled, chill in the refrigerator for 4 hours.

4. To prepare the syrup, place the water, sugar, and rose water in a saucepan and bring to a boil, stirring to dissolve the sugar. Stir in the food coloring, boil for another 2 minutes, and remove the pan from heat. Let the syrup cool completely.

5. When the malabi has chilled for 4 hours, pour 1 to 2 tablespoons of the syrup over each portion, and garnish with the peanuts or pistachios and shredded coconut.

Classic Malabi
SEE PAGE 353

Blueberry & Ginger Malabi

YIELD: 4 SERVINGS | **ACTIVE TIME:** 30 MINUTES | **TOTAL TIME:** 5 HOURS

2 CUPS LIGHT CREAM

1 TABLESPOON SUGAR

1 TEASPOON GRATED FRESH
GINGER

½ CUP BLUEBERRIES

¼ CUP COLD WATER

2 TABLESPOONS
CORNSTARCH

1. Place the cream, sugar, ginger, and blueberries in a small saucepan and warm the mixture over medium heat. When the mixture begins to bubble at the edge, reduce the heat to low and let it simmer for 30 minutes.

2. Puree the mixture using an immersion blender (or a food processor). Strain the mixture, place the liquid in a clean saucepan, and warm it over medium-high heat.

3. In a small bowl, combine the water and cornstarch. While stirring continually, gradually add the slurry to the cream mixture. As the mixture starts to thicken, reduce the heat to medium. Cook until the mixture acquires a pudding-like consistency, about 5 minutes.

4. Divide the mixture among 4-oz. ramekins or mason jars, place them in the refrigerator, and chill for 4 hours before serving.

Keto Chocolate Pudding

YIELD: 6 SERVINGS | **ACTIVE TIME:** 15 MINUTES | **TOTAL TIME:** 3 HOURS

¼ CUP STEVIA OR PREFERRED KETO-FRIENDLY SWEETENER

1¼ OZ. BAKER'S CHOCOLATE, GRATED

¼ CUP UNSWEETENED COCOA POWDER

¼ CUP ALMOND FLOUR

½ TEASPOON KOSHER SALT

2 CUPS WHOLE MILK

¼ CUP HEAVY CREAM

4 TABLESPOONS UNSALTED BUTTER, DIVIDED INTO TABLESPOONS

2 TEASPOONS PURE VANILLA EXTRACT

¾ OZ. UNSWEETENED SHREDDED COCONUT (OPTIONAL)

2½ OZ. RASPBERRIES (OPTIONAL)

1¼ OZ. SUGAR-FREE CHOCOLATE, GRATED (OPTIONAL)

1. Place the sweetener, chocolate, cocoa powder, almond flour, and salt in a saucepan and whisk to combine. Cook over medium heat and slowly add the milk, whisking continually. Cook until the mixture thickens and comes to a boil, approximately 8 to 10 minutes.

2. Reduce the heat to low and simmer the mixture for 1 to 2 minutes. Remove the saucepan from heat and stir in the cream.

3. Incorporate the butter 1 tablespoon at a time and then stir in the vanilla.

4. Transfer the pudding into the serving dishes and place plastic wrap directly on the surface to prevent a skin from forming. Refrigerate the pudding for 2 hours before serving and top with the shredded coconut, raspberries, and/or chocolate shavings, if desired.

Nutritional Info Per Serving: Calories: 153; Fat: 12 g; Net Carbs: 7 g; Protein: 5.2 g

Keto Eton Mess

YIELD: 4 SERVINGS | **ACTIVE TIME:** 10 MINUTES | **TOTAL TIME:** 1 HOUR

2 EGG WHITES

¼ TEASPOON CREAM OF TARTAR

1 TEASPOON PURE VANILLA EXTRACT

1½ TEASPOONS POWDERED ERYTHRITOL

5.3 OZ. HEAVY CREAM

STEVIA OR PREFERRED KETO-FRIENDLY SWEETENER, TO TASTE

3½ OZ. STRAWBERRIES, HULLED AND DICED

1. Preheat the oven to 245°F and line a baking sheet with parchment paper. Place the egg whites in a bowl and beat until they are frothy. Add the cream of tartar and beat until the mixture holds soft peaks. Add half of the vanilla and the erythritol and whisk to combine.

2. Transfer the meringue to the baking sheet and bake until it is cooked through and dry to the touch, 30 to 35 minutes. Remove the meringue from the oven and let the meringue cool for 15 minutes before removing it from the parchment paper.

3. While the meringue is in the oven, place the heavy cream, sweetener, and remaining vanilla in a bowl and beat until the mixture holds soft peaks. Refrigerate for 15 minutes and then fold the strawberries into the mixture. Break the meringue into pieces, add it to the strawberries and cream, and serve.

Nutritional Info Per Serving: Calories: 146; Fat: 14 g; Net Carbs: 2 g; Protein: 3 g

Chocolate Pots de Crème

YIELD: 6 SERVINGS | **ACTIVE TIME:** 30 MINUTES | **TOTAL TIME:** 6 HOURS AND 30 MINUTES

5 OZ. CHOCOLATE

2 CUPS HEAVY CREAM

4 OZ. SUGAR

4 EGG YOLKS

1 TABLESPOON CHOCOLATE LIQUEUR

¼ TEASPOON KOSHER SALT

1. Preheat the oven to 325°F. Bring 8 cups of water to a boil and then set aside.

2. Place the chocolate in a heatproof mixing bowl. Place the heavy cream in a saucepan and bring it to a simmer over medium heat. Pour the cream over the chocolate and whisk until the chocolate has melted and the mixture is combined. Set the mixture aside.

3. In the work bowl of a stand mixer fitted with the whisk attachment, combine the sugar, egg yolks, liqueur, and salt and whip on high until the mixture is pale yellow and ribbony, about 10 minutes.

4. Pour the mixture into the chocolate mixture and fold to incorporate.

5. Fill six 8-oz. ramekins three-quarters of the way with the custard.

6. Place the ramekins in a 13 x 9–inch baking pan and pour the boiling water into the pan until it reaches halfway up the sides of the ramekins. Place the pan in the oven and bake until the custards are set at their edges and jiggle slightly at their centers, about 50 minutes. Remove the custards from the oven and carefully transfer the ramekins to a wire rack. Let them cool for 1 hour.

7. Place the ramekins in the refrigerator and chill them for 4 hours before enjoying.

Quick Chocolate Mousse

YIELD: 3 CUPS | **ACTIVE TIME:** 15 MINUTES | **TOTAL TIME:** 15 MINUTES

1½ CUPS HEAVY CREAM

½ LB. CHOCOLATE

½ CUP WATER

2 TABLESPOONS COCOA POWDER

1 TABLESPOON CONFECTIONERS' SUGAR

1 TEASPOON PURE VANILLA EXTRACT

PINCH OF KOSHER SALT

1. Place the heavy cream in the work bowl of a stand mixer fitted with a whisk attachment and whip it on medium until the cream holds stiff peaks.

2. Fill a small saucepan halfway with water and bring it to a gentle simmer.

3. Combine the chocolate, water, cocoa powder, confectioners' sugar, vanilla, and salt in a heatproof mixing bowl. Place the bowl over the simmering water and whisk until the chocolate has melted and the mixture is smooth.

4. Remove the bowl from heat, add the whipped cream, and fold until incorporated. Transfer the mousse to ramekins or a piping bag, if using it as a cake filling. If not using immediately, place the mousse in an airtight container and store it in the refrigerator, where it will keep for up to 2 weeks.

Lemon Posset

YIELD: 6 SERVINGS | **ACTIVE TIME:** 30 MINUTES | **TOTAL TIME:** 4 HOURS

2 CUPS HEAVY CREAM

⅔ CUP SUGAR

1 TABLESPOON LEMON ZEST

6 TABLESPOONS FRESH LEMON JUICE

2 CUPS CHANTILLY CREAM (SEE PAGE 518)

FRESH BLUEBERRIES, FOR TOPPING

1. Place the heavy cream, sugar, and lemon zest in a saucepan and bring the mixture to a simmer over medium heat, stirring constantly. Cook until the sugar has dissolved and the mixture has reduced slightly, about 10 minutes.

2. Remove the saucepan from heat and stir in the lemon juice. Let the mixture stand until a skin forms on the top, about 20 minutes. Strain the mixture through a fine sieve and transfer it to the refrigerator. Chill the posset until it is set, about 3 hours.

3. About 10 minutes before you are ready to serve the posset, remove the mixture from the refrigerator and let it come to room temperature. Cover the bottom of the serving dishes with the Chantilly Cream and then alternate layers of the posset and Chantilly Cream. Top each serving with a generous amount of blueberries and enjoy.

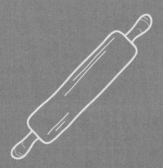

Passion Fruit Curd

YIELD: 3 CUPS | **ACTIVE TIME:** 25 MINUTES | **TOTAL TIME:** 2 HOURS

¾ CUP PASSION FRUIT JUICE

4 EGGS

½ CUP SUGAR

⅛ TEASPOON KOSHER SALT

¼ TEASPOON PURE VANILLA EXTRACT

4 OZ. UNSALTED BUTTER, SOFTENED

1. Fill a small saucepan halfway with water and bring it to a gentle simmer.

2. Place the passion fruit juice in a small saucepan and warm it over low heat.

3. Combine the eggs, sugar, salt, and vanilla in a metal mixing bowl. Place the bowl over the simmering water and whisk the mixture continually until it is 135°F on an instant-read thermometer.

4. When the passion fruit juice comes to a simmer, gradually add it to the egg mixture while whisking constantly.

5. When all of the lemon juice has been incorporated, whisk the curd until it has thickened and is 155°F. Remove the bowl from heat, add the butter, and stir until thoroughly incorporated.

6. Transfer the curd to a mason jar and let it cool. Once cool, store the curd in the refrigerator, where it will keep for up to 2 weeks.

Grape-Nut Custard

YIELD: 12 SERVINGS | **ACTIVE TIME:** 15 MINUTES | **TOTAL TIME:** 1 HOUR AND 15 MINUTES

4 CUPS WHOLE MILK, WARMED

½ CUP GRAPE-NUTS CEREAL

5 EGGS

1 TEASPOON PURE VANILLA EXTRACT

½ CUP SUGAR

1 TEASPOON CINNAMON

FRESHLY GRATED NUTMEG, TO TASTE

MAPLE SYRUP, FOR SERVING

CHANTILLY CREAM (SEE PAGE 518), FOR SERVING

1. Preheat the oven to 350°F. Place the milk, cereal, eggs, vanilla, and sugar in a bowl and stir until thoroughly combined.

2. Transfer the mixture to a baking dish, and then place the dish in a roasting pan. Fill the roasting pan with hot water until it reaches halfway up the sides of the baking dish. Place the custard in the oven and bake for 15 minutes.

3. Remove the baking dish from the oven and stir the custard. Return to the oven and cook until it is golden brown and a cake tester inserted into the center comes out clean, about 15 minutes.

4. Remove the custard from the oven, sprinkle with the cinnamon, and grate nutmeg over the top. Let the custard cool completely.

5. When the custard is cool, top each serving with a drizzle of maple syrup and a dollop of Chantilly Cream.

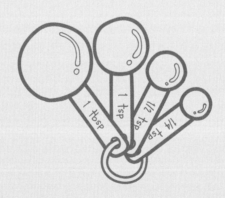

Dark Chocolate Mousse

YIELD: 6 SERVINGS | **ACTIVE TIME:** 45 MINUTES | **TOTAL TIME:** 2 HOURS AND 45 MINUTES

17 OZ. DARK CHOCOLATE
(55 TO 65 PERCENT)

19 OZ. HEAVY CREAM

2 EGG YOLKS

1 OZ. SUGAR

½ CUP WHOLE MILK

¼ TEASPOON KOSHER SALT

CHANTILLY CREAM (SEE
PAGE 518), FOR SERVING

1. Fill a small saucepan halfway with water and bring it to a simmer. Place the dark chocolate in a heatproof mixing bowl and place it over the simmering water. Stir until the chocolate is melted and then set aside.

2. In the work bowl of a stand mixer fitted with the whisk attachment, whip 15 oz. of the heavy cream until it holds soft peaks. Transfer the whipped cream to another bowl and place it in the refrigerator.

3. Place the egg yolks and sugar in a mixing bowl, whisk to combine, and set the mixture aside.

4. In a small saucepan, combine the milk, salt, and remaining cream and bring the mixture to a simmer. Remove the pan from heat.

5. Whisking constantly, gradually add the warm mixture to the egg yolk mixture. When all of the warm mixture has been incorporated, add the tempered egg yolks to the saucepan and cook over low heat, stirring constantly, until the mixture thickens enough to coat the back of a wooden spoon.

6. Remove the pan from heat, pour the mixture into the melted chocolate, and whisk until thoroughly combined. Add half of the whipped cream, fold until incorporated, and then fold in the rest of the whipped cream.

7. Divide the mousse among six 8-oz. ramekins and lightly tap the bottom of each one to settle the mousse and remove any air bubbles. Transfer the mousse to the refrigerator and chill for 2 hours.

8. To serve, top each mousse with Chantilly Cream.

Dark Chocolate Mousse
SEE PAGE 365

Meyer Lemon Curd

YIELD: 3 CUPS | **ACTIVE TIME:** 25 MINUTES | **TOTAL TIME:** 2 HOURS

¾ CUP FRESH MEYER LEMON JUICE

4 EGGS

¾ CUP SUGAR

⅛ TEASPOON KOSHER SALT

¼ TEASPOON PURE VANILLA EXTRACT

½ CUP UNSALTED BUTTER, SOFTENED

1. Fill a small saucepan halfway with water and bring it to a gentle simmer.

2. Place the lemon juice in a small saucepan and warm it over low heat.

3. Combine the eggs, sugar, salt, and vanilla in a metal mixing bowl. Place the bowl over the simmering water and whisk the mixture continually until it is 135°F on an instant-read thermometer.

4. When the lemon juice comes to a simmer, gradually add it to the egg mixture while whisking constantly.

5. When all of the lemon juice has been incorporated, whisk the curd until it has thickened and is 155°F. Remove the bowl from heat, add the butter, and stir until thoroughly incorporated.

6. Transfer the curd to a mason jar and let it cool. Once cool, store the curd in the refrigerator, where it will keep for up to 2 weeks.

Coconut Flan

YIELD: 6 SERVINGS | **ACTIVE TIME:** 30 MINUTES | **TOTAL TIME:** 6 HOURS AND 30 MINUTES

½ CUP SUGAR

2 TABLESPOONS WATER

12 OZ. EVAPORATED MILK

1 (14 OZ.) CAN OF COCONUT MILK

1 (14 OZ.) CAN OF SWEETENED CONDENSED MILK

3 EGGS

3 EGG YOLKS

1½ TEASPOONS PURE VANILLA EXTRACT

½ TEASPOON KOSHER SALT

1. Preheat the oven to 350°F. Bring 8 cups of water to a boil and set aside.

2. Place the sugar and water in a small saucepan and bring to a boil over high heat, swirling the pan instead of stirring. Cook until the caramel is a deep golden brown, taking care not to burn it. Remove the pan from heat and add the evaporated milk a little at a time, whisking constantly to prevent the sugar from seizing. When all of the evaporated milk has been added, incorporate the coconut milk and condensed milk in the same fashion.

3. Whisk the eggs, egg yolks, vanilla, and salt into the mixture. Divide the mixture among six 8-oz. ramekins, filling each one about three-quarters of the way.

4. Place the ramekins in a 13 x 9–inch roasting pan. Pour the boiling water into the roasting pan until it reaches halfway up the sides of the ramekins.

5. Place the pan in the oven and bake until the flan is just set, 45 to 50 minutes. The flan should still be jiggly without being runny. Remove from the oven, place the roasting pan on a cooling rack, and let it cool for 1 hour.

6. Place the flan in the refrigerator and chill for 4 hours before serving.

Orange & Coconut Panna Cotta

YIELD: 6 SERVINGS | **ACTIVE TIME:** 30 MINUTES | **TOTAL TIME:** 4 HOURS AND 30 MINUTES

4 SHEETS OF SILVER GELATIN

2½ CUPS HEAVY CREAM

1 CUP COCONUT MILK

4½ OZ. CONFECTIONERS' SUGAR

1¼ CUPS ORANGE JUICE

ZEST OF 1 ORANGE

SEEDS OF 1 VANILLA BEAN, POD RESERVED

6 FRESH PASSION FRUITS, FOR GARNISH

1. Place the gelatin sheets in a small bowl. Add 1 cup of ice and water until the sheets are submerged. Let the mixture rest.

2. Combine the heavy cream, coconut milk, confectioners' sugar, orange juice, orange zest, vanilla seeds, and half of the vanilla bean pod in a saucepan and bring to a simmer. Cook for 15 minutes and then remove the pan from heat. Remove the vanilla bean pod and discard it.

3. Remove the bloomed gelatin from the ice water. Squeeze to remove as much water from the sheets as possible, add them to the warm mixture, and whisk until they have completely dissolved.

4. Strain the mixture into a bowl through a fine-mesh sieve and divide it among six 8-oz. ramekins, leaving about ½ inch of space at the top. Carefully transfer the ramekins to the refrigerator and chill until the panna cottas are fully set, about 4 hours.

5. Split the passion fruits in half and scoop the insides into a small bowl to remove their seeds and juice. Garnish the top of each panna cotta with about 1 tablespoon of passion fruit juice and seeds, and chill the panna cottas in the refrigerator until ready to serve.

Quark Panna Cotta with Rosé Raspberry Sauce

YIELD: 6 SERVINGS | **ACTIVE TIME:** 40 MINUTES | **TOTAL TIME:** 24 HOURS

FOR THE PANNA COTTA

2½ CUPS HEAVY CREAM

⅔ CUP WHOLE MILK

⅔ CUP SUGAR

½ TEASPOON FINE SEA SALT

1 TEASPOON PURE VANILLA EXTRACT

2 CUPS QUARK CHEESE

½ OZ. GELATIN (2 ENVELOPES)

6 TABLESPOONS HONEY

RASPBERRIES, FOR GARNISH

TOASTED ALMONDS, FOR GARNISH

MINT LEAVES, FOR GARNISH

FOR THE SAUCE

2 CUPS ROSÉ

⅓ CUP SUGAR

¼ TEASPOON FINE SEA SALT

2 CUPS RASPBERRIES

1. To prepare the panna cotta, place the cream, milk, sugar, salt, and vanilla in a saucepan and bring to a simmer over medium heat, taking care that the mixture does not come to a boil. Remove the pan from heat.

2. Place the quark in a small mixing bowl and ladle about 1 cup of the warm milk mixture into the bowl. Whisk to combine and then pour the tempered quark into the saucepan.

3. Bring the mixture to a boil and then remove the saucepan from heat. Place the gelatin in a large mixing bowl and pour the warmed mixture into it, whisking constantly to prevent lumps from forming. Pour the mixture into six ramekins and place them in the refrigerator to set overnight.

4. Approximately 2 hours before you will serve the panna cotta, prepare the sauce. Place the Rosé in a small saucepan and cook over medium-high heat until it has reduced by half. Add the remaining ingredients, bring the mixture to a boil, and then reduce the heat so that the mixture simmers. Simmer for 20 minutes.

5. Transfer the mixture to a blender and puree until smooth. Strain through a fine sieve and place the sauce in the refrigerator to cool completely.

6. When the panna cottas are set, pour 1 tablespoon of honey over each serving. Pour the sauce on top of the honey and garnish with raspberries, toasted almonds, and mint.

Tiramisu

YIELD: 8 TO 10 SERVINGS | **ACTIVE TIME:** 20 MINUTES | **TOTAL TIME:** 3 HOURS AND 30 MINUTES

2 CUPS FRESHLY BREWED ESPRESSO

½ CUP PLUS 1 TABLESPOON SUGAR

3 TABLESPOONS KAHLÚA

4 LARGE EGG YOLKS

2 CUPS MASCARPONE CHEESE

1 CUP HEAVY CREAM

30 LADYFINGERS (SEE PAGE 539)

2 TABLESPOONS COCOA POWDER

1. Place the espresso, 1 tablespoon of sugar, and the Kahlúa in a bowl and stir to combine. Set the mixture aside.

2. Place 2 inches of water in a saucepan and bring to a simmer. Place the remaining sugar and egg yolks in a metal mixing bowl and set the bowl over the simmering water. Whisk the mixture continually until it has nearly tripled in size, approximately 10 minutes. Remove from heat, add the mascarpone, and fold to incorporate.

3. Pour the heavy cream into a separate bowl and whisk until soft peaks start to form. Gently fold the whipped cream into the mascarpone mixture.

4. Place the Ladyfingers in the espresso mixture and briefly submerge them. Place an even layer of the soaked Ladyfingers on the bottom of a 13 x 9-inch baking pan. This will use up approximately half of the Ladyfingers. Spread half of the mascarpone mixture on top of the Ladyfingers and then repeat until the Ladyfingers and mascarpone have been used up.

5. Cover with plastic and place in the refrigerator for 3 hours. Sprinkle the cocoa powder over the top before serving.

Tiramisu
SEE PAGE 373

Coconut Pudding Pancakes

YIELD: 30 PANCAKES | **ACTIVE TIME:** 20 MINUTES | **TOTAL TIME:** 50 MINUTES

1½ CUPS COCONUT MILK

1½ CUPS RICE FLOUR

½ CUP SWEETENED SHREDDED COCONUT

5 TABLESPOONS CASTER (SUPERFINE) SUGAR

½ TEASPOON FINE SEA SALT

1 CUP COCONUT CREAM

½ TABLESPOON TAPIOCA STARCH OR CORNSTARCH

2 TABLESPOONS CANOLA OIL

¼ CUP CORN KERNELS (OPTIONAL)

1. Preheat the oven to 350°F and coat an aebleskiver pan with nonstick cooking spray.

2. Place the coconut milk, 1 cup of the rice flour, the coconut, 1 tablespoon of the sugar, and the salt in a bowl and whisk vigorously until the sugar has dissolved. Set the mixture aside.

3. Place the coconut cream, remaining rice flour, remaining sugar, and tapioca starch or cornstarch in another bowl and whisk until the starch has dissolved. Add this mixture to the coconut milk mixture and stir until combined.

4. Coat the wells of the aebleskiver pan with the canola oil, fill them with the batter, and top with some of the corn, if using.

5. Place the pan in the oven and bake the pancakes until they are firm, 15 to 20 minutes. Remove from the oven, transfer the cooked pancakes to a platter, and tent it with aluminum foil to keep them warm. Repeat Steps 4 and 5 with any remaining batter.

Indian Pudding

YIELD: 8 SERVINGS | **ACTIVE TIME:** 30 MINUTES | **TOTAL TIME:** 9 HOURS

3 CUPS WHOLE MILK

1 CUP HEAVY CREAM

½ CUP CORNMEAL

½ CUP BLACKSTRAP MOLASSES

½ CUP LIGHT BROWN SUGAR

½ TEASPOON GROUND GINGER

½ TEASPOON FRESHLY GRATED NUTMEG

½ TEASPOON ALLSPICE

2 TEASPOONS CINNAMON

2 TEASPOONS FINE SEA SALT

5 EGGS

5 TABLESPOONS UNSALTED BUTTER

CHANTILLY CREAM (SEE PAGE 518), FOR SERVING

1. Preheat the oven to 275°F and coat a baking dish with nonstick cooking spray.

2. Place the milk in a large saucepan and cook over medium-high heat until it comes to a simmer. Remove the saucepan from heat and set it aside.

3. Place all of the remaining ingredients, except for the eggs, butter, and Chantilly Cream, in a mixing bowl and stir to combine. Whisk this mixture into the warm milk, place the saucepan over medium-low heat, and cook, stirring, until the mixture begins to thicken.

4. Remove the saucepan from heat, crack the eggs into a bowl, and whisk them until combined. While whisking, add the hot molasses-and-cornmeal mixture ½ cup at a time until all of it has been incorporated. Add the butter and whisk until it has been incorporated.

5. Pour the pudding into the prepared baking dish. Place the dish in a roasting pan and fill the roasting pan with warm water until it reaches halfway up the sides of the baking dish. Place the pudding in the oven and bake until it is set, about 2 hours.

6. Remove the pudding from the oven and let it cool to room temperature. When cool, transfer to the refrigerator and chill for at least 6 hours before serving with the Chantilly Cream.

Strawberry Consommé
with Cardamom Panna Cotta

YIELD: 4 SERVINGS | **ACTIVE TIME:** 30 MINUTES | **TOTAL TIME:** 7 HOURS

FOR THE CONSOMMÉ

2 QUARTS OF STRAWBERRIES, HULLED AND CHOPPED

½ CUP SUGAR

SEEDS OF 1 VANILLA BEAN

1 CINNAMON STICK

1 STAR ANISE POD

JUICE AND ZEST OF 2 LEMONS

1 SPRIG OF FRESH MINT

2 TABLESPOONS GRAND MARNIER

FOR THE PANNA COTTA

¾ CUP BUTTERMILK

¾ CUP HEAVY CREAM

SEEDS AND POD OF ½ VANILLA BEAN

SEEDS OF 2 CARDAMOM PODS, CHOPPED

2 TABLESPOONS SUGAR

1¼ TEASPOONS GELATIN

SCOTTISH SHORTBREAD (SEE PAGE 85), FOR SERVING

1. To begin preparations for the consommé, place all of the ingredients in a heatproof mixing bowl, stir to combine, and cover with plastic wrap.

2. Bring 2 cups of water to a boil in a saucepan. Place the bowl over the saucepan and reduce the heat so that the water simmers. Cook the consommé for 1 hour, turn off the burner, and let stand for 1 hour.

3. After 1 hour, strain the mixture through a fine sieve and place it in the refrigerator for 1 hour.

4. While the consommé is chilling in the refrigerator, begin preparations for the panna cotta. Place half of the buttermilk in a bowl and set it aside. Place the remaining buttermilk, heavy cream, vanilla seeds and pod, cardamom, and sugar in a small saucepan and bring to a simmer over medium-low heat. Remove the pan from heat and let the mixture steep for 10 minutes.

5. Place the gelatin in the bowl of cold buttermilk and stir briskly to combine. Bring the contents of the saucepan to a boil over medium heat and add the buttermilk-and-gelatin mixture. Remove the pan from heat and stir gently for 2 minutes. Strain through a fine sieve and chill in the refrigerator for 15 minutes, removing to stir every 5 minutes. Pour the panna cotta into ramekins and refrigerate for 3 hours.

6. To serve, ladle the consommé over the panna cotta and serve with Scottish Shortbread.

The Perfect Flan

YIELD: 6 SERVINGS | **ACTIVE TIME:** 30 MINUTES | **TOTAL TIME:** 6 HOURS AND 30 MINUTES

2 CUPS SUGAR

¼ CUP WATER

5 EGG YOLKS

5 EGGS

5 OZ. CREAM CHEESE, SOFTENED

1 (14 OZ.) CAN OF SWEETENED CONDENSED MILK

1 (12 OZ.) CAN OF EVAPORATED MILK

1½ CUPS HEAVY CREAM

½ TEASPOON ALMOND EXTRACT

½ TEASPOON PURE VANILLA EXTRACT

1. Preheat the oven to 350°F. Bring 2 quarts of water to a boil and set it aside.

2. Place the 1 cup of the sugar and the water in a small saucepan and bring to a boil over high heat, swirling the pan instead of stirring. Cook until the caramel is a deep golden brown, taking care not to burn it. Remove the pan from heat and pour the caramel into a round 8-inch cake pan. Place the cake pan on a cooling rack and let it sit until it has set.

3. Place the egg yolks, eggs, cream cheese, remaining sugar, condensed milk, evaporated milk, heavy cream, almond extract, and vanilla in a blender and puree until emulsified.

4. Pour the mixture over the caramel and place the cake pan in a roasting pan. Pour the boiling water into the roasting pan until it reaches halfway up the side of the cake pan.

5. Place the flan in the oven and bake until it is just set, 60 to 70 minutes. The flan should still be jiggly without being runny. Remove from the oven, place the cake pan on a cooling rack, and let it cool for 1 hour.

6. Place the flan in the refrigerator and chill for 4 hours.

7. Run a knife along the edge of the pan and invert the flan onto a plate so that the caramel layer is on top. Slice the flan and serve.

Kataifi Pudding

YIELD: 8 SERVINGS | **ACTIVE TIME:** 15 MINUTES | **TOTAL TIME:** 1 HOUR AND 30 MINUTES

SALT, TO TASTE

½ LB. ANGEL HAIR PASTA

3½ OZ. UNSALTED BUTTER

1 TEASPOON CINNAMON

¾ CUP SLIVERED ALMONDS

¾ CUP RAISINS

¾ CUP CHOPPED PISTACHIOS

¾ CUP CASTER (SUPERFINE) SUGAR

¼ CUP ICE WATER

CHANTILLY CREAM (SEE PAGE 518), FOR SERVING

1. Preheat the oven to 300°F and coat a square 8-inch cake pan with nonstick cooking spray.

2. Bring a large saucepan of water to a boil. When the water is boiling, add salt and the pasta and cook for 3 minutes less than the directed time. Reserve ¼ cup of the pasta water, drain the pasta, and set it aside.

3. Return the empty pan to the stove. Immediately turn the heat to high and add half of the butter and all of the reserved pasta water. Add the drained pasta and cook. Add the cinnamon and cook, while tossing to coat, for 1 to 2 minutes. Remove from heat.

4. Transfer one-third of the cooked pasta to the prepared pan. Sprinkle half of the almonds, raisins, pistachios, and ¼ cup of the sugar on top. Add half of the remaining pasta and sprinkle with the remaining almonds, raisins, pistachios, and another ¼ cup of the sugar. Top with the remaining pasta. Cut the remaining butter into small pieces and dot the mixture with them.

5. Place the pan in the oven and bake for 25 minutes.

6. While it bakes, put the remaining sugar in a small saucepan over low heat and stir until it melts and turns golden brown. Remove from heat and very slowly and carefully (the mixture will splatter a bit) add the ice water. Return the pan to heat and stir until the mixture thickens, about 4 minutes.

7. After 25 minutes, remove the dish from the oven and pour the sauce evenly over the top. Return to the oven and bake until the top is golden brown, about 5 minutes. Let cool briefly before serving with Chantilly Cream.

Beet Panna Cotta

YIELD: 4 SERVINGS | **ACTIVE TIME:** 30 MINUTES | **TOTAL TIME:** 4 HOURS AND 30 MINUTES

4 SHEETS OF SILVER GELATIN

13 OZ. HEAVY CREAM

9 OZ. MILK

4 OZ. SUGAR

1.8 OZ. HONEY

¾ LB. RED BEETS, PEELED AND FINELY DICED

4 OZ. GOAT CHEESE, CRUMBLED

1. Place the gelatin sheets in a small bowl. Add 1 cup of ice and water until the sheets are submerged. Let the mixture rest.

2. Combine the heavy cream, milk, sugar, honey, and beets in a saucepan and bring to a simmer. Cook for 15 minutes and then remove the pan from heat.

3. Remove the bloomed gelatin from the ice water. Squeeze to remove as much water from the sheets as possible, add them to the warm mixture, and whisk until they have completely dissolved.

4. Transfer the mixture to a blender, add the goat cheese, and puree until emulsified, about 45 seconds.

5. Strain the mixture into a bowl through a fine-mesh sieve and divide it among four 8-oz. ramekins, leaving about ½ inch of space at the top. Carefully transfer the ramekins to the refrigerator and chill until the panna cottas are fully set, about 4 hours.

Tapioca Pudding

YIELD: 6 SERVINGS | **ACTIVE TIME:** 15 MINUTES | **TOTAL TIME:** 4 HOURS AND 15 MINUTES

2 LARGE EGGS

1 CUP SUGAR

½ CUP INSTANT TAPIOCA

SEEDS AND POD OF 1 VANILLA BEAN

4 CUPS HALF-AND-HALF

½ TEASPOON FINE SEA SALT

¼ TEASPOON FRESHLY GRATED NUTMEG

1. Place the eggs, sugar, tapioca, and vanilla seeds and pod in a saucepan and whisk until the mixture is frothy.

2. Stir in the half-and-half and bring the mixture to a simmer over medium-low heat while stirring constantly. Cook until the mixture has thickened considerably, about 10 minutes, taking care not to let it come to a boil.

3. Remove the pan from heat, remove the vanilla pod, and discard it. Transfer the mixture to a bowl and stir in the salt and nutmeg. Place the pudding in the refrigerator and chill for 4 hours before serving.

Zabaglione

YIELD: 6 SERVINGS | **ACTIVE TIME:** 20 MINUTES | **TOTAL TIME:** 20 MINUTES

4 EGG YOLKS

¼ CUP SUGAR

½ CUP DRY MARSALA WINE

FRESH RASPBERRIES, FOR GARNISH

1. Fill a small saucepan halfway with water and bring it to a gentle simmer. Combine the egg yolks and sugar in a heatproof bowl and place it over the simmering water. Whisk the mixture until it is pale yellow and creamy.

2. While whisking continually, slowly add the Marsala. The mixture will begin to foam and then it will swell considerably. Whisk until it is very soft with a number of gentle peaks and valleys. Ladle into the serving glasses and garnish with fresh raspberries.

Maple Pots de Crème

YIELD: 4 SERVINGS | **ACTIVE TIME:** 30 MINUTES | **TOTAL TIME:** 6 HOURS AND 30 MINUTES

18 OZ. HEAVY CREAM

6 OZ. MAPLE SUGAR

¼ TEASPOON KOSHER SALT

5 EGG YOLKS

1. Preheat the oven to 325°F. Bring 8 cups of water to a boil and then set it aside.

2. Place the heavy cream, two-thirds of the maple sugar, and the salt in a saucepan and bring it to a simmer over medium heat.

3. Place the egg yolks and remaining maple sugar in a mixing bowl and whisk until the sugar has dissolved.

4. Whisking constantly, gradually add the warm mixture to the egg yolk mixture. When all of the warm mixture has been incorporated, pour the custard into four 8-oz. ramekins until they are three-quarters full.

5. Place the ramekins in a 13 x 9–inch baking pan and pour the boiling water into the pan until it reaches halfway up the sides of the ramekins. Place the pan in the oven and bake until the custards are set at their edges and jiggle slightly at their centers, about 50 minutes. Remove from the oven and carefully transfer the ramekins to a wire rack. Let cool for 1 hour.

6. Place the ramekins in the refrigerator and chill for 4 hours before enjoying.

Chocolate Pudding

YIELD: 8 SERVINGS | **ACTIVE TIME:** 15 MINUTES | **TOTAL TIME:** 2 HOURS AND 15 MINUTES

3 LARGE EGG YOLKS

¼ CUP SUGAR

½ CUP SWEETENED COCOA POWDER

2 TABLESPOONS CORNSTARCH

¾ TEASPOON FINE SEA SALT

2½ CUPS WHOLE MILK

6 TABLESPOONS UNSALTED BUTTER, SOFTENED

2 TEASPOONS PURE VANILLA EXTRACT

1. Place the egg yolks in a heatproof bowl and whisk to combine.

2. Place the sugar, cocoa powder, cornstarch, and salt in a saucepan and whisk to combine. Cook over medium heat and, whisking continually, gradually add the milk. Cook until the mixture thickens and comes to a simmer, approximately 8 to 10 minutes.

3. Reduce the heat to low and simmer for 1 to 2 minutes. Remove the saucepan from heat and stir in the butter and vanilla.

4. While whisking continually, gradually add the warm milk mixture to the egg yolks. When all of the milk mixture has been incorporated, transfer the pudding into serving dishes and place plastic wrap directly on the pudding's surface to prevent a skin from forming. Place in the refrigerator and chill for 2 hours before serving.

Vanilla Pudding

YIELD: 8 SERVINGS | **ACTIVE TIME:** 20 MINUTES | **TOTAL TIME:** 2 HOURS AND 20 MINUTES

3 LARGE EGG YOLKS

⅓ CUP SUGAR

2 TABLESPOONS CORNSTARCH

¼ TEASPOON FINE SEA SALT

2 CUPS WHOLE MILK

2 TABLESPOONS UNSALTED BUTTER, SOFTENED

2 TABLESPOONS PURE VANILLA EXTRACT

1. Place the egg yolks in a bowl and beat until combined.

2. Place the sugar, cornstarch, and salt in a saucepan, stir to combine, and warm over medium heat. Slowly add the milk and whisk constantly as the mixture comes to a simmer.

3. Remove the saucepan from heat and, whisking continually, add approximately one-third of the warm mixture into the beaten egg yolks. Pour the tempered egg yolks into the saucepan, place it back over medium heat, and cook for 1 minute while stirring constantly. Remove from heat.

4. Stir in the butter and vanilla. Transfer the pudding into serving dishes and place plastic wrap directly on the surface of each one to prevent a skin from forming. Place the pudding in the refrigerator and chill for 2 hours before serving.

Crema Catalana

YIELD: 4 SERVINGS | **ACTIVE TIME:** 30 MINUTES | **TOTAL TIME:** 6 HOURS AND 30 MINUTES

8 EGG YOLKS

1½ CUPS HEAVY CREAM

7 OZ. MILK

SEEDS OF ½ VANILLA BEAN

1 CUP SUGAR

ZEST OF ½ ORANGE

¼ TEASPOON KOSHER SALT

1. Place the egg yolks in a mixing bowl, whisk to combine, and set them aside.

2. Combine the heavy cream, milk, vanilla seeds, three-quarters of the sugar, the orange zest, and salt in a saucepan and bring the mixture to a simmer. Remove the pan from heat and strain the mixture into a clean bowl through a fine-mesh sieve.

3. Whisking constantly, gradually add the warm mixture to the egg yolk mixture. When all of the warm mixture has been incorporated, place the custard in the refrigerator and chill for 4 hours.

4. Preheat the oven to 325°F. Bring 8 cups of water to a boil and then set it aside.

5. Fill four 8-oz. ramekins three-quarters of the way with the custard.

6. Place the ramekins in a 13 x 9–inch baking pan and pour the boiling water into the pan until it reaches halfway up the sides of the ramekins. Place the pan in the oven and bake until the custards are set at their edges and jiggle slightly at their centers, about 50 minutes. Remove from the oven and carefully transfer the ramekins to a wire rack. Let cool for 1 hour.

7. Place the ramekins in the refrigerator and chill for 4 hours.

8. Divide the remaining sugar between the ramekins and spread evenly on top. Use a kitchen torch to caramelize the sugar and serve.

Caramel Bread Pudding

YIELD: 16 SERVINGS | **ACTIVE TIME:** 45 MINUTES | **TOTAL TIME:** 24 HOURS

8 CUPS TORN CHALLAH OR BRIOCHE

9 OZ. HEAVY CREAM

3 OZ. MILK

1 TEASPOON CINNAMON

¼ TEASPOON GROUND CLOVES

3 OZ. SUGAR

¼ TEASPOON KOSHER SALT

3 EGGS

½ TEASPOON PURE VANILLA EXTRACT

2 CUPS BOURBON TOFFEE SAUCE (SEE PAGE 530)

1. Place the bread in a mixing bowl and let it rest overnight at room temperature, uncovered, to dry out.

2. Place the cream, milk, cinnamon, cloves, sugar, and salt in a medium saucepan and bring the mixture to a simmer. Remove the pan from heat.

3. Place the eggs and vanilla in a heatproof mixing bowl and whisk to combine. Whisking constantly, gradually add the warm mixture. When half of the warm mixture has been incorporated, add the tempered eggs to the saucepan and whisk to combine.

4. Coat a 13 x 9–inch baking pan with cooking spray and then distribute the bread pieces in it. Slowly pour the custard over the bread and gently shake the pan to ensure it is evenly distributed. Press down on the bread with a rubber spatula so that it soaks up the custard. Cover the baking pan with aluminum foil, place it in the refrigerator, and chill for 2 hours.

5. Preheat the oven to 350°F.

6. Place the baking pan in the oven and bake for 45 minutes. Remove the aluminum foil and bake until the bread pudding is golden brown on top, about 15 minutes. Remove from the oven and let the bread pudding cool slightly before slicing and serving with the toffee sauce.

Chocolate & Sourdough Bread Pudding

YIELD: 16 SERVINGS | **ACTIVE TIME:** 45 MINUTES | **TOTAL TIME:** 24 HOURS

8 CUPS SOURDOUGH BREAD PIECES

2 CUPS CHOCOLATE CHIPS

3 CUPS WHOLE MILK

3 TABLESPOONS UNSALTED BUTTER

2¼ CUPS SUGAR

¾ CUP HEAVY CREAM

1½ TEASPOONS CINNAMON

½ TEASPOON FRESHLY GRATED NUTMEG

¼ TEASPOON KOSHER SALT

3 EGGS

1½ TEASPOONS PURE VANILLA EXTRACT

1. Place the bread in a mixing bowl and let it rest overnight at room temperature, uncovered, to dry out.

2. Place the chocolate chips in a heatproof mixing bowl. Place the milk, butter, sugar, cream, cinnamon, nutmeg, and salt in a medium saucepan and bring the mixture to a simmer. Remove the pan from heat, pour it over the chocolate chips, and stir until the chocolate has melted and the mixture is combined.

3. Place the eggs and vanilla in a heatproof mixing bowl and whisk to combine. Whisking constantly, gradually add the melted chocolate mixture until all of it has been incorporated.

4. Coat a 13 x 9–inch baking pan with cooking spray and then distribute the bread pieces in it. Slowly pour the custard over the bread and gently shake the pan to ensure it is evenly distributed. Press down on the bread with a rubber spatula so that it soaks up the custard. Cover the baking pan with aluminum foil, place it in the refrigerator, and chill for 2 hours.

5. Preheat the oven to 350°F.

6. Place the baking pan in the oven and bake for 45 minutes. Remove the aluminum foil and bake until the bread pudding is golden brown on top, about 15 minutes. Remove from the oven and let the bread pudding cool slightly before slicing and serving.

Gingerbread Mousse

YIELD: 6 SERVINGS | **ACTIVE TIME:** 30 MINUTES | **TOTAL TIME:** 2 HOURS AND 45 MINUTES

10½ OZ. WHITE CHOCOLATE

14 OZ. HEAVY CREAM

2 OZ. MOLASSES

1 OZ. CONFECTIONERS' SUGAR

2 EGG YOLKS

2 WHOLE EGGS

1 TEASPOON PURE VANILLA EXTRACT

1 TEASPOON CINNAMON

1 TEASPOON ALLSPICE

1 TEASPOON CARDAMOM

1 TEASPOON FRESHLY GRATED NUTMEG

½ TEASPOON GROUND GINGER

2 CUPS CHANTILLY CREAM (SEE PAGE 518)

1. Fill a small saucepan halfway with water and bring it to a simmer. Place the white chocolate in a heatproof mixing bowl and place it over the simmering water. Stir until the white chocolate is melted and then set it aside.

2. In the work bowl of a stand mixer fitted with the whisk attachment, whip the heavy cream until it holds soft peaks. Transfer the whipped cream to another bowl and place it in the refrigerator.

3. Wipe out the work bowl of the stand mixer, add the molasses, confectioners' sugar, egg yolks, eggs, vanilla, cinnamon, allspice, cardamom, nutmeg, and ginger, and whip until the mixture has doubled in size and is pale, about 15 minutes. Transfer the mixture to a mixing bowl. Add the white chocolate and whisk to incorporate. Add the whipped cream and fold to incorporate.

4. Divide the mousse among six 8-oz. ramekins and lightly tap the bottom of each one to settle the mousse and remove any air bubbles. Transfer to the refrigerator and chill for 2 hours.

5. To serve, top each mousse with the Chantilly Cream.

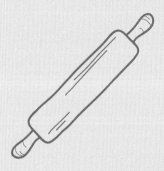

Eggnog Mousse

YIELD: 6 SERVINGS | **ACTIVE TIME:** 30 MINUTES | **TOTAL TIME:** 2 HOURS AND 30 MINUTES

4 EGG WHITES

4 CUPS HEAVY CREAM

1 CUP CONFECTIONERS' SUGAR

2 TEASPOONS PURE VANILLA EXTRACT

2 TABLESPOONS FRESHLY GRATED NUTMEG, OR TO TASTE

2 TABLESPOONS CINNAMON

1 TABLESPOON GROUND GINGER, OR TO TASTE

2 CUPS CHANTILLY CREAM (SEE PAGE 518)

1. In the work bowl of a stand mixer fitted with the whisk attachment, whip the egg whites on high until they hold stiff peaks. Transfer the egg whites to another bowl and place it in the refrigerator.

2. Wipe out the work bowl of the stand mixer, add the heavy cream, confectioners' sugar, vanilla, nutmeg, cinnamon, and ginger, and whip until the mixture holds stiff peaks.

3. Transfer the whipped cream to a mixing bowl. Add the whipped egg whites and fold to incorporate.

4. Divide the mousse among six 8-oz. ramekins and lightly tap the bottom of each one to settle the mousse and remove any air bubbles. Transfer to the refrigerator and chill for 2 hours.

5. To serve, top each mousse with the Chantilly Cream.

Pumpkin Mousse

YIELD: 6 SERVINGS | **ACTIVE TIME:** 30 MINUTES | **TOTAL TIME:** 2 HOURS AND 30 MINUTES

15 OZ. PUMPKIN PUREE

3 CUPS HEAVY CREAM

¾ CUP SUGAR

1 TABLESPOON CINNAMON

1 TEASPOON FRESHLY GRATED NUTMEG

1 TEASPOON GROUND CLOVES

1 TABLESPOON PURE VANILLA EXTRACT

2 CUPS CINNAMON CHANTILLY CREAM (SEE PAGE 518)

1. Place the pumpkin puree, 1 cup of the heavy cream, and the sugar in a saucepan and bring the mixture to a simmer, stirring to combine. Remove the pan from heat, pour the mixture into a heatproof bowl, and set it aside.

2. In the work bowl of a stand mixer fitted with the whisk attachment, add the cinnamon, nutmeg, cloves, vanilla, and remaining heavy cream and whip on medium speed until the mixture holds medium peaks.

3. Transfer the whipped cream to the bowl containing the pumpkin mixture and fold to incorporate.

4. Divide the mousse among six 8-oz. ramekins and lightly tap the bottom of each one to settle the mousse and remove any air bubbles. Transfer to the refrigerator and chill for 2 hours.

5. To serve, top each mousse with the Cinnamon Chantilly Cream.

ICE CREAM & OTHER FROZEN DELIGHTS

Custard Ice Cream Base

YIELD: 1 QUART | **ACTIVE TIME:** 30 MINUTES | **TOTAL TIME:** 5 HOURS

2 CUPS HEAVY CREAM

1 CUP WHOLE MILK

⅔ CUP SUGAR

⅛ TEASPOON FINE SEA SALT

6 LARGE EGG YOLKS

1. In a small saucepan, combine the heavy cream, milk, sugar, and salt and bring to a simmer over medium-low heat, stirring until the sugar completely dissolves, about 5 minutes.

2. Remove the saucepan from heat. Place the egg yolks in a heatproof mixing bowl and whisk them until combined. While whisking constantly, slowly whisk about a third of the hot cream mixture into the yolks. Whisk the tempered egg yolks into the saucepan.

3. Warm the mixture over medium-low heat, stirring constantly, until the mixture is thick enough to coat the back of a wooden spoon (about 170°F on an instant-read thermometer).

4. Strain the custard through a fine-mesh sieve into a bowl and let it cool to room temperature. Cover the bowl, place it in the refrigerator, and let it chill for at least 4 hours.

5. Flavor the custard as desired and churn it in an ice cream maker until it has the desired consistency.

Philadelphia Ice Cream Base

YIELD: 1 QUART | **ACTIVE TIME:** 10 MINUTES | **TOTAL TIME:** 5 HOURS

3 CUPS HEAVY CREAM

1 CUP WHOLE MILK

½ CUP SUGAR

½ CUP LIGHT CORN SYRUP OR ⅓ CUP HONEY

½ TEASPOON FINE SEA SALT

1. In a saucepan, combine the cream, milk, sugar, corn syrup or honey, and salt and bring the mixture to a simmer, stirring until the sugar has dissolved.

2. Pour the mixture into a heatproof bowl and let it cool to room temperature. Cover it with plastic wrap and store in the refrigerator for at least 4 hours.

3. Flavor the ice cream base as desired and churn it in an ice cream maker until it has the desired consistency.

Vegan Ice Cream Base

YIELD: 1 QUART | **ACTIVE TIME:** 15 MINUTES | **TOTAL TIME:** 4 HOURS AND 15 MINUTES

2 (14 OZ.) CANS OF COCONUT MILK

¾ CUP MAPLE SYRUP

SEEDS OF 2 VANILLA BEANS

1 TEASPOON FINE SEA SALT

1. Place the coconut milk, maple syrup, vanilla seeds, and salt in a blender or food processor and blitz until combined. Transfer the mixture to a bowl, cover it, and refrigerate for 4 hours.

2. Flavor the base as desired and churn in an ice cream maker until it has the desired consistency.

Vanilla Ice Cream

YIELD: 1 QUART | **ACTIVE TIME:** 30 MINUTES | **TOTAL TIME:** 9 HOURS

1 QUART ICE CREAM BASE

2 VANILLA BEANS

1. While preparing the ice cream base, halve the vanilla beans, scrape the seeds into the saucepan, and add the pods as well. When the base is ready, pour it into a bowl and let steep for 1 hour.

2. Remove the vanilla bean pods, cover the bowl, and place it in the refrigerator for 4 hours.

3. Churn the mixture in an ice cream maker until it is the desired texture. Place the ice cream in an airtight container and freeze it for 4 to 6 hours before serving.

Chocolate Ice Cream

YIELD: 1 QUART | **ACTIVE TIME:** 30 MINUTES | **TOTAL TIME:** 9 HOURS

1 QUART ICE CREAM BASE

¾ CUP HEAVY CREAM

3 TABLESPOONS COCOA POWDER

4 OZ. CHOCOLATE, CHOPPED

¾ CUP CRÈME FRAÎCHE

1 TEASPOON PURE VANILLA EXTRACT

1. While the ice cream base is still warm, combine the cream and cocoa powder in a saucepan and bring to a simmer over medium-low heat.

2. Place the chocolate in a heatproof bowl and pour the warm cream mixture over it. Stir until melted and smooth.

3. Stir the melted chocolate mixture, crème fraîche, and vanilla into the base. Let the mixture cool to room temperature. Strain into a bowl through a fine-mesh sieve, cover the bowl, and store in the refrigerator for 4 hours.

4. Churn the mixture in an ice cream maker until it reaches the desired consistency. Place the ice cream in an airtight container and freeze it for 4 to 6 hours before serving.

Pistachio Ice Cream

YIELD: 1 QUART | **ACTIVE TIME:** 30 MINUTES | **TOTAL TIME:** 9 HOURS

1 QUART ICE CREAM BASE

1 CUP PISTACHIO PASTE
(SEE PAGE 538)

¼ TEASPOON ALMOND
EXTRACT

PISTACHIOS, CHOPPED, TO
TASTE

1. Add your preferred ice cream base to the ice cream maker and churn for 5 minutes.

2. Add the paste and almond extract and churn for 5 minutes.

3. Gradually add the chopped pistachios to the mixture and churn until they have been evenly distributed. Transfer the ice cream to an airtight container and freeze for 4 to 6 hours before serving.

Coconut Ice Cream

YIELD: 1 QUART | **ACTIVE TIME:** 30 MINUTES | **TOTAL TIME:** 9 HOURS

1 QUART ICE CREAM BASE

1 CUP COCONUT MILK OR COCONUT CREAM

1 CUP SHREDDED UNSWEETENED COCONUT, TOASTED

½ CUP SHREDDED SWEETENED COCONUT, TOASTED

1. While preparing your preferred ice cream base, add the coconut milk and toasted unsweetened coconut to the pot and proceed with the preparation as normal.

2. After removing the pan from heat, let the mixture steep for 1 hour.

3. Strain into a bowl through a fine-mesh sieve, pressing down on the coconut to extract as much liquid from it as possible. Cover the bowl and refrigerate for 4 hours.

4. Place the mixture in an ice cream maker and churn until it almost has the desired consistency. Add the toasted sweetened coconut and churn for 2 minutes, or until it is equally distributed. Place the ice cream in an airtight container and freeze for 4 to 6 hours before serving.

Coffee Ice Cream

YIELD: 1 QUART | **ACTIVE TIME:** 30 MINUTES | **TOTAL TIME:** 9 HOURS

1 QUART ICE CREAM BASE

½ CUP COFFEE BEANS, COARSELY GROUND

1. While the base is still warm, stir in the ground coffee and let the mixture steep for 1 hour.

2. Strain into a bowl through a fine-mesh sieve, cover the bowl, and store in the refrigerator for 4 hours.

3. Churn the mixture in an ice cream maker until it reaches the desired consistency. Place the ice cream in an airtight container and freeze it for 4 to 6 hours before serving.

Mint Chocolate Chip Ice Cream

YIELD: 1 QUART | **ACTIVE TIME:** 30 MINUTES | **TOTAL TIME:** 9 HOURS

1 CUP FRESH MINT LEAVES

½ CUP SUGAR

1 QUART ICE CREAM BASE (NO SUGAR)

1 CUP CHOPPED DARK CHOCOLATE

1. Place the mint leaves and sugar in a food processor and pulse until well combined.

2. Prepare the base, adding the mint-and-sugar mixture in place of the plain sugar in your chosen preparation. When the base is ready, pour the mixture into a heatproof bowl and let it steep for 30 minutes.

3. Strain into a bowl through a fine-mesh sieve, cover the bowl, and refrigerate for 4 hours.

4. Churn the mixture in an ice cream maker until it is almost the desired consistency. Add the chocolate and churn until evenly distributed. Place the ice cream in an airtight container and freeze it for 4 to 6 hours before serving.

Banana Ice Cream

YIELD: 1 QUART | **ACTIVE TIME:** 30 MINUTES | **TOTAL TIME:** 9 HOURS

1 QUART ICE CREAM BASE

4 VERY RIPE BANANAS

2 TABLESPOONS SUGAR

1 TEASPOON FRESH LEMON JUICE

PINCH OF FINE SEA SALT

½ CUP CRÈME FRAÎCHE

1. While the ice cream base is still warm, place all of the remaining ingredients, except for the crème fraîche, in a blender and puree until smooth. Stir the puree and crème fraîche into the base and let the mixture cool to room temperature. Strain into a bowl, cover the bowl, and store in the refrigerator for 4 hours.

2. Churn the mixture in an ice cream maker until it reaches the desired consistency. Place the ice cream in an airtight container and freeze it for 4 to 6 hours before serving.

Affogato

YIELD: 4 SERVINGS | **ACTIVE TIME:** 5 MINUTES | **TOTAL TIME:** 5 MINUTES

1 PINT OF VANILLA ICE CREAM (SEE PAGE 399 FOR HOMEMADE)

¼ CUP SAMBUCA

1 TEASPOON FRESHLY GRATED NUTMEG

1¼ CUPS FRESHLY BREWED ESPRESSO OR VERY STRONG COFFEE

CHANTILLY CREAM (SEE PAGE 518), FOR GARNISH

1. Scoop ice cream into four small glasses. Pour some of the liqueur over each scoop and sprinkle a bit of the nutmeg on top.

2. Pour the espresso or coffee over the ice cream. Top each portion with Chantilly Cream and serve.

Cranberry Sorbet

YIELD: 1 QUART | **ACTIVE TIME:** 40 MINUTES | **TOTAL TIME:** 6 HOURS

½ LB. FRESH CRANBERRIES

2¾ CUPS WATER

13 TABLESPOONS SUGAR

1 CUP ORANGE JUICE

½ TEASPOON CORNSTARCH

1. Place the cranberries, 9 oz. of the water, and 5 tablespoons of the sugar in a medium saucepan and cook over medium heat until all of the cranberries burst. Transfer the mixture to a blender and puree until smooth, starting at a low speed and increasing to high. Strain into a bowl through a fine-mesh sieve and place in the refrigerator until chilled.

2. Place the remaining water and sugar in a saucepan and bring to a boil, while stirring, until the sugar is dissolved. Remove from heat and let cool completely.

3. Place the cranberry puree, simple syrup, orange juice, and cornstarch in a bowl and stir until combined.

4. Pour the mixture into an ice cream maker and churn until it has the desired texture. Place the sorbet in an airtight container and freeze for 4 to 6 hours.

Almond Granita

YIELD: 1 PINT | **ACTIVE TIME:** 15 MINUTES | **TOTAL TIME:** 2 HOURS AND 15 MINUTES

1¼ CUPS WHOLE MILK

1¼ CUPS WATER

3 OZ. SLIVERED ALMONDS, TOASTED, COOLED, AND CHOPPED

2.7 OZ. SUGAR

2½ OZ. ALMOND PASTE

1 TEASPOON ALMOND EXTRACT

1. Place all of the ingredients in a blender and puree until smooth.

2. Place a fine-mesh sieve over a square metal 9-inch baking pan. Strain the puree into the pan, pressing down on the solids to extract as much liquid as possible. Discard the solids.

3. Cover the pan with plastic wrap and freeze until the mixture is firm, about 2 hours.

4. Using a fork, vigorously scrape the mixture until it is a collection of icy flakes. Cover with aluminum foil and store in the freezer. Scrape again with a fork before enjoying.

Strawberry & Balsamic Ice Cream

YIELD: 1 QUART | **ACTIVE TIME:** 30 MINUTES | **TOTAL TIME:** 9 HOURS

1 QUART ICE CREAM BASE (NO MILK USED)

1 LB. STRAWBERRIES

3 TABLESPOONS SUGAR

½ TEASPOON BALSAMIC VINEGAR

PINCH OF FINE SEA SALT

1. While the base is warm, place the strawberries, sugar, vinegar, and salt in a blender and puree until smooth. Taste and adjust the amount of sugar or vinegar as desired.

2. Stir the puree into the base and let the mixture cool to room temperature. Cover the bowl with plastic wrap and refrigerate for 4 hours.

3. Place the mixture in an ice cream maker and churn until it is the desired consistency. Place the ice cream in an airtight container and freeze it for 4 to 6 hours before serving.

Lemon Gelato

YIELD: 1 PINT | **ACTIVE TIME:** 30 MINUTES | **TOTAL TIME:** 6 HOURS

2 CUPS WHOLE MILK

ZEST OF ½ LEMON

5 LARGE EGG YOLKS

½ CUP SUGAR

1. In a small saucepan, combine the milk and lemon zest and warm over medium-low heat until the mixture starts to steam. Remove the pan from heat, cover it, and let the mixture steep for about 20 minutes.

2. Put a few inches of ice water in a large bowl. In a mixing bowl, whisk together the egg yolks and sugar. Strain the infused milk into a pitcher, then whisk it into the yolk mixture.

3. Pour the mixture into a clean saucepan and place it over medium-low heat. While stirring constantly with a wooden spoon, warm until it forms a custard thick enough to coat the back of the spoon, about 10 minutes. Take care not to overheat the mixture; it will curdle.

4. Place the pan in the ice water bath and stir until cool. Transfer to a bowl, cover it, and refrigerate for about 1 hour.

5. Pour the mixture into an ice cream maker and churn until it has the desired consistency. Transfer to an airtight container and freeze for 4 to 6 hours before serving.

Salted Caramel Ice Cream

YIELD: 1 QUART | **ACTIVE TIME:** 30 MINUTES | **TOTAL TIME:** 9 HOURS

1 QUART ICE CREAM BASE

¾ CUP SUGAR

3 TABLESPOONS WATER

¼ TEASPOON FLAKY SEA SALT

1. While the ice cream base is still warm, place the sugar and water in a saucepan and warm over medium heat, swirling the pan frequently, until the mixture is a deep golden brown. Add the mixture to the base and let the mixture cool to room temperature. Cover the bowl and store in the refrigerator for 4 hours.

2. Churn the mixture in an ice cream maker until it is approaching the desired consistency. Sprinkle the salt into the ice cream and churn for another 2 minutes. Place the ice cream in an airtight container and freeze it for 4 to 6 hours before serving.

Keto Chocolate Ice Cream

YIELD: 6 SERVINGS | **ACTIVE TIME:** 10 MINUTES | **TOTAL TIME:** 8 HOURS

1½ CUPS HEAVY CREAM

¾ CUP WHOLE MILK

¼ CUP UNSWEETENED COCOA POWDER

½ CUP STEVIA OR PREFERRED KETO-FRIENDLY SWEETENER

3 LARGE EGG YOLKS, LIGHTLY BEATEN

1¾ OZ. BAKER'S CHOCOLATE, CHOPPED

½ TEASPOON PURE VANILLA EXTRACT

PINCH OF FLAKY SEA SALT

1½ TABLESPOONS VODKA (OPTIONAL)

1. Prepare an ice bath in a large bowl. Place the cream, ½ cup of the milk, the cocoa powder, and sweetener in a saucepan and warm the mixture over medium heat, stirring continually. Once the sugar has dissolved, take approximately 1 cup from the mixture in the saucepan and whisk it into the bowl containing the egg yolks. Add the tempered egg yolks to the saucepan and continue cooking over medium heat, stirring continually, until the custard has thickened to where it will coat the back of a wooden spoon. Remove the pan from heat.

2. Stir the chocolate into the custard, let the mixture cool for 5 minutes, and then stir until it is smooth. Pour the custard into a metal bowl and then set the bowl in the ice bath. Stir occasionally until the mixture is smooth, about 10 minutes. Cover the bowl with plastic wrap and refrigerate for 3 hours.

3. Stir the remaining milk, the vanilla, salt, and vodka (if using) into the chilled custard. Pour the custard into an ice cream maker and churn until the ice cream has the desired consistency, about 20 minutes. Pour the ice cream into an airtight container, cover, and freeze until firm, about 4 hours.

Tips: Using the vodka will help prevent the formation of ice crystals in the ice cream without affecting the flavor, ultimately yielding a smoother texture.

Nutritional Info Per Serving: Calories: 311; Fat: 29.6 g; Net Carbs: 6.8 g; Protein: 5.2 g

Keto Avocado Ice Cream

YIELD: 4 SERVINGS | **ACTIVE TIME:** 10 MINUTES | **TOTAL TIME:** 8 HOURS

FLESH OF 2 AVOCADOS

1 CUP COCONUT MILK

1 TABLESPOON FRESH LEMON JUICE

1 TABLESPOON MCT OIL

2 TABLESPOONS STEVIA OR PREFERRED KETO-FRIENDLY SWEETENER

PINCH OF KOSHER SALT

UNSWEETENED COCONUT FLAKES, TOASTED, FOR GARNISH

1. Place the avocados, coconut milk, lemon juice, MCT oil, sweetener, and salt in a food processor and puree until smooth, scraping down the sides of the work bowl as needed.

2. Transfer the mixture to an ice cream maker and churn until the ice cream has the desired consistency, about 20 minutes. Transfer the mixture to an airtight container, cover, and freeze for 4 hours.

3. To serve, garnish each portion with some coconut.

   Nutritional Info Per Serving: Calories: 259; Fat: 24.5 g; Net Carbs: 3 g; Protein: 2.9 g

Cinnamon Ice Cream

YIELD: 1 QUART | **ACTIVE TIME:** 30 MINUTES | **TOTAL TIME:** 9 HOURS

1 CINNAMON STICK, CHOPPED

½ CUP SUGAR

1 QUART ICE CREAM BASE (NO SUGAR)

1. Place the cinnamon stick and sugar in a food processor and pulse until finely ground.

2. Prepare the base, adding the cinnamon sugar in place of the plain sugar in your chosen preparation. When the base is ready, pour the mixture into a heatproof bowl and let it steep for 30 minutes.

3. Strain into a bowl through a fine-mesh sieve, cover the bowl, and refrigerate for 4 hours.

4. Churn the mixture in an ice cream maker until it is the desired consistency. Place the ice cream in an airtight container and freeze it for 4 to 6 hours before serving.

Rosé Sorbet

YIELD: 6 SERVINGS | **ACTIVE TIME:** 30 MINUTES | **TOTAL TIME:** 7 HOURS

1⅓ CUPS SUGAR

1 (750 ML) BOTTLE OF ROSÉ

1 CUP WATER

1. Place all of the ingredients in a saucepan and cook, while stirring, over medium-low heat until the sugar has dissolved. Raise the heat and bring to a boil.

2. Remove the pan from heat and let the mixture cool completely. Cover and place the mixture in the refrigerator for 2 hours.

3. Pour the mixture into an ice cream maker and churn until the desired consistency has been achieved. Transfer to the freezer and freeze for 4 to 6 hours before serving.

Paleta

YIELD: 12 POPS | **ACTIVE TIME:** 30 MINUTES | **TOTAL TIME:** 24 HOURS

8 EARS OF CORN, SHUCKED

4 CUPS HEAVY CREAM

6 CUPS MILK

1½ CUPS EGG YOLKS

2 CUPS SUGAR

2 TEASPOONS PURE
VANILLA EXTRACT

⅛ TEASPOON FINE SEA SALT

1. Prepare an ice bath. Grate the corn kernels into a saucepan and discard the cobs. Add the cream and milk and bring the mixture to a simmer.

2. Place the egg yolks and sugar in the work bowl of a stand mixer fitted with the whisk attachment and whip until the mixture is pale and thick.

3. Add the milk mixture to the whipped yolks a little bit at a time, whisking continually. When all of the milk mixture has been incorporated, return the tempered mixture back to the pan and cook over low heat until the mixture has thickened, enough that it coats the back of a wooden spoon.

4. Remove the pan from heat, stir in the vanilla and salt, and strain the mixture into a bowl.

5. Place the bowl in the ice bath and stir until the custard is cool.

6. Pour the custard into popsicle molds and chill them in the freezer overnight.

Lavender Ice Cream

YIELD: 1 QUART | **ACTIVE TIME:** 30 MINUTES | **TOTAL TIME:** 9 HOURS

1 QUART ICE CREAM BASE

2 TABLESPOONS DRIED LAVENDER

PINCH OF FINE SEA SALT

1. While the base is still warm, stir in the lavender and let it steep for 30 minutes.

2. Strain into a bowl through a fine-mesh sieve, cover the bowl with plastic wrap, and refrigerate for 4 hours.

3. Churn the mixture in an ice cream maker until it almost has the desired consistency. Sprinkle in the sea salt and churn for another 2 minutes. Place the ice cream in an airtight container and freeze for 4 to 6 hours before serving.

Peach Ice Cream

YIELD: 1 QUART | **ACTIVE TIME:** 30 MINUTES | **TOTAL TIME:** 9 HOURS

1 QUART ICE CREAM BASE
(NO MILK USED)

1½ LBS. PEACHES, PITTED

¼ CUP SUGAR

½ CUP CRÈME FRAÎCHE

2 DROPS OF ALMOND
EXTRACT

1. While the base is warm, place the peaches and sugar in a saucepan and warm over medium heat. Simmer gently for 10 minutes and then stir the mixture into the base along with the crème fraîche and almond extract. Let the mixture cool to room temperature, cover the bowl with plastic wrap, and refrigerate it for 4 hours.

2. Churn the mixture in an ice cream maker until it is the desired consistency. Place the ice cream in an airtight container and freeze it for 4 to 6 hours before using.

Roasted Parsnip Ice Cream

YIELD: 6 SERVINGS | **ACTIVE TIME:** 30 MINUTES | **TOTAL TIME:** 9 HOURS

1 QUART ICE CREAM BASE

3½ CUPS ROASTED PARSNIP
TRIMMINGS

1. While the base is still warm, stir in the roasted parsnip trimmings and let the mixture steep for 1 hour.

2. Strain into a bowl through a fine-mesh sieve, pressing down on the pieces of parsnip to extract as much liquid from them as possible. Cover the bowl with plastic wrap and refrigerate for 4 hours.

3. Churn the mixture in an ice cream maker until it has the desired consistency. Place the ice cream in an airtight container and freeze for 4 to 6 hours before serving.

Hot Fudge Sundaes

YIELD: 4 SERVINGS | **ACTIVE TIME:** 5 MINUTES | **TOTAL TIME:** 5 MINUTES

HOT FUDGE (SEE PAGE 527)

2 PINTS OF VANILLA ICE CREAM (SEE PAGE 399 FOR HOMEMADE)

CHANTILLY CREAM (SEE PAGE 518)

½ CUP CHOPPED PECANS OR WALNUTS

4 MARASCHINO CHERRIES, FOR GARNISH

1. Place the Hot Fudge in the bottom of four tulip sundae dishes or bowls.

2. Scoop the ice cream into the bowls.

3. Top each portion with Chantilly Cream, pecans or walnuts, and a maraschino cherry and serve.

Gingerbread Ice Cream

YIELD: 1 QUART | **ACTIVE TIME:** 30 MINUTES | **TOTAL TIME:** 9 HOURS

1 QUART ICE CREAM BASE

2 TEASPOONS GRATED GINGER

2 TEASPOONS CINNAMON

1 TEASPOON FRESHLY GRATED NUTMEG

¼ TEASPOON GROUND CLOVES

2 TABLESPOONS MOLASSES

PINCH OF FINE SEA SALT

1. While the base is still warm, stir in the remaining ingredients and let the mixture steep for 1 hour.

2. Strain into a bowl through a fine-mesh sieve, cover the bowl, and refrigerate for 4 hours.

3. Churn the mixture in an ice cream maker until it has the desired consistency. Place in an airtight container and freeze for 4 to 6 hours before serving.

Black Raspberry Ice Cream

YIELD: 4 CUPS | **ACTIVE TIME:** 30 MINUTES | **TOTAL TIME:** 9 HOURS

1 QUART ICE CREAM BASE

1 TEASPOON PURE VANILLA EXTRACT

5 CUPS BLACK RASPBERRIES

1. While the ice cream base is still warm, stir in the vanilla.

2. Place the raspberries in a blender and puree until smooth. Strain to remove the seeds and stir the puree into the ice cream base. Let the mixture cool completely, cover it, and refrigerate for 4 hours.

3. Churn the mixture in an ice cream maker until it has the desired consistency. Place in an airtight container and freeze for 4 to 6 hours before serving.

Strawberry Sorbet

YIELD: 1 QUART | **ACTIVE TIME:** 30 MINUTES | **TOTAL TIME:** 9 HOURS

1 CUP SUGAR

½ CUP WATER

3 PINTS OF FRESH STRAWBERRIES, HULLED

¼ CUP FRESH LEMON JUICE

½ TEASPOON FINE SEA SALT

1 TEASPOON LEMON ZEST

1. Place the sugar and water in a saucepan and cook over medium heat, while stirring, until the sugar has dissolved. Remove from heat and let cool completely.

2. Place the strawberries, lemon juice, salt, and lemon zest in a food processor and puree until smooth. Add the cooled simple syrup and blitz to incorporate. Place the mixture in a bowl, cover it, and refrigerate for 4 hours.

3. Churn the mixture in an ice cream maker until it has the desired consistency. Place the sorbet in an airtight container and freeze for 4 to 6 hours.

Honey & Ginger Frozen Yogurt

YIELD: 3 CUPS | **ACTIVE TIME:** 15 MINUTES | **TOTAL TIME:** 7 HOURS

2½ CUPS FULL-FAT GREEK YOGURT

½ CUP EVAPORATED MILK

¼ TEASPOON PURE VANILLA EXTRACT

1 TEASPOON GRATED GINGER

2 TABLESPOONS LIGHT CORN SYRUP

½ TEASPOON FINE SEA SALT

⅓ CUP HONEY

1. Place the yogurt, evaporated milk, vanilla, ginger, corn syrup, salt, and honey in a mixing bowl and stir to combine.

2. Pour the mixture into an ice cream maker and churn until it has the desired consistency. Transfer to the freezer and freeze for 4 to 6 hours before serving.

Black Raspberry Ice Cream
SEE PAGE 424

Classic Ice Cream Sandwiches

YIELD: 4 SERVINGS | **ACTIVE TIME:** 10 MINUTES | **TOTAL TIME:** 1 HOUR AND 45 MINUTES

DOUGH FROM CHOCOLATE CHIP COOKIES (SEE PAGE 14)

1 PINT OF ICE CREAM

1. Preheat the oven to 350°F and line two baking sheets with parchment paper.

2. Drop 4-oz. portions of the dough on the baking sheets, making sure to leave enough space between them. Place them in the oven and bake until golden brown and the edges are set, 14 to 18 minutes.

3. Remove the cookies from the oven and transfer them to wire racks to cool completely.

4. When the cookies have cooled completely, scoop ice cream onto half of the cookies. Carefully press down with the other cookies to assemble the sandwiches and store in the freezer until ready to serve.

CANDIES & OTHER DECADENT CONFECTIONS

Peanut Butter Cups

YIELD: 12 CUPS | **ACTIVE TIME:** 15 MINUTES | **TOTAL TIME:** 1 HOUR AND 15 MINUTES

1 CUP CREAMY PEANUT BUTTER

½ CUP CONFECTIONERS' SUGAR

½ TEASPOON FINE SEA SALT

¼ TEASPOON PURE VANILLA EXTRACT

¾ LB. MILK CHOCOLATE, CHOPPED

1. Line a 12-well cupcake pan with paper liners and coat them with nonstick cooking spray. Place the peanut butter, confectioners' sugar, salt, and vanilla in a mixing bowl and stir to combine. Set the mixture aside.

2. Fill a small saucepan with water and bring it to a gentle simmer. Place the chocolate in a heatproof bowl, place it over the simmering water, and stir until it is melted.

3. Place a spoonful of the melted chocolate in each muffin liner and then use a spoon to drag the chocolate halfway up the sides. When you have done this for each liner, place the pan in the refrigerator and let it chill until the chocolate has hardened, 15 to 20 minutes.

4. Remove from the refrigerator, scoop the peanut butter mixture into each chocolate shell, and smooth it with a rubber spatula. Return to the refrigerator and chill for 10 to 15 minutes.

5. Remove from the refrigerator, top each filled shell with another spoonful of melted chocolate, and smooth the top with a rubber spatula. Return to the refrigerator and chill for 25 to 30 minutes before serving.

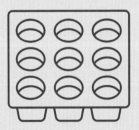

Sweet & Spicy Pecans

YIELD: 4 CUPS | **ACTIVE TIME:** 30 MINUTES | **TOTAL TIME:** 1 HOUR AND 30 MINUTES

4 CUPS PECANS HALVES

2 EGG WHITES

PINCH OF KOSHER SALT

¾ CUP SUGAR

½ TEASPOON CINNAMON

¼ TEASPOON FRESHLY GRATED NUTMEG

⅛ TEASPOON CAYENNE PEPPER

1. Preheat the oven to 350°F. Place the pecans on a parchment-lined baking sheet, place them in the oven, and toast until fragrant, about 15 minutes.

2. Remove the pecans from the oven, set the pan on a cooling rack, and let the pecans cool. Leave the oven on.

3. In the work bowl of a stand mixer fitted with the whisk attachment, whip the egg whites and salt on high until the mixture holds stiff peaks.

4. Reduce the speed to medium and gradually incorporate the sugar. When all of the sugar has been added, raise the speed to high, and whip until the meringue is glossy, about 2 minutes. Reduce the speed to low, add the cinnamon, nutmeg, and cayenne pepper, and beat until incorporated.

5. Remove the work bowl from the mixer, add the toasted pecans, and fold until evenly distributed in the meringue.

6. Line an 18 x 13–inch baking sheet with a silicone baking mat. Place the frosted pecans on the baking sheet in a single layer, place them in the oven, and bake for 30 minutes, removing the pan from the oven every 10 minutes to stir the pecans and ensure that they cook evenly.

7. Remove the pecans from the oven and let them cool completely before enjoying.

Strawberry Fruit Leather

YIELD: 40 SERVINGS | **ACTIVE TIME:** 30 MINUTES | **TOTAL TIME:** 4 HOURS AND 30 MINUTES

½ LB. STRAWBERRIES, HULLED

2 TABLESPOONS CONFECTIONERS' SUGAR

1 TEASPOON FRESH LEMON JUICE

1. Preheat the oven to 180°F. Line an 18 x 13–inch baking sheet with a silicone baking mat.

2. Place the strawberries, confectioners' sugar, and lemon juice in a blender and puree until smooth.

3. Spread the strawberry puree over the silicone mat. It should be an even layer that is about ⅛ inch thick.

4. Place in the oven and bake until the leather is tacky but no longer sticky, about 3 hours.

5. Remove the pan from the oven and place it on a wire rack to cool completely.

6. Carefully remove the fruit leather from the silicone mat and place it on a piece of parchment paper. Use a pizza cutter to cut the leather into the desired shapes and sizes. The fruit leather can be stored in an airtight container at room temperature for up to 1 week.

Raspberry Fruit Leather

YIELD: 40 SERVINGS | **ACTIVE TIME:** 30 MINUTES | **TOTAL TIME:** 4 HOURS AND 30 MINUTES

2 PINTS OF RASPBERRIES

2 TABLESPOONS CONFECTIONERS' SUGAR

1 TEASPOON FRESH LEMON JUICE

1. Preheat the oven to 180°F. Line an 18 x 13–inch baking sheet with a silicone baking mat.

2. Place the raspberries, confectioners' sugar, and lemon juice in a blender and puree until smooth.

3. Spread the raspberry puree over the silicone mat. It should be an even layer that is about ⅛ inch thick.

4. Place in the oven and bake until the leather is tacky but no longer sticky, about 3 hours.

5. Remove the pan from the oven and place it on a wire rack to cool completely.

6. Carefully remove the fruit leather from the silicone mat and place it on a piece of parchment paper. Use a pizza cutter to cut the leather into the desired shapes and sizes. The fruit leather can be stored in an airtight container at room temperature for up to 1 week.

Halvah

YIELD: 12 SERVINGS | **ACTIVE TIME:** 20 MINUTES | **TOTAL TIME:** 36 HOURS

1½ CUPS TAHINI PASTE, STIRRED WELL

2 CUPS HONEY

2 CUPS SLICED ALMONDS, TOASTED

1. Coat a loaf pan with nonstick cooking spray. Place the tahini in a small saucepan.

2. Place the honey in a saucepan fitted with a candy thermometer and warm it over medium heat until it reaches 240°F. Remove the pan from heat.

3. Warm the tahini to 120°F.

4. Add the warmed tahini to the honey and stir the mixture with a wooden spoon. It will look broken at first, but after a few minutes the mixture will come together smoothly.

5. Add the almonds and continue to stir the mixture until it starts to stiffen, 6 to 8 minutes.

6. Pour the mixture into the loaf pan and let it cool to room temperature.

7. Cover the pan tightly with plastic wrap and refrigerate for 36 hours. This will allow sugar crystals to form, which will give the halvah its distinctive texture.

8. Invert the halvah to remove it from the pan and use a sharp knife to cut it into the desired portions.

Tang Yuan Dango

YIELD: 6 SERVINGS | **ACTIVE TIME:** 30 MINUTES | **TOTAL TIME:** 2 HOURS

4 CUPS FRESH STRAWBERRIES, HULLED AND CHOPPED

8¾ OZ. SUGAR

8¾ OZ. SWEET RICE FLOUR (GLUTINOUS RICE FLOUR), PLUS MORE AS NEEDED

⅓ CUP WATER, PLUS MORE AS NEEDED

2 TABLESPOONS CANOLA OIL

FREEZE-DRIED STRAWBERRIES, FOR GARNISH

1. Place the fresh strawberries and sugar in a glass mixing bowl and stir to combine. Place 1 inch of water in a small saucepan and bring it to a boil. Cover the bowl with plastic wrap, place it over the saucepan, and let cook for 1 hour. Check the water level every 15 minutes and add more if it has evaporated. After 1 hour, turn off the heat and let the syrup cool. When cool, strain and discard the solids.

2. Bring water to a boil in a large saucepan. Place the flour, water, and ¾ cup of the syrup in a large mixing bowl and use a fork to work the mixture until it is combined and very dry. Remove 2 tablespoons of the mixture and roll each tablespoon into a ball.

3. Place the balls in the boiling water and cook until they float to the surface and double in size, about 5 minutes. Return the balls to the mixture, add the canola oil, and use the fork to incorporate.

4. Bring the water back to a boil and prepare an ice water bath. Place the mixture on a flour-dusted work surface and knead until it is a smooth and slightly tacky dough. If the dough is too dry or too sticky, incorporate water or flour as needed.

5. Divide the dough into 18 pieces, roll them into balls, and use a slotted spoon to gently lower them into the pot. Gently stir to keep them from sticking to the bottom, and then cook until they float to the surface and double in size, about 8 minutes.

6. Remove with a slotted spoon, refresh in the ice water bath, drain, and thread the balls onto 6 wooden skewers, placing 3 balls on each skewer. Garnish with the freeze-dried strawberries, drizzle some of the remaining syrup over the top, and enjoy.

Mango con Chile Pâte de Fruit

YIELD: 60 CANDIES | **ACTIVE TIME:** 25 MINUTES | **TOTAL TIME:** 3 HOURS AND 30 MINUTES

3 TABLESPOONS APPLE PECTIN

20.1 OZ. SUGAR, PLUS MORE TO TASTE

1½ TEASPOONS CITRIC ACID

1½ TEASPOONS WATER

17.6 OZ. MANGO PUREE

3½ OZ. CORN SYRUP

PINCH OF LIME ZEST

TAJÍN SEASONING, TO TASTE

SALT, TO TASTE

1. Line a baking sheet with a silicone baking mat and place a silicone candy mold on it. Place the pectin and a little bit of the sugar in a mixing bowl and stir to combine. Add the citric acid to the water and let it dissolve.

2. Place the puree in a saucepan and warm it to 120°F. Add the pectin-and-sugar mixture and whisk to prevent any clumps from forming. Bring the mixture to a boil and let it cook for 1 minute.

3. Stir in the corn syrup and remaining sugar and cook the mixture until it is 223°F. The mixture should have thickened and should cool quickly and hold its shape when a small portion of it is dropped from a rubber spatula.

4. Stir in the lime zest and citric acid-and-water mixture and cook for another minute or so. Remove the pan from heat, strain the mixture, and pour it into the candy mold.

5. Let it cool for at least 3 hours before cutting into the desired shapes. Toss in Tajín seasoning, sugar, and salt and enjoy.

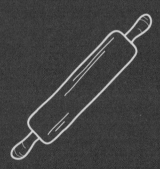

Blueberry Cobbler

YIELD: 16 SERVINGS | **ACTIVE TIME:** 15 MINUTES | **TOTAL TIME:** 1 HOUR

3 PINTS OF FRESH BLUEBERRIES

½ CUP SUGAR

1 TABLESPOON CORNSTARCH

¼ TEASPOON KOSHER SALT

ZEST AND JUICE OF 1 LEMON

1 TEASPOON PURE VANILLA EXTRACT

DOUGH FROM BUTTERMILK BISCUITS (SEE PAGE 532)

1 EGG, BEATEN

SANDING SUGAR, FOR TOPPING

1. Preheat the oven to 375°F. Place the blueberries, sugar, cornstarch, salt, lemon zest, lemon juice, and vanilla in a mixing bowl and toss to combine.

2. Transfer the blueberry mixture to a 13 x 9–inch baking dish.

3. Break the dough into large chunks and cover the mixture with them.

4. Brush the chunks of dough with the egg and sprinkle sanding sugar over them.

5. Place the cobbler in the oven and bake until the biscuits are golden brown and the blueberry mixture is bubbling and has thickened, 30 to 35 minutes.

6. Remove from the oven and let the cobbler cool briefly before serving.

Classic Chocolate Truffles

YIELD: 36 TRUFFLES | **ACTIVE TIME:** 20 MINUTES | **TOTAL TIME:** 24 HOURS

1 LB. DARK CHOCOLATE (55 TO 65 PERCENT)

PINCH OF FINE SEA SALT

1¼ CUPS HEAVY CREAM

½ CUP COCOA POWDER

1. Break the chocolate into small pieces, place it in a food processor, and blitz until it is finely chopped. Place it in a heatproof bowl and add the salt.

2. Place the cream in a saucepan and bring to a simmer over medium heat, stirring frequently. Pour the warm cream over the chocolate and whisk until it has melted and the mixture is smooth. Transfer the chocolate to a square 9-inch baking pan and let it cool completely. Cover with plastic wrap and refrigerate overnight.

3. Line two baking sheets with parchment paper and place the cocoa powder in a shallow bowl. Form heaping tablespoons of the chocolate mixture into balls and roll them in the cocoa powder. Place them on the baking sheets and refrigerate for 30 minutes before serving.

Peppermint Bark

YIELD: 24 SERVINGS | **ACTIVE TIME:** 15 MINUTES | **TOTAL TIME:** 1 HOUR

¾ CUP CRUSHED
PEPPERMINT CANDIES

¾ LB. SEMISWEET
CHOCOLATE CHIPS

2 TEASPOONS CANOLA OIL

¾ LB. WHITE CHOCOLATE
CHIPS

1. Line a rimmed baking sheet with parchment paper and place the crushed peppermint candies in a mixing bowl.

2. Fill a small saucepan halfway with water and bring it to a gentle simmer. Place the semisweet chocolate chips in a heatproof bowl, place it over the simmering water, and stir until melted. Keep the water at a simmer.

3. Stir 1 teaspoon of the canola oil into the melted chocolate and then pour the chocolate onto the baking sheet, using a rubber spatula to distribute evenly. Place in the refrigerator until it has set, about 30 minutes.

4. Place the white chocolate chips in a heatproof bowl, place it over the simmering water, and stir until melted. Stir in the remaining oil and pour the melted white chocolate on top of the hardened semisweet chocolate, using a rubber spatula to distribute evenly.

5. Sprinkle the peppermint pieces liberally over the white chocolate and press down on them lightly. Refrigerate until set, about 30 minutes. Break the bark into pieces and refrigerate until ready to serve.

Pralines

YIELD: 24 PRALINES | **ACTIVE TIME:** 30 MINUTES | **TOTAL TIME:** 1 HOUR AND 30 MINUTES

3 CUPS PECANS

10 OZ. SUGAR

¾ CUP DARK BROWN SUGAR

½ TEASPOON BAKING SODA

¼ TEASPOON KOSHER SALT

3 OZ. MILK

3 OZ. HEAVY CREAM

2 TABLESPOONS UNSALTED BUTTER

1 TABLESPOON BOURBON

1. Preheat the oven to 350°F. Place the pecans on a parchment-lined baking sheet, place them in the oven, and toast until fragrant, about 15 minutes. Remove from the oven and let the pecans cool.

2. Line an 18 x 13–inch baking sheet with a silicone baking mat.

3. Combine the sugar, brown sugar, baking soda, salt, milk, and heavy cream in a medium saucepan fitted with a candy thermometer and cook over medium-high heat, stirring occasionally, until the thermometer reads 242°F. Remove the pan from heat, stir in the butter and bourbon, and then add the pecans. Fold until the pecans are completely coated and evenly distributed.

4. Scoop 2-oz. portions of the mixture onto the silicone mat, leaving ½ inch between each praline. Place the baking sheet on a wire rack and let the pralines set for 1 hour before enjoying.

Honey Nut Truffles

YIELD: 16 TRUFFLES | **ACTIVE TIME:** 10 MINUTES | **TOTAL TIME:** 2 HOURS

½ CUP CREAMY PEANUT BUTTER

¼ CUP HONEY

¼ TEASPOON FINE SEA SALT

4 OZ. DARK CHOCOLATE (55 TO 65 PERCENT), CHOPPED

1. Place the peanut butter, honey, and salt in a mixing bowl and stir until well combined. Drop teaspoons of the mixture on a parchment-lined baking sheet and then place it in the refrigerator for 1 hour.

2. Remove the baking sheet from the refrigerator. Fill a small saucepan with water and bring it to a gentle simmer. Place the chocolate in a heatproof bowl, place it over the simmering water, and stir until it is melted.

3. Dip the balls into the melted chocolate until completely covered. Place them back on the baking sheet. When all of the truffles have been coated, place them in the refrigerator and chill until the chocolate is set, about 45 minutes.

Chocolate & Walnut Fudge

YIELD: 16 SERVINGS | **ACTIVE TIME:** 15 MINUTES | **TOTAL TIME:** 2 HOURS AND 30 MINUTES

1 CUP CHOPPED WALNUTS

1 LB. QUALITY BITTERSWEET CHOCOLATE, CHOPPED

4 OZ. UNSALTED BUTTER

2 CUPS SUGAR

1 TEASPOON PURE VANILLA EXTRACT

1. Preheat the oven to 350°F and line a square 8-inch baking pan with heavy-duty aluminum foil, making sure the foil extends over the sides. Coat the foil with nonstick cooking spray.

2. Cover a baking sheet with the walnuts, place it in the oven, and toast the walnuts until they are fragrant and lightly browned, about 5 to 7 minutes. Remove from the oven and set the walnuts aside.

3. Place the chocolate and butter in a heatproof mixing bowl and set aside. Place the sugar in a large saucepan fitted with a candy thermometer and cook over medium heat until it has dissolved and is boiling. Continue to cook, stirring constantly, until the sugar reaches 236°F on a candy thermometer. Carefully pour the sugar over the chocolate-and-butter mixture in the mixing bowl. Whisk until the mixture is smooth and then stir in the toasted walnuts and the vanilla.

4. Spread the fudge in an even layer in the baking pan. Refrigerate the fudge until it is set, about 2 hours. Use the foil to lift the fudge out of the pan and cut it into squares.

Almond Meringue Kisses

YIELD: 24 KISSES | **ACTIVE TIME:** 15 MINUTES | **TOTAL TIME:** 1 HOUR AND 45 MINUTES

3 EGG WHITES, AT ROOM TEMPERATURE

1 TEASPOON PURE ALMOND EXTRACT

¼ TEASPOON KOSHER SALT

⅓ CUP SUGAR

1 TABLESPOON FINE ALMOND FLOUR

1. Preheat the oven to 250°F and line two baking sheets with parchment paper. Place the egg whites, almond extract, and salt in the work bowl of a stand mixer fitted with the whisk attachment and beat at medium speed until soft peaks form. Incorporate the sugar 1 tablespoon at a time and beat until the mixture holds stiff peaks.

2. Add the almond flour and fold to incorporate. Spoon the meringue mixture into a piping bag fitted with a plain tip and pipe the mixture onto the baking sheets.

3. Place the kisses in the oven and bake until set, about 30 minutes. Turn off the oven and allow the meringues to dry in the oven for 45 minutes. Remove the baking sheets from the oven, gently remove the meringues from the parchment paper, and transfer them to wire racks to cool completely before enjoying.

Nougat

YIELD: 24 SERVINGS | **ACTIVE TIME:** 30 MINUTES | **TOTAL TIME:** 1 HOUR AND 30 MINUTES

3 LARGE EGG WHITES

3 CUPS SUGAR

⅓ CUP LIGHT CORN SYRUP

1 CUP HONEY

1 CUP WATER

ZEST OF 1 LEMON

SEEDS OF 2 VANILLA BEANS

¾ TEASPOON FINE SEA SALT

1 CUP CHOPPED ALMONDS, TOASTED

1. Coat a rimmed baking sheet with nonstick cooking spray. Place the egg whites in the work bowl of a stand mixer fitted with the whisk attachment and beat until frothy. Set aside.

2. Place the sugar, corn syrup, honey, and water in a saucepan fitted with a candy thermometer and bring to a boil over medium-high heat. Cook until the mixture is 300°F.

3. With the mixer running on low, gradually add the hot syrup to the egg whites. When half of the syrup has been incorporated, pour the rest of the hot syrup into the mixture and gradually increase the speed until the mixture is light and frothy. Add the lemon zest, vanilla seeds, salt, and slivered almonds and continue to run the mixer until the mixture has cooled considerably, about 15 to 20 minutes.

4. Pour the mixture onto the baking sheet and let it cool completely before slicing into bars, about 1 hour.

Keto Chia & Sesame Bliss Balls

YIELD: 12 SERVINGS | **ACTIVE TIME:** 10 MINUTES | **TOTAL TIME:** 30 MINUTES

½ CUP COCONUT OIL, MELTED

½ CUP COCONUT BUTTER, MELTED

¼ CUP UNSWEETENED COCOA POWDER

1 TEASPOON PURE ALMOND EXTRACT

½ TEASPOON PURE VANILLA EXTRACT

½ TEASPOON LIQUID STEVIA OR PREFERRED KETO-FRIENDLY SWEETENER

2.8 OZ. WHITE CHIA SEEDS

2 TABLESPOONS SESAME SEEDS

1. Place the coconut oil and coconut butter in a bowl and stir to combine. Stir in the cocoa powder, extracts, and sweetener, cover the bowl, and freeze until the mixture is set, about 20 minutes.

2. Combine the chia seeds and sesame seeds in a shallow dish. Form 2-tablespoon portions of the coconut mixture into balls and roll them in the seed mixture until completely coated. Enjoy immediately or store in the refrigerator.

Nutritional Info Per Serving: Calories: 199; Fat 18.9 g; Net Carbs: 1.5 g; Protein: 3 g

Keto Coconut Bliss Balls

YIELD: 12 SERVINGS | **ACTIVE TIME:** 10 MINUTES | **TOTAL TIME:** 30 MINUTES

½ CUP COCONUT OIL, MELTED

½ CUP ALMOND BUTTER, MELTED

2 TABLESPOONS REAL MAPLE SYRUP

3.2 OZ. UNSWEETENED SHREDDED COCONUT

1¾ OZ. ALMONDS, CHOPPED

½ TEASPOON PURE VANILLA EXTRACT

PINCH OF KOSHER SALT

1. Place the coconut oil, almond butter, and maple syrup in a bowl and stir to combine. Stir in two-thirds of the coconut, the almonds, vanilla, and salt, cover the bowl, and freeze the mixture until it is set, about 20 minutes.

2. Place the remaining coconut in a shallow dish. Form 2-tablespoon portions of the almond butter mixture into balls and roll them in the coconut until completely coated. Enjoy immediately or store in the refrigerator.

Nutritional Info Per Serving: Calories: 212; Fat: 20.7 g; Net Carbs: 4.3 g; Protein: 3 g

Macadamia Brittle

YIELD: 24 SERVINGS | **ACTIVE TIME:** 40 MINUTES | **TOTAL TIME:** 2 HOURS AND 30 MINUTES

1½ CUPS MACADAMIA NUTS

1 TABLESPOON UNSALTED BUTTER, SOFTENED

½ CUP LIGHT CORN SYRUP

3½ OZ. BROWN SUGAR

1 LB. SUGAR

½ TEASPOON KOSHER SALT

½ CUP WATER

½ TEASPOON PURE VANILLA EXTRACT

¾ TEASPOON BAKING SODA

1. Preheat the oven to 350°F. Line a baking sheet with parchment paper and place the macadamia nuts on it. Place in the oven and roast until golden brown and fragrant, about 15 minutes. Remove the nuts from the oven and let them cool for 30 minutes.

2. Place the nuts in a food processor and pulse until roughly chopped.

3. Make sure all of the ingredients are measured out, as you must work quickly once the sugar caramelizes. Place two 18 x 13–inch silicone mats on the counter, along with one rolling pin and a cooling rack.

4. In a large saucepan fitted with a candy thermometer, combine the butter, corn syrup, brown sugar, sugar, and salt and cook over medium heat, swirling the pan occasionally, until the caramel reaches 248°F.

5. Remove the pan from heat and carefully whisk in the water and vanilla.

6. Add the baking soda and toasted macadamia nuts and work quickly, whisking the mixture to deflate the bubbling up of the caramel.

7. Pour the mixture over one of the mats, using a rubber spatula to remove all of the caramel from the pan. Place the second mat on top. Using the rolling pin, roll the caramel out until it is the length and width of the mats.

8. Carefully transfer the mats to the cooling rack. Allow the brittle to set for at least an hour before breaking it up.

Meringue Kisses

YIELD: 50 KISSES | **ACTIVE TIME:** 30 MINUTES | **TOTAL TIME:** 1 HOUR AND 30 MINUTES

4 EGG WHITES

7 OZ. SUGAR

PINCH OF KOSHER SALT

2 DROPS OF GEL FOOD
COLORING (OPTIONAL)

1 TEASPOON PURE VANILLA
EXTRACT (OPTIONAL)

1. Preheat the oven to 200°F and line two baking sheets with
   parchment paper.

2. Fill a small saucepan halfway with water and bring it to a gentle
   simmer. In the work bowl of a stand mixer, combine the egg
   whites, sugar, and salt. Place the work bowl over the simmering
   water and whisk continually until the sugar has dissolved.
   Remove the bowl from heat and return it to the stand mixer.

3. Fit the mixer with the whisk attachment and whip the mixture
   on high speed until it holds stiff peaks. If using food coloring or
   vanilla, add it now and whisk to incorporate.

4. Transfer the meringue to a piping bag fit with a round tip.

5. Pipe the meringue onto the baking sheets, leaving about 1
   inch between them. Place the sheets in the oven and bake the
   meringues until they can be pulled off the parchment cleanly and
   are no longer sticky in the center, about 1 hour. If the meringues
   need a little longer, crack the oven door and continue cooking.
   This will prevent the meringues from browning.

6. Remove from the oven and enjoy immediately.

Caramel Apples

YIELD: 12 APPLES | **ACTIVE TIME:** 30 MINUTES | **TOTAL TIME:** 4 HOURS

12 HONEYCRISP APPLES

½ CUP UNSALTED BUTTER

14 OZ. LIGHT BROWN SUGAR

1 CUP LIGHT CORN SYRUP

1 (14 OZ.) CAN OF SWEETENED CONDENSED MILK

1 TEASPOON PURE VANILLA EXTRACT

1. Line a large baking sheet with parchment paper and coat it with nonstick cooking spray.

2. Insert 6-inch wooden dowels in the bottoms of the apples and push up until they are secure. Place the apples on the baking sheet and chill in the refrigerator for 2 hours.

3. In a medium saucepan fitted with a candy thermometer, combine the butter, brown sugar, corn syrup, and sweetened condensed milk and cook over medium heat, swirling the pan occasionally, until the mixture is 248°F. Remove the pan from heat and whisk in the vanilla extract.

4. While working quickly, grab the apples by the end of the dowels and dip them into the caramel until evenly coated. Let any excess caramel drip off.

5. Place the apples back on the baking sheet and let them set before enjoying.

Smoked Apple Crisp

YIELD: 8 TO 10 SERVINGS | **ACTIVE TIME:** 35 MINUTES | **TOTAL TIME:** 2 HOURS AND 30 MINUTES

1 CUP HICKORY OR APPLEWOOD CHIPS

4 LBS. APPLES, SLICED (BALDWIN OR GRANNY SMITH RECOMMENDED)

1 CUP SUGAR

1 CUP ALL-PURPOSE FLOUR

1 TABLESPOON CINNAMON

1 CUP ROLLED OATS

1 CUP BROWN SUGAR

¼ TEASPOON BAKING SODA

¼ TEASPOON BAKING POWDER

½ CUP UNSALTED BUTTER, SOFTENED

1 TEASPOON FRESHLY GRATED NUTMEG

1. Soak the wood chips in a bowl of water 1 hour before you are ready to cook the apples.

2. Bring your smoker to 250°F. Place the soaked wood chips in the smoking tray and place the apples in the smoker. Smoke for 8 to 10 minutes. Remove the apples and set aside.

3. Preheat the oven to 350°F and coat a baking pan with nonstick cooking spray. Place the sugar, flour, 2 teaspoons of the cinnamon, the oats, brown sugar, baking soda, and baking powder in a mixing bowl and mix by hand until combined. Add the butter and mix until the butter has been incorporated and the mixture is a coarse, crumbly meal.

4. Place the apples in a bowl with the remaining cinnamon, the nutmeg, and half of the crumble. Toss until the apples are evenly coated. Evenly distribute this mixture into a greased baking dish, top with the remaining crumble, and bake until golden brown, about 35 to 45 minutes. Remove from the oven and let the apple crisp cool slightly before serving.

Raspberry Pâte de Fruit

YIELD: 6 SERVINGS | **ACTIVE TIME:** 45 MINUTES | **TOTAL TIME:** 3 HOURS

1 OZ. APPLE PECTIN

6¼ CUPS SUGAR, PLUS MORE AS NEEDED

14.2 OZ. RASPBERRIES, PUREED

28½ OZ. WATER

1. Line a 13 x 9–inch baking pan with parchment paper and coat it with nonstick cooking spray.

2. Place the pectin and ¼ cup of the sugar in a mixing bowl and whisk to combine.

3. In a large saucepan fitted with a candy thermometer, combine the raspberry puree and water and warm the mixture over high heat. While whisking continually, gradually add the pectin mixture and bring the mixture to a boil.

4. Once boiling, add 4 cups of the sugar and whisk until dissolved. Lower the heat to medium and cook the mixture until it is 230°F.

5. Remove the pan from heat and carefully pour the mixture into the prepared baking pan. Transfer the pan to a cooling rack and let it sit at room temperature until cool and set, about 2 hours.

6. Dust a cutting board with sugar, transfer the candy onto the board, and cut it into 1-inch squares.

7. Place the remaining sugar in a medium bowl, add the candies, and toss until coated.

Baked Apples

YIELD: 6 SERVINGS | **ACTIVE TIME:** 15 MINUTES | **TOTAL TIME:** 1 HOUR

6 PINK LADY APPLES

3 TABLESPOONS UNSALTED BUTTER, MELTED

6 TABLESPOONS BLACKBERRY JAM

2 OZ. GOAT CHEESE, SOFTENED, CUT INTO 6 ROUNDS

1. Preheat the oven to 350°F. Slice the tops off of the apples and set the tops aside. Use a paring knife to cut out the apples' cores and then scoop out the centers, leaving a ½-inch-thick wall inside each apple.

2. Rub the inside and outside of the apples with some of the melted butter. Place the jam and goat cheese in a mixing bowl and stir to combine. Fill the apples' cavities with the mixture, place the tops back on the apples, and set them aside.

3. Coat a baking pan with the remaining butter and then arrange the apples in the pan. Place in the oven and bake until tender, 25 to 30 minutes. Remove from the oven and let cool briefly before serving.

Pear & Ginger Crumble

YIELD: 4 SERVINGS | **ACTIVE TIME:** 30 MINUTES | **TOTAL TIME:** 1 HOUR AND 30 MINUTES

4½ OZ. UNSALTED BUTTER, CHILLED

4 PEARS

1 TEASPOON GRATED FRESH GINGER

1 CUP ALL-PURPOSE FLOUR

½ CUP PACKED DARK BROWN SUGAR

½ CUP ROLLED OATS

VANILLA ICE CREAM (SEE PAGE 399 FOR HOMEMADE), FOR SERVING

1. Preheat the oven to 350°F. Place 1 tablespoon of the butter in a large cast-iron skillet and melt it over medium heat.

2. Trim the tops and bottoms from the pears, cut them into quarters, remove the cores, and cut each quarter in half. Lay the slices in the melted butter. Sprinkle the ginger over the pears, cook until they start to brown, and remove the skillet from heat.

3. Place the flour and brown sugar in a bowl and stir to combine. Cut the remaining butter into slices, add them to the bowl, and use your fingers to work the mixture until it comes together as a coarse, crumbly meal. Stir in the rolled oats and then spread the mixture on top of the pears.

4. Put the skillet in the oven and bake until the filling is bubbling and the topping is golden brown, about 25 minutes. Remove the skillet from the oven and let cool for a few minutes before serving with ice cream.

Grilled Peaches with Bourbon Caramel

YIELD: 6 SERVINGS | **ACTIVE TIME:** 20 MINUTES | **TOTAL TIME:** 20 MINUTES

½ CUP SUGAR

¼ CUP PLUS 2 TABLESPOONS BOURBON

¼ CUP HEAVY CREAM, WARMED

1 TABLESPOON UNSALTED BUTTER

1 TEASPOON FINE SEA SALT

6 PEACHES, PITS REMOVED, HALVED

2 PINTS OF VANILLA ICE CREAM (SEE PAGE 399 FOR HOMEMADE), FOR SERVING

1. Preheat your gas or charcoal grill to medium heat (about 425°F). Place the sugar and ¼ cup of bourbon in a small saucepan and cook over medium heat until the sugar has dissolved. Reduce the heat and add the heavy cream, stirring constantly and being careful, as the mixture will splatter. Add the remaining bourbon, the butter, and salt, remove from heat, and pour into a heatproof mixing bowl.

2. When the grill is ready, place the peaches, cut side down, on the grill and cook until the flesh becomes tender and starts to caramelize, about 5 minutes. Turn the peaches over and cook for another 4 to 5 minutes. Place 2 to 3 peach halves in each bowl, drizzle the caramel over them, and top with ice cream.

Peach Cobbler

YIELD: 4 TO 6 SERVINGS | **ACTIVE TIME:** 30 MINUTES | **TOTAL TIME:** 1 HOUR

DOUGH FROM BUTTERMILK BISCUITS (SEE PAGE 532)

1 TO 2 TABLESPOONS ALL-PURPOSE FLOUR, PLUS MORE AS NEEDED

5 OR 6 PEACHES, PITTED AND SLICED

¼ CUP SUGAR

1 TEASPOON CINNAMON

CHANTILLY CREAM (SEE PAGE 518), FOR SERVING (OPTIONAL)

VANILLA ICE CREAM (SEE PAGE 399 FOR HOMEMADE), FOR SERVING (OPTIONAL)

1. Preheat the oven to 400°F and place a cast-iron skillet in the oven as it warms. Place the dough on a flour-dusted work surface and pat it out into a 1-inch-thick rectangle. Use a flour-dusted biscuit cutter or mason jar to cut the dough into rounds.

2. To prepare the filling, place the peaches, sugar, and flour in a bowl and stir to combine. The amount of flour you use will depend on how juicy the peaches are; more juice means more flour is required. Remove the skillet from the oven, transfer the filling into the skillet, and bake for 10 minutes.

3. Remove the skillet from the oven and place the biscuits on top of the filling, making sure they are evenly distributed. Sprinkle the cinnamon on top and return the skillet to the oven. Bake until the biscuits are golden brown and the filling is bubbling, about 12 minutes. Make sure not to burn the topping. Remove from the oven, let cool briefly, and serve with Chantilly Cream or ice cream.

Cherry & Watermelon Soup

YIELD: 4 SERVINGS | **ACTIVE TIME:** 20 MINUTES | **TOTAL TIME:** 24 HOURS

2½ CUPS WATERMELON CUBES

1 TABLESPOON KIRSCH

ZEST AND JUICE OF 1 LIME

SEEDS AND POD OF ½ VANILLA BEAN

¾ CUP CHERRIES, PITTED

1 CUP RIESLING

1 CUP CHAMPAGNE

1. Place 1 cup of the watermelon cubes, the kirsch, lime zest, lime juice, and vanilla seeds and pod in a mixing bowl, stir to combine, and chill in the refrigerator for 1 hour.

2. Spread the mixture evenly over a rimmed baking sheet, place in the freezer, and freeze overnight.

3. Place the remaining watermelon, the cherries, and Riesling in a food processor and puree until smooth. Strain through a fine sieve and place the puree in the refrigerator until ready to serve.

4. Remove the baking tray from the freezer and cut the mixture into cubes. Add these cubes and the Champagne to the puree, ladle the soup into chilled bowls, and enjoy.

Muddy Buddies

YIELD: 8 TO 10 SERVINGS | **ACTIVE TIME:** 5 MINUTES | **TOTAL TIME:** 50 MINUTES

1 CUP SEMISWEET CHOCOLATE CHIPS

¾ CUP CREAMY PEANUT BUTTER

1 TEASPOON PURE VANILLA EXTRACT

9 CUPS RICE CHEX

1½ CUPS CONFECTIONERS' SUGAR

1. Fill a small saucepan halfway with water and bring it to a gentle simmer. Place the chocolate chips and peanut butter in a heatproof bowl and microwave on medium for 30 seconds. Remove from the microwave, add the vanilla, and stir until the mixture is smooth.

2. Place the Chex in a large mixing bowl and pour the peanut butter-and-chocolate mixture over the cereal. Carefully stir until all of the Chex are coated.

3. Place the mixture into a large resealable plastic bag and add the confectioners' sugar. Seal the bag and shake until each piece is coated with sugar.

4. Pour the mixture onto a parchment-lined baking sheet. Place the sheet in the refrigerator and chill for 45 minutes before enjoying.

Bananas Foster

YIELD: 6 SERVINGS | **ACTIVE TIME:** 10 MINUTES | **TOTAL TIME:** 10 MINUTES

½ LB. UNSALTED BUTTER

1 CUP PACKED LIGHT BROWN SUGAR

6 BANANAS, CUT LENGTHWISE AND HALVED

½ CUP DARK RUM

½ CUP HEAVY CREAM

VANILLA ICE CREAM (SEE PAGE 399 FOR HOMEMADE), FOR SERVING

CINNAMON, FOR TOPPING

1. Place a large cast-iron skillet over medium-high heat and add the butter and brown sugar. Once the butter and sugar are melted, add the bananas to the pan and cook until they start to caramelize, about 3 minutes. Shake the pan and spoon some of the sauce over the bananas.

2. Remove the pan from heat and add the rum. Using a long match or wand lighter, carefully light the rum on fire. Place the pan back on the heat and shake the pan until the flames are gone. Add the cream and stir to incorporate.

3. Divide the bananas and sauce among the serving dishes. Top each portion with ice cream and sprinkle cinnamon over the top.

Chocolate & Coconut Soup with Brûléed Bananas

YIELD: 4 SERVINGS | **ACTIVE TIME:** 25 MINUTES | **TOTAL TIME:** 1 HOUR

2 CUPS WHOLE MILK

1 (14 OZ.) CAN OF UNSWEETENED COCONUT MILK

1 CUP HEAVY CREAM

SEEDS AND POD OF 1 VANILLA BEAN

2 BANANAS

¾ CUP SUGAR, PLUS MORE AS NEEDED

½ FRESH COCONUT

½ CUP WATER

¾ LB. DARK CHOCOLATE (55 TO 65 PERCENT), CHOPPED

1. Place the milk, coconut milk, cream, and vanilla seeds and pod in a saucepan and bring to a simmer over medium heat. Turn off the heat and let the mixture stand for 20 minutes.

2. Cut the bananas on a bias. Dip one side into a dish of sugar and then use a kitchen torch to caramelize the sugar. Set aside.

3. Preheat the oven to 350°F. Remove the outer shell of the coconut and use a spoon to remove the meat. Slice the coconut meat very thin and set aside. In a small saucepan, add the sugar and the water and bring to a boil. Remove the syrup from heat and let stand until cool.

4. When the syrup is cool, dip the coconut slices into the syrup and place on a parchment-lined baking sheet. Place the sheet in the oven and bake until the coconut is golden brown, about 8 minutes. Remove and set aside.

5. After 20 minutes, remove the vanilla pod from the soup and return to a simmer. Turn off the heat, add the chocolate, and stir until the chocolate is melted. Strain the soup through a fine sieve and serve with the bruléed bananas and candied coconut.

DRINKS

Chocolate Milkshakes

YIELD: 4 SERVINGS | **ACTIVE TIME:** 2 MINUTES | **TOTAL TIME:** 2 MINUTES

2 PINTS OF CHOCOLATE ICE CREAM (SEE PAGE 401 FOR HOMEMADE)

½ CUP WHOLE MILK

½ TEASPOON FINE SEA SALT

2 TEASPOONS PURE VANILLA EXTRACT

CHANTILLY CREAM (SEE PAGE 518), FOR GARNISH

CHOCOLATE, GRATED, FOR GARNISH

1. Place all of the ingredients, other than the garnishes, in a blender and puree until combined.

2. Pour the milkshakes into tall glasses, garnish each one with the Chantilly Cream and chocolate, and enjoy.

Irish Coffee

YIELD: 1 DRINK | **ACTIVE TIME:** 2 MINUTES | **TOTAL TIME:** 2 MINUTES

½ CUP FRESHLY BREWED COFFEE

DASH OF SUGAR

1 OZ. IRISH WHISKEY

1 OZ. BAILEYS IRISH CREAM

CHANTILLY CREAM (SEE PAGE 518), FOR GARNISH

1. Pour the coffee into an Irish Coffee glass and add the sugar. Stir until the sugar has dissolved.

2. Add the whiskey and stir again. Top with the Baileys Irish Cream. If desired, pour the Baileys over the back of an upturned spoon to layer it on top. Garnish with a dollop of Chantilly Cream and enjoy.

Strawberry Daiquiri

YIELD: 2 SERVINGS | **ACTIVE TIME:** 2 MINUTES | **TOTAL TIME:** 2 MINUTES

1 LB. FROZEN STRAWBERRIES

½ CUP FRESH LIME JUICE

2 TABLESPOONS CASTER (SUPERFINE) SUGAR

1 TABLESPOON HONEY

½ CUP WHITE RUM

1. Place all of the ingredients in a blender and puree until smooth.

2. Pour the cocktail into tall glasses and enjoy.

Piña Colada

YIELD: 4 SERVINGS | **ACTIVE TIME:** 2 MINUTES | **TOTAL TIME:** 2 MINUTES

1 CUP FROZEN PINEAPPLE CHUNKS

1 CUP ICE

½ CUP PINEAPPLE JUICE

½ CUP CREAM OF COCONUT

½ CUP WHITE RUM

½ CUP DARK RUM

1 TEASPOON FRESHLY GRATED NUTMEG

1. Place all of the ingredients in a blender and puree until smooth.

2. Pour the cocktail into tall glasses and enjoy.

Marathon Man

YIELD: 1 DRINK | **ACTIVE TIME:** 2 MINUTES | **TOTAL TIME:** 2 MINUTES

1 OZ. FEW BOURBON

¾ OZ. KAHLÚA

2 TEASPOONS ORGEAT (SEE PAGE 531)

¾ OZ. FRANGELICO

¾ OZ. MOZART DARK CHOCOLATE LIQUEUR

1 TABLESPOON PEANUT BUTTER

1½ OZ. WHOLE MILK

1 MINIATURE SNICKERS BAR

1. Add all of the ingredients to a blender along with two large ice cubes and pulverize until there are fine bubbles throughout and all of the ice has been thoroughly incorporated.

2. Pour over ice into a rocks glass and enjoy.

Sgroppino Plagiato

YIELD: 1 DRINK | **ACTIVE TIME:** 2 MINUTES | **TOTAL TIME:** 2 MINUTES

1 SCOOP OF STRAWBERRY
SORBET (SEE PAGE 425 FOR
HOMEMADE)

1¾ OZ. SELECT APERITIVO

PROSECCO, TO TOP

1. Place the scoop of sorbet in a goblet and pour in the Select
   Aperitivo.

2. Slowly pour Prosecco into the goblet and enjoy.

Rum Ba Ba

YIELD: 1 DRINK | **ACTIVE TIME:** 2 MINUTES | **TOTAL TIME:** 2 MINUTES

1½ OZ. APPLETON ESTATE RUM

1½ OZ. HEAVY CREAM

1 OZ. ORGEAT (SEE PAGE 531)

½ OZ. FRESH LEMON JUICE

1¼ OZ. PASSION FRUIT PUREE

2 DASHES OF PEYCHAUD'S BITTERS

1 SLICE OF PASSION FRUIT, FOR GARNISH

1 SPRIG OF FRESH MINT, FOR GARNISH

1. Add all of the ingredients, except for the garnishes, to a cocktail shaker, fill it two-thirds of the way with ice, and shake vigorously until chilled.

2. Double-strain the cocktail over ice into a rocks glass.

3. Garnish with the passion fruit slice and sprig of mint and enjoy.

Mexican Hot Chocolate

YIELD: 4 SERVINGS | **ACTIVE TIME:** 15 MINUTES | **TOTAL TIME:** 15 MINUTES

3 CUPS WHOLE MILK

1 CUP HALF-AND-HALF

3 CINNAMON STICKS

1 RED CHILE PEPPER, STEM AND SEEDS REMOVED

¼ CUP SWEETENED CONDENSED MILK

1½ LBS. SEMISWEET CHOCOLATE CHIPS

½ TEASPOON PURE VANILLA EXTRACT

1 TEASPOON FRESHLY GRATED NUTMEG

½ TEASPOON FINE SEA SALT

CHANTILLY CREAM (SEE PAGE 518), FOR GARNISH

1. Place the milk, half-and-half, cinnamon sticks, and chile in a saucepan and warm it over medium-low heat for 5 to 6 minutes, making sure the mixture does not come to a boil. When the mixture starts to steam, remove the cinnamon sticks and chile pepper.

2. Add the sweetened condensed milk and whisk until combined. Add the chocolate chips and cook, stirring occasionally, until they have melted. Stir in the vanilla, nutmeg, and salt.

3. Ladle the hot chocolate into warmed mugs, top with Chantilly Cream, and enjoy.

Campfire S'Mores

YIELD: 1 DRINK | **ACTIVE TIME:** 2 MINUTES | **TOTAL TIME:** 2 MINUTES

GRAHAM CRACKER CRUMBS, FOR THE RIM

CHOCOLATE SHAVINGS, FOR THE RIM

1½ OZ. BOURBON

1½ OZ. GIFFARD CRÈME DE CACAO (WHITE)

12 OZ. STOUT, TO TOP

1 TOASTED MARSHMALLOW, FOR GARNISH

1. Place the graham cracker crumbs and chocolate shavings in a dish and stir to combine. Wet the rim of a pint glass and dip it into the mixture.

2. Add the bourbon and crème de cacao to a cocktail shaker, fill it two-thirds of the way with ice, shake vigorously until chilled, and strain into the rimmed pint glass.

3. Top the cocktail with the stout, garnish with the toasted marshmallow, and enjoy.

Café Mocha

YIELD: 10 SERVINGS | **ACTIVE TIME:** 10 MINUTES | **TOTAL TIME:** 20 MINUTES

8 CUPS WHOLE MILK

1 CUP HEAVY CREAM

½ CUP SUGAR, PLUS MORE TO TASTE

½ CUP FRESHLY BREWED ESPRESSO

½ LB. BITTERSWEET CHOCOLATE, CHOPPED

1 TABLESPOON ORANGE ZEST

½ TEASPOON FINE SEA SALT

CHANTILLY CREAM (SEE PAGE 518), FOR GARNISH

1. Place the milk, cream, sugar, and espresso in a saucepan and warm it over medium heat.

2. Place the chocolate in a heatproof bowl. When the milk mixture is hot, ladle 1 cup of it over the chocolate and whisk until the chocolate is completely melted, adding more of the warm milk mixture if the melted chocolate mixture is too thick.

3. Pour the melted chocolate mixture into the pot of warm milk and whisk to combine. Add the orange zest and salt and stir to combine.

4. Pour the beverage into mugs, top with Chantilly Cream, and enjoy.

Cake Boss

YIELD: 1 DRINK | **ACTIVE TIME:** 2 MINUTES | **TOTAL TIME:** 2 MINUTES

2 OZ. PINNACLE CAKE VODKA

1 OZ. MARIE BRIZARD CHOCOLAT ROYAL LIQUEUR

BAILEYS IRISH CREAM, TO TOP

CAKE CRUMBS, FOR GARNISH

1. Place a cocktail glass in the freezer.

2. Add the vodka and chocolate liqueur to a cocktail shaker, fill it two-thirds of the way with ice, and shake vigorously until chilled.

3. Strain the cocktail into the chilled cocktail glass.

4. Pour the Baileys over the back of an upturned spoon to float it on top of the cocktail. Garnish with the cake crumbs and enjoy.

Gourmet Lemon

YIELD: 1 DRINK | **ACTIVE TIME:** 2 MINUTES | **TOTAL TIME:** 2 MINUTES

1½ OZ. SILVER TEQUILA

¾ OZ. LIMONCELLO

¾ OZ. FRESH LIME JUICE

2 DASHES OF LEMON BITTERS

ITALIAN MERINGUE (SEE PAGE 508), TO TOP

1 SPRIG OF FRESH MINT, FOR GARNISH

1 DEHYDRATED LEMON WHEEL, FOR GARNISH

1. Add the tequila, limoncello, lime juice, and bitters to a mixing glass, fill it two-thirds of the way with ice, and stir until chilled.

2. Strain the cocktail into a coupe, top it with the meringue, and torch the meringue until it is browned.

3. Garnish with the sprig of mint and dehydrated lemon wheel and enjoy.

Elevated Irish Coffee

YIELD: 1 DRINK | **ACTIVE TIME:** 2 MINUTES | **TOTAL TIME:** 2 MINUTES

¾ OZ. BUSHMILLS BLACK BUSH IRISH WHISKEY

½ OZ. SIMPLE SYRUP (SEE PAGE 539)

½ TEASPOON PEDRO XIMÉNEZ SHERRY

2 OZ. FRESHLY BREWED MEDIUM-ROAST ESPRESSO

HOT WATER, TO TOP

HEAVY CREAM, LIGHTLY WHIPPED, FOR GARNISH

1. Fill an Irish Coffee glass with boiling water. When the glass is warm, discard the water.

2. Add the whiskey, syrup, and sherry to the glass and stir to combine.

3. Add the espresso and hot water—reserving room for the cream—and stir to incorporate.

4. Layer the lightly whipped cream on top by pouring it over the back of an upturned spoon and enjoy.

Chocolate Burdock Martini

YIELD: 1 DRINK | **ACTIVE TIME:** 2 MINUTES | **TOTAL TIME:** 2 MINUTES

2 OZ. BURDOCK & CACAO NIB BRANDY (SEE PAGE 540)

½ OZ. CHOCOLATE LIQUEUR

2 BAR SPOONS OF PEDRO XIMÉNEZ SHERRY

1 BAR SPOON OF MAPLE SYRUP

3 DASHES OF ORANGE BITTERS

1. Add all of the ingredients to a cocktail shaker, fill it two-thirds of the way with ice, and shake vigorously until chilled.

2. Strain the cocktail into a coupe containing 1 large block of ice and enjoy.

Brandy Alexander

YIELD: 1 DRINK | **ACTIVE TIME:** 2 MINUTES | **TOTAL TIME:** 2 MINUTES

1½ OZ. BRANDY OR COGNAC

1 OZ. CRÈME DE CACAO

¾ OZ. HEAVY CREAM

1. Chill a cocktail glass in the freezer.

2. Place the ingredients in a cocktail shaker, fill it two-thirds of the way with ice, and shake vigorously until chilled.

3. Strain the cocktail into the chilled cocktail glass and enjoy.

Dwight's Friend

YIELD: 1 DRINK | **ACTIVE TIME:** 2 MINUTES | **TOTAL TIME:** 2 MINUTES

2 OZ. BOURBON

½ OZ. KAHLÚA

2 DASHES OF ORANGE BITTERS

1 ORANGE TWIST, FOR GARNISH

1. Place the bourbon, Kahlúa, and bitters in a mixing glass, fill it two-thirds of the way with ice, and stir until chilled.

2. Strain the cocktail over ice into a rocks glass, garnish with the orange twist, and enjoy.

Arcadia

YIELD: 1 DRINK | **ACTIVE TIME:** 2 MINUTES | **TOTAL TIME:** 2 MINUTES

⅔ OZ. FINLANDIA VODKA

2 BAR SPOONS OF MIDORI MELON LIQUEUR

2 BAR SPOONS OF KAHLÚA

⅔ OZ. HEAVY CREAM

1 EGG YOLK

DARK CHOCOLATE, CRUSHED, FOR GARNISH

1 SPRIG OF FRESH MINT, FOR GARNISH

1. Place all of the ingredients, except for the garnishes, in a cocktail shaker, fill it two-thirds of the way with ice, and shake vigorously until chilled.

2. Strain the cocktail into a coupe, garnish with crushed chocolate and the sprig of fresh mint, and enjoy.

At the Mercy of Inertia

YIELD: 1 DRINK | **ACTIVE TIME:** 2 MINUTES | **TOTAL TIME:** 2 MINUTES

2 OZ. BOURBON

4 OZ. WHOLE MILK

DASH OF SIMPLE SYRUP
(SEE PAGE 539)

2 DROPS OF PURE VANILLA
EXTRACT

FRESHLY GRATED NUTMEG,
FOR GARNISH

1. Place the bourbon, milk, syrup, and vanilla in a cocktail shaker, fill it two-thirds of the way with ice, and shake vigorously until chilled.

2. Strain the cocktail into a coupe, garnish with a dash of nutmeg, and enjoy.

Ice Age

YIELD: 1 DRINK | **ACTIVE TIME:** 2 MINUTES | **TOTAL TIME:** 2 MINUTES

SPLASH OF SIMPLE SYRUP (SEE PAGE 399)

DASH OF PEYCHAUD'S BITTERS

2 OZ. BOURBON

4 OZ. ICED COFFEE

1. Add all of the ingredients to a rocks glass filled with ice, stir until chilled, and enjoy.

Root Beer Floats

YIELD: 4 SERVINGS | **ACTIVE TIME:** 5 MINUTES | **TOTAL TIME:** 5 MINUTES

2 PINTS OF VANILLA ICE CREAM (SEE PAGE 399 FOR HOMEMADE)

4 (12 OZ.) BOTTLES OF QUALITY ROOT BEER

CHANTILLY CREAM (SEE PAGE 518), FOR GARNISH

1. Place 2 scoops of ice cream in the bottom of 4 tall glasses.

2. Slowly pour a bottle of root beer into each glass, top with the Chantilly Cream, and enjoy.

Godfather

YIELD: 1 DRINK | **ACTIVE TIME:** 2 MINUTES | **TOTAL TIME:** 2 MINUTES

2 OZ. BLENDED SCOTCH WHISKY

⅔ OZ. AMARETTO

1 ORANGE TWIST, FOR GARNISH

1. Place the whisky and Amaretto in a mixing glass, fill it two-thirds of the way with ice, and stir until chilled.

2. Strain the cocktail over ice into a rocks glass, garnish with the orange twist, and enjoy.

Snow Bowl

YIELD: 1 DRINK | **ACTIVE TIME:** 2 MINUTES | **TOTAL TIME:** 2 MINUTES

2 OZ. GIN

2 OZ. WHITE CHOCOLATE LIQUEUR

SPLASH OF WHITE CRÈME DE MENTHE

FRESHLY GRATED NUTMEG, FOR GARNISH

1. Place the gin, chocolate liqueur, and crème de menthe in a cocktail shaker, fill it two-thirds of the way with ice, and shake vigorously until chilled.

2. Strain the cocktail over ice into a rocks glass, garnish with a dusting of nutmeg, and enjoy.

White Russian

YIELD: 1 DRINK | **ACTIVE TIME:** 2 MINUTES | **TOTAL TIME:** 2 MINUTES

2 OZ. VODKA

1 OZ. KAHLÚA

HEAVY CREAM, TO TOP

1. Place a few ice cubes in a rocks glass.

2. Add the vodka and Kahlúa and stir until chilled. Top with a generous splash of heavy cream, slowly stir until incorporated, and enjoy.

Cooper's Café

YIELD: 1 DRINK | **ACTIVE TIME:** 2 MINUTES | **TOTAL TIME:** 2 MINUTES

1 OZ. FRESHLY BREWED ESPRESSO

2 OZ. MEZCAL

½ OZ. CINNAMON SYRUP (SEE PAGE 540)

1 STRIP OF ORANGE PEEL, FOR GARNISH

1. Place the espresso, mezcal, and syrup in a cocktail shaker, fill it two-thirds of the way with ice, and shake vigorously until chilled.

2. Strain the cocktail into a Nick & Nora glass, garnish with the strip of orange peel, and enjoy.

Mudslide

YIELD: 1 DRINK | **ACTIVE TIME:** 2 MINUTES | **TOTAL TIME:** 2 MINUTES

1½ OZ. VODKA

1½ OZ. KAHLÚA

1½ OZ. BAILEYS IRISH CREAM

¾ CUP VANILLA ICE CREAM (SEE PAGE 399 FOR HOMEMADE)

½ CUP ICE

COCOA POWDER, FOR GARNISH

1. Place the vodka, liqueurs, ice cream, and ice in a blender and puree to the desired consistency.

2. Pour the cocktail into a tumbler, garnish with a dusting of cocoa powder, and enjoy.

Crosseyed & Painless

YIELD: 1 DRINK | **ACTIVE TIME:** 2 MINUTES | **TOTAL TIME:** 2 MINUTES

2 OZ. CHIPOTLE RUM (SEE PAGE 541)

1 OZ. CREAM OF COCONUT

1 OZ. ORANGE JUICE

4 OZ. PINEAPPLE JUICE

FRESHLY GRATED NUTMEG, FOR GARNISH

1 ORANGE SLICE, FOR GARNISH

1. Place the rum, cream of coconut, orange juice, and pineapple juice in a cocktail shaker, fill it two-thirds of the way with crushed ice, and shake until chilled.

2. Pour the contents of the shaker into a glass, grate nutmeg over the cocktail, garnish with the orange slice, and enjoy.

My Silks & Fine Array

YIELD: 1 DRINK | **ACTIVE TIME:** 2 MINUTES | **TOTAL TIME:** 2 MINUTES

1 OZ. VODKA

1 OZ. CHOCOLATE LIQUEUR

1 OZ. KAHLÚA

2 OZ. MILK

1. Add all of the ingredients to a cocktail shaker, fill it two-thirds of the way with ice, and shake vigorously until chilled.

2. Strain the cocktail over ice into a rocks glass and enjoy.

Creamsicle

YIELD: 1 DRINK | **ACTIVE TIME:** 2 MINUTES | **TOTAL TIME:** 2 MINUTES

1½ OZ. ORANGE JUICE

1½ OZ. VODKA

2 SCOOPS OF VANILLA ICE CREAM (SEE PAGE 399 FOR HOMEMADE)

SPLASH OF TRIPLE SEC

½ CUP ICE

1 ORANGE SLICE, FOR GARNISH

1. Add all of the ingredients, except for the garnish, to a blender and puree until smooth.

2. Pour the cocktail into a glass, garnish with the orange slice, and enjoy.

All the Hearts

YIELD: 1 DRINK | **ACTIVE TIME:** 2 MINUTES | **TOTAL TIME:** 2 MINUTES

1 OZ. AGED RUM

1 OZ. KAHLÚA

1 OZ. IRISH CREAM

DASH OF WHITE CRÈME DE MENTHE

1 SPRIG OF FRESH MINT, FOR GARNISH

1. Place the rum, Kahlúa, and Irish cream in a cocktail shaker, fill it two-thirds of the way with ice, and shake until chilled.

2. Strain the cocktail over ice into a rocks glass, add the dash of crème de menthe, garnish with the sprig of mint, and enjoy.

Tom & Jerry

YIELD: 1 DRINK | **ACTIVE TIME:** 2 MINUTES | **TOTAL TIME:** 2 MINUTES

1 OZ. SIMPLE SYRUP (SEE PAGE 539)

1 OZ. DARK RUM

1 OZ. BRANDY

2 OZ. EGGNOG, WARMED

1 CINNAMON STICK, FOR GARNISH

1. Place the syrup, rum, brandy, and eggnog in an Irish Coffee glass and stir to combine.

2. Garnish the cocktail with the cinnamon stick and enjoy.

Grasshopper

YIELD: 1 DRINK | **ACTIVE TIME:** 2 MINUTES | **TOTAL TIME:** 2 MINUTES

1 OZ. GREEN CRÈME DE MENTHE

1 OZ. WHITE CRÈME DE CACAO

1 OZ. HEAVY CREAM

1. Chill a cocktail glass in the freezer.

2. Place the ingredients in a cocktail shaker, fill it two-thirds of the way with ice, and shake until chilled.

3. Strain the cocktail into the chilled glass and enjoy.

BUILDING BLOCKS

Perfect Piecrusts

YIELD: 2 (9-INCH) PIECRUSTS | **ACTIVE TIME:** 15 MINUTES | **TOTAL TIME:** 2 HOURS AND 15 MINUTES

1 CUP UNSALTED BUTTER, CUBED

12½ OZ. ALL-PURPOSE FLOUR, PLUS MORE AS NEEDED

½ TEASPOON KOSHER SALT

4 TEASPOONS SUGAR

½ CUP ICE WATER

1. Transfer the butter to a small bowl and place it in the freezer.

2. Place the flour, salt, and sugar in a food processor and pulse a few times until combined.

3. Add the chilled butter and pulse until the mixture is crumbly, consisting of pea-sized clumps.

4. Add the water and pulse until the mixture comes together as a dough.

5. Place the dough on a flour-dusted work surface and fold it over itself until it is a ball. Divide the dough in two and flatten each piece into a 1-inch-thick disc. Envelop each piece in plastic wrap and place in the refrigerator for at least 2 hours before rolling out to fit your pie plate.

Graham Cracker Crust

YIELD: 1 (9-INCH) CRUST | **ACTIVE TIME:** 10 MINUTES | **TOTAL TIME:** 1 HOUR

1½ CUPS GRAHAM CRACKER CRUMBS

2 TABLESPOONS SUGAR

1 TABLESPOON REAL MAPLE SYRUP

3 OZ. UNSALTED BUTTER, MELTED

1. Preheat the oven to 375°F. Place the graham cracker crumbs and sugar in a large mixing bowl and stir to combine. Add the maple syrup and 5 tablespoons of the melted butter and stir until thoroughly combined.

2. Grease a 9-inch pie plate with the remaining butter. Pour the dough into the pie plate and gently press into shape. Line the crust with aluminum foil, fill it with uncooked rice, dried beans, or pie weights, and bake for about 10 minutes, until the crust is firm.

3. Remove from the oven, remove the foil and weight, and allow the crust to cool completely before filling.

Cookie Crust

YIELD: 1 (9-INCH) CRUST | **ACTIVE TIME:** 20 MINUTES | **TOTAL TIME:** 1 HOUR AND 15 MINUTES

1 CUP UNSALTED BUTTER, SOFTENED

5.3 OZ. LIGHT BROWN SUGAR

5.3 OZ. SUGAR

1 TABLESPOON PURE VANILLA EXTRACT

¾ CUP SEMISWEET CHOCOLATE CHIPS, MELTED

½ CUP COCOA POWDER

1 TEASPOON BAKING SODA

½ TEASPOON KOSHER SALT

8¾ OZ. ALL-PURPOSE FLOUR, PLUS MORE AS NEEDED

½ EGG WHITE

1. Preheat the oven to 300°F and grease an 18 x 13–inch baking sheet with nonstick cooking spray. Place three-quarters of the butter and the sugars in the work bowl of a stand mixer fitted with the paddle attachment and beat the mixture until it is light and fluffy, about 5 minutes. Add the vanilla and melted chocolate chips and beat to combine, scraping down the work bowl as needed.

2. Sift the cocoa powder, baking soda, salt, and flour into a separate mixing bowl. Add the dry mixture to the wet mixture and beat until just combined. Place the dough on a flour-dusted work surface and roll it out so that it will fit the baking sheet and is approximately ⅛ inch thick.

3. Place in the oven and bake until firm, about 20 minutes. Check the crust after 15 minutes to make sure you don't overcook it—it is ready when you don't leave an impression while gently pressing down in the middle. Remove and let cool. While the crust is cooling, place the remaining butter in a saucepan and melt over medium-low heat. Leave the oven at 300°F.

4. Use a rolling pin or food processor to break the crust up into crumbs. Place the crumbs in a mixing bowl, add the melted butter and egg white, and work the mixture with your hands until it becomes sticky.

5. Press the crumbs into a greased 9-inch pie plate and bake for 5 to 6 minutes, until the crust is firm. Remove from the oven and let cool before filling.

Crimping a Piecrust

Crimping creates a decorative edge on your piecrust. It also defines it, keeping it from folding over in the oven. To crimp a piecrust, place your left thumb and left index finger approximately 1 inch from each other. Crook your right index finger and work your way around the pie plate, pressing your right index finger into that 1-inch space and against the inside edge of the piecrust.

Cocoa Crust

YIELD: 1 (9-INCH) CRUST | **ACTIVE TIME:** 20 MINUTES | **TOTAL TIME:** 2 HOURS

5 OZ. ALL-PURPOSE FLOUR, PLUS MORE AS NEEDED

2 TABLESPOONS COCOA POWDER

2 TABLESPOONS SUGAR

½ TEASPOON FINE SEA SALT

2 OZ. UNSALTED BUTTER

2 TABLESPOONS SHORTENING

1 LARGE EGG YOLK

2 TO 3 TABLESPOONS ICE WATER

1. Place the flour, cocoa powder, sugar, and salt in a food processor and pulse until combined. Add the butter and shortening and pulse until the mixture resembles coarse crumbs. Add the egg yolk and water and pulse until the mixture comes together as a dough.

2. Form the dough into a disc, envelop it in plastic wrap, and refrigerate for 1 hour.

3. Preheat the oven to 350°F. Remove the dough from the refrigerator and let it rest at room temperature for 5 to 10 minutes. Place the dough on a flour-dusted work surface and roll it out to ¼ inch thick. Place the crust in a greased 9-inch pie plate, line it with aluminum foil, and fill it with uncooked rice, dried beans, or pie weights. Place in the oven and bake for 15 to 20 minutes, until firm.

4. Remove from the oven, remove the weight and foil, and let the crust cool completely before filling it.

Nutty Crust

YIELD: 1 (9-INCH) CRUST | **ACTIVE TIME:** 10 MINUTES | **TOTAL TIME:** 45 MINUTES

1 OZ. UNSALTED BUTTER, CHILLED AND CHOPPED, PLUS MORE AS NEEDED

1½ CUPS NUTS

1½ TABLESPOONS HONEY

1. Preheat the oven to 400°F and generously grease a 9-inch pie plate with butter. Place the nuts in a food processor and pulse until you have a coarse meal.

2. Transfer the nuts to a bowl and add the honey and butter. Work the mixture with a pastry blender or your hands until combined. Press the mixture into the pie plate, place it in the oven, and bake for about 10 minutes, until the nuts look browned and smell toasted. Remove from the oven, transfer to a wire rack, and let the crust cool completely before filling.

Meringue Shell

YIELD: 1 (9-INCH) SHELL | **ACTIVE TIME:** 20 MINUTES | **TOTAL TIME:** 2 HOURS AND 45 MINUTES

BUTTER, AS NEEDED

3 EGG WHITES, AT ROOM TEMPERATURE

¼ TEASPOON CREAM OF TARTAR

5¼ OZ. SUGAR

½ TEASPOON PURE VANILLA EXTRACT

1. Preheat the oven to 225°F and grease a 9-inch pie plate with butter. Place the egg whites and cream of tartar in the work bowl of a stand mixer fitted with the whisk attachment and beat on high until foamy. With the mixer running, incorporate the sugar 2 tablespoons at a time, waiting until the sugar has dissolved before adding the next increment. Beat until the mixture is glossy and holds stiff peaks.

2. Add the vanilla, beat to incorporate, and spread the meringue over the pie plate, making sure to extend it all the way up the side. Place in the oven and bake for about 1 hour, until the meringue is firm and a toothpick inserted into the center comes out clean. Turn off the oven and allow the shell to rest in the oven for 1 hour.

3. Remove from the oven, transfer the pie plate to a wire rack, and let cool completely before filling.

Gluten-Free Piecrust

YIELD: 1 (9-INCH) PIECRUST | **ACTIVE TIME:** 15 MINUTES | **TOTAL TIME:** 1 HOUR

5.3 OZ. GLUTEN-FREE FLOUR, PLUS MORE AS NEEDED

1 TABLESPOON SUGAR

½ TEASPOON XANTHAN GUM

½ TEASPOON FINE SEA SALT

3 OZ. UNSALTED BUTTER, CHILLED AND CUT INTO SMALL PIECES

1 LARGE EGG

2 TEASPOONS FRESH LEMON JUICE

ICE WATER, AS NEEDED

1. Place the flour, sugar, xanthan gum, and salt in a large mixing bowl. Add the butter and work the mixture with a pastry blender until it is a coarse meal. Place the egg and lemon juice in a separate bowl and whisk until the mixture is very foamy. Add it to the dry mixture and stir until the mixture just comes together as a dough.

2. If the dough isn't quite holding together, add water in 1-tablespoon increments until it does. Form the dough into a disc, envelop it in plastic wrap, and refrigerate for 30 minutes.

3. Remove the dough from the refrigerator and let it rest at room temperature for 10 minutes. Place it on a flour-dusted work surface, roll it out to ¼ inch thick, and place it in a greased 9-inch pie plate. Fill as desired.

Pâté Sucrée

YIELD: 2 (9-INCH) CRUSTS | **ACTIVE TIME:** 15 MINUTES | **TOTAL TIME:** 2 HOURS AND 15 MINUTES

1 CUP UNSALTED BUTTER, SOFTENED

½ LB. SUGAR

¼ TEASPOON KOSHER SALT

1 EGG

2 EGG YOLKS

1 LB. ALL-PURPOSE FLOUR, PLUS MORE AS NEEDED

1. In the work bowl of a stand mixer fitted with the paddle attachment, cream the butter, sugar, and salt on medium speed until the mixture is creamy, light, and fluffy, about 5 minutes.

2. Add the egg and egg yolks and beat until incorporated. Add the flour and beat until the mixture comes together as a dough.

3. Place the dough on a flour-dusted work surface and fold it over itself until it is a ball. Divide the dough in two and flatten each piece into a 1-inch-thick disc. Envelop each piece in plastic wrap and place in the refrigerator for at least 2 hours before rolling out to fit your pie plate.

Blind Baking

The technique of baking a piecrust before filling it is also known as "blind baking." When working with a custard filling, as in a lemon meringue or pumpkin pie, baking the crust ahead of time has several advantages. It prevents pockets of steam from forming in the crust once it is filled, which can cause the crust to become puffy and uneven. Blind baking also keeps the bottom of the crust from becoming soggy, and allows the edge of the pie to be sturdy. Uncooked rice is the most typical weight when blind baking a pie, though dried beans and weights designed specifically for the task can also be utilized. To blind bake a crust, prick it with a fork, line it with aluminum foil, and fill with your chosen weight. Place the crust in a 350°F oven, and bake for 15 to 20 minutes, until it is golden brown and firm. Remove, remove the weight, and let the crust cool completely before filling.

Royal Icing

YIELD: 3 CUPS | **ACTIVE TIME:** 5 MINUTES | **TOTAL TIME:** 5 MINUTES

6 EGG WHITES

1 TEASPOON PURE VANILLA EXTRACT

2 LBS. CONFECTIONERS' SUGAR

2 DROPS OF GEL FOOD COLORING (OPTIONAL)

1. Place the egg whites, vanilla, and confectioners' sugar in a mixing bowl and whisk until the mixture is smooth.

2. If desired, add the food coloring. If using immediately, place the icing in a piping bag. If making ahead of time, store in the refrigerator, where it will keep for 5 days.

Frangipane

YIELD: 4 CUPS | **ACTIVE TIME:** 10 MINUTES | **TOTAL TIME:** 10 MINUTES

¾ LB. ALMOND PASTE

4 OZ. UNSALTED BUTTER, SOFTENED

¼ TEASPOON KOSHER SALT

4 EGGS

1¾ OZ. ALL-PURPOSE FLOUR

1. In the work bowl of a stand mixer fitted with the paddle attachment, cream the almond paste, butter, and salt on medium speed until the mixture is light and fluffy, about 5 minutes.

2. Reduce the speed to low, add the eggs one at a time, and beat until incorporated, again scraping the work bowl as needed. Add the flour and beat until incorporated. Use immediately or store in the refrigerator for up to 2 weeks.

Pound Cake

YIELD: 1 CAKE | **ACTIVE TIME:** 20 MINUTES | **TOTAL TIME:** 2 HOURS AND 15 MINUTES

1 CUP UNSALTED BUTTER, CHILLED AND DIVIDED INTO TABLESPOONS, PLUS MORE AS NEEDED

3 LARGE EGGS

3 LARGE EGG YOLKS

2 TEASPOONS PURE VANILLA EXTRACT

7 OZ. CAKE FLOUR, PLUS MORE AS NEEDED

½ TEASPOON FINE SEA SALT

8¾ OZ. SUGAR

1. Place the butter in the work bowl of a stand mixer and let it stand until it is room temperature, about 25 minutes.

2. Place the eggs, egg yolks, and vanilla in a mixing bowl and beat until combined. Set the mixture aside.

3. Preheat the oven to 325°F and generously butter a 9 x 5–inch loaf pan, dust it with flour, and knock out any excess.

4. Attach the paddle attachment to the stand mixer. Add the salt to the butter and beat on medium until the mixture is smooth and creamy, 2 to 3 minutes. Gradually add the sugar and beat until the mixture is fluffy and almost white, 5 to 8 minutes. Scrape down the bowl as needed while mixing the batter.

5. Gradually add the egg mixture in a steady stream and beat the mixture until light and fluffy, 3 to 4 minutes. Remove the work bowl from the mixer and scrape it down with a rubber spatula.

6. Working in three or four increments, sift the cake flour over the mixture and use a rubber spatula to fold the mixture and thoroughly incorporate the flour before adding the next increment.

7. Transfer the batter to the prepared loaf pan and smooth the top with a rubber spatula. Place the cake in the oven and bake until golden brown and a toothpick inserted into the center of the cake comes out clean, about 1 hour and 15 minutes.

8. Remove the pan from the oven and let the cake cool in the pan on a wire rack for 15 minutes. Invert the cake onto the wire rack and let it cool completely before serving.

French Meringue

YIELD: 4 CUPS | **ACTIVE TIME:** 10 MINUTES | **TOTAL TIME:** 10 MINUTES

4 EGG WHITES

PINCH OF KOSHER SALT

½ CUP SUGAR

1. In the work bowl of a stand mixer fitted with the whisk attachment, whip the egg whites and salt on medium until soft peaks form.

2. Add the sugar 1 tablespoon at a time and whisk to incorporate. Wait about 10 seconds between additions.

3. When all of the sugar has been incorporated, whip until the mixture holds stiff peaks. Use immediately.

Swiss Meringue

YIELD: 3 CUPS | **ACTIVE TIME:** 20 MINUTES | **TOTAL TIME:** 20 MINUTES

4 EGG WHITES

1 CUP SUGAR

PINCH OF KOSHER SALT

1. Fill a small saucepan halfway with water and bring it to a gentle simmer.

2. Place the egg whites, sugar, and salt in the work bowl of a stand mixer. Place the bowl over the simmering water and whisk until the mixture reaches 115°F.

3. Return the bowl to the stand mixer and fit it with the whisk attachment. Whip on high until the meringue is shiny, glossy, and holds stiff peaks, about 5 minutes. For best results, use the meringue the day you make it.

Italian Meringue

YIELD: 3 CUPS | **ACTIVE TIME:** 15 MINUTES | **TOTAL TIME:** 30 MINUTES

1 CUP SUGAR

¼ CUP WATER

4 EGG WHITES

PINCH OF KOSHER SALT

1. Place the sugar and water in a small saucepan that is fit with a candy thermometer and bring the mixture to a boil.

2. While the syrup is coming to a boil, place the egg whites and salt in the work bowl of a stand mixer fitted with the whisk attachment and whip on medium speed until the mixture holds stiff peaks.

3. Cook the syrup until the thermometer reads 245°F. Immediately remove the pan from heat. Once the syrup stops bubbling, let it sit for 30 seconds.

4. Reduce the speed of the mixer to medium-low and slowly pour the syrup down the side of the mixing bowl until all of it has been incorporated. Raise the speed to high and whip until the meringue is glossy and holds stiff peaks.

American Buttercream

YIELD: 3 CUPS | **ACTIVE TIME:** 10 MINUTES | **TOTAL TIME:** 10 MINUTES

1 LB. UNSALTED BUTTER, SOFTENED

2 LBS. CONFECTIONERS' SUGAR

⅛ TEASPOON KOSHER SALT

¼ CUP HEAVY CREAM

½ TEASPOON PURE VANILLA EXTRACT

1. In the work bowl of a stand mixer fitted with the paddle attachment, combine the butter, confectioners' sugar, and salt and beat on low speed until the sugar starts to be incorporated into the butter. Raise the speed to high and beat until the mixture is smooth and fluffy, about 5 minutes.

2. Reduce the speed to low, add the heavy cream and vanilla, and beat until incorporated. Use immediately, or store in the refrigerator for up to 2 weeks. If refrigerating, return to room temperature before using.

Italian Buttercream

YIELD: 3 CUPS | **ACTIVE TIME:** 20 MINUTES | **TOTAL TIME:** 30 MINUTES

2 CUPS SUGAR

½ CUP WATER

8 EGG WHITES

¼ TEASPOON FINE SEA SALT

1½ LBS. UNSALTED BUTTER, SOFTENED

1 TEASPOON PURE VANILLA EXTRACT

1. Place the sugar and water in a small saucepan, fit it with a candy thermometer, and bring the mixture to a boil.

2. While the syrup is coming to a boil, place the egg whites and salt in the work bowl of a stand mixer fitted with the whisk attachment and whip on medium speed until the mixture holds stiff peaks.

3. Cook the syrup until the thermometer reads 245°F. Immediately remove the pan from the heat. Once the syrup stops bubbling, let it sit for 30 seconds.

4. Reduce the speed of the mixer to medium-low and slowly pour the syrup down the side of the mixing bowl until all of it has been incorporated. Raise the speed to high and whip until the meringue is glossy and holds stiff peaks.

5. Add the butter 4 oz. at a time and whip until the mixture has thickened.

6. Reduce the speed to medium, add the vanilla, and beat until incorporated. Use immediately, or store in the refrigerator for up to 2 weeks. If refrigerating, return to room temperature before using.

Cream Cheese Frosting

YIELD: 3 CUPS | **ACTIVE TIME:** 10 MINUTES | **TOTAL TIME:** 10 MINUTES

1 CUP UNSALTED BUTTER, SOFTENED

1 CUP CREAM CHEESE, SOFTENED

2 LBS. CONFECTIONERS' SUGAR

⅛ TEASPOON KOSHER SALT

¼ CUP HEAVY CREAM

½ TEASPOON PURE VANILLA EXTRACT

1. In the work bowl of a stand mixer fitted with the paddle attachment, combine the butter, cream cheese, confectioners' sugar, and salt and beat on low speed until the sugar starts to be incorporated into the butter. Raise the speed to high and beat until the mixture is smooth and fluffy, about 5 minutes.

2. Reduce the speed to low, add the heavy cream and vanilla extract, and beat until incorporated. Use immediately, or store in the refrigerator for up to 2 weeks. If refrigerating, return to room temperature before using.

Pastry Cream

YIELD: 2½ CUPS | **ACTIVE TIME:** 15 MINUTES | **TOTAL TIME:** 2 HOURS AND 15 MINUTES

2 CUPS WHOLE MILK

1 TABLESPOON UNSALTED BUTTER

½ CUP SUGAR

3 TABLESPOONS CORNSTARCH

2 LARGE EGGS

PINCH OF FINE SEA SALT

½ TEASPOON PURE VANILLA EXTRACT

1. Place the milk and butter in a saucepan and bring to a simmer over medium heat.

2. As the milk mixture is coming to a simmer, place the sugar and cornstarch in a small bowl and whisk to combine. Add the eggs and whisk until the mixture is smooth and creamy.

3. Slowly pour half of the hot milk mixture into the egg mixture and stir until incorporated. Add the salt and vanilla, stir to incorporate, and pour the tempered egg mixture into the saucepan. Cook, while stirring constantly, until the mixture is very thick and about to come to a boil.

4. Remove from heat and pour the pastry cream into a bowl. Place plastic wrap directly on the surface to prevent a skin from forming. Place in the refrigerator and chill for about 2 hours.

Classic Chocolate Frosting

YIELD: 1½ CUPS | **ACTIVE TIME:** 15 MINUTES | **TOTAL TIME:** 1 HOUR AND 30 MINUTES

1 LB. MILK CHOCOLATE, CHOPPED

⅔ CUP HEAVY CREAM

1 CUP UNSALTED BUTTER, DIVIDED INTO TABLESPOONS AND SOFTENED

1. Fill a small saucepan halfway with water and bring it to a simmer over medium heat.

2. Place the chocolate and cream in a large heatproof bowl and place it over the simmering water. Stir occasionally until the mixture is smooth and glossy.

3. Remove the bowl from heat, add the butter, and stir briefly. Let the mixture stand until the butter is melted, about 5 minutes, and then stir until the mixture is smooth.

4. Place the frosting in the refrigerator until it is cool and has thickened, 30 minutes to 1 hour.

Autumn-Spiced Pastry Cream

YIELD: 2½ CUPS | **ACTIVE TIME:** 30 MINUTES | **TOTAL TIME:** 2 HOURS AND 30 MINUTES

½ CUP SUGAR

3 TABLESPOONS CORNSTARCH

6 EGG YOLKS

2 CUPS WHOLE MILK

1½ TEASPOONS CINNAMON

1 TEASPOON FRESHLY GRATED NUTMEG

½ TEASPOON GROUND GINGER

⅛ TEASPOON GROUND CLOVES

¼ TEASPOON KOSHER SALT

1½ TEASPOONS PURE VANILLA EXTRACT

4 TABLESPOONS UNSALTED BUTTER, SOFTENED

1. In a mixing bowl, add the sugar, cornstarch, and egg yolks and whisk until combined, about 2 minutes. Set the mixture aside.

2. Place the milk, cinnamon, nutmeg, ginger, and cloves in a saucepan and bring to a simmer over medium heat. Remove the pan from heat.

3. Slowly pour half of the hot milk mixture into the egg mixture and stir until incorporated. Add the salt and vanilla, stir to incorporate, and pour the tempered egg mixture into the saucepan. Cook, while stirring constantly, until the mixture is very thick and about to come to a boil.

4. Remove the pan from heat, add the butter, and stir until thoroughly incorporated.

5. Strain the pastry cream through a fine-mesh strainer into a small bowl.

6. Place plastic wrap directly on the surface to prevent a skin from forming. Place in the refrigerator and chill for about 2 hours. This will keep in the refrigerator for up to 5 days.

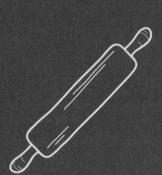

Butterscotch Pastry Cream

YIELD: 2½ CUPS | **ACTIVE TIME:** 30 MINUTES | **TOTAL TIME:** 2 HOURS AND 30 MINUTES

3 TABLESPOONS CORNSTARCH

6 EGG YOLKS

½ CUP LIGHT BROWN SUGAR

2 TABLESPOONS WATER

2 CUPS MILK

¼ TEASPOON KOSHER SALT

1½ TEASPOONS PURE VANILLA EXTRACT

4 TABLESPOONS UNSALTED BUTTER, SOFTENED

1. In a small bowl, combine the cornstarch and egg yolks and whisk for 2 minutes. Set the mixture aside.

2. Place the brown sugar and water in a saucepan, fit the pan with a candy thermometer, and cook over high heat until the thermometer reads 290°F.

3. Remove the pan from the heat. While whisking, slowly add the milk to the sugar. Be careful, as the mixture will most likely splatter. Place the pan over high heat and bring the mixture back to a simmer. Remove the pan from heat.

4. Slowly pour half of the hot milk mixture into the egg mixture and stir until incorporated. Add the salt and vanilla extract, stir to incorporate, and pour the tempered egg mixture into the saucepan. Cook, while stirring constantly, until the mixture is very thick and about to come to a boil. Remove the pan from heat.

5. Add the butter and whisk until fully incorporated.

6. Strain the pastry cream through a fine-mesh strainer into a small bowl.

7. Place plastic wrap directly on the surface to prevent a skin from forming. Place in the refrigerator and chill for about 2 hours. This will keep in the refrigerator for up to 5 days.

Caramelized White Chocolate

YIELD: 1 CUP | **ACTIVE TIME:** 25 MINUTES | **TOTAL TIME:** 1 HOUR AND 30 MINUTES

1 LB. WHITE CHOCOLATE

PINCH OF FINE SEA SALT

2 TABLESPOONS CANOLA
OIL

1. Preheat the oven to 250°F.

2. Line a rimmed 18 x 13–inch baking sheet with a Silpat mat.

3. Chop the white chocolate into small pieces and spread them over the pan. Add the salt and oil and stir to coat the chocolate pieces.

4. Place the pan in the oven and bake for 10 minutes.

5. Use a rubber spatula to spread the chocolate until it covers the entire pan. Place back in the oven and bake until the white chocolate has caramelized to a deep golden brown, about 30 to 50 minutes, removing to stir every 10 minutes.

6. Carefully pour the caramelized white chocolate into a heatproof container. Store at room temperature for up to 1 month.

Butterfluff Filling

YIELD: 4 CUPS | **ACTIVE TIME:** 10 MINUTES | **TOTAL TIME:** 10 MINUTES

½ LB. MARSHMALLOW CREME

10 OZ. UNSALTED BUTTER, SOFTENED

11 OZ. CONFECTIONERS' SUGAR

1½ TEASPOONS PURE VANILLA EXTRACT

¾ TEASPOON KOSHER SALT

1. In the work bowl of a stand mixer fitted with the paddle attachment, cream the marshmallow creme and butter on medium speed until the mixture is light and fluffy, about 5 minutes.

2. Add the confectioners' sugar, vanilla, and salt, reduce the speed to low, and beat for 2 minutes. Use immediately, or store in the refrigerator for up to 1 month.

Chantilly Cream

YIELD: 2 CUPS | **ACTIVE TIME:** 5 MINUTES | **TOTAL TIME:** 5 MINUTES

2 CUPS HEAVY CREAM

3 TABLESPOONS SUGAR

1 TEASPOON PURE VANILLA EXTRACT

1. In the work bowl of a stand mixer fitted with the whisk attachment, whip the heavy cream, sugar, and vanilla on high until the mixture holds soft peaks.

2. Use immediately, or store in the refrigerator for up to 3 days.

Cinnamon Chantilly Cream

YIELD: 2 CUPS | **ACTIVE TIME:** 5 MINUTES | **TOTAL TIME:** 5 MINUTES

2 CUPS HEAVY CREAM

¼ CUP CONFECTIONERS' SUGAR

1 TABLESPOON CINNAMON

1 TEASPOON PURE VANILLA EXTRACT

1. In the work bowl of a stand mixer fitted with the whisk attachment, whip the heavy cream, sugar, cinnamon, and vanilla on high until the mixture holds soft peaks.

2. Use immediately, or store in the refrigerator for up to 3 days.

Vanilla Glaze

YIELD: 1½ CUPS | **ACTIVE TIME:** 5 MINUTES | **TOTAL TIME:** 5 MINUTES

½ CUP MILK, PLUS MORE AS NEEDED

¼ TEASPOON PURE VANILLA EXTRACT

1 LB. CONFECTIONERS' SUGAR, PLUS MORE AS NEEDED

1. In a mixing bowl, whisk all of the ingredients until combined.

2. If the glaze is too thick, incorporate tablespoons of milk until it reaches the desired consistency. If it's too thin, incorporate tablespoons of confectioners' sugar. Use immediately, or store in the refrigerator for up to 5 days.

Honey Glaze

YIELD: 1½ CUPS | **ACTIVE TIME:** 5 MINUTES | **TOTAL TIME:** 5 MINUTES

½ CUP MILK, PLUS MORE AS NEEDED

1 TABLESPOON HONEY

¼ TEASPOON KOSHER SALT

1 LB. CONFECTIONERS' SUGAR, PLUS MORE AS NEEDED

1. In a mixing bowl, whisk all of the ingredients until combined.

2. If the glaze is too thick, incorporate tablespoons of milk until it reaches the desired consistency. If it's too thin, incorporate tablespoons of confectioners' sugar. Use immediately, or store in the refrigerator for up to 5 days.

Milk Chocolate Crémeux

YIELD: 4 CUPS | **ACTIVE TIME:** 30 MINUTES | **TOTAL TIME:** 24 HOURS

2 SHEETS OF SILVER GELATIN

10.7 OZ. MILK CHOCOLATE

¼ CUP SUGAR

4 EGG YOLKS

¾ CUP MILK

¾ CUP HEAVY CREAM

1. Place the gelatin sheets in a small bowl and add 1 cup of ice and enough cold water that the sheets are completely covered. Set aside.

2. Place the chocolate in a heatproof mixing bowl.

3. Place half of sugar and the egg yolks in a small bowl and whisk for 2 minutes. Set the mixture aside.

4. In a small saucepan, combine the milk, heavy cream, and remaining sugar and bring to a simmer over medium heat.

5. Slowly pour half of the hot milk mixture into the egg mixture and stir until incorporated. Pour the tempered egg mixture into the saucepan. Cook, while stirring constantly, until the mixture thickens and is about to come to a full simmer (if you have an instant-read thermometer, 175°F). Remove the pan from heat.

6. Remove the bloomed gelatin from the ice water. Squeeze to remove as much water as possible from the sheets. Add the sheets to the hot milk mixture base and whisk until they have completely dissolved.

7. Pour the hot milk mixture over the chocolate and let the mixture sit for 1 minute. Whisk to combine, transfer to a heatproof container, and let it cool to room temperature.

8. Store in the refrigerator overnight before using.

Rhubarb Jam

YIELD: 3 CUPS | **ACTIVE TIME:** 20 MINUTES | **TOTAL TIME:** 3 HOURS

4 CUPS CHOPPED RHUBARB

1 CUP WATER

¾ CUP SUGAR

½ TEASPOON FINE SEA SALT

1 TEASPOON PECTIN

1. Place the rhubarb, water, sugar, and salt in a saucepan and cook the mixture over high heat, stirring occasionally to keep it from sticking, until nearly all of the liquid has evaporated.

2. Add the pectin and stir the mixture for 1 minute. Transfer it to a sterilized mason jar and let it cool completely before using or storing in the refrigerator.

Almond Syrup

YIELD: ½ CUP | **ACTIVE TIME:** 10 MINUTES | **TOTAL TIME:** 1 HOUR

½ CUP WATER

½ CUP SUGAR

¼ TEASPOON ALMOND EXTRACT

1. Place the water and sugar in a small saucepan and bring to a boil over medium heat, stirring to dissolve the sugar.

2. Remove the saucepan from heat, stir in the almond extract, and let the syrup cool completely before using or storing in the refrigerator.

Brown Butter

YIELD: 1 LB. | **ACTIVE TIME:** 10 MINUTES | **TOTAL TIME:** 10 MINUTES

1½ LBS. UNSALTED BUTTER

1. Place the butter in a large saucepan and melt it over medium heat, stirring frequently, until the butter starts to give off a nutty smell and turn golden brown (let your nose lead the way here, frequently wafting the steam toward you).

2. Remove the pan from heat and strain the butter through a fine sieve. Let the butter cool and solidify before using or storing in the refrigerator.

Chocolate Ganache

YIELD: 1½ CUPS | **ACTIVE TIME:** 10 MINUTES | **TOTAL TIME:** 2 HOURS AND 30 MINUTES

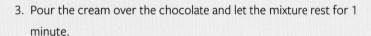

½ LB. CHOCOLATE (DARK, MILK, OR WHITE)

1 CUP HEAVY CREAM

1. Place the chocolate in a heatproof mixing bowl and set it aside.

2. Place the heavy cream in a small saucepan and bring to a simmer over medium heat.

3. Pour the cream over the chocolate and let the mixture rest for 1 minute.

4. Gently whisk the mixture until thoroughly combined. Use immediately if drizzling over a cake or serving with fruit. Let the ganache cool for 2 hours if piping. The ganache will keep in the refrigerator for up to 5 days.

Hazelnut Mousseline

YIELD: 3 CUPS | **ACTIVE TIME:** 20 MINUTES | **TOTAL TIME:** 2 HOURS AND 30 MINUTES

½ CUP SUGAR

6 EGG YOLKS

3 TABLESPOONS CORNSTARCH

2 CUPS WHOLE MILK

¼ TEASPOON KOSHER SALT

1½ TEASPOONS PURE VANILLA EXTRACT

2 OZ. UNSALTED BUTTER, SOFTENED

¼ CUP HAZELNUT PRALINE PASTE (SEE OPPOSITE PAGE)

1. Place the sugar, egg yolks, and cornstarch in a mixing bowl and whisk for 2 minutes, so that the mixture is thoroughly combined. Set it aside.

2. Place the milk in a medium saucepan and bring it to a simmer over medium heat. While whisking continually, gradually add the warm milk to the egg yolk mixture until it has all been incorporated.

3. Pour the tempered egg yolks into the saucepan and cook over medium heat, stirring constantly. When the custard has thickened and begins to simmer, cook for another 30 seconds and then remove the pan from heat.

4. Whisk in the remaining ingredients, strain the mousseline into a bowl through a fine-mesh sieve, and place plastic wrap directly on the top to keep a skin from forming. Place the mousseline in the refrigerator and chill for 2 hours before using. The mousseline will keep in the refrigerator for 5 days.

Hazelnut Praline Paste

YIELD: 3 CUPS | **ACTIVE TIME:** 25 MINUTES | **TOTAL TIME:** 2 HOURS

2 CUPS HAZELNUTS

1 CUP SUGAR

3 TABLESPOONS WATER

2 TEASPOONS CANOLA OIL

¼ TEASPOON FINE SEA SALT

1. Place the hazelnuts in a large, dry skillet and toast over medium heat until they just start to brown, about 5 minutes. Transfer the nuts to a clean, dry kitchen towel, fold the towel over the nuts, and rub them together until the skins have loosened. Place the toasted nuts on a parchment-lined baking sheet and discard the skins.

2. Place the sugar and water in a small saucepan and warm the mixture over medium heat, swirling the pan occasionally instead of stirring the mixture. Cook until the mixture is a deep golden brown and then pour it over the toasted hazelnuts. Let the mixture sit at room temperature until it has set.

3. Break the hazelnut brittle into pieces, place them in a blender, and add the canola oil and salt. Puree until the mixture is a smooth paste and use immediately or store in the refrigerator.

Gianduja Crémeux

YIELD: 4 CUPS | **ACTIVE TIME:** 30 MINUTES | **TOTAL TIME:** 24 HOURS

2 SHEETS OF SILVER GELATIN

¾ LB. GIANDUJA CHOCOLATE, CHOPPED

¼ CUP SUGAR

4 EGG YOLKS

¾ CUP MILK

¾ CUP HEAVY CREAM

1. Place the gelatin sheets in a small bowl and add 1 cup of ice and enough cold water that the sheets are completely covered. Set aside.

2. Place the chocolate in a heatproof mixing bowl.

3. Place half of sugar and the egg yolks in a small bowl and whisk for 2 minutes. Set the mixture aside.

4. In a small saucepan, combine the milk, heavy cream, and remaining sugar and bring to a simmer over medium heat.

5. Slowly pour half of the hot milk mixture into the egg mixture and stir until incorporated. Pour the tempered egg mixture into the saucepan. Cook, while stirring constantly, until the mixture thickens and is about to come to a full simmer (if you have an instant-read thermometer, 175°F). Remove the pan from heat.

6. Remove the bloomed gelatin from the ice water. Squeeze to remove as much water as possible from the sheets. Add the sheets to the hot milk mixture base and whisk until they have completely dissolved.

7. Pour the hot milk mixture over the chocolate and let the mixture sit for 1 minute. Whisk to combine, transfer to a heatproof container, and let it cool to room temperature.

8. Store in the refrigerator overnight before using.

Hot Fudge

YIELD: 2 CUPS | **ACTIVE TIME:** 15 MINUTES | **TOTAL TIME:** 15 MINUTES

⅔ CUP HEAVY CREAM

½ CUP LIGHT CORN SYRUP

⅓ CUP DARK BROWN SUGAR

¼ CUP COCOA POWDER

½ TEASPOON FINE SEA SALT

½ LB. BITTERSWEET CHOCOLATE, CHOPPED

½ TEASPOON ESPRESSO POWDER

2 TABLESPOONS UNSALTED BUTTER

1 TEASPOON PURE VANILLA EXTRACT

1. Place the cream, corn syrup, brown sugar, cocoa powder, salt, half of the chocolate, and the espresso powder in a saucepan and cook over medium heat until the chocolate is melted.

2. Reduce the heat and simmer for 5 minutes. Remove the pan from heat and whisk in the remaining chocolate, the butter, and the vanilla. Serve immediately.

Cajeta

YIELD: 1½ CUPS | **ACTIVE TIME:** 1 HOUR | **TOTAL TIME:** 5 HOURS

4 CUPS GOATS' MILK

1 CUP SUGAR

1 CINNAMON STICK

⅛ TEASPOON KOSHER SALT

¼ TEASPOON BAKING SODA

1½ TEASPOONS WATER

1. Place the goat milk, sugar, cinnamon stick, and salt in a medium saucepan and bring to a simmer over medium-low heat.

2. In a small bowl, combine the baking soda and water. Whisk the mixture into the saucepan.

3. Continue to simmer for 1 to 2 hours, stirring frequently.

4. When the mixture has turned a caramel color and is thick enough to coat the back of a wooden spoon, remove the pan from heat and let the cajeta cool for 1 hour.

5. Transfer to a mason jar and refrigerate until set. This will keep in the refrigerator for up to 1 month.

Caramel Sauce

YIELD: 2 CUPS | **ACTIVE TIME:** 15 MINUTES | **TOTAL TIME:** 1 HOUR AND 30 MINUTES

1 CUP SUGAR

¼ CUP WATER

½ CUP HEAVY CREAM

6 TABLESPOONS UNSALTED BUTTER, SOFTENED

½ TEASPOON KOSHER SALT

½ TEASPOON PURE VANILLA EXTRACT

1. Place the sugar and water in a small saucepan and bring to a boil over high heat. Resist the urge to whisk the mixture; instead, swirl the pan occasionally.

2. Once the mixture turns a dark amber, turn off the heat and, whisking slowly, drizzle in the heavy cream. Be careful, as the mixture may splatter.

3. When all of the cream has been incorporated, add the butter, salt, and vanilla and whisk until smooth. Pour the hot caramel into a mason jar to cool. The caramel sauce can be stored for 1 week at room temperature.

Bourbon Toffee Sauce

YIELD: 4 CUPS | **ACTIVE TIME:** 10 MINUTES | **TOTAL TIME:** 20 MINUTES

7 OZ. UNSALTED BUTTER

¾ CUP PACKED LIGHT BROWN SUGAR

¾ CUP MAPLE SYRUP

¼ CUP HEAVY CREAM

¼ TEASPOON KOSHER SALT

2 TABLESPOONS BOURBON

1. Place the butter, light brown sugar, maple syrup, heavy cream, and salt in a medium saucepan and bring the mixture to a boil over medium heat.

2. Let the mixture boil for 30 seconds, while continually whisking.

3. Remove the pan from heat and whisk in the bourbon.

4. Use immediately, or store in the refrigerator for up to 1 month. If storing in the refrigerator, reheat before using.

Coating Chocolate

YIELD: 1 CUP | **ACTIVE TIME:** 10 MINUTES | **TOTAL TIME:** 10 MINUTES

½ LB. DARK CHOCOLATE (55 TO 65 PERCENT)

4 OZ. COCONUT OIL

½ TEASPOON PURE VANILLA EXTRACT

⅛ TEASPOON KOSHER SALT

1. Combine all of the ingredients in a small saucepan and place it over low heat.

2. Stir constantly until the chocolate has melted and the mixture is smooth. Use immediately.

Summary Berry Compote

YIELD: 2 CUPS | **ACTIVE TIME:** 20 MINUTES | **TOTAL TIME:** 1 HOUR

4 PINTS OF ASSORTED BERRIES

ZEST AND JUICE OF 1 LEMON

1 CUP SUGAR

3 TABLESPOONS CORNSTARCH

¼ TEASPOON KOSHER SALT

2 TEASPOONS PURE VANILLA EXTRACT

1. Place the berries, lemon juice, lemon zest, and sugar in a medium saucepan and cook over medium heat until the berries begin to burst and release their liquid, about 10 minutes.

2. Stir in the cornstarch, salt, and vanilla and reduce the heat to medium-low. Cook, stirring occasionally, until the mixture thickens slightly.

3. Remove the pan from heat and let the compote cool completely before storing in an airtight container. The compote can be served warm or chilled. It will keep in the refrigerator for up to 1 week.

Orgeat

YIELD: 1½ CUPS | **ACTIVE TIME:** 20 MINUTES | **TOTAL TIME:** 7 HOURS

2 CUPS ALMONDS

1 CUP SIMPLE SYRUP (SEE PAGE 539)

1 TEASPOON ORANGE BLOSSOM WATER

2 OZ. VODKA

1. Preheat the oven to 400°F. Place the almonds on a baking sheet, place them in the oven, and toast until they are fragrant, 6 to 8 minutes. Remove the almonds from the oven and let them cool completely.

2. Place the nuts in a food processor and pulse until they are a coarse meal. Set the almonds aside.

3. Place the syrup in a saucepan and warm it over medium heat. Add the almond meal, remove the pan from heat, and let the mixture steep for 6 hours.

4. Strain the mixture through cheesecloth and discard the solids. Stir in the orange blossom water and vodka. Use the orgeat immediately or store it in an airtight container.

Buttermilk Biscuits

YIELD: 12 BISCUITS | **ACTIVE TIME:** 30 MINUTES | **TOTAL TIME:** 1 HOUR

2 CUPS PLUS ½ CUP BUTTERMILK

¼ CUP HONEY

26 OZ. ALL-PURPOSE FLOUR, PLUS MORE AS NEEDED

1 TABLESPOON KOSHER SALT

3 TABLESPOONS BAKING POWDER

½ LB. UNSALTED BUTTER, CHILLED AND CUBED

1. Preheat the oven to 425°F. Line a baking sheet with parchment paper.

2. Place 2 cups of the buttermilk and the honey in a measuring cup and whisk to combine. Set the mixture aside.

3. Place the flour, salt, baking powder, and butter in the work bowl of a stand mixer fitted with the paddle attachment and beat the mixture until combined and the butter has been reduced to pea-sized pieces, 5 to 10 minutes. Gradually add the buttermilk mixture and beat the mixture until it comes together as a slightly crumbly dough.

4. Transfer the dough to a flour-dusted work surface. Working with generously flour-dusted hands and a roller, roll the dough into a ¾-inch-thick rectangle.

5. Using a bench scraper, cut the dough into thirds and stack them on top of each other. Roll the dough out again into a ¾-inch-thick rectangle.

6. Cut the dough into twelve 3-inch squares and arrange them on the baking sheet. Brush the tops of the biscuits with the ½ cup of buttermilk.

7. Place the biscuits in the oven and bake until they are golden brown, 15 to 17 minutes.

8. Remove the biscuits from the oven and place them on a wire rack to cool slightly before serving.

Raspberry Jam

YIELD: 2 CUPS | **ACTIVE TIME:** 30 MINUTES | **TOTAL TIME:** 3 HOURS

1 LB. FRESH RASPBERRIES

1 LB. SUGAR

ZEST AND JUICE OF 1
LEMON

1. Place the ingredients in a large saucepan fitted with a candy thermometer and cook over medium-high heat until the mixture is 220°F. Stir the jam occasionally as it cooks.

2. Pour the jam into jars and let it cool completely before using or storing in the refrigerator.

Lemon Glaze

YIELD: 4 SERVINGS | **ACTIVE TIME:** 5 MINUTES | **TOTAL TIME:** 5 MINUTES

3 TABLESPOONS FRESH
LEMON JUICE

2 TABLESPOONS FULL-FAT
GREEK YOGURT

2 CUPS CONFECTIONERS'
SUGAR

SEEDS OF ½ VANILLA BEAN

1. Place all of the ingredients in a mixing bowl and whisk to combine.

Roasted Vanilla Cherries

YIELD: 4 SERVINGS | **ACTIVE TIME:** 25 MINUTES | **TOTAL TIME:** 24 HOURS

24 CHERRIES

PINCH OF FINE SEA SALT

¼ CUP BRANDY

SEEDS OF ½ VANILLA BEAN OR 1 TEASPOON PURE VANILLA EXTRACT

2 TABLESPOONS DEMERARA SUGAR

1. Place the cherries, salt, brandy, and vanilla in a bowl and let the mixture marinate at room temperature overnight.

2. Preheat the oven to 400°F. Strain the cherries, reserve the liquid, and place the cherries on a baking sheet. Sprinkle the sugar over the cherries, place them in the oven, and roast until the sugar starts to caramelize, 8 to 10 minutes, making sure that the sugar does not burn.

3. Remove the cherries from the oven, pour the reserved liquid over them, and place them back in the oven. Roast for another 5 minutes, remove the cherries from the oven, and let them cool. When they are cool enough to handle, remove the pits from the cherries. Chill the cherries in the refrigerator until ready to use.

Granola

YIELD: 3 CUPS | **ACTIVE TIME:** 10 MINUTES | **TOTAL TIME:** 45 MINUTES

2 CUPS ROLLED OATS

¼ CUP REAL MAPLE SYRUP

1 CUP PECAN HALVES

2 TEASPOONS KOSHER SALT

1 TEASPOON CINNAMON

⅔ CUP DRIED CRANBERRIES

1. Preheat the oven to 350°F and line a baking sheet with a Silpat mat. Place all of the ingredients in a mixing bowl and toss to combine.

2. Spread the mixture on the baking sheet in an even layer. Place it in the oven and bake until browned and fragrant, about 20 minutes. Remove from the oven and let the granola cool completely before serving.

Lemon Crème

YIELD: 4 SERVINGS | **ACTIVE TIME:** 20 MINUTES | **TOTAL TIME:** 20 MINUTES

ZEST AND JUICE OF 2 LEMONS

½ CUP SUGAR

3 EGGS

6 TABLESPOONS UNSALTED BUTTER

PINCH OF FINE SEA SALT

1. Place the lemon zest, lemon juice, and half of the sugar in a small saucepan and bring the mixture to a boil, stirring to dissolve the sugar. Remove the pan from heat.

2. Place the remaining sugar and the eggs in a small mixing bowl and whisk until combined. While whisking vigorously, slowly pour the hot syrup into the mixture. Place the tempered mixture in the saucepan, place it over low heat, and stir until it starts to thicken, about 5 minutes.

3. Remove the pan from heat and incorporate the butter 1 tablespoon at a time. When all of the butter has been incorporated, stir in the salt and then pour the crème into a bowl. Place plastic wrap directly on the surface to prevent a skin from forming and chill the crème in the refrigerator until ready to use.

Blueberry Compote

YIELD: 4 SERVINGS | **ACTIVE TIME:** 10 MINUTES | **TOTAL TIME:** 30 MINUTES

1½ CUPS FROZEN BLUEBERRIES, THAWED

2 TABLESPOONS SUGAR

JUICE OF 1 ORANGE

2 CINNAMON STICKS

1 STAR ANISE POD

1. Place all of the ingredients in a small saucepan and cook over low heat, stirring occasionally, until the mixture has thickened and most of the liquid has evaporated, 5 to 7 minutes.

2. Remove the cinnamon sticks and star anise and let the compote cool.

3. When the compote has cooled, use immediately or store in the refrigerator until needed.

Coffee Cake Topping

YIELD: 3 CUPS | **ACTIVE TIME:** 10 MINUTES | **TOTAL TIME:** 10 MINUTES

7 OZ. ALL-PURPOSE FLOUR

9 OZ. LIGHT BROWN SUGAR

¼ TEASPOON KOSHER SALT

¾ TEASPOON CINNAMON

6 OZ. UNSALTED BUTTER, CHILLED AND CUBED

1. In the work bowl of a stand mixer fitted with the paddle attachment, add the flour, brown sugar, salt, and cinnamon and beat until the mixture is combined.

2. Turn off the mixer and add the butter. Raise the speed to medium and beat until the mixture is crumbly and the butter is being absorbed by the dry mixture. Take care not to overwork the mixture—you want it to be crumbly, not creamy.

3. Use as desired or store in the refrigerator, where it will keep for up to 1 week.

Strawberry Preserves

YIELD: 2 CUPS | **ACTIVE TIME:** 30 MINUTES | **TOTAL TIME:** 2 HOURS AND 30 MINUTES

1 LB. STRAWBERRIES, HULLED

1 LB. SUGAR

ZEST AND JUICE OF 1 LEMON

SEEDS AND POD OF 1 VANILLA BEAN

¼ TEASPOON KOSHER SALT

1. Place all of the ingredients in a large saucepan and warm it over low heat, using a wooden spoon to occasionally fold the mixture. Cook until the sugar has dissolved and the strawberries are starting to collapse, about 15 minutes.

2. Remove the pan from heat and transfer the preserves to a sterilized mason jar. Let them cool at room temperature for 2 hours before using or storing in the refrigerator.

Apricot Glaze

YIELD: 2 CUPS | **ACTIVE TIME:** 10 MINUTES | **TOTAL TIME:** 40 MINUTES

2 CUPS APRICOT JAM

¼ CUP WATER

1. Place the apricot jam and water in a saucepan and warm the mixture over medium heat until it is about to come to a simmer, stirring occasionally.

2. Strain the mixture through a fine-mesh strainer and let it cool until just above room temperature before using or storing in the refrigerator. If storing in the refrigerator, add a little water and warm it in a saucepan before using.

Cream Cheese Danish Filling

YIELD: 4 CUPS | **ACTIVE TIME:** 20 MINUTES | **TOTAL TIME:** 20 MINUTES

½ LB. ALMOND PASTE

1 CUP SUGAR

1 LB. CREAM CHEESE, SOFTENED

1½ TEASPOONS PURE VANILLA EXTRACT

½ TEASPOON KOSHER SALT

1. Place the almond paste in the work bowl of a stand mixer fitted with the paddle attachment and beat it on medium until it has softened, about 5 minutes.

2. Add the sugar and cream the mixture for 5 minutes.

3. Add the cream cheese, vanilla, and salt and cream until the mixture is very smooth, about 10 minutes. Use immediately or store in the refrigerator.

Lemon Syrup

YIELD: ½ CUP | **ACTIVE TIME:** 10 MINUTES | **TOTAL TIME:** 1 HOUR

½ CUP FRESH LEMON JUICE

½ CUP SUGAR

1. Place the lemon juice and sugar in a small saucepan and bring the mixture to a simmer over medium heat, stirring to dissolve the sugar.

2. Remove the pan from heat and let the syrup cool completely before using or storing in the refrigerator.

Pistachio Paste

YIELD: 2 CUPS | **ACTIVE TIME:** 10 MINUTES | **TOTAL TIME:** 10 MINUTES

9 OZ. RAW PISTACHIOS, BLANCHED AND PEELED

10 OZ. CONFECTIONERS' SUGAR

½ TEASPOON KOSHER SALT

¼ TEASPOON ORANGE BLOSSOM WATER

2 OZ. ROASTED PISTACHIO OIL

1. Place the pistachios in a food processor and blitz until they are a smooth, oily paste.

2. Add the confectioners' sugar, salt, and orange blossom water and blitz until the paste is smooth and thick.

3. With the food processor running, drizzle in the pistachio oil and blitz until the paste is silky. Use immediately or store in the refrigerator, where the paste will keep for up to 1 month.

Ladyfingers

YIELD: 30 LADYFINGERS | **ACTIVE TIME:** 15 MINUTES | **TOTAL TIME:** 1 HOUR

⅔ CUP ALL-PURPOSE FLOUR, PLUS MORE AS NEEDED

3 EGGS, SEPARATED

½ CUP PLUS 1 TABLESPOON SUGAR

1 TEASPOON PURE VANILLA EXTRACT

PINCH OF FINE SEA SALT

¾ CUP CONFECTIONERS' SUGAR

1. Preheat the oven to 300°F. Line two baking sheets with parchment paper and dust them with flour.

2. Place the egg yolks in a mixing bowl and gradually incorporate the sugar, using a handheld mixer at high speed. When the mixture is thick and a pale yellow, whisk in the vanilla.

3. In the work bowl of a stand mixer fitted with the whisk attachment, beat the egg whites and salt until the mixture holds soft peaks. Scoop one-quarter of the whipped egg whites into the egg yolk mixture and sift one-quarter of the flour on top. Fold to combine. Repeat until all of the egg whites and flour have been incorporated and the mixture is light and airy.

4. Spread the batter in 4-inch-long strips on the baking sheets, leaving 1 inch between them. Sprinkle the confectioners' sugar over each strip and place the ladyfingers in the oven.

5. Bake the ladyfingers until they are lightly golden brown and just crispy, about 20 minutes. Remove them from the oven and transfer the ladyfingers to a wire rack to cool completely before using.

Simple Syrup

YIELD: ½ CUP | **ACTIVE TIME:** 10 MINUTES | **TOTAL TIME:** 1 HOUR

½ CUP SUGAR

½ CUP WATER

1. Combine the sugar and water in a saucepan and bring the mixture to a boil over medium heat, stirring to dissolve the sugar.

2. When the sugar has dissolved, remove the pan from heat, pour the syrup into a mason jar, and let it cool before using or storing in the refrigerator, where it will keep for up to 1 month.

Burdock & Cacao Nib Brandy

YIELD: 3 CUPS | **ACTIVE TIME:** 10 MINUTES | **TOTAL TIME:** 3 DAYS

1 PIECE OF BURDOCK ROOT
⅓ OZ. CACAO NIBS
23¾ OZ. BRANDY

1. Combine all of the ingredients in a mason jar and let the mixture steep at room temperature for 3 days.

2. Strain and use immediately or store in an airtight container.

Cinnamon Syrup

YIELD: 1½ CUPS | **ACTIVE TIME:** 10 MINUTES | **TOTAL TIME:** 2 HOURS

1 CUP SUGAR
1 CUP WATER
3 CINNAMON STICKS

1. Place the sugar and water in a saucepan and bring the mixture to a boil, stirring to dissolve the sugar.

2. When the sugar has dissolved, add the cinnamon sticks, cook for another minute, and remove the pan from heat. Let it steep for 1 hour.

3. Strain the syrup into a mason jar and let it cool completely before using or storing in the refrigerator.

Chipotle Rum

YIELD: 1 CUP | **ACTIVE TIME:** 5 MINUTES | **TOTAL TIME:** 3 HOURS

1 CUP AGED RUM

1 DRIED CHIPOTLE CHILE PEPPER, TORN

1. Place the rum and chipotle in a mason jar and let the mixture steep at room temperature for 3 hours.

2. Strain and use immediately or store in the refrigerator.

Streusel Topping

YIELD: 3 CUPS | **ACTIVE TIME:** 10 MINUTES | **TOTAL TIME:** 10 MINUTES

9 OZ. ALL-PURPOSE FLOUR

6 OZ. SUGAR

6 OZ. LIGHT BROWN SUGAR

4 OZ. ROLLED OATS

2¼ TEASPOONS CINNAMON

¾ TEASPOON KOSHER SALT

½ LB. UNSALTED BUTTER, CHILLED AND DIVIDED INTO TABLESPOONS

1. In the work bowl of a stand mixer fitted with the paddle attachment, beat the flour, sugar, brown sugar, oats, cinnamon, and salt on low speed until combined.

2. Turn off the mixer and add the butter.

3. Raise the speed to medium and beat the mixture until the mixture is crumbly and the butter has been absorbed by the dry ingredients. Make sure not to overwork the mixture.

4. Store in the refrigerator for a week and place on muffins before baking.

METRIC CONVERSION CHART

US Measurement	Approximate Metric Liquid Measurement	Approximate Metric Dry Measurement
1 teaspoon	5 ml	—
1 tablespoon or ½ ounce	15 ml	14 g
1 ounce or ⅛ cup	30 ml	29 g
¼ cup or 2 ounces	60 ml	57 g
⅓ cup	80 ml	—
½ cup or 4 ounces	120 ml	113 g
⅔ cup	160 ml	—
¾ cup or 6 ounces	180 ml	—
1 cup or 8 ounces or ½ pint	240 ml	227 g
1½ cups or 12 ounces	350 ml	—
2 cups or 1 pint or 16 ounces	475 ml	454 g
3 cups or 1½ pints	700 ml	—
4 cups or 2 pints or 1 quart	950 ml	—

INDEX

About Cider Mill Press Book Publishers

Good ideas ripen with time. From seed to harvest, Cider Mill Press brings fine reading, information, and entertainment together between the covers of its creatively crafted books. Our Cider Mill bears fruit twice a year, publishing a new crop of titles each spring and fall.

"Where Good Books Are Ready for Press"

501 Nelson Place
Nashville, Tennessee 37214

cidermillpress.com